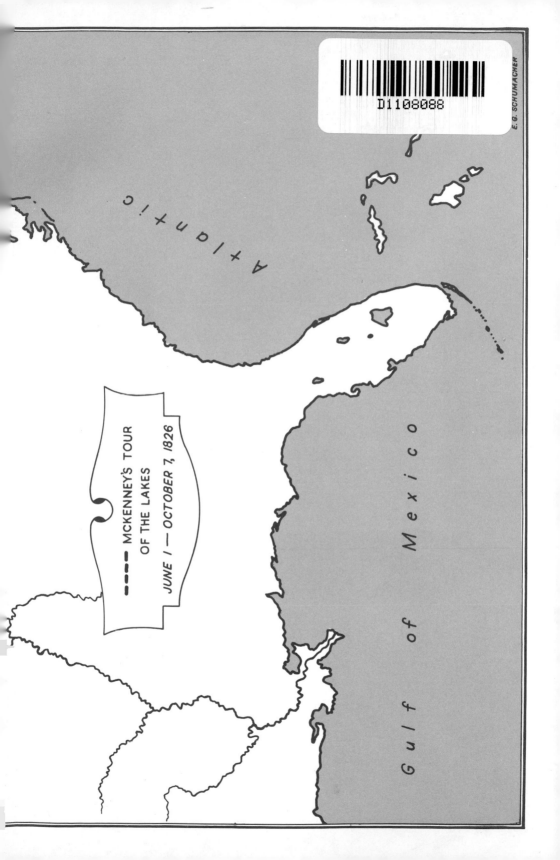

MCKENNEY'S TOUR
OF THE LAKES

JUNE 1 — OCTOBER 7, 1826

Atlantic

Gulf of Mexico

Thomas L. McKenney

Architect of America's Early Indian Policy: 1816-1830

HERMAN J. VIOLA

SAGE BOOKS

THE SWALLOW PRESS INC.
CHICAGO

First Edition
First Printing

Sage Books are published by
The Swallow Press Incorporated
1139 South Wabash Avenue
Chicago, Illinois 60605

The frontispiece is from a painting of Thomas L. McKenney
at age seventy-one, by Charles Loring Elliott, 1856.
Courtesy Corcoran Gallery of Art, Washington, D.C.

ISBN 0-8040-0668-7
LIBRARY OF CONGRESS CATALOG CARD NUMBER 74-18075

To my parents,
who believed in the American dream,
and to Susan, Joseph, Paul, and Peter,
who helped me make it come true.

Contents

Illustrations

Maps

Preface

Thomas Loraine McKenney is one of the most significant yet least known figures in the history of the American Indian. For almost fourteen years, between 1816 and 1830, he administered the nation's Indian affairs, first as superintendent of Indian trade and then as head of the Office of Indian Affairs. Not only was McKenney a pioneer in the study of North American ethnology, establishing in his office a remarkable collection of books, manuscripts, artifacts, and paintings, which he called his "archives of the American Indian," he was also the major architect of two government programs that had tremendous impact on the native Americans: Indian reform and Indian removal. Largely through his efforts, Congress in 1819 passed the Indian Civilization Act, which provided $10,000 annually for the support of schools in the Indian country; eleven years later Congress passed the Indian Removal Act, which provided for the resettlement of eastern tribes west of the Mississippi River.

Following his dismissal from office in 1830, McKenney, with the collaboration of James Hall, published the monumental *History of the Indian Tribes of North America*. The three folio

xi

volumes of biographical sketches and hand-colored lithographs of 120 famous Indians have long been recognized by anthropologists and historians as a unique source for the study of the native Americans.

Although McKenney has been characterized as a vacillating, self-seeking opportunist who used the Indians as stepping stones to political prominence, this interpretation is not supported by the evidence. McKenney was a sincere humanitarian who espoused many of the reform causes of early nineteenth-century America. He was concerned about cruelty to animals; he advocated the establishment of orphanages, Sunday schools, and Bible societies; he spoke out against the evils of dueling, whiskey, and slavery. But the bulk of his humanitarian energies, he spent on behalf of the American Indian. Some of his actions, particularly with respect to the Indian removal program, leave him open for criticism, but overall he appears to have been a man of honor and integrity, more idealistic than practical, who did his best to maintain a balance between national desires and national honor by just treatment of the Indians.

1
Preparation
for Office

A**N AIR OF ANTICIPATION** marked the inauguration of James Madison as fourth president of the United States. Visitors in record numbers trekked to the capital city being carved out of inhospitable marshlands at the confluence of the Potomac and Anacostia Rivers, and by noon that March Saturday in 1809 fully ten thousand people had gathered on Capitol Hill, while thousands more crowded the tree-lined avenue to the President's House. President Thomas Jefferson arrived at the recently completed House of Representatives shortly before noon; Madison, escorted by units of the Georgetown and Washington cavalry, followed a few minutes later. Madison delivered a barely audible inaugural address to the packed gallery and then took the oath of office from Chief Justice John Marshall. Minute guns boomed as James and Dolley Madison returned to their home on F Street to hold an open house that attracted such crowds that carriages clogged streets for blocks around. That evening at Long's Hotel in Georgetown the Madisons entertained four hundred citizens, government officials, and foreign dignitaries at America's first inaugural ball. John Quincy Adams complained that "the crowd was excessive—the heat oppressive, and the entertainment bad," but the *National Intelligencer* assured its readers that the new first lady "looked a queen" in her yellow velvet dress, pearls, and turban with bird-of-paradise plumes.[1]

Madison's inauguration greatly impressed Thomas Loraine McKenney who was visiting Washington for the first time. Tall, with the red hair and hooked nose of his Scottish ancestors, the young Maryland merchant had been among the throng at the capitol. He was almost twenty-four, and his future seemed uncertain. His father had died only four months earlier, and McKenney was visiting a sister in Georgetown. More than once civic ceremonies were to inspire McKenney; this one was a turning point in his life. The inauguration and its cast of characters, including some of the most influential and respected political figures of the early years of the republic, fired McKenney's imagination. He contrasted the glittering social festivities to his own quiet life on Maryland's Eastern Shore and decided to make the nation's capital his home. It is appropriate that a national civic occasion was the background for this critical personal decision, for the capital was the background for the most significant accomplishments of McKenney's public career—his service as superintendent of Indian trade and as the first head of the Bureau of Indian Affairs.

Inaugurations aside, the capital itself was not appealing. Washington had been the seat of government less than a decade, and the city reflected its youth. Paved streets were nonexistent; roads were dustbowls or quagmires depending on the weather. Mosquitoes thrived in the marshy ground, hogs rooted in the garbage-strewn roadways, and cattle grazed in the open meadows. Although several handsome residences, occupied chiefly by members of the diplomatic corps, were clustered near the President's House, for the most part the few federal buildings stood like stark sentinels in a barren landscape.[2] Nevertheless, the older communities of the District of Columbia—Alexandria and Georgetown—were established trading centers; the profitable commerce in flour and tobacco there, the shipping and manufacturing, and the bright prospects of the federal government attracted many merchants like McKenney to the infant capital.

McKenney was born March 21, 1785, at Hopewell, an estate in Somerset County, Maryland. He was named for his father's great-uncle Thomas Loraine, a wealthy sea captain of nearby Chestertown. There his father, William McKenney, moved the rapidly growing family in 1786. William and Anne Barber McKenney had five sons and two daughters; after his first wife's death in 1795, William married Hannah Hines and fathered seven more children, again five sons and two daughters.[3]

The most significant influence in Thomas McKenney's childhood was his Quaker upbringing. His maternal grandmother was Sarah Grub, a celebrated Quaker preacher of the eighteenth century. His mother, Anne Barber, reared her son in the faith until her death. He remained a Quaker, he later stated, in spirit if not in dress or demeanor.[4]

Intellectually McKenney was a man of scholarly interests and considerable imagination. He had a fine education, attending Washington College, a local school of good reputation where well-to-do young men of the Eastern Shore studied mathematics, English, Latin, and Greek. He wrote three books and at least four pamphlets in the course of his long life. In 1826 he predicted that man would fly within twenty years, and in 1842 he suggested using balloons in the war against the Seminoles in Florida.[5] His avocation was medicine, and he had a corresponding interest in all the natural sciences, particularly mineralogy. McKenney had wanted to be a physician but, he explained, "the delicate appearance of my physical powers led my Father to change [t]his purpose. He feared the consequence of the exposures to a Country practice." Instead, "he took me into his compting House, and I was bred a merchant."[6]

William McKenney's prosperous firm in Chestertown was a combination bank and store, the largest of its kind on the Eastern Shore, including warehouses, docks, and a seagoing vessel. By 1804, at age nineteen, Thomas McKenney had charge of the entire business. Two years later he married Editha Gleaves, an "exemplary and truly estimable lady."[7] They had two children, a daughter, Maria, who died in infancy, and a son, George William, always referred to by his father as William.

McKenney appeared well settled in the quiet, prosperous life of a Maryland merchant when his forty-six-year-old father died suddenly and intestate. Claims of creditors forced a sale of realty, and a handsome inheritance melted away. "I found there would not be much more left," McKenney later wrote,

Thomas L. McKenney, 1806.
Courtesy Eleanor McKenney Gibson, Charlottesville, Va.

Editha Gleaves McKenney.
Courtesy Eleanor McKenney Gibson, Charlottesville, Va.

"after sett'ling up the mercantile concern, than would support my step-mother, and her four young children. I remembered my Father's dying words—'My Son, take care of your Mother, & her little children.' I drew up a paper, and procured the signatures of my Brother's and Sisters, to it, giving the Farm to our step-mother, & her children, with its stock &c."[8]

Shortly thereafter McKenney brought his own young family to Georgetown where his sister Henrietta and her husband, Samuel Groome Osborne, lived. Osborne, also a merchant, offered his brother-in-law a partnership, and McKenney spent several uneventful years as a storekeeper. When the War of 1812 broke out, he rallied to the colors. Despite his Quaker background, McKenney was no stranger to military duty, for he had been an officer in the Kent County militia. During the war he served in various units, usually as liaison officer, adjutant, or aide-de-camp, finishing with the permanent rank of major.[9] He participated in the battle of Bladensburg, saw Washington burn, then shouldered a musket and marched to the defense of Baltimore. Although later McKenney was often addressed as colonel, no evidence indicates that he achieved the rank during the war. He subsequently joined the District of Columbia militia, and the title may derive from that service.[10]

McKenney certainly looked like a colonel. He was tall and slender, outgoing and friendly, fastidious in dress, and, according to one contemporary, "characterized by great amenity of manners, as well as ready business tact."[11] His hair grayed prematurely. The Indians called him White Eagle and sometimes, because of his strong features and military bearing, mistook him for Andrew Jackson. His friends dubbed him the White Hawk—partly for his appearance, partly for his temperament, for McKenney never retreated from a fight.

A few months before hostilities with Great Britain ended, McKenney began seeking a position of public trust suited to his talents. Failing in a bid for the post of secretary of the Senate, he settled for a partnership with Joseph C. Hall, who owned a dry-goods store on Pennsylvania Avenue. They wrote their contract for five years, but McKenney tired early of the arrangement—profits the first year amounted to less than $1,000—and by 1816 he was again searching for federal employment.[12] On March 20 his name was suggested for the office of accountant of the navy, but nothing came of it. Nine days later, several of McKenney's friends (no doubt at his urging) sent President Madison a petition recommending him for the recently vacated position of superintendent of Indian trade.[13] The president, who had first met McKenney during the war and now patronized his store, offered him the superintendency, which the congenial merchant accepted "with great pleasure."[14]

Although he was eager to begin work, McKenney had first to post a $20,000 surety bond and withdraw from his partnership with Hall. More than a week passed before McKenney finally appeared at the comptroller's office with William Whann, cashier of the Bank of Columbia, and John Cox, a prominent Georgetown merchant, his cosigners for the bond. McKenney swore "faithfully and honestly [to] execute the trust committed to me as Superintendent of Indian Trade," signed his bond, and went home and prayed.[15]

April 12, 1816 was Good Friday, and the thirty-one-year-old McKenney felt deeply the responsibility he had just accepted. "Almighty God!" he wrote, "this day I have sworn faithfully and honestly, to discharge the duties of Superintendent of Indian Trade—but as man in his best estate is weak and helpless, always liable to err; and continually subject to the casualties which often involve his good name, and his dearest interests,— I do most humbly beseech Thee to grant me in all my labors the assistance of thy Holy Spirit, through Jesus Christ our Lord. Amen." McKenney's premonitions of the pitfalls of public office were correct, but his plea for deliverance went unanswered.[16]

2

Superintendent of Indian Trade

THE NETWORK OF government-owned trading houses called the factory system had a checkered and controversial history long before McKenney became superintendent of Indian trade.[1] Under the prodding of President George Washington, Congress had established two experimental factories in 1795 for the ostensible purpose of creating "harmony with the Indian nation."[2] Advocates of the factory system viewed it primarily as a means to control the tribes, attract the fur trade to the Americans, and counteract foreign influence among the Indians. The welfare of the Indians was at best a secondary consideration, although the factories did have that side effect.

The experience of the American Revolution inspired the factories. In the years following the fall of France in North America, British colonial administrators fostered and won Indian friendship by convincing the natives that the crown wished to be the benefactor and protector of the tribes, desiring only their furs and not their lands. The success of this policy was manifested during the Revolutionary War when many of the eastern tribes joined the English against the colonists; the woodland warriors made loyal and effective allies of the royal cause as they ravaged frontier settlements with tomahawk and torch. Americans paid dearly for their failure to recognize early enough the value of Indian friendship, and the mistake haunted them after the war, for the British retained control of the Great Lakes, the fur trade, and the Indians. Consequently, a solution of the Indian problem was a pressing need of the newly formed United States. Rather than undertake a war of conquest against the tribes arrayed along its borders—a war the country could not afford—the federal government embarked on a policy of conciliation that included the trading houses as a major component.[3]

The factory system, as conceived, should have fulfilled its goals. The trading houses were to stock the finest merchandise and offer it at little more than cost to the Indians in a fair exchange for furs. Factors were to be literate and trustworthy and interested in the welfare of the Indians. In time a network of factories serving all the tribes would make the Indians completely dependent on government trade goods. Thus the factories, rather than costly military garrisons dotting the frontier, could be used to control the tribes: the threat of deprivation supposedly would keep the Indians peaceful.

Only if the government monopolized the fur trade could so grandiose a program succeed. The idea, however, was repugnant to most Americans even though the fur industry in this period was, as an employee of the Hudson's Bay Company aptly described, "a loose dissipated, jealous sort of thing—jealous not only of British rivalry, but of American rivalry—and eager to grasp at any article, however worthless, and by any means, however unworthy."[4] A government monopoly perhaps could have prevented the evils that characterized so much of the American fur trade. The factories might even have counteracted British influence in the Northwest. Wrote one Canadian observer in 1812: "Of all the projects of Genl Washington, after effecting the separation of those Colonies from the mother country; I apprehend this of the Trading houses, best calculated to undermine the influence of Great Britain, with the Indians."[5] Only congressional parsimony, the Canadian believed, hindered the factories from developing vigorously.

Indeed, despite the potential of the factory system, Congress gave it only halfhearted support. The success of the two factories opened in 1795 encouraged Congress the following year to give definite organization to the factory system; the president, through an appropriation of $150,000, was authorized to establish additional trading houses in the Indian country. But the 1796 law expired three years later, and the factories were allowed to continue only because direct legislative action was necessary to abolish the system. The enabling act renewed in 1802 lapsed after three years, and for a year the system again operated without proper authorization. From 1806 to 1822 Congress maintained the factories without interruption, but only by enabling acts of one or two years' duration.[6]

The legislative ambivalence is clearly reflected in the failure of Congress to provide an effective administrative structure for the factory system. As late as February 1822, just three months before the system was abolished, the secretary of war was urging Congress to place the Office of Indian Trade completely under his jurisdiction so as to combine all functions relating to Indian affairs under one administrative head. "At present," he informed the chairman of the Committee on Public Expenditures, "the Office . . . is not connected with, or under the control of any of the Departments of the Government, tho' in its operations it is so intimately blended with the management of Indian affairs as to render it desirable that it should be under the same general control with that Department. So much of the disbursements of the Indian Department is made through the Superintendent of Indian Trade, that if no other cause for the union of the two existed, that alone would render it desirable."[7]

At first the Purveyor of Public Supplies "and others" had administered the factory system under the direction of the secretary of war, but in 1806 Congress established the position of superintendent of Indian trade and moved the office from Philadelphia to Georgetown the following year. Inexplicably, however, Congress failed to fix administrative responsibility for the new officer. For example, as a disbursing officer, the superintendent had to submit his Indian trade accounts and those of his factors to the Treasury Department for review, but he had to receive the approval of the secretary of war for the dates on which he auctioned off the furs received in trade. For other matters, such as the appointment of factors and the moving, opening, or closing of trading houses, he needed the approval of the president. In 1811 the administrative entanglement became even more acute, for Congress made the superintendent responsible for purchasing and shipping all merchandise the government disbursed annually as annuities or presents to the Indians. The superintendent had to submit the accounts for these transactions to the War Department, although the Treasury Department continued to handle his trade accounts. Nevertheless, if for no other reason than courtesy, the superintendent of Indian trade normally recognized the authority of the secretary of war in most matters.[8]

The factory system, if it did not flourish, at least functioned under this strange and complex arrangement. By 1809 the capital fund totaled almost $300,000, and the factories that ranged along the American frontier from Mackinac to Fort St. Stephens, a few miles above Mobile Bay, seemed permanently established.

The War of 1812, however, dealt harshly with the trading houses. Of the ten in operation when hostilities began, the British and their Indian allies destroyed or forced the abandonment of five, and two others suspended business for varying periods. Property damage was officially assessed at $43,369.61, but this sum—which Congress never restored to the operating capital—did not take into account the disruptive effect of the war on the Indian trade.[9] Moreover, the best trade goods were manufactured in Britain, and the war made those unobtainable; the substituted American products were shoddy, expensive, and unmarketable once normal trade relations were restored. Thousands of dollars worth of useless merchandise remained on hand until abolition of the factory system and then could only be given away.

After 1814 there was a tremendous surge of American interest in the fur trade, particularly in the Great Lakes region. With England's influence among the tribes at its lowest ebb, American investors more confidently ventured capital into the former British stronghold. An 1816 law barring foreigners from the Indian trade also encouraged the influx. Private fur interests now had only to contend with the factory system; yet they feared even its weak competition. The fur business, one trader wrote, "is too precarious for anybody to hazard in it unless the factories were to be abolished."[10] The traders' attack on the system was supported by other critics who saw no further need for the factories since the war had ended the Indian threat to national security. When McKenney took control in 1816, the factory system was doomed. That the death struggle lasted until 1822 is tribute to his tenacity, energy, and ability.

McKenney, of course, realized none of this at the time. He readily admitted knowing little about Indians or Indian affairs before he had accepted the office, and he was then politically unsophisticated. At best he had a casual acquaintance with the trading houses, having sometimes sold goods to John Mason, whom he succeeded as superintendent, but his limited mercantile experience had scarcely prepared him for supervising a nation-wide business with a working capital of more than a quarter of a million dollars. Fortunately, the routine of conducting factory operations had been well established by his predecessor, and the new superintendent had only to learn the system.

The Office of Indian Trade occupied the former Bank of Columbia building, which the trustees rented to the government for $350 a year. The three-story, red brick building still stands on M Street adjacent to the City Tavern in the heart of Georgetown. Wagons passed through an archway just west of the building to reach a basement entrance in the rear; a wharf and a brick warehouse on the Potomac River were a short distance beyond. For at least three months of the year the premises rang with the sound of the cooper's mallet as he fashioned the casks needed for packing and transporting the trade goods to the distant factories. Odors of all sorts wafted through the building—of woolen goods, medicines, tobacco, and, most noticeably, the "exceptionable smell" of the furs and skins stored in the paved cellar for sale at the next auction.[11] Merchants and visitors continually passed through the rooms, and occasionally hungry and ill-clad Indians would appear at the front door hoping for a handout. McKenney always gave them some bounty from the government supplies but never without a sermon on the virtues of thrift and industry.

Typical of the federal bureaucracy in the first quarter of the nineteenth century, McKenney's staff was small, underpaid, and male. The superintendent of Indian trade received $2,000 annually. The salary of his chief clerk, Jeremiah Bronaugh, was half that. For keeping the books John W. Rich was paid $800, and Meade Fitzhugh, the copy clerk, received $700. John W. Bronaugh, the transportation clerk, earned $400 annually for shipping and receiving the merchandise and furs, while McKenney's "trusty" messenger and janitor, William Miles, subsisted on $360. Also typical of the bureaucracy in this period, the staff was remarkably stable. These men had worked for the Office of Indian Trade since it had opened in Georgetown in 1807, and they remained at their posts, except for Rich who died in 1821, until the factory system was abolished. Then, McKenney recalled, "we parted as we had met—*friends*."[12]

Working hours at the Office of Indian Trade were 9 A.M. to 3 P.M., six days a week, except in the spring when goods were packed and shipped to the factories and in the fall when the furs were prepared for the annual auction. Long hours were the rule in those seasons, although no work was ever done on Sunday. To ease the burden on his staff during periods of peak activity, McKenney called on John Kelly who would bring as many as seven blacks to the Georgetown warehouse to pack trade goods, load wagons, or clean, sort, and bundle the foul-smelling furs and peltries. Kelly received each day $2 for his own services and $.75 for each of his slaves.[13]

Except for its mercantile character, the daily routine in the Office of Indian Trade differed little from other federal agencies in this uncomplicated era. It revolved around correspondence. Miles would bring the morning mail to McKenney who broke the wax seals, read the letters, and then passed them over to Jeremiah Bronaugh who maintained the correspondence files. Bronaugh refolded each letter into thirds, wrote a brief of the contents on the back fold, and entered in a register the correspondent's name, the date of the letter, and an abstract of its contents. After registering the letters, Bronaugh filed them above his desk in pigeon holes labelled according to subject. When a hole was full, he took out the letters, bundled them neatly with red tape, and stacked them on a shelf.

Meade Fitzhugh transcribed all outgoing correspondence. With quill pen and ink, he painstakingly copied each letter McKenney drafted—an unknown blessing to correspondents, because the superintendent by his own admission had "villainous handwriting."[14] When McKenney needed many copies of a letter—he frequently sent circulars to every factor—Fitzhugh copied by hand the letter and whatever enclosures as often as necessary. Even for single letters Fitzhugh made second copies in the bound letterbooks that constituted the office files. Compared with McKenney's later output as superintendent of Indian affairs, the volume of correspondence of the Office of Indian Trade was not considerable. In six years as superintendent McKenney filled three letterbooks, roughly half the amount of correspondence he generated in an equivalent time as head of the Indian office.

Conducting the basic factory business was simple. Each fall McKenney sent order blanks to his factors, who determined their needs for the coming year. The superintendent purchased the requested items during the winter and forwarded them in the spring. As furs or other goods were received in trade, the factors shipped them to Georgetown for sale. The income from the fur sales supported the purchase of additional trade goods. Making the business function well, however, proved far less simple. The factory system depended on the cooperation of dozens of individuals, the weather, and the vagaries of the domestic market. Even under ideal conditions, problems were inevitable; in the declining years of the trade McKenney's headaches were legion.

Routine duties, like purchasing merchandise, consumed an inordinate amount of McKenney's time. The factories stocked more than 150 different kinds of cloth as well as blankets, guns, pipe tomahawks, knives, brooches, rings, toys, spectacles—almost everything except playing cards and alcohol. McKenney also purchased the goods the government distributed annually as annuities and presents to the Indians. His first assignment as superintendent, in fact, was to obtain and transport to various tribes $133,166 worth of annuity goods due since 1812, when the war had disrupted normal relations with them. The annuity goods were kept in the brick warehouse on the wharf, which McKenney's predecessor, John Mason, rented to the government for $300 a year.[15]

Since the trade fund could not afford an inventory of unsold goods, McKenney spared no pains to obtain merchandise of the best quality and price available. "My rule in regard to purchasing was a fixed one," he claimed. "It was, to give as wide a range as I could to the demand, its nature, and variety; and to produce all the competition I could, I gave samples of the kinds of articles which were required in the Indian trade—even, for the purpose of making them portable, to the cutting of guns in two." In his search for suitable goods, McKenney relied on agents like Joseph Lopez Diaz of New York, who kept him informed about market conditions, new products, and the arrival of merchant ships from abroad and who purchased goods for a 1½ percent commission. McKenney's letters contain many references to the "excellent supply" of goods he was shipping, and the factors, in turn, complimented him on the quality of the merchandise. Governor Lewis Cass of Michigan Territory claimed the annuity goods McKenney sent in 1816 were the finest ever seen in his region.[16]

Although foreign-made goods generally were better and cheaper, McKenney would buy American products whenever possible. He gladly would have limited all his purchases to domestic industry, he explained to one manufacturer, but the Indians were "so long used to foreign fabricks and the dressing which is given them" that their tastes would lead them away from the factories and into the arms of the traders "whose business it would be of course, to supply them with what they have been used to." The Indians were so perceptive that McKenney, agreeing to buy some American vermilion, cautioned the manufacturer to package the order "in papers resembling the Chinese methods & marks, as nearly as possible."[17]

McKenney's difficulty in finding suitable guns and blankets was indicative of American reliance on foreign manufactures. These items were the backbone of the Indian trade, but McKenney could seldom find domestically produced guns and blankets to compare favorably in price and quality with British goods. Henry Deringer of Philadelphia made a fine musket that sold for $12.50 including accessories. British Tower muskets, on the other hand, were prized by the Indians and could sometimes be purchased in lots for as little as $10 each. Nevertheless, McKenney established Deringer as the major contractor for factory muskets, and the gunsmith later became one of the leading weapons manufacturers in the United States. The popular, blue-striped, three-point blankets sold by the British-owned Northwest Company were the finest available. McKenney bought similar blankets from George Patterson of New Jersey in 1820, but the $5,000 price was 15 percent more than the cost of the Northwest blankets.[18]

Necessity, of course, often dictated purchases regardless of the manufacturer, especially in the case of wampum. The demand for the cylindrical beads made from clam and conch shells seemed to be insatiable. Blue wampum was the scarcest and most valuable, but at times McKenney would welcome any color. At one point he offered Diaz twice the normal commission for any wampum he could find.[19]

Although McKenney normally sent only goods the factors ordered, he occasionally selected a few items he thought might do well at a particular factory. For the most part he used sound judgment, rejecting offers from merchants of ladies' hats, gold lace, and silver headdresses. His resistance broke down, however, at a Chinese "Mandarine dress." He first considered presenting the dress as a gift from the government to some important chief. Then he decided to add feathers for the cap and sent the ensemble to the Osage factory because the Osages had "splendid notions." The dress might prove difficult to sell, McKenney admitted in his accompanying letter, but it should at least "serve to excite curiosity and draw attention."[20]

After purchasing the goods, McKenney had to see them safely to the factories. Eight were in operation in the spring of 1816: Green Bay, Chicago, and Prairie du Chien, near the confluence of the Wisconsin and Mississippi Rivers, in the north; Fort Osage on the Missouri River just east of present-day Kansas City; Chickasaw Bluffs at the site of Memphis on the Mississippi; Natchitoches on the Red River; Fort St. Stephens on the Tombigbee in Alabama; and Fort Hawkins on the Ocmulgee at the present site of Macon, Georgia.[21] Goods for the Chicago and Green Bay factories went by wagon through Pittsburgh to Lake Erie and the rest of the way by boat. Goods for the factories on the Mississippi and Missouri went by boat up the Potomac River to Cumberland, by wagon over the mountains to Brownsville, and then by keelboat to St. Louis, down the Monongahela and Ohio Rivers. Goods for the southern factories—Natchitoches (later Sulphur Fork on the Arkansas border), Fort Hawkins, and Fort St. Stephens—went by sea to New Orleans. Transportation agents at Pittsburgh, St. Louis, and New Orleans forwarded the goods to the respective factories.

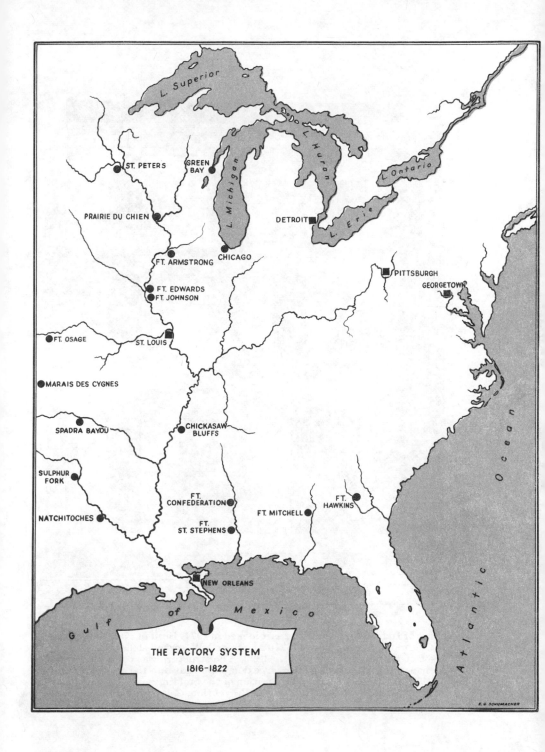

THE FACTORY SYSTEM
1816-1822

Office of Indian Trade building as it looked in 1974. Built in 1796 as the Bank of Columbia, the building, at 3210 M Street NW, served as headquarters for the factory system from 1807 to 1822. The structure was converted into a firehouse in 1883, when the two large doors were cut into the original facade. In 1972 Congress authorized restoration of the building as the National Fire-fighting Museum and Center for Fire Prevention. *Courtesy Charles Photographers.*

For shipping trade goods, McKenney preferred tierces, casks somewhat larger than standard barrels. Packed with a screw press and wrapped in tarpaulin, the oak containers were so tightly secured they were almost waterproof. Hundreds were needed every spring. Some were made at the Office of Indian Trade. Others were manufactured by J. Hill and Company and by Zachariah Green, both of Alexandria, for $3.50 each, not including $.25 each for freight to Georgetown. McKenney later recalled that he packed and shipped so many trade goods and presents in his first year as superintendent "that the tierces required for their transportation were found, on being measured, to extend in length over one mile and a quarter."[22]

The transportation costs in time and money can easily be imagined. Freight charges were exorbitant, often equaling the value of the merchandise, and the goods passed through so many hands that the opportunities for loss, theft, and damage multiplied. A fully loaded wagon held nine tierces and carried as much as three thousand pounds of freight. As many as sixty wagons each season made the three-week trip to Pittsburgh; the annuity goods alone in 1816 required fifty-two wagons. McKenney would send Rich, his bookkeeper, scouring nearby communities for available vehicles, and even then he could not be assured of securing a sufficient number. Each teamster was paid $180—half in advance, the rest upon safe delivery of his cargo to the Pittsburgh transportation agent. In Baltimore in 1817 Rich tried for four days to hire twenty "large bedded" wagons but could find no takers even at $200. McKenney in desperation authorized him to offer $210 for four or five, "provided they *come on immediately*. Wagons must be had—as you know there is [no] making progress without them."[23]

When space permitted, McKenney allowed congressmen, clergymen, and benevolent organizations to ship personal baggage with the public goods, although the congressmen were charged $5.75 per hundredweight.[24] Ironically, in the closing months of the factory system this courtesy enabled McKenney to ship the reduced quantities of trade goods requested by his factors. By the spring of 1821, some of the wagons that left Georgetown carried little but trunks of western congressmen.

Water routes were cheaper and faster than overland roads, but they also exposed the merchandise to more danger. Factory goods sent by sea to New Orleans were lost in storms, damaged by salt water, and once stolen by pirates. Even on inland water routes cargoes were frozen in ice, damaged by capsizing, and stolen. Most perplexing were delays caused by *"low water,"* an excuse McKenney heard so often he claimed he could "make a River." McKenney attributed many of his troubles to boatmen; in his opinion they all were worthless characters. So consistently were his goods delayed, damaged, or stolen that McKenney finally concluded the boatmen "were hired to a detention of them by Men whose *interest* it is to shackle our policy."[25]

McKenney also enjoyed only indifferent success with the transportation agents who handled factory merchandise in transit. For a commission, they were to see that factors received goods promptly and that furs reached Georgetown with a minimum of spoilage. Abraham R. Wolley, the Pittsburgh agent, was competent and reliable, but James Kennerly at St. Louis and Joseph Saul at New Orleans demonstrated a carelessness and a disregard for factory property that bordered on the criminal. McKenney discovered Kennerly had kept several tierces in his warehouse for months; one was there for two years. Kennerly also admitted selling furs locally—at a loss—instead of sending them to Georgetown. Despite his negligence, Kennerly, perhaps because his brother-in-law was William Clark, the superintendent of Indian affairs at St. Louis, remained at his post. Such tolerance, however, was not extended to Saul, who was responsible for $10,000 damage to a shipment of deerskins. This "extraordinary & I believe hitherto unequalled loss" led to Saul's dismissal in May 1820.[26]

McKenney was more fortunate with his eight factors. George S. Gaines at Fort St. Stephens had served for eleven years, six factors were veterans of at least five years, and one was a novice —Daniel Hughes at Fort Hawkins, who like McKenney received his appointment in April 1816. George C. Sibley at Fort Osage was a factor from 1808 to 1822, a record for tenure. McKenney regarded Sibley so highly that as late as 1841 he wrote of him: "I know no better, or more honourable man. Few men are ... [his] equal in business habits, and talents. He is to be *implicitly relied on*."[27]

The factor had to be a man of many talents, for he was at once merchant, bookkeeper, correspondent, and ambassador.

Moreover, under McKenney at least, he had to be a man of "Industry, and personal activity, and *sound morals,*" for the superintendent viewed the factor as a civilizing influence as well as a storekeeper. He screened carefully the men he recommended to the president for appointment. Perhaps his nominees knew. little about Indians, but they were all competent businessmen of impeccable character. Barak Owens, a Virginian acquaintance of eight years, McKenney considered "peculiarly fitted for the business of factor, from his knowledge of accounts, and mercantile affairs—his practical experience, his known industry, and his unimpeachable morals." McKenney had known Marylander John Hersey for ten years before nominating him in 1819. Not only was Hersey "a merchant and a man of business [with] . . . considerable experience in mechanicks," but he also was "a minister of religion & approved by the Church of which he is a member." Hersey was assigned to the Choctaw factory after it was moved to Fort Confederation, about ninety miles above Fort St. Stephens on the Tombigbee River. Within a year McKenney was writing to the chairman of the Senate Committee on Indian Affairs of the wisdom of the appointment, claiming that Hersey spent "his sabbath days . . . in the department of morals & religious instruction" and that the Indians "are flocking from their haunts of idleness & dissipation to hear his councils." Not all factors, of course, were so dedicated to their work. Although John W. Johnson at Prairie du Chien was married to an Indian woman, he confided in a letter to Sibley his desire to get away from "the cursed stinking Indians."[28]

Johnson perhaps voiced a bitterness shared but not expressed by most of his colleagues, for a factor's life was difficult and discouraging, especially in the declining years of the system. For help the factor had only an interpreter and, rarely, an assistant or clerk. Four factors owned slaves, including Sibley who had five. Although the pay was adequate—$1,300 a year—living conditions were deplorable. Johnson likened one factor's quarters to the "pig pens on a gentleman's farm." Ideally, each trading house had at least two buildings—quarters for the factor and his family and a store with cellar for the furs. Most factories, however, were housed within the stockade of a fort, which meant store and quarters were crowded under one roof, a disagreeable arrangement considering the odor that emanated from curing skins. McKenney was sympathetic but helpless. He could spare no funds to provide more than minimum shelter for the factors or the trade goods, and he would authorize only essential repairs, such as "plaster[ing] up the leaky places" and "nailing on of boards, & propping to keep the buildings from falling down."[29]

Adding to the discomfort of the factors was the open hostility of the soldiers with whom they were closely associated. If factories were not located in military posts, then soldiers were detailed to guard them. The soldiers were expected not only to protect the public property but also to keep the buildings in repair and to tend the furs, receiving a gill of whiskey and fifteen cents a day for the extra duty. Instead of assistance, the factors often endured abuse from the soldiers who had no relish for the work and held the "storekeepers" in contempt. As a rule the harassment was petty, but John Fowler was virtually a prisoner of the ten-man sergeant's guard at the Sulphur Fork factory in southern Arkansas. Fowler was so terrorized that he finally abandoned the factory until a "proper" officer could take command. "At the time I close this every soldier here is drunk and they are quarrelling & fighting," Fowler wrote in May 1820, informing McKenney of his decision.[30] Officers were little better, however, for they objected to detailing troops for factory duty and ignored or circumvented regulations requiring their cooperation. McKenney continually petitioned the secretary of war for assistance but to no avail; the officers and enlisted men in the frontier garrisons merely winked at the War Department directives.[31]

No less frustrating to the factors was the antagonism expressed by the agents with whom they shared responsibility for Indian administration. The factors' duties were primarily mercantile and they answered directly to McKenney; all other aspects of Indian affairs, including the licensing of private traders, were handled by a loose network of agents and superintendents responsible to the secretary of war. The lines of demarcation between the civilian branches of the Indian service were understandably hazy. Confusion was even greater when factors and agents were stationed at the same place, as was the case at Chicago, Green Bay, and Fort Osage, and when factors served as agents for brief periods.

Agents resented the factors, perhaps because the licensing function gave the agents close contact with the private traders. Indian agents and superintendents volunteered some of the most persuasive arguments against the factories during the congressional hearings in the spring of 1822 that ended in the abolition of the system.[32]

Furs and peltries were the factor's first responsibility, since they required constant attention and provided the main income for the factory system. The furs were highly susceptible to moths, mildew, worms, and water damage; excessive heat caused rot. Sprinkling with turpentine effectively controlled moths, but in warm weather only beating could combat worms. Shipping the furs was even riskier than storing them. When the factor accumulated furs for a large bundle, he packed them tightly with a press and sent them to the nearest transportation agent who in turn forwarded them to Georgetown. In transit the furs had to be regularly unpacked, beaten, and dried in the sun. To ensure against damage, McKenney advised his factors to send the furs to Georgetown by northern routes in summer and to avoid steamboats whenever possible. "There is not room enough in a steam boat to unpack and beat the skins; and the heat of her works breed worms faster than they could be got out—nor will she stop for a time long enough to perform this unpleasant and tedious operation on shore."[33] In spite of precautions, some loss was expected on every shipment.

McKenney sold the furs at auction, normally every November. If the factories sent many furs, he held another auction in April. Weeks of preparation preceded the sales, primarily in cleaning, sorting, and bundling the furs. John Kelly's slave gang did this disagreeable work, while McKenney and his clerks graded the skins as to first or second quality; damaged pelts they graded and bundled separately. The number of skins in a pack varied: the small muskrat pelts were packed in lots of a hundred, the popular beaver in lots of fifty, and the massive bearskins in lots of ten.

McKenney advertised the dates of the auctions and the types and quantities of furs in newspapers as far away as Boston. On auction day, the slaves hauled the packs up from the cellar to Edward Davis, the auctioneer, a Georgetown merchant who received $100 for his services. Davis described each lot in detail

to the buyers assembled in the yard behind the M Street building. If the furs were particularly fine and the market good, the
auction secured sufficient capital to operate the factories the
coming year. McKenney held two auctions in 1817. The April
sale grossed $11,877 from only 135 lots; the November sale
grossed $29,951 from twenty buyers who bid on 641 lots. Sub-
sequent sales were less frequent and less lucrative, reflecting
both the decline in the quality of furs and factory business and
the effects of the depression of 1819. The auction held in November 1820, for instance, attracted seventeen buyers for 307
lots and grossed only $8,905, although McKenney offered a
wide variety of furs and skins—muskrat, raccoon, mink, fisher,
wildcat, fox, wolf, ground hog, rabbit, beaver, otter—as well as
thirty-five reed mats from Prairie du Chien.[34]

The mats were by no means unique sales items. Furs may
have been the mainstay of the factory system, but the trading
houses received feathers, nets, baskets, beeswax, lead, vege-
tables, even cotton. McKenney, in fact, urged the factors to
accept anything that could be sold without loss—except stolen
property, such as the mules a band of Comanche warriors
offered Fowler. Agricultural commodities most pleased Mc-
Kenney, because agriculture was "a branch of the great scheme
of civilization" and he soon came to regard the government trade
as a humanitarian endeavor designed to civilize and Christianize
the Indians. Until the "great object" had been attained, the
factories were to be the link for the Indians between the wilderness and civilized life—"a shield to protect, and a fountain to
sustain, and refresh, and bless the Indians."[35]

3
The Factories and Indian Reform

Although McKenney was responsible only for the government trading houses, the Office of Indian Trade gradually became an informal focus for many aspects of Indian affairs. Its expanding function reflected McKenney's own broadening concern for the Indians, a concern that came to dominate his private as well as public life. He advised the secretary of war and members of Congress about Indian matters; he corresponded with humanitarians and church groups throughout the country; and he conferred with and entertained many of the missionaries, agents, and Indians who visited the nation's capital.

One wonders what Editha McKenney thought of the constant stream of guests her husband brought home for dinner or for conversation by the fireside. She evidently approved, for the McKenneys led an active social life throughout their years in Washington, especially those they spent at Weston, the magnificent one-hundred-acre estate on Georgetown Heights that McKenney rented from Walter S. Chandler. Three white laborers tended the gardens and crops, while Editha was mistress of a household that included six black servants, four of whom were slaves.[1] In the elegantly furnished mansion with its handsome beamed ceilings, McKenney extended the lavish hospitality of the aristocrat he yearned to be.

Always welcome were Indians, whether urbane and polished leaders of the southern tribes or *"very raw* folks" like the seventeen members of the Pawnee, Oto, Kansa, Omaha, and Missouri delegation that visited Washington in the autumn of 1821. The warmth and sincerity of the McKenneys greatly impressed the travelers. "I am not insensible of the kind regard manifested to me at all times at Weston by my invaluable friends," wrote the Cherokee chief Elijah Hicks in July 1824. "My truest affection for yourself and Lady having taken my heart for its foundation that altho, we are separated by space no time nor power can succeed from my immortal Soul to eradicate; the flame of happiness which necessarily fires the breast at Weston." Less florid but equally earnest was the tribute written two years later by David Folsom, a principal chief of the Choctaws. "When I became acquainted with you in your City, I was pleased to find that you were friend to the red people, & the relation which you stand with your Government, have actuated me to write you in a private manner, and not official."[2]

McKenney's greater participation in the administration of Indian affairs was encouraged by John C. Calhoun. When he became secretary of war in December 1817, Calhoun found the nation's largest executive department in chaos. Faced with a staggering accumulation of housekeeping problems, including the management of Indian affairs, he came early to respect McKenney's knowledge and accepted his help and advice. In October 1818, for instance, McKenney sent him a letter from John Fowler, the Natchitoches factor, reporting rumors of an impending Indian uprising. "When I had the honor of a conversation with you the other day," McKenney wrote in the covering letter, "you mentioned your purposes of throwing a portion of the Military on the western boundaries of Louisiana —Your object if I recollect was to keep down the adventurous and warlike spirit of the Natives in that quarter." If Calhoun acted promptly, perhaps he could "effectually arrest" the outbreak. Fowler's "means *of gathering information* is very good," McKenney assured the secretary of war, and in his "representations the most implicit reliance may be placed."[3]

Four months later, McKenney confided to Calhoun his grave doubts about a pending agreement between the Cherokee Indians and the federal government. The Cherokees would agree to a partial cession of the tribal holdings in Georgia and Tennessee in return for firm title to their remaining lands. McKenney was afraid the Cherokee request would not be honored. "I speak of my *understanding* of their wishes—which, however, may not be critically correct." If made, the cession would throw open to settlement a large tract of valuable land. "A numerous body of *coarse, bad people*" already occupied much of that land illegally. "My fear," McKenney wrote Calhoun in his "unofficial" letter, "is, that this wretched set of men, finding their squatting places (Knickerbocker, I think it is, calls such folks squatters) to have fallen into the possession of men who will [purchase them legally],... will force themselves upon the lands which the present negotiations may reserve for the Indians. The impunity with which they have so long held the lands, now occupied by them, seems to warrant this apprehension. If they shall do so," McKenney warned, "there will still be no relief to the Indians, *whose principal curse has flowed from this source.*" To guarantee the sanctity of the remaining Cherokee lands would be, McKenney concluded, "I am sure, a source of great consolation to both you & myself."[4]

In time, humanitarians and Indians alike learned a good way to reach Calhoun was through McKenney. Typical was the request from Charles Hicks of the Eastern Cherokees, who sought removal of the tribe's newly appointed assistant agent. "With real pleasure I sit down to address this letter to your notice on the Affairs of this Nation.... The only reason I have for troubling you with the above contents is that its tenour may be safely conveyed to the honourble Secretary of War. And trust your excuse, of being troublesome of which a red man is too much so." McKenney gave the request little heed and simply forwarded it to Calhoun.[5]

Much more spirited was McKenney's defense of the Reverend Elias Cornelius, a member of the American Board of Commissioners for Foreign Missions accused of undermining government efforts to remove the Cherokees from Tennessee and Georgia. On February 7, 1818, Samuel Worcester, corresponding secretary of the board, sought McKenney's intercession on the missionary's behalf. McKenney immediately dashed off a strong letter to Calhoun, who had then been in office only three months. The superintendent admitted knowing nothing more about the affair than Worcester had reported, yet his acquaintance with the missionary convinced him Cornelius had been unjustly accused. "Mr. Cornelius & myself have conversed largely on our Indian relations, at my house, when on his way to the Indian Country," wrote McKenney, "—and I am satisfied he is incapable of the conduct that has been attributed to him." McKenney sent Worcester a copy of his letter and promised to see Calhoun at "some early opportunity." The meeting was unnecessary; Calhoun replied in less than three days. The secretary of war was pleased that Cornelius seemed blameless, but he included a warning that McKenney relayed to Worcester. "While the government extends every encouragement to render the efforts of Missionaries successful in reclaiming even in a limited degree, the Indians from their barbarous state, it expects from them a proper support of all its measures growing out of our relations with the Tribes, and prompted by our best policy." Worcester thanked McKenney profusely and asked him to reassure Calhoun that the American Board considered the government's Indian policy "highly satisfactory" and that "to 'afford a proper support of its measures,' will be our pleasure as well as our duty."[6]

McKenney's paramount interest while superintendent of Indian trade was Indian reform. On this subject he did more than advise Calhoun; he initiated programs and shaped policy according to what he conceived to be the government's primary obligation—to civilize and Christianize the Indians. "It is enough to know that Indians are Men," he wrote to Cornelius, "that like ourselves they are susceptible of pleasure, and of pain—that they have souls; . . . that like us they must live forever; and that we have the power not only to enhance their happiness in this world, but in the next also; and by our councils, and guidance, save souls that otherwise must perish!"[7] Although McKenney's own conversion to the cause of Indian reform dated only from his appointment to office, he emerged within a remarkably short period as one of the most able and active proponents of the movement.

Calhoun must have marveled at McKenney's machinations

for the cause, for the unwary secretary of war soon found himself hailed as a patron of reform. "It is a work in which he has taken deep interest," the superintendent would assure his missionary friends. Interested or not, Calhoun became involved in McKenney's ever-growing circle of clergymen and humanitarians dedicated to saving the Indians. McKenney reported in October 1821 to the Reverend Philip Milledoler of the United Foreign Missionary Society of New York, who wished to establish an Indian mission, "the Secy of War . . . & Gov. Cass dined with me a few days ago—and 'we talked the subject oer'—I felt like 'shouldering my crutch & shewing how fields were won.' Missions—Missions—Missions," exclaimed McKenney. "These are the moral artillery that are ordained to level the Citadels of error & crime; & those who conduct them will enter, amidst the ruins, building the waste places, but of new materials."[8]

McKenney and his fellow humanitarians believed the salvation of the tribes could best be achieved through agriculture. Farming would give the Indians an appreciation for private property, an incentive for personal industry, and the stability needed for organized society and self-government. Agriculture would also require the settled existence the missionaries considered essential before the Indians could benefit from the gospel; successful conversions depended on regular school and church attendance.

Accordingly, as superintendent of Indian trade McKenney did his utmost to promote agriculture among the tribes. On June 18, 1816, for instance, he wrote to each factor and Indian agent requesting his help in determining "what particular implements of husbandry" the various tribes wished to receive either in trade or in annuity payments. "The Government, and Society in General, would be happy to learn that our border neighbors were quickening in their advances to a state of Civilization; and growing fond of the agricultural life," McKenney explained. Only the Chickasaw agent responded, but his letter was very encouraging. "The Indians are very desirous to get plenty of good Corn hoes, light barshear or shovel ploughs, axes, grubbing hoes, and every useful implement of husbandry," the agent informed McKenney. "I sincerely recommend that a very considerable part of the annuity for the years 1817 and 1818, be of articles of that valuable kind." Delighted, McKenney "took great care" to select a fine assortment of agricultural tools, which the Chickasaws then refused to accept. They demanded their annuity payments in cash and denied ever asking for the farm goods.[9]

McKenney was not disheartened, and he continued to send seeds, hoes, and plows to the factories. To encourage the Indians to trade for the equipment, McKenney urged his factors to plant gardens. "Little farms around the factories are useful," McKenney informed one factor. "The family of the factor is benefited; and the example seems to impress the Indians with notions of providing for their own wants." To another McKenney wrote: "I will also send you some wheat for seed, that the Indians may be encouraged in the growth of this article. This is the way you will most effectually promote the *great object of the Govt.* towards these unenlightened people. Invite their attention to agriculture and the arts, and help them, for they are helpless. Our object is not to keep these Indians hunters eternally," McKenney explained. "We want to make citizens out of them, and they must be first anchored in the soil, else they will be fliting about whilst there is any room for them in the wilderness or an animal to be trapped."[10]

McKenney also used his position as superintendent of Indian trade to promote and sustain missionary activities among the Indians. "I am aware that I am not acting under any special authority of law in these matters," he admitted to Calhoun, "but somehow or other I am believed by those who are so deeply interested in the matter to be *duty bound* to act &c. And I am prepared to comply with what appears to be the wishes of these friends to these unfortunate people."[11]

One tangible benefit the religious societies realized from McKenney's liberal interpretation of his duties was the privilege of sending letters and packages to their missionaries under the frank of the superintendent of Indian trade. Parcels too large for the mails traveled free of charge with the trade goods and annuities McKenney sent into the Indian country. "I most cheerfully open the way for their transmission thro' this office," he informed one inquirer. "Portable packages ... put under cover to me by the mail conveyance shall be duely forwarded; and presents of any kind, or larger packages that may be provided for our Brothers of the forest, by being shipped to this

office, shall also be forwarded." Although the American Board
of Commissioners for Foreign Missions made the most extensive use of McKenney's "obliging proposal," several other eastern
churches and philanthropic organizations took advantage of the
offer, including a group of Philadelphia ladies who collected
clothing for needy Indian children.[12]

McKenney's efforts on behalf of the United Foreign Missionary Society well illustrate the nature and extent of the
cooperation he gave the philanthropic organizations. In the
spring of 1819 Milledoler wrote that two society members, Job
B. Vinal and Epaphras Chapman, would soon leave New York
to visit the Cherokees and Delawares who had recently emigrated
to Arkansas Territory and to find a suitable site for an Indian
mission. McKenney wrote Superintendent Clark at St. Louis,
soliciting "any service which you may have in your power to
bestow in furthering their mission, whether in relation to those
tribes or any others they may be led to visit." He wrote similar
letters to the Fort Osage, Sulphur Fork, and Chicago factors
instructing them to furnish in addition interpreters and "friendly
Indians" as guides. "These Gentlemen represent a most respectable body of benevolent men who have associated to promote
the best interests of our Indians.—I know their credentials are
genuine, and from my heart wish them success." McKenney also
obtained for the travelers a War Department pass suggesting
that superintendents of Indian affairs and "all other agents in
the service of the United States" show their "special favor and
protection."[13]

Armed with these impressive recommendations, Chapman
and Vinal journeyed to Arkansas only to discover that the
American Board had already begun laboring in the Cherokee
vineyard. The two missionaries continued on to the Arkansas
River where they met the Little Osages. Vinal died shortly thereafter, but Chapman returned to New York the following January
enthusiastic about the favorable prospects of an Osage mission.
The only apparent obstacle was the tribe's lack of an Indian
agent; the nearest one was more than five hundred miles away.
The problem seemed serious to the society, which hoped to draw
on the resources of an agency while establishing the mission; an
interpreter's salary was one expense the society especially wished
to avoid.

Milledoler turned to McKenney. Would the government consider appointing an agent to the Osages? If so, the society was prepared to send twenty missionaries to the Arkansas—"Males and Females, in the prime of life, most of them married persons, furnished with the most respectable testimonials, and so far as we can judge entirely devoted to the work." The clergyman asked the superintendent of Indian trade to use his influence with the secretary of war to have an Osage agency established and also to obtain funds and supplies. The missionaries would pass through Washington on their way west if McKenney thought conferring with their friends in the government would improve their chances. "You see dear Sir," Milledoler admitted with some candor, "how much we can venture on your goodness and philanthropy?"[14]

McKenney was eager to help and immediately discussed the requests with Calhoun. "I approve, myself, of the purpose of this agency—and think the design will be promoted by the change of location [from the Cherokees to the Osages]. The subject gathers interest every day, & promises the happiest results, if it be *suitably sustain'd*, and if it shall not be, I am sure it will be no fault of yours." The secretary of war, who interpreted his duties less liberally than the impulsive superintendent, endorsed the enterprise but offered little material aid. Equipment and money were out of the question. Congress controlled the appointment of Indian agents; Calhoun could only make recommendations. Nevertheless, the secretary did agree to instruct William Clark to assign a subagent to the Little Osages, thereby presenting the missionaries with an interpreter and much of the logistical support they needed.[15] Calhoun also indicated his approval of the venture by giving Chapman and his fellow immigrants a "general Circular" addressed to the superintendents of Indian affairs and all other federal officials whom they might meet; a brief testimonial to the Osage chiefs of the Arkansas; and letters of introduction to Clark, Governor James T. Miller of Arkansas Territory, and Major William Bradford, commandant of Fort Smith.

McKenney doubtless drafted these letters as well as his own, which were much more expansive and reflected his fervent hopes for the success of the mission. "I avail myself of the agency of the Revd. E. Chapman who is on his way to the Osage Indians, in

company with a large missionary family, to present to you my
remembrances; and to solicit for this mission, your countenance
and best feelings," McKenney wrote to Miller. The mission had
"the confidence of the Government" he assured the governor,
while "for myself, I look for the best results, when I consider
that the Indians among whom Mr. Chapman is going are within
your agency; and that your countenance & friendly councils &
interpositions, are always at hand in behalf of the great cause
of justice & benevolence." McKenney appealed to the Indian
agents for "aid in the furtherance of this benevolent work. I do
this with the greater confidence that the Agents are men of kind
& benevolent feelings and will delight in the promotion of what-
soever shall tend to the amelioration of human misery." To
David Brearly, who had just been appointed agent to the Cherokee Indians west of the Mississippi, the superintendent wrote:
"I am gratified to have the opportunity to address you by the
Revd. Mr. Chapman, who will hand you this. I sincerely rejoice
in your appointment... because I rely upon your known disposition of benevolence which you may now so advantageously
exercise in promoting the welfare of the Indians. Mr. Chapman's
mission is known to you—I sincerely wish him well, and [on]
your aid I rely much."[16]

McKenney saved his most ardent language for the Osage
chiefs. "Brothers, I live a great distance from you towards the
rising Sun, yet I know you, and I am your friend. . . . I want to
council and advise you." White brothers from the great city of
New York were coming to instruct the Osages "in those things
which are important for you to know." They were not like the
fur traders who would only cheat and defraud Indians. "These
good men will teach you how to till the ground—how to make
fields and gardens, where all things necessary for you to live
upon will grow." The missionary women would teach the little
girls to spin, weave, knit, and sew. All the Osage children would
learn to read, write, cipher, and "pray and sing praises to the
Great Spirit." Their Great Father, the president, approved of
this important work and wished his Osage children to accept
the missionaries and to heed their words. "Brothers," McKenney
wrote, "I shake hands with you—and put my seal upon this
talk. I pray the Great Spirit to make you and your children
happy."[17]

Meanwhile, the Great Osages, the other branch of the tribe, were forming a small delegation to visit Washington to discuss a mission of their own. Led by the aged but articulate Sans Nerf, the three-member delegation reached the nation's capital in late June. McKenney invited the Indians to Weston for dinner. The old chief seemed so troubled and preoccupied during the evening that his host, hoping to cheer him up, told him about the missionaries who were at that very moment traveling to the Little Osage village. His people, McKenney said, would soon receive the same favors. "Brother," Sans Nerf replied, "I have long been ready—But I will make you a talk soon."[18]

A few days later Sans Nerf visited the Office of Indian Trade to "pour out his complaints." As soon as the Indian left, McKenney wrote to both Milledoler and to Samuel Worcester describing the interview. "I have this moment parted from the Osage deputation consisting of their principle chief—Councellor, & warrior. The address of the Chief, to me, was eloquent beyond description." In 1806 Sans Nerf had met President Thomas Jefferson, who had promised the Osages many favors if they remained peaceful and friendly. They had done so, but the Great Father had chosen instead to bestow blessings on tribes whose hands were bloody. "Poor fellow," McKenney wrote, "he seemed more sensible than any with whom I have conversed, of their sad state, and of their wrongs, and the Justice that is due them."

McKenney hoped to persuade the United Foreign Missionary Society or the American Board to establish a mission for the Great Osages. He preferred that Milledoler's group accept the responsibility, since the society had already begun work among the Osages, but, he explained to Worcester, "if they cannot move in the work *speedily*, I think it important that some other hand of our great system of kindness should be organized amongst these people, *without delay*. They are anxious about it—and to hear that the work would be immediately undertaken would give them joy indescribable." McKenney urged both men to come to Washington before the Osages left so they could judge for themselves the sincerity of the Indians. Sans Nerf's speech alone "was worth a ride from Boston to hear," he claimed.

McKenney concluded his busy day by briefing Calhoun on his activities. "I have thought it proper to pass this in review before you," he explained, "as in the great talk which I learn the Chief intends to have with his *Father* [the secretary of war], the same or nearly the same ground will be gone over." McKenney also felt obliged to tell Calhoun he had offered— "for you"—the complete cooperation of the War Department in establishing the mission.[19]

The United Foreign Missionary Society must have had some qualms about assuming responsibilities beyond its capacity. Nevertheless, Milledoler two weeks later visited Washington, interviewed Sans Nerf, and agreed to establish a second mission among the Osages by autumn. Milledoler may have been worried, but McKenney was overjoyed. "I sincerely wish you success in the noble work in which you are engaged, as I do all others who have undertaken its promotion," he wrote after learning the good news. "I know that any aid which it may be in the power of the President to afford; and which will be furnished thro' the Secretary of War, whose good feelings and hearty co-operation in this benevolent design is known to you, will be most cheerfully granted. As for myself, if I can help in my feeble way to forward this cause of suffering humanity, I promise the best service I may have the ability to render. And these you are authorised at all times freely to command."[20]

McKenney kept his word. By the fall of 1821 the government had appointed an agent for the Osages, headquartered at St. Louis; in another two years both the Little and Great Osages had resident subagents as well. In the meantime the United Foreign Missionary Society had established two stations for the tribe: Union Mission for the Little Osages was situated on the west bank of the Grand River about forty-five miles above its confluence with the Arkansas; Harmony Mission for the Great Osages was near the Missouri River approximately 170 miles north of Union and eighty-five miles below the Fort Osage factory.

Much to everyone's disappointment, however, the missions did not prosper. The Osages welcomed the missionaries joyously, exclaiming on their arrival that it was "a bright day" and "a good morning without clouds." But it soon became evident that the Osages wanted the missionaries not for religious guidance but for political influence with the federal government and help in combating their bitter enemies, the Cherokees. "When we attempt to evade their requests, by referring them to their

Agent," reported William F. Vaill, superintendent of Union Mission, "they reply 'he is at a great distance; we want advice to day; you are all one as ourselves; you come to do us good; when we need the advice of wise men, will you refuse to counsel us?' " When the Osage leaders met the blacksmith, they "wondered if they could not be instructed by us, how to make powder and guns." The profane situation improved little with time. "The Chiefs are friends to us as citizens and as the representatives of a great nation which they *respect*," a somewhat discouraged Vaill reported two years later. "But they cannot as yet be considered as fathers to the school. They have not realised the benefit of civilization; have many fears lest they shall lose their influence by changing their habits; and have done very little, if any thing to make the school popular among their people."[21]

It had not taken the superintendent of Indian trade long to realize that his efforts for Indian reform were inadequate. Eight factories and a handful of missions could have little impact on the thousands of Indians scattered across the American frontier; something far more comprehensive and organized was needed. A proposal from the Reverend Cyrus Kingsbury of the American Board of Commissioners for Foreign Missions suggested an answer. In the spring of 1816 Kingsbury appealed for federal aid to establish a Cherokee school. The American Board wished to test the feasibility of instructing Indian children in farming, weaving, and carpentry. The secretary of war authorized the Cherokee agent to build a schoolhouse and quarters for a teacher and to purchase plows, hoes, spinning wheels, and whatever else the board needed. If the experiment failed, all property would revert to the government.[22]

Known as Brainerd, the school, which was located east of Chattanooga on Chickamauga Creek, opened in January 1817. Within a year, fifty acres under cultivation surrounded a mission house, schoolhouse, dining hall, kitchen, gristmill, sawmill, barn, stable, and five long domitories. Moreover, forty-seven "promising Cherokee children" ranging in age from six to eighteen and in extraction "from full blooded Cherokees to those apparently white" were receiving "a christian and civilized education."[23]

Kingsbury used the Lancasterian system of instruction at Brainerd. Devised by a Quaker schoolmaster to provide cheap

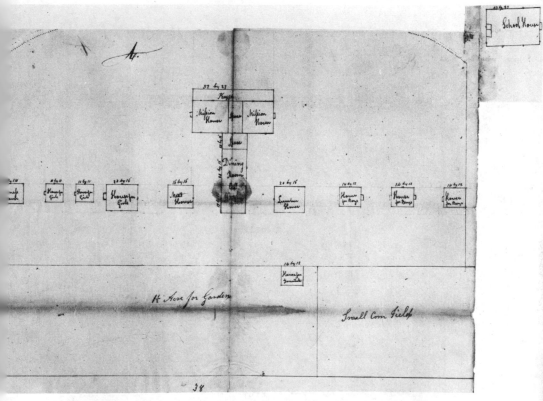

Diagram of the grounds and buildings at Brainerd school, submitted by Cyrus Kingsbury with his first annual report, June 10, 1818. *Courtesy National Archives.*

Specimens of handwriting by Indian children at Brainerd, submitted by Cyrus Kingsbury with his first annual report, June 10, 1818. *Courtesy National Archives.*

education for England's poor, Lancasterian schools usually consisted of one large room with lesson cards suspended from the wall. The students were divided into squads of ten, each under the direction of a quick-learning child called a monitor. The teacher taught the monitors and they in turn drilled their squads.[24] Although the Lancasterian system was efficient and adequate for lessons that could be mastered through memorization, it broke down when the subject matter required thought or analysis. Using children to teach children was an inherent weakness. But despite its defects, the economical Lancasterian educational program appealed to thrifty philanthropists of the nineteenth century.

Kingsbury followed the system quite closely at Brainerd. He called the squads companies and the monitors captains. The students first learned to print the alphabet in sand, then to write on slates, then to read. By May 1818 eighteen Cherokee scholars had attained the final step—writing on paper—and Kingsbury proudly announced in his first annual report that fifteen students who had been enrolled only six to twelve months could now read very well from the Bible. Kingsbury also regimented the time the Cherokee children spent outside the classroom. The girls were placed under the care of a female teacher who instructed them in sewing, knitting, and spinning; the boys cut wood in the winter and worked in the fields during the summer. As incentives, the students received printed tickets for good conduct, which they could redeem for useful and necessary articles. "This has had a very happy influence, both on their learning & industry," reported Kingsbury, who considered the experiment at Brainerd a remarkable success. "We are confident we have never seen so many children in one school, who accomplished so much work as ours."[25]

McKenney was so taken with Kingsbury's idea that he proposed the federal government establish a network of identical schools throughout the Indian country. Fortuitously, President Madison in his state of the union message of December 3, 1816, charged Congress with resuming "the work of civilization" interrupted by the War of 1812. A week later Congressman Isaac Thomas of Tennessee, chairman of the House Committee on Indian Affairs, asked McKenney for information respecting the "particular situation" of the tribes and for "a plan, if any, . . .

best calculated to effect the humane object recommended to Congress."[26]

McKenney responded immediately. In a series of lengthy letters to Thomas, he outlined a comprehensive program to expand the factory system and "serve the great object of humanity." McKenney admitted the condition of the Indians remained almost unchanged from earlier eras. "The same devotion to the chase, and those irregular habits which have characterised the sons of our forests yet predominate." Only those tribes bordering the frontier settlements or utilizing the trading houses had shown any cultural improvement. Indeed, McKenney declared in a rash statement he would later contradict repeatedly when agitating for Indian removal, "all cases of advancement, may be traced to their contiguity to, and intercourse with the whites." Therefore, the best way to serve the "great object of humanity" would be to increase the number of factories, making them available to more distant Indian tribes. With an additional appropriation of $200,000 McKenney could build eight new factories west of the Mississippi and establish a supply depot at St. Louis under the administration of an assistant superintendent of Indian trade.[27]

An important auxiliary to McKenney's plan was a system of schools, which he would oversee but which the various benevolent associations would run. "However ineffectual this means of instruction might be in its operations on the adult Indians," McKenney told Thomas, "the rising generation would insensibly imbibe from such a source of improvement, and transmit them to their successors those ingredients without which it seems impossible with any thing like human exertion to teach them a knowledge of, or make them familiar with (at least in any reasonable time) the excellent principles of our Government; the ties which unite and bind society together, with the great advantages of that state over that of the savage; or impress them with the importance of the observance of those great moral lessons, in the practise of which results so much security and happiness to man." The Indians' knowledge of those principles would be worth as much to the United States as to the tribes. Moreover, continued McKenney, the government could teach such principles at relatively little expense. Lancasterian schools would be an ideal method for teaching Indian children the basic rudiments of writing and farming "as well on account of its simplicity, as its economy." The schools would cost only $1,000 each to run, McKenney figured—$200 for rude but sturdy log cabins large enough to hold one hundred children, $8 for lesson cards, another $50 for slates and pencils; a competent teacher could be hired for $700 or $800 annually.[28]

As with so many of his proposals, McKenney's motives were not entirely unselfish. Although genuinely concerned about Indian reform, he anticipated tangible benefits for himself. The movement to abolish the factory system was gathering momentum in Congress. Perhaps by associating the factories with Indian civilization he could forestall threats to their survival. What congressman would oppose benevolence and Christian charity? McKenney also desperately needed the increased salary he expected the expanded Office of Indian Trade would command.

Throughout his life McKenney lived beyond his means. The Georgetown tax assessment records show that his personal property was worth $750 in 1811; by 1815 this modest sum had dwindled to $615. His mercantile venture with Hall had not been very profitable. Now, only nine months in office, McKenney was seeking a raise. His salary of $2,000 was simply inadequate, he informed Thomas. Every gentleman knows how expensive it is to live in Washington. "Does he want a house to live in?— If it be a good one, he must give $500 for it annually. His Beef 15¢ his Pork, 10¢ his Butter from 50 to 75¢ per lb—and his fire wood from $8 to 10 Dollars the cord.—What can a man do who has to pay those prices when he is limitted, and tied down by the sacred obligation of an oath—on $2000.—per year?" McKenney asked. "'Tis true he may live; but he can do no more."[29]

McKenney's letters to Thomas were effective, for on February 4, 1817, the congressman introduced a bill increasing the trade fund by $200,000. Specifically, it proposed eight new trading houses, a depot at St. Louis under an assistant superintendent of Indian trade, and raises for McKenney and his entire staff. Schools were not mentioned. The bill was read twice and referred to the House Committee of the Whole but received no further action.[30] No matter. McKenney felt certain the measure would succeed in the next Congress. He was so confident, in fact, that a few months later—after borrowing $16,750 from the Bank of Columbia—he purchased Weston from Chandler for $15,000.[31]

What sparked McKenney's optimism was a circular he received from the Kentucky Baptist Society for Propagating the Gospel among the Heathen, which appealed to government officials to persuade the Indians "to permit some of their children to be brought into this country for the purpose of being educated; and ultimately to have schools established among them." The society wished to teach three or four children from each tribe the three Rs and, "where genius warrants it, the higher branches of literature." The boys in addition would learn husbandry, the girls the domestic arts. Graduates, accompanied by teachers, would return to their villages to help instruct other children.[32]

The circular must have seemed providential to McKenney, who used it to launch a campaign urging congressional adoption of his proposal. Although Indian agents were not under his jurisdiction, he sent each a copy. "I have long believed the *Key* to the civilization of our *Aborigines*, to be the *knowledge* of some Christian language—but especially the English in this case—inasmuch as information would be conveyed to these people through this channel. This can be furnished only by the agency of *schools of instruction*," he wrote. "I sollicit, on the part of humanity, and in behalf of the Christian religion . . . that you circulate these good tidings amongst the Indians within your agency; and by means of all your persuasion, endeavour to influence them to accept the generous offer." McKenney also sent copies to the superintendents of Indian affairs. "If I do not mistake the signs of the times," he said, "a change is about to happen in the condition of our aborigines. There is a spirit gone forth amongst many tribes, corresponding to that which influences the Kentucky Babtist society, and others, who are engaged in the same work. The result must be favourable— It only needs to be anticipated in the use of active means to produce it." Therefore, he asked the superintendents to urge their agents to cooperate. A letter to each "would add vigor to their efforts."[33]

At the same time, McKenney asked Cornelius of the American Board to help in the campaign. The federal government was anxious to further the work of reform, he assured the clergyman. If any measures could be devised offering happiness to any portion of its human family, "those who constitute this Government stand ready to furnish the means." A school system administered by the Office of Indian Trade was such a measure. The best tactic for bringing the idea to the attention of Congress, McKenney thought, was for the Indians themselves to petition the president for schools. "If schools of instruction shall appear to them the best remedy for their distress, (*and they are the only direct remedy in my view*), let them be petitioned for." The petitions should "set forth their *sufferings*, their *hopelessness*, and their *dependance* on him as their father," McKenney advised. "Such an appeal, and especially if coming from several tribes, or nations, would not be lost. My word for it the President would lay the subject before the Congress, in whom alone is lodged the power to act on it." As for himself, McKenney told Cornelius, "there are no means within my controul, which, to promote such a work, I would not gladly put in immediate requisition."[34]

The value of having in government someone so friendly to their cause was not lost upon the religious groups. The Kentucky Baptist Society immediately made McKenney an honorary member of its board of directors, while the American Board appointed him to the two-member "Committee of correspondence and general agency near the seat of the National Government." The American Board took this action, it explained, because of the "very lively interest with which you enter into the design of winning up the Aborigines of our country from ignorance & wretchedness to an elevated condition of civilized & christianized life."[35] Suitably impressed by these honors, McKenney prepared for his forthcoming struggle with the Congress.

Whether McKenney discussed his plan with James Monroe, or whether some tribes did in fact petition for schools, the new president's first state of the union message could scarcely have been more favorable. Monroe gave the Congress a clear mandate. "It is our duty to make new efforts for the preservation, improvement, and civilization of the native inhabitants," he said. Some provision must be made "for the advancement of the liberal and humane policy of the United States towards all tribes within our limits, and more particularly for their improvement in the arts of civilized life."[36]

With the encouragement of the president and at least two missionary societies, McKenney wasted little time proceeding with his plans. Isaac Thomas had not been re-elected, but fortunately Henry Southard of New Jersey, who became chairman of the House Committee on Indian Affairs, was also sympathetic to Indian reform. Indeed, Southard became one of McKenney's strongest supporters, defending well the interests of the factory system throughout the next two Congresses. His retirement in 1821 was a severe loss to the friends of the factories.

McKenney was pleasantly surprised at the warmth with which the New Jersey congressman greeted his proposal. "I have had much pleasure in witnessing your friendly feelings towards these unfortunate people, and am happy to learn that a similar spirit actuates the members of the Committee generally," McKenney wrote when presenting Southard with a copy—"in its renewed form"—of his proposed bill. "It will need only a little activity in dispensing previous information among the members of the house to beget an interest there also."[37]

Southard could not have been adequately prepared for the massive document McKenney gave him. Meade Fitzhugh, McKenney's copy clerk, had drafted twenty-one clauses on thirteen legal-size sheets of paper. If adopted, the bill would have reorganized the government trade with the Indians. The proposal called for eight new trading houses and, of course, salary increases for McKenney and his staff, but the idea of an assistant superintendent and warehouse at St. Louis was dropped. The most important new provisions concerned the schools. Profits from the expanded factory system were to be applied "in the organization and endowment of schools . . . for the instruction and improvement of Indian children . . . on the Lancasterian plan." In addition, a fund would be established to aid the benevolent associations engaged in Indian education. The superintendent of Indian trade would apportion the money to the societies according to the enrollments of the schools. With the draft bill McKenney sent Southard letters from two missionaries, a copy of the Kentucky Baptist Society circular, and the assurance that the congressman could count on the active support of his colleagues Henry R. Storrs and Oliver Cromwell

Comstock of New York and Richard M. Johnson of Kentucky. "I certainly think," McKenney concluded, "Congress has it completely in its power to erect out of the materials of Indian reform a monument more durable and towering than those of ordinary dimensions, a monument as indestructible as justice; interesting as humanity—and lasting as time. Who would not help to build it?" Southard laid the cornerstone a week later when he introduced McKenney's bill in the House.[38]

McKenney now began lobbying in earnest. The day the bill was introduced, he wrote Congressman Storrs. "Seeing the sad condition of our Indians; and believing that it can be bettered; and very speedily too, by the adoption of proper means, I have felt the obligation to use my exertions to promote so humane an object. The bill... promises great advantages to the Indians." McKenney also pressed Senator George M. Troup of Georgia to back the schools. "This mode of civilizing & Christianizing the Indians, is one which would best apply to ourselves were we natives of the wilderness—and why should it not be equally applicable to other branches of our species? It were impossible for me to tell you, how fervently I wish this experiment adopted."[39]

At the same time, McKenney appealed to his missionary friends. "A bill is before the house, which promises much—I may be partial to it, perhaps because it is a pet of mine," he informed Samuel Worcester. "Whether it will pass, is one of those mysteries which it requires time to solve." Various church groups and benevolent associations across the country could aid passage by petitioning their representatives in Congress "to notice the subject." Worcester evidently did not have time to marshal such help, but he did send McKenney two sets of American Board annual reports and ten copies of the society's *Missionary Herald*. One of the reports went to President Monroe who, McKenney told Worcester, "possesses, among other noble qualities, a very sincere, and anxious solicitude for the welfare of the Indians." The copies of the *Herald* went to Southard for "such use of them as may best promote the success of his bill."[40]

Despite McKenney's exertions, the bill fared poorly. An amendment eliminated participation by the missionary societies and the school fund was limited to $10,000. Even with these changes the bill was defeated.[41]

Circumstances, however, worked to the benefit of Mc-Kenney's plans. On February 16, 1818, Philip E. Thomas, corresponding secretary of the Yearly Meeting of Friends at Baltimore, informed Calhoun that the War Department since 1813 had been financing the education of a Choctaw boy named James Lawrence McDonald. The Quakers considered the seventeen-year-old McDonald well qualified for government employment and wished to send him to Washington. "He has during the whole time of his being under our care conducted himself remarkably well, has an excellent understanding, and promises to become a useful & valuable man," Thomas wrote. When six weeks passed and Calhoun had not responded, Thomas sent the boy to Washington with Isaac Tyson and Andrew Ellicott. Calhoun referred the trio to McKenney, suggesting that the Office of Indian Trade might be a suitable place to prepare McDonald for eventual employment at the Choctaw agency. "It will afford me very great pleasure to second... this very judicious suggestion respecting the Youth," McKenney replied after meeting McDonald. "All the routines of book keeping and of accounts, with a knowledge of such other branches as may be necessary to prepare him for an agency shall be taught him." Only one aspect of the arrangement troubled McKenney. Unless the boy were placed "in some worthy family" who would supervise his leisure time, the idle young men of Georgetown might corrupt him and undo all his accomplishments.[42] No doubt the worthy family McKenney had in mind was his own.

The following day McKenney saw Calhoun, then wrote Tyson and Ellicott: "He will be committed to my charge, and in all respects." McKenney had reason to be pleased with his good fortune, for he knew McDonald would be invaluable in convincing doubting congressmen that Indians could profit from education. He admitted as much in his letter to the Quakers. "The acquirements of this young Indian afford a gratifying evidence of Indian capacity, and aptness for the attainment of the principles of Civilization, and of science.... To such as question the capacity of Indians for Civilization and improvement in science, no better argument need be offered (even tho' there were not thousands in addition) than that which a bare reference to this youth would demonstrate."[43]

McDonald moved to Georgetown on April 8, 1818, five days after the House tabled the school bill. McKenney put the young Choctaw to work in the Office of Indian Trade and boarded him at Weston. Since McKenney's son, William, was about the same age, he raised the two like brothers. "I made no distinction between [them] . . . in dress or attentions," he claimed. McDonald "had a horse at his service, when he chose to ride; took a seat with my family in the coach, rode with us to church, and visited where we did; and was never overlooked, in any of those social relations in which we indulged, whether in or out of Washington." The arrangement was ideal. The War Department gave McKenney $330 a year for the boy's room and board and paid for his wardrobe, books, and incidentals as well.[44] At the office McDonald spent most of his time copying letters for McKenney's signature, especially correspondence to federal officials, missionaries, and anyone else who might aid the school bill. For instance, to John McKee, the Choctaw agent, McKenney wrote: "I have with me in this office, and indeed living with me, James L. McDonald, a choctaw youth, whose friends are near your Agency. Tell them he is doing well—and that the U. States Gov't. are doing the part of a kind parent for him. I hope he may live to prove a blessing to himself & to his countrymen." A letter to Calhoun written a week after McDonald's arrival bears this notation: "This letter is copied *in haste* by our little Indian."[45] Similar notes can be found on McKenney's letters to Worcester written in this period.

McKenney was shrewd enough to know that he would need more than McDonald's help to get his bill through the next session of Congress. This time he based his strategy primarily on a privately printed circular dated July 4, 1818, and headed "Weston." "I turn to the religious community and beg for help for our distressed and afflicted brothers—the heathen of our country," he wrote. "I turn to those whose motto is 'peace and good will towards men.' I lay the claims of our Indians at the feet of the Christians in America." The circular asked every Christian to petition his congressman for his *"special attention, in adding to the existing system [of Indian trade], whatever else may tend to better the condition of our Indians."* Suggest no means—a variety of plans would only confuse the issue and "produce perplexity." Petitioners were simply to urge the adoption of the "grand object"—"the *security, preservation,* and *improvement* of the Indians." The method by which it would be achieved would be "attended to at Washington."[46]

McKenney sent copies to every religious association known to him. He warned Worcester to keep "its *origin* from the public view. Such things are said to smell of the Government, if they are known to come from a Government agent. I shall communicate upon this subject to no one else of your Church but shall leave all to be done by you, and by the time the Congress shall have assembled: There is no time therefore to be lost."[47]

The response probably surprised even McKenney. Petitions from all parts of the country flooded Congress. The First Baptist Church and Congregation of Philadelphia, the Mississippi Baptist Association, the Blue River Baptist Association of Indiana, and Quakers from New England, New York, New Jersey, Delaware, Maryland, Pennsylvania, Ohio, Indiana, Illinois, and Virginia all asked Congress to help the Indians. Typical was the petition sent by the Kentucky Bracken Association of Baptists, representing eleven hundred adult members in fourteen churches, which beseeched Congress to "make such provisions and appropriations, for educating the Indians, males, and females, in the English language, and instructing them in the useful arts and manners of civilized life, as the importance of the case demands."[48] Citizens from thirteen states presented their memorials in person.

Congress could not ignore the petitioners. In January 1819 Southard introduced a bill authorizing the president to select the tribes he thought prepared for the change to civilized life and to use whatever means necessary to educate them. When the House tabled the measure, McKenney feared his bill would suffer the same fate as the others. His concern was dispelled by Jeremiah Morrow, chairman of the Senate Committee on Indian Affairs, who summoned the superintendent to his office. "I never shall forget the good old Gentleman's excitement," McKenney later wrote. "He began by saying that a very great degree of interest had pervaded the Country in behalf of the Indians, . . . (I appeared not to know anything of the popular movement)."

"Something must be done," the senator declared. "I have sent for you to get your opinion as to the sum which should be appropriated annually, for the Civilization of the Indians."

"One hundred thousand dollars, annually," came McKenney's quick reply "It is little enough since we got the Indians' land for an average of 2¾ cents the acre."

"I agree with you," Morrow responded, "but as a *prudent* step, had we not better begin with $10,000 annually? If it succeeds, we can afterwards add to the sum."[49] McKenney assented, and Morrow introduced his own bill, which replaced the House version and became law on March 3, 1819. It provided $10,000 annually for the "civilization of the tribes adjoining the frontier settlements" and authorized the president "to employ capable persons of good moral character, to instruct them in the mode of agriculture suited to their situation; and for teaching their children in reading, writing, and arithmetic, and for performing such other duties, as the President may give and prescribe for the regulation of their conduct, in the discharge of their duties."[50]

With passage of the school bill McKenney turned his attention to its proper implementation. Three weeks later he sent an "entirely unofficial" letter to Worcester, asking for information about the American Board's activities among the Indians. "Believing that the money will be directed through the benevolent channels that have been opened," he wrote, "it is important that I be able to point them out. I am decided as to this—And shall so recommend it." McKenney believed the small appropriation would do the most good used in conjunction with existing schools. "And I further think, that its application should be made where *Letters, The Christian Religion, & Agriculture*, are taught." But, he stressed, "I need not tell you how exactly your Brainard establishment comes up to my way of thinking." In a month McKenney again wrote to Worcester. "You may expect a share of the 10.000$—and your undertaking will justify, in my mind, a pretty large slice. It shall be my pleasure, & business, to help, in the direction of the instrument that is to divide it.'[51]

The instrument was two printed War Department circulars announcing the ground rules for distributing the money. The appropriation would be applied "in co-operation with the exertions of benevolent associations, or individuals, who may choose to devote their time or means to effect the object contemplated by the act of Congress." The schools were expected to teach not only reading, writing, and arithmetic but also the mechanical and domestic arts. Groups interested in sharing in the appropriation were to describe to the War Department the locations of their schools, funds available, numbers of teachers and children, curriculums, and the amounts of money desired. The government agreed to pay two-thirds of the expense of erecting the necessary school buildings, but no money was to be given until construction had begun, and one-fourth of the grant was to be reserved until the buildings were completed. In addition, the government would contribute annually to each school a sum proportionate to its enrollment. Reports listing the number of students, teachers, amount of disbursements, and value and description of property on hand were due every October. Not only were the administrators of the schools expected to be sober and upright people, the second circular warned, but they had "as far as practicable, to impress on the minds of the Indians, the friendly and benevolent views of the government towards them, and the advantage to them in yielding to the policy of the government, and co-operating with it, in such measures as it may deem necessary for their civilization and happiness."[52]

McKenney's experience with the gifted McDonald greatly reinforced his belief that the schools would teach the Indians to live like white people. McDonald was born in Hinds County, Mississippi, near Jackson. Nothing is known of his white father, but his Choctaw mother, Molly, was a person of means, owning land and several slaves. By the time McKenney met the boy he had already received more than a decade of education, first at a school in Jackson and then with the Quakers in Baltimore. McDonald was by no means a typical student, and he certainly should not have been used as a gauge for measuring the educational potential of the average Indian. Nevertheless, what McDonald could do, his benefactor believed, his brethren could do just as easily and just as well. This naiveté was later to bring anguish to both McKenney and his protégé. In the meantime, the boy's accomplishments made McKenney's predictions seem possible.

McKenney grew increasingly impressed with McDonald's intellectual capacity. "No young man in the District writes more, or with apparently more pleasure," McKenney claimed. "He loves to keep his intelligence in operation—but dislikes drudgery, & forms." Instead of returning him to Mississippi, suggested McKenney, why not teach him a profession such as law, medicine, or theology? Since the professions required a knowledge of Latin, McKenney offered to send McDonald to a preparatory school until he learned the language. Calhoun agreed and so did McDonald, who preferred school to working in the Office of Indian Trade. Moreover, the Choctaw later wrote, "there did not seem any necessity implied, in learning the Latin language, of my becoming a Lawyer, Doctor, or Divine."[53]

Accordingly, with Calhoun's approval and the War Department's money, McKenney a month after passage of the school bill began grooming the boy for a career of distinction. Georgetown's finest clothiers, tailors, and cobblers outfitted McDonald with an enviable wardrobe—"1 pr. worsted suspenders, 6 Superfine Cravats, 5 yds Domestic for drawers, 1 pair of Beaver gloves, 2 pair Lambs wool 1/2 hose, 1 pair of shoes," as well as trousers, suits, and vests made of Irish linen and "super London cassimere." At the same time McKenney took the boy out of the Indian office and placed him in a Georgetown school to learn Latin from the Reverend William Carnahan, later president of Princeton University. To aid him in his studies McDonald received "1 Latin Grammar, Introduction & grammar, Selectae e verteri, Caesar Delphini, 1 Blank Book & 2 Copy books, Homers Iliad & Odyssey, Lempriere's Classical Dictionary, [and] *Rollins Ancient History.*"[54]

By August 1819, after only five months with Carnahan, McDonald had done so well that McKenney thought the boy was ready to choose a profession and asked him for a decision. "I must confess," McDonald replied, "I have some ambition to distinguish myself, some disposition to be useful,—and a desire to free the character of educated Indian Youth (with some degree of Justice cast upon it) of a proneness to relapse into Savagism." Nevertheless, he did not want to learn a profession. "I have been raised on a Farm. . . . I have a partiality for a Farmer's life, and did I believe my choice unconnected with the interest of others I might probably give it the preference, and return to a Farm." Perhaps, he continued, "it might be that after a sight once more of my country, & of my Friends, (whom I feel as if I must see again) I might so far divest myself of Family attachments & recollections, as to return, and turn my eyes to an honourable profession with pleasure." But he did not think it likely. McDonald did, however, agree to remain in Washington until spring to complete his study of Latin.[55]

By spring Calhoun and McKenney had interested McDonald in law. The young Choctaw would remain in Washington another year and then, in February 1821, go to Lebanon, Ohio, to read law with John McLean, later a Supreme Court justice. Until McDonald completed his education, the War Department would continue to bear his expenses. "I am delighted at the promise of this young man," McKenney exclaimed, when telling Calhoun of the boy's decision. "And it cannot be otherwise than gratifying to you to know, that his destiny, which so far promises so much of every thing that enables and distinguishes the Human character, is inscribed to your decisions over his pursuits, without which, he could have received no guidance from me. Whatever I may have thought, or desired in relation to him must have been powerless. You have been his patron, and I trust he may live to illustrate the wisdom which was employed in ordering his course."[56]

Passage of the civilization act marked the apex of McKenney's influence. His plans for an expanded factory system and a salary increase had been blunted, but already he had grander schemes in mind. His success with the school bill had enhanced his prestige both in and out of government; now he viewed the measure as the first step and himself as the architect of a major federal program of Indian reform. The rapid improvement of the condition of the tribes because of the schools, which McKenney anticipated, would add even greater luster to his reputation, enabling him eventually to direct all the nation's Indian affairs, not just those relating to trade. Little did McKenney suspect that within the decade his hopes for McDonald and the schools were to founder completely. He had little time to reflect or to speculate. Even as McDonald was preparing for his sojourn in Ohio, opponents of the factory system launched a determined campaign to abolish the trading houses.

4

Defending
the Factories

WHEN MCKENNEY BECAME superintendent of Indian
trade in the spring of 1816, the factory system was
in a state of decline. Although the government trading
houses were never prosperous nor universally popular, they did
not face sustained criticism and organized opposition until after
the War of 1812. The conflict crippled the factories financially
and at the same time opened the vast fur resources of the Old
Northwest to exploitation by independent American traders
and fur companies. Each year thereafter the system came under
stronger and stronger attack from the private traders who resented the government competition and brought economic and
political pressure to bear on the factories. The opposition of
the vested interest groups was supported by the spirit of nationalism that swept the country after the war; the nationalists
favored a laissez faire economic policy and therefore disapproved of the government's participation in the realm of private
enterprise. Then, to compound McKenney's problems, just as
the factories appeared to be recovering from the effects of the
war, the devastating depression of 1819 caused a near total
collapse of the economy and forced Congress to seek ways of

curbing federal spending. Accusations of waste and inefficiency were hurled most often at the War Department. As Secretary of State John Quincy Adams noted in his diary, "the falling off in the revenue has stirred up the spirit of economy and retrenchment, and as the expenditures of the War Department are those upon which the considerable reduction can be made, it is at them that the economists level their first and principal batteries."[1]

The factory system was particularly vulnerable to congressional scrutiny. To McKenney's dismay, few of the trading houses met expenses and the situation worsened with each passing year. The income from fur sales dwindled from a postwar high of $73,305 in 1816 to $28,482 in 1819. "I have hardly done a sufficiency of business this season to clear the wages of my interpreter," Jacob Varnum, the Chicago factor, complained in December 1818. Two years later George Sibley admitted trade at the Fort Osage factory had "almost intirely ceased—not more than a dozen Indians has been in to trade during the fall & winter."[2]

"Why do the factories lose money?" members of Congress would ask. Patiently McKenney would try to explain. The eight factories were too few and scattered—only one was across the Missouri—and the Indians were apprehensive of the "long knives" who guarded them. Moreover, renewing the enabling act one year at a time weakened faith in the permanency of the system and precluded major improvements or innovations. McKenney's analysis was correct, but more fundamental problems also hampered the trading houses.

One impediment was the Indian desire for presents and credit. Lack of funds to finance properly even day-to-day factory operations made it impossible to give more than token presents. The Indians did not view favorably this apparent stinginess, especially when they compared it to the generosity of the private traders. Presents were basic to Indian culture, and many of the tribes regarded the trade relationship more as gift-giving than economic exchange.[3] The same was true of credit. Indians grasped poorly the concept of repaying debts, and the usual wilderness hazards made them even greater credit risks. Yet a warrior needed his supplies before he left on his winter hunt and he could not be expected to pay for them until his return.

Although McKenney tried to discourage the practice, the factors were forced to give the Indians merchandise on credit. As one of them explained to McKenney after receiving a consignment of muskets, "unless I am permitted to give a few of them on credit to some particular Indians I fear I shall not be able to dispose of them to advantage." McKenney replied, "I have no objection that a few of the Rifles be let out on time—but regard the punctuality of the buyers."[4] When the factories closed in the summer of 1822 they held $37,416—more than 10 percent of the capital fund—in unpaid bills; debts due the Choctaw factory alone totaled $12,702.48.[5] No more than a few hundred dollars was ever recovered.

McKenney's reluctance to give credit was not based solely on the financial shakiness of the factory system. The superintendent feared giving the Indians "free" merchandise would make them idle and shiftless; eventually they might depend entirely on government bounty for subsistence. Even civilized men, he reasoned, found it difficult to work if they were materially independent. Of course, destitute individuals were to be helped, but McKenney considered pampering Indians bad policy. Humanity required the government to encourage self-reliance.[6]

Overshadowing credit as a serious handicap to the factory system was the prohibition against liquor. Although exceptions had been made in the past, McKenney was inflexible. "The bane of the Indian was wholly excluded from the United States trade," he later boasted. "Not a drop of brandy, rum or whiskey [was] permitted to pass through the factories."[7] Low prices and honest treatment were poor substitutes for "mad water," however, which partially explains why Indians did their trading elsewhere. Established and reputable fur companies preferred low but consistent profits over a period of time to the brief, spectacular gains the free use of whiskey brought. Smaller companies and most independent traders, on the other hand, found alcohol to be the best means of competing with the larger fur companies, and whiskey became the independent trader's leading article of exchange. To retaliate, the large companies poured liquor into the Indian country, theorizing that the trader with the most whiskey would get the most furs.

Day after day reports documenting the extent of the whiskey traffic crossed McKenney's desk. "Intoxication among the In-

dians who have visited here this season has been so common
... that I feel it my duty as a public officer once more to address
you on the subject," wrote John Johnson from Prairie du Chien
in 1820. McKenney knew one source was responsible for introducing forty barrels of whiskey into the Green Bay area alone,
and he reported that whiskey peddlers secured five thousand
pounds of lead from the Sac and Fox "without the Indians receiving for their toils *a solitary remuneration beside.*" In the
southwest, John Fowler said, whiskey vendors pursued the Indians like wolves. "I am in the neighbourhood of Men who are
in the daily and regular habit of ... [leaving] Natchitoches with
their Perogues loaded with whiskey, for the avowed purpose of
trade with Indians, & trade wherever they please without any
regard, whatever, to the agent at Natchitoches."[8]

Whiskey should not have been so pervasive considering the
many federal, state, and territorial regulations prohibiting its
sale to Indians. Indian agents were in fact specifically charged
—"as far as practicable"—with preventing the traffic. But enforcing the regulations was another matter. For one thing,
Indians could not testify in court. "It admits of no doubt that
the Traders do sell in very considerable quantities spiritous
liquors to the Indians," Johnson informed McKenney, "but
they do it in so secret a manner, taking care to have no other
witness present than the Indian, whose testimony would not be
legal evidence, that it is impossible to convict them." Mathew
Irwin at Green Bay echoed this complaint. "The Indians are
frequently kept in a state of intoxication giving their furs, etc.,
at great sacrifices for whiskey," he said, but "it is deemed illegal
to accept Indian testimony, so that the British and American
traders ... may deal in whiskey without the smallest chance of
detection."[9]

Loopholes in the law caused further complications. Fur
companies could give their employees daily liquor rations, since
the prohibition against spirits applied only to Indians. To cir-
cumvent the law, the fur companies simply padded their lists
of employees. The American Fur Company needed no subter-
fuge in the Northwest. Claiming that it required liquor to com-
pete effectively with British traders, the company received permission from the president to use alcohol. This authority, wrote
one employee, enabled the company to bring into the Lake

Superior region a "liberal & quite sufficient" quantity of whiskey.[10]

Despite strenuous efforts, the harried McKenney had scant success stemming the flow. Only the most drastic measures could end this degenerating traffic, he insisted. "Experience has demonstrated how inefficient are the most promising regulations, when they are intended to govern men bent upon such enterprises, and especially when the means of evading the agents whose duty it is made to enforce them, are so numerous; and when the opportunities of escape and security are rendered so certain by the unsearchable intricacies of the surrounding forests," McKenney complained to Secretary of War Calhoun. "Upon these incendiaries among the Indians—these murderers of the Indian's health, and peace, and life—the law should have always, and ought now, to be armed with such frightful vengence as to deter them from the exercise of their avarice." At the very least, he told Southard, federal regulations should provide *the severest penalties of forfeiture . . .* against the vending of whiskey or spirituous liquor of any kind."[11] Neither laws of frightful vengeance nor severe penalties were enacted. Moreover, it is doubtful that laws alone could ever have effectively controlled the whiskey traffic. Too many Indians were anxious to procure alcohol, and too many whites were willing to supply it.

The final breakdown of the factory system was a result of the opposition of the private traders, especially John Jacob Astor, owner of the American Fur Company, director of the Bank of the United States, and one of the richest men in the country. As early as 1808 Astor began to plan the downfall of the factory system, and by the time of McKenney's appointment he had become its principal antagonist. While the fur baron lobbied in Washington for abolition of the trading houses on the grounds that they were incapable of fulfilling their goals, a condition for which Astor was largely responsible, a vast network of agents directed by his lieutenants Ramsay Crooks and Robert Stuart harassed factory operations in the field. Astor's agents told the Indians the "damned Yankee peddlars" at the factories were selling goods the president actually intended as gifts. They claimed the factories were no more than a clever trick to cheat the Indians out of their lands; the government would force the tribes to cede their domain to pay factory debts.

"As falacious and improbable as such an idea should have been, yet it ... [is] widely diffused ... and generally believed," reported one of the factors.[12]

At first McKenney did not realize Astor was behind the troubles of the factory system. He blamed foreigners—"generally British, or British agents, who [during the War of 1812] were doing immense injury—and promoting the destruction even of our Citizens, whose scalps were bought and sold in the village of Prairie du Chien, & strung on poles, & carried in triumph to Mackinac in 1816." British traders were indeed active in the Great Lakes area, and McKenney's factors at Prairie du Chien, Chicago, and Green Bay complained bitterly of the competition of these formidable rivals. Most of the traders had served with the British frontier militia during the war. They were also lifelong residents of the region, married to Indian women. Their influence with the tribesmen, who preferred British trade goods to those of American manufacture, was enormous.[13]

Continued British activity in the Northwest after the war challenged American nationalism and led to passage in April 1816 of the law barring noncitizens from the fur trade. President Madison suspended the law for the Great Lakes region because American traders were unable to supply the needs of the tribes there. McKenney was incredulous at this action. These men, "with the worst of views," should not be allowed to trade with the Indians, he wrote in January 1817 to Isaac Thomas, chairman of the House Committee on Indian Affairs. "They are not organized bodies of men—but who in separate and small detachments traverse our Western territories inflaming and spurring the untutored savage on to deeds, which but for their agency would not exist." For emphasis, McKenney enclosed a recent letter from the Prairie du Chien factor who complained that "the large number of British Traders *admitted here this fall* destroys my calculation, ... & strange it is to say 5/6ths of those British Traders are of the very worst characters,—men who have hired the Indians to kill our women & helpless children on the frontier." Astor also urged the House committee to exclude foreigners, but for good measure he added the hope that Congress would abolish the factories as well. They "answer *no* good purpose and they prevent many from engaging in the trade," he declared.[14]

The committee treated McKenney's objections seriously and a month later reported a bill "to regulate trade and intercourse with the Indian tribes, and to exclude foreigners from a participation therein." The committee condemned the discretionary authority the act of 1816 gave the president, explaining that although the provision seemed appropriate, it in fact admitted to the trade "men of the most inflammable and vicious habits."[15]

Congress did not act on the bill, but McKenney almost succeeded anyway. President Monroe issued a new order that was interpreted to mean all foreigners, including employees of American-owned firms, were excluded. But this was not what the private fur interests wanted. How could they find enough American citizens to serve as boatmen and interpreters? Immediately Ramsay Crooks appealed to Astor to have the order revised. "You must try hard to get clerks & interpreters... giving assurances that proper care will be taken to keep from among the Indians, all whom there is reason to believe unfriendly to the Government." Astor at least was to obtain permission to hire Canadian boatmen. "These people are indispensable to the successful prosecution of the trade, their places cannot be supplied by Americans, who are for the most part too independent to submit quietly to a proper controul...."[16] Accordingly, President Monroe, who owed Astor $5,000, agreed "on further information and reflection" to allow foreign engagees into the Northwest. Calhoun sent Governor Cass the change in orders on March 25, 1818, with careful directions to ensure a tight supervision and to prevent foreigners in the guise of interpreters or boatmen from participating in the trade itself; anyone who had fought against the United States was not to be admitted in any capacity.[17]

A partial restriction was better than none at all, and McKenney relayed the welcome news to his factors. "Whenever you detect any person or persons, engaged in trade who are shut out by this letter you will report him or them immediately to the Governor, or the Sub agent—sending me copies of your letters," he wrote. Yet McKenney was sending his people on a fool's errand, for Calhoun's order had little effect. If possible, the problem became worse. "I believe," McKenney wrote in July 1820, "it may now be taken for granted that such persons are not to be controul'd except by some suitable & summary process that shall take from them *and their employers*, their assumed right thus to annoy the Indians, and trample on the authority of the United States."[18]

The employers McKenney meant were the Chouteau brothers of the Missouri Fur Company and Astor, whose adversary role was now becoming evident. "I do not mean to intimate that he, purposely, occasions these excitements," McKenney explained to Calhoun, "far from it; but he certainly employs the most hostile Agents, and those, too, who not only have no American feeling in them; but those who during the late War did us much mischief." McKenney was not as certain about the Missouri Fur Company, which operated out of St. Louis, but he was suspicious. "The organization of the south too, I presume, is a machine constituted of very few parts," he declared.[19]

Rather than combat these giants of the fur trade, a wiser superintendent would have let the factories die quietly. But this was not McKenney's nature. If the trading houses were to be way stations for the Indians on their road to civilized life, they had to thrive. Dismissing the clamor to abolish the system as "the workings of *avarice*," McKenney marshaled the same forces he had used so ably in behalf of his school bill and conducted a sustained, almost inspired, two-front campaign to save the factories. While trying to counteract the harassment of the private traders in the field, he lobbied for passage of measures that would eliminate or at least restrict their competition.

McKenney drew on his own mercantile experience in his efforts to revive the slumping government trade. Where the competition of private traders was particularly keen, he authorized his factors to cut prices "if you can do no better; and if to do this will be necessary to preserve your influence with the Indians." He also urged his factors to advertise. "Do you ever procure runners to notify the tribes of the movement of handsome supplies?" he asked Sibley. "How would such a policy, especially if it be novel; operate against the private traders, and in favor of the factory?" He even tried propaganda. Believing "all correct means that may tend to expel those traders" would be "of service to humanity and justice," he urged Sibley to impress the Osages "with the belief that such is the design of

those traders . . . that [the Indians] must get rid of them; & hope
not to be accountable for their own efforts to drive them out."
McKenney gave similar advice to Johnson at Prairie du Chien.
"I should judge, with your long acquaintance with the Indian
tempers, you might upon the most humane and honourable
grounds, turn their prejudices against these their enemies."[20]

More practical was Johnson's suggestion to employ subtraders—men supplied with factory goods who would travel into
the Indian country like private traders. "It will be necessary for
you to use extreme caution in trusting out goods to traders,"
McKenney warned when agreeing to the experiment. "Boats
may get upset . . . and even if . . . they should escape being
drowned, the tommahawk may put them to rest—and relieve
you from the trouble of counting their returns." McKenney
came to admire the idea of subtraders and judged its implementation at Chicago and Green Bay a success; he claimed that the
results of the experiment had been "an encrease of factory business—peace with and among the Indians, *and a failure in the
plans of these Private adventurers.*" It was only a temporary
triumph at best. Once the agents of the American Fur Company
recovered from their initial surprise, they harassed the factory
traders from the fur country.[21]

The only sure way to help the factories was to control the
private traders. McKenney knew this. He also knew it would
not be easy. At the time he took office, the government, through
the War Department, regulated trade with the Indians by license. Any United States citizen who posted a $1,000 bond could
obtain from a superintendent or Indian agent a license valid for
two years. If a trader failed to observe the regulations governing the trade, the issuing agent was authorized to recall his
license and put his bond in suit. An unlicensed trader was subject to a $100 fine and thirty days imprisonment and was also
liable to forfeit his goods, one half to the informer, the other
to the United States. Theoretically, licensing kept known criminals, whiskey peddlers, and other undesirable individuals from
the fur trade; actually, the regulations were ineffectual. Since
licenses were issued at many scattered locations, nothing prevented a trader who was refused a permit at one place from going
elsewhere. The irresponsible and degenerate characters at whom
the laws were primarily directed did not even bother; unlicensed

traders stood little risk of arrest or conviction. During his administration of the Indian trade, McKenney said, no one was
successfully prosecuted for selling whiskey to Indians or for
trading without a license.[22]

The extent of the illicit trade was appalling. McKenney
scarcely saw a week pass without a complaint from one of his
factors concerning the "constant, and the most flagrant violations of the law regulating Indian trade." William Bowen, the
assistant factor at Fort Mitchell, claimed "the spirit of intrusion
and contraband trade, appears to pervade the whole Georgia
frontier, smugglers, or private traders have uninterrupted, introduced their merchandize into the very heart of the [Creek]
nation, and into almost every Indian village. . . . Packhorses,
carts, and other vehicles of light description truck goods . . . into
all corners where the profits warrant, and these have become
frequent and considerable." Those who attempted to enforce the
laws placed their jobs and lives in jeopardy. Irwin at Green Bay
reported in 1819 that the agents of the American Fur Company
"hold out an idea that they will, ere long, be able to break down
the factories; and they menace the Indian agents and others
who may interfere with them, with dismission from office through
Mr. Astor." John Fowler was even more disturbed. He said legal
evidence against the traders was almost impossible to obtain;
even then "they are so numerous in this quarter and of such
bad character I have been repeatedly told a witness would risk
both life and property by giving evidence against them in a
court of Justice."[23]

McKenney knew how to solve the problem: give the factory
system exclusive rights to the fur trade. As early as December
1816 he made this recommendation to the House Committee on
Indian Affairs; he renewed it in various forms at every session
of Congress until the factories were abolished. Essentially, he
wanted Congress to increase the trade fund from $300,000 to
$500,000. The additional money would enable him to double
the number of factories and to establish his supply center at
St. Louis under an assistant superintendent of Indian trade.
The only individuals allowed to trade with Indians would be
American citizens employed by the assistant superintendent to
reach tribes beyond the range of the factory system. These
traders would receive their outfits at the St. Louis depot and

return there with their furs. McKenney also privately admitted
his hopes to purchase a steamboat to cut transportation costs.[24]

In 1818 McKenney expressed candidly his ambitions for a
government monopoly of the fur trade. The present system,
"which grew up . . . under the two fold view of conveying articles
of necessity amongst the Indians, and to promote peace, as well
in the Forests as along our borders, has not failed in its original
design," he wrote Henry Southard, chairman of the House Committee on Indian Affairs. Where factories operated without the
interference of foreign or domestic traders, "the result has been
manifest." Indians received "ameliorating and peaceful lessons"
as well as articles suited to their wants and tastes. If private
traders had the same noble motives "of bettering the condition
of our native Inhabitants; of diverting them from their propensity for war," McKenney would not object to their competition.
In fact, there would be no need for factories. But the private
trader had no such motives. "He has been, and is yet, subversive
of all the objects [the] Government had in view in the adoption
of the present system of commercial intercourse with the Indians." Give the factory system control of the fur trade, Mc-
Kenney urged. "I know of no check that could be devised having
such a powerful influence as that which this sort of dependence
would impose on the Indians. Armies themselves would not be
so effectual in regulating the native Inhabitants as would a state
of dependence on the Government for their *commercial intercourse*." McKenney realized a monopoly "embraces the idea of
compulsion," but who would object? "The power over the Indians is covetted only for their good—and also to prevent them
from doing harm."[25]

The House Committee on Indian Affairs would not entertain McKenney's demands for a government monopoly of the
fur trade, but it greeted warmly his proposal for reorganizing
and expanding the factory system, which he included in his
program for Indian reform. Congressman Isaac Thomas in February 1817 had introduced a bill authorizing an increase of
$200,000 in the trade fund and eight new trading houses as well
as an assistant superintendent and depot at St. Louis. The bill
died in committee. McKenney persuaded Southard to reintro-
duce the measure the following year, but the bill was sent to
committee and received no further action.[26] It was the closest

McKenney came to reviving the factories.

McKenney's efforts to invigorate the factory system had not gone unnoticed by the American Fur Company. Ramsay Crooks and Robert Stuart, writing Astor in January 1818, expressed their grave concern at the aggressive spirit of the government trading houses. "The factories ... have become so numerous, and are of late provided with such extensive means," they claimed, "as threatens in a very few years more, to annihilate private competition, and throw the whole trade into the hands of Government." Crooks and Stuart mentioned specifically Johnson's and Irwin's factory traders, who were "depriving the most persevering [private trader] of the advantage he gained by travelling to remote districts." Astor's agents urged him to seek the abolition of the factory system, otherwise "it will in our opinion be imprudent in you to continue interested in the trade."[27] The fur magnate soon complained to Secretary of War Calhoun of his "difficulties" in prosecuting the trade because of federal interference. "We have been great sufferers," he wrote, "so much so, that it would indeed be ruinous to continue the Trade under such circumstances." In fact, Astor continued, he was sending Ramsay Crooks to Washington to explain "to your entire satisfaction the difficulties which we have hitherto encountered, and which I am sure will be obviated, when the subject shall be properly explained to you."[28]

Crooks was more than a mail carrier. From the moment he arrived in the nation's capital he worked feverishly to kill McKenney's bill. Succeeding, he turned next to destroying the factory system itself. Until the abolition of the government trade four years later, Crooks was in Washington during each session of Congress lobbying against the factories. A short month after Crooks arrived in March 1818, Congressman Jesse Slocum of North Carolina introduced a resolution directing the secretary of war to report at the next session "a system for providing for the abolition of the existing Indian trading establishments."[29]

Calhoun referred the resolution to his superintendent of Indian trade. "I am aware that the resolution of the house of Representatives calls for a system, providing for the opening of the trade to Individuals under 'suitable regulation,' " McKenney responded. "But I am aware also of the impractability, in my opinion, of framing any system, that shall be so suitable as to overrule the consequences." The factory system "has its foundation in *benevolence, and reform.*" The only objective of the private trader was personal gain. McKenney had an alternate plan. Congress should place all Indian affairs in the control of a general superintendent. The network of Indian agents under him would administer the fur trade on the local level. The superintendent would issue annual licenses for $100 each. All applicants would post $5,000 bonds and present notarized certificates of "good character." Anyone issued a license would then "select his spot, build his factory, & locate himself." The sale of liquor would be, of course, strictly prohibited. "Those are the outlines of a system which appear to me . . . as being more likely than any other to provide against the abuses which are to be dreaded, even under its adoption."[30]

Calhoun's report of December 5, 1818, followed McKenney's outline closely, suggesting the appointment of a superintendent to direct all Indian affairs. The superintendent would issue trade licenses to citizens of good moral character who posted bonds of sufficient security. Licensed traders would be restricted to specified locations that could not be changed without the superintendent's consent. A separate license would be required for each trading house, and accurate records would be kept for Indian agents to inspect. "The reasons for most of these provisions are so obvious as to require no illustration," Calhoun declared. "The trade should, as far as practicable, be put effectually under the control of the Government, in order that . . . [the Indians] may be protected against the fraud and the violence to which their ignorance and weakness would, without such protection, expose them."[31]

Congress did not abolish the factory system, but it came close. The enabling act expired on March 1, 1819, and not until two days later did the friends of the factories muster enough support to approve a new statute. A relieved McKenney relayed the news to one of his factors. "You have seen doubtless, that the Gov't. trade is continued for another year, when, (such is my opinion,) it will be renewed under a more enlarged character."[32]

McKenney's optimism was not well founded. He had the firm backing of Secretary of War Calhoun, and he could count on a few friends in Congress, particularly Henry Southard who remained chairman of the House Committee on Indian Affairs. But the factories were fortunate even to survive the year because of the panic of 1819. Shaved deerskins, one of the staples of the government trade, fell in price from $.50 to $.12½ per pack.[33] Moreover, pressure from private traders increased to such an extent that the Fort Osage, Chicago, and Green Bay factories virtually stopped doing business.

Even in these dark moments McKenney tenaciously clung to the belief that Congress would not let the factory system fail. A month into the next session, McKenney sent Southard a scorching report on the activities of the private traders—"blood naturally follows in the track of these men"—and on the urgent need for legislation to save the factories. The report, which appeared in the National Intelligencer on February 25, 1820, criticized the lax licensing law that permitted unscrupulous traders to debauch the impoverished Indians with liquor. Free enterprise did not give one group of individuals the right to prey on another. "I do think," McKenney wrote, "if the object of the Government be to civilize and preserve our Aborigines, (and I am convinced it is,) that all such pernicious intercourse ... should be made to cease." At the very least Congress should enact a stringent licensing law and require private traders to build factories of their own.[34]

McKenney's report to the House was followed three weeks later by one on the same subject from Calhoun to the Senate. "The Indian traders are with some exceptions of a character not at all calculated to secure peace with the Indians or to advance their prosperity," it noted. "They are believed to be in many instances the most abandoned characters; and such it is feared will continue to be the case under the present mode of granting licenses." The report urged Congress to place the licensing function "immediately under the eye of the Government" and enclosed a draft bill giving that power to the superintendent of Indian trade; only applicants of good moral character who posted bonds up to $10,000 would have the right to trade.[35]

The bill was introduced in the Senate, passed, and on March 1 sent to the House where it raised a storm of protest.[36] Delegate William Woodbridge of Michigan Territory immediately wrote Governor Cass, a trusted friend of the fur traders. "What is this but giving to the Secy at War power to create a Monopoly?" Woodbridge asked. "You have seen a part of the same plan in the mischievous & malicious letter of McKenney which was published some time ago in the Intelligencer. . . . The plain English is that all our citizens are if possible to be excluded from the Indian trade & Either the Military & Factory Gen[tleme]n are to take it all—or there is to be a great . . . Company established to monopolise the whole." Ramsay Crooks viewed matters in the same light. Although he planned to leave Washington in early March, he promptly changed his mind. "New arrangements being in contemplation which if carried into effect will materially injure the trade," he informed Astor on March 22, "I have been induced to tarry here this long with the view of defeating them, and have great hopes of succeeding—several members of Congress have promised their aid."[37]

Opponents of the bill were aided by an anonymous "Backwoodsman" who published in late March an eight-page pamphlet entitled *A Letter Addressed to Thomas L. M'Kenney . . . in reply to his Report of January, 1820.* The Backwoodsman charged McKenney with "unwarrantable perversion of facts" respecting the private traders whose only crimes were to expose the ineptness of the factory system and to render its abolition probable, thereby jeopardizing "the snug situation, (I had almost said sinecure,) you enjoy at Georgetown, as Superintendent of Indian Trade." The writer had extensive knowledge of the fur trade and the factories; he struck down McKenney's objections to private traders and ridiculed the philosophy behind the factory system. "It never drove a foreign trader from the country; it never ministered to the wants, or relieved the necessities of the Indians in the day of distress; and no instance can be adduced, of its ever composing the differences of contending tribes."[38]

Ramsay Crooks did his work well. "The new-fangled obnoxious Indian system, died a natural death," he reported to Astor on May 30. "The House of Representatives pleading a press of more important business refused to act on the bill from the Senate and from the interest our friends took in the explanations given them." Nevertheless, he assured his employer, "had Mr. Secretary Calhoun carried his point in getting the proposed law passed, it is no longer concealed that his first step was to license so few traders that the factories were sure of re-viving." McKenney could take comfort only in the fact that the renewal bill for the factory system passed midway through the session with a minimum of difficulty, tribute no doubt to his own tireless efforts. Even then, it was difficult for him to remain optimistic. "Our trade is spun out for another year," he told Sibley. "This is bad policy." Although still convinced "the time is at hand when all will go right," he promised to help his factor find another post if the factories were abolished.[39]

For the factories, 1820 was another grim year. The price of furs continued to fall and so did income. The Chicago and Green Bay factories could not hold much longer. "Your business in that quarter hardly warrants a continuance of the factory," McKenney wrote Irwin in December. "I have been hoping that Congress would act in relation to the trade system and purge it from its importunities. As yet nothing is done."[40]

Inaction was not McKenney's fault. On November 30, only two weeks into the second session of the Sixteenth Congress, with a persistence born of desperation, McKenney sent Southard a long and stirring letter that detailed the ills besetting the factory system. He admitted the depression had "arrested the slow, but gradual increase of profit," but, he also pointed out, "gain . . . is not one of the characteristics of this system." Fur-thermore, the factory system should not be evaluated on the basis of a few thousand dollars. "Greater objects than such as are included in making gains out of an impoverished people were in the view of those who originated this intercourse with our Indians." Justice, humanity, political influence, "the civilization and preservation of these helpless people," were more appropriate objectives. Rather than again detail the sins of the private traders, McKenney referred Southard to his letter of the previous January, "barely remarking, that the experience of another year has been added, demonstrating the pernicious effects which continue to result." McKenney thought the government could profitably spend a million dollars improving the Indians and expanding the factory system; he would gladly settle for $63,000, the sum owed the trade fund from unpaid debts and losses incurred during the War of 1812. "Great reliance," Mc-Kenney concluded, "is placed on a well devised system of trade, as an auxiliary in promoting the benevolent scheme of civilization which appears to have met the approbation, and secured the co-operation, of so many thousands of our most respectable citizens."[41]

What Southard thought of McKenney's remarks is not known; the Backwoodsman published his opinion in *On the Indian Trade*. Comparing the superintendent's latest endeavor to his "master effort of 7th January," the pamphleteer noted McKenney had again bestowed "the same villainous character" on the private traders. "You must have presumed, that in addressing the chairman of the Indian committee, you were speaking to a dunce," the Backwoodsman exclaimed. "Why, sir, do you not state explicitly what it is the traders do? What crimes they commit against the government, and wherein they violate the conditions of their licenses?" Obviously, the writer continued, the only explanation for McKenney's attitude was the Indians' preference for private traders. "I believe you are perfectly aware of the ticklish situation you now occupy, and that nothing short of curbing or cramping the traders in their operations will save the factory system from destruction." The Backwoodsman also attacked McKenney's program of Indian reform. "I will not so far insult your understanding as to believe for a moment that you, in reality, think the United States' public trading houses have, or can, ever be of the least possible use in civilizing the Indians." Rather, "I do most sincerely believe all your apparent solicitude about saving the unfortunate Indians is merely a stalking horse for more substantial gains."[42]

The identity of the Backwoodsman remains a mystery, although probably he was Ramsay Crooks. Despite his efforts, the factory system once again weathered the opposition, but the enabling act was not approved until the last day of the session. Actually, time had run out for McKenney; on that day Henry Southard retired from Congress. McKenney owed him much and would sorely feel his absence. "You have contributed your part," McKenney wrote thanking him for his assistance to the cause. "This alone would have ensured to your retirement the repose to which a long life of public services in other matters, without this, would have entitled you to enjoy. Take with you my Dear Sir, into your retirement my best wishes for your health & happiness."[43]

During the summer and fall of 1821 McKenney prepared for

the next Congress which he realized might be his last as superintendent of Indian trade. "The system will die of itself soon," he wrote in June, "by the very policy of the Congress, and then it will be charged upon those who have had the care of it." But he refused to surrender. First, he closed the Green Bay and Chicago factories. Anticipating a close scrutiny of factory operations at the forthcoming session, he could no longer afford to maintain the unproductive facilities. Nevertheless, it was a painful decision. "This state of things is owing entirely to the unsuitable provisions which exist for the regulation of the trade," he announced angrily to Calhoun. To Irwin at Green Bay, McKenney wrote, "I am led to it entirely from considerations growing out of the duty which my trust imposes on me ... to keep the capital from diminution, and not from considerations of policy." Next, he attempted to marshal popular support for the system. "I expect *the people* will speak at the next session," he confided to Sibley. "They may be heard."[44]

As usual McKenney was relying heavily on his missionary friends. Even before the end of the spring session he had sent Milledoler a pamphlet that contained "the skeleton of the only *just system* of commercial intercourse with our Indians. If you think so," he said, "use it in the best manner you can to bring out the *public opinion*. And should it be deemed proper to memorialize Congress at its next session, let this be the basis. You will no doubt recognize in this little affair your friend— Thos L. McKenney." A month later he wrote John Emory, an Ohio clergyman, seeking help in arranging memorials and petitions to save the factories. McKenney disclaimed any other motive than concern for the Indians. "My place would not be disturbed by any change," he assured Emory, "whilst a head would be required for our Indian relations of *any sort*."[45]

Milledoler willingly lent his support to the cause. By October he had drafted a "noble" memorial, which he sent to McKenney for approval. "I have nothing to suggest in addition to your own views," responded McKenney, who was more concerned about "the number & respectability of the memorialists; & on their locations." The appeal to Congress must be *"general,"* he cautioned, and, "if I might suggest to your better skill, I would say, that some variety in the form of the memorials, coming from distant places, might obviate the impression of the *oneness*

of their origin." The artless clergyman evidently missed Mc-
Kenney's point; his printed petitions included this notation:
"The Gentleman who may receive this paper is requested to
procure signatures to it without delay, and return it to the Rev.
Dr. Milledoler, No. 20, Rutgers-Street, New-York."[46]

Meanwhile, Ramsay Crooks had also been preparing for the
anticipated conflict. "I shall follow your advice . . . and will use
every fair means to obtain a decision on the Public Trading
House system," he promised Astor in November 1821, a week
before the session opened. "It [the bill to abolish the factories]
will be brought forward early this session, and I have every
reason to think will be warmly supported." His expectations
were justified. In the House, Churchill Cambreleng, Joel Poin-
sett, and John B. Floyd had already promised their aid, while
in the Senate the fur company could count on newly elected
Thomas Hart Benton, who was on the Astor payroll as a "legal
representative." It was no coincidence that Crooks and Russell
Farnham, another American Fur Company employee, were staying at Brown's Hotel, the residence of Benton and Floyd. The
acquaintance of the fur traders "was naturally made by Western
men like us—in fact, I knew them before," Benton later admitted, "and their conversation, rich in information upon a new
and interesting country, was eagerly devoured by the ardent
spirit of Floyd."[47]

The westerners obviously did more than swap yarns, for
Floyd and Benton spearheaded the attack on the factories. A
week after the session began, Floyd introduced a resolution in
the House calling for a committee "to inquire into the expediency
of occupying the Columbia river and the territory of the United
States adjacent thereto, and of regulating the trade with the
Indian tribes." The House passed this oblique assault on the
factories and asked Floyd to chair the committee. His purpose
was obvious to McKenney, who immediately sent an urgent
appeal for help to Milledoler, Judge John McLean, Jeremiah
Evarts of the American Board of Commissioners for Foreign
Missions, Philip E. Thomas of the Yearly Meeting of the Society
of Friends at Baltimore, and Thomas Eddy, a prominent philanthropist. The superintendent's anxiety is clearly evident in
the hastily scribbled draft of his letter. "You see how the Indian
compass is working," he wrote. "Floyd of Virginia who is hostile

to every thing Indian, and to the improvement of these people
. . . has coupled in a resolve into the expediency of occupying
the Columbia, *the regulating of trade with the Indians.*" Mc-
Kenney requested, besides the memorials which must not be
delayed, letters to members of Congress "calling their attention
to Floyd's designs." Only in this way could friends of the Indians
hope to counteract those few in Congress who were bent on
destroying them. "The people must speak for the Indians, &
then the Congress will hear."[48]

The petitions came. Concerned citizens from Ohio, Pennsylvania, Maryland, New Jersey, and New York beseeched their
congressmen to exclude private individuals from the fur trade,
to prohibit the sale of liquor to Indians, and to continue and
expand the factory system. "By occupying an intermediate space
in the fur trade between them and men whose private interest
has ever been at war with Indian happiness . . . [the factories]
have thrown a shield over them worthy of the government,"
wrote petitioners from New Jersey, whose sentiments were
shared by the trustees of Dickinson College, the inhabitants of
Carlisle, the citizens of Baltimore, the Reverend William De
Witt of Harrisburg, and the ministers attending the Annual
Conference of the Methodist Episcopal Church. One petition
from Ohio had 166 signatures.[49] The people were speaking for
the Indians, but Congress would not listen. Ramsay Crooks had
again prevailed.

Benton pursued even more vigorously in the Senate the same
destructive course that Floyd charted in the House. Indeed, his
attack was so spirited and vindictive that McKenney thought
the senator's purpose was "not to abolish the factory system
only, but to demolish my humble self along with it."[50] Benton,
conveniently, was a member of the Senate Committee on Indian
Affairs, which immediately launched into an extensive investigation of the government trade. From McKenney the committee
wanted to know the value—"estimated at the original cost
prices"—of the property on hand at each trading post, his
opinion of the advantages of the factory system compared to
private commerce, the improvements that could be made in the
general conduct of the trade, and "such other views" he might
have "illustrative of the present state of our Indian relations,
and the best methods to preserve the peace with them." Mc-

Kenney responded with facts, figures, and an earnest essay on the importance of the factory system. He presented nothing new; he was uncompromising as ever. In his opinion the government trade had four basic advantages: "the disinterestedness which characterizes it and the superior advantages . . . over any other system originating in plans of gain, the harmony which is the natural consequence of such a system, the tranquility and peace which are the fruits of this harmony, [and] the consequently easy access under its benevolent operations to the confidence and friendship of the Indians, and in the state of preparation which it secures for the introduction of those intellectual and moral lessons which, in the presence of any other system of commercial intercourse, it were useless to attempt to enforce them."

McKenney was not opposed to continuing the present system of mixed public and private competition if Congress would meet certain conditions. First, require all private traders to operate from fixed locations approved by the president and then only after they posted a $10,000 bond and secured a license renewable annually for $200. Second, use the revenue from the license fees to support the work of civilizing and improving the Indians. Third, require all traders to submit quarterly reports to the superintendent of Indian trade detailing articles sold, goods received, and profits realized. *"Spirituous liquors should be excluded under the severest penalties."* At the same time, McKenney urged repayment of the $63,000 trade fund deficit, which would enable him to expand the factory system and extend its benevolent policies to other tribes. McKenney also considered it essential to fund the system more than one year at a time. Three years would be sufficient, five better. If Congress adopted his suggestions, then McKenney could promise both peace with the Indians and their introduction into the blessings of civilized life.[51]

McKenney was the first in a series of witnesses to appear before the Senate committee. Unfortunately, he was the only one who favored the factories. In January the committee heard testimony from Crooks and from Indian agents John R. Bell, John Biddle, and Benjamin O'Fallon, each a one-time resident of St. Louis and each a personal friend of Benton. All agreed the factories were useless and should be abolished; O'Fallon added the opinion, held "by almost every officer with whom I have been stationed on the frontiers, that the superintendent and factors are growing rich in the service." The committee gave McKenney an opportunity to reply. The documents and statement he supplied in rebuttal amounted to twenty-two printed pages. He was convincing, but he could no longer stem the tide. The outcome was so obvious that Farnham and Crooks both left Washington at the end of January, confident their services were no longer needed. "Congress seems disposed to act seriously this session," Crooks reported a few days after his departure, and "there is every appearance that the Factories will be abolished."[52]

A month later Benton felt strong enough to move against the factories. On February 25 the committee reported a bill to abolish the factory system that passed its first and second readings. Before the third and final reading Benton introduced an amendment authorizing the appointment of persons other than McKenney and his factors to liquidate the trading houses, lest the incumbents somehow manage to cover up their illegal manipulations.

Benton introduced his amendment on March 25 with a speech of filibustering proportions that has few rivals for invective and sarcasm. Drawing arguments from the statements of Bell, Biddle, Crooks, and O'Fallon, the Missouri senator attacked the system on three main points: McKenney's conduct in purchasing trade goods, the conduct of the factors in selling them, and McKenney's handling of the furs and peltries received in trade. The factors, Benton claimed, sold more goods to whites than to Indians, and they overpriced the merchandise regardless of the purchaser. What few furs they received in trade McKenney sold at a loss because he held his auctions in Georgetown, "perhaps the last place in America that any man would think of for a fur market." Benton was at his best describing McKenney's inappropriate purchases, particularly eight gross of jew's harps sent to the factories in 1820. Their use puzzled the senator, who wondered how they could expel British traders from American soil. "I know!" he exclaimed. "They are part of McKenney's schemes to amend the heads and hearts of the Indians, to improve their moral and intellectual faculties, to draw them from the savage and hunter state, and induct them into the innocent pursuits of civilized life." Had Benton checked, he would have discovered that jew's harps were a common trade item; Ramsay Crooks himself had supplied one of his men with four gross a short time earlier. But Benton made his point. "I hope I have now fully shown to the Senate, by unimpeachable testimony, that the factory system is worse than useless; that every public consideration requires it to be immediately abolished, the accounts of all concerned be settled up and closed, the capital be returned to the public treasury, the salaries of all officers be stopped, and that its profit and loss be shown at the next session of Congress. My Amendment," he concluded, "will accomplish these purposes."[53] Debate on the bill and on Benton's amendment raged in the Senate for the next three days. The superintendent and the factories were not without friends. Richard M. Johnson of Kentucky refused to countenance any attack on McKenney's character. "His integrity stands high and from the best information I can obtain he has fulfilled the duties of his office with ability, and perhaps as well as any other man could have performed them." Walter Lowrie of Pennsylvania said, "For two years I was a member of the Senate Committee on Indian Affairs, which gave me a good opportunity of knowing McKenney. It is but justice to him to state, that I consider him an able and a faithful officer, and, what is of as much esteem with me, an honest and an upright man." Even so, the Senate on March 28 voted 17 to 11 in favor of Benton's amendment. The following day the bill to abolish the factories was read a third time and passed without debate.[54]

By then the entire Washington community had become interested in the fate of the factories. As the bill went through the House, the columns of the *National Intelligencer* featured the controversy. On April 10 the paper carried Benton's speech of March 25. A week later it published a letter from George Sibley, who had come from the Fort Osage factory to Washington to assist McKenney in his fight. McKenney's rebuttal of Benton's speech appeared on May 3. The superintendent claimed he purchased only items Indians asked for, including jew's harps. He admitted that goods of poor quality had been purchased, but only during the War of 1812 when no others were available. He challenged Benton's contention that Georgetown was a poor supply center and fur market. "I trust," McKenney concluded, "the practice and policy of this office have been freed from, at least, many of the imputations which have been, with so little ceremony, and with less justice, heaped upon them." The rebuttal was able and eloquent—but too late. The House passed the bill the following day, and President Monroe signed it two days later. "Thank God for all his mercies," Crooks exclaimed.[55]

McKenney had no reason to cheer. Ignominiously cashiered, his reputation irreparably and unfairly tarnished, he faced an uncertain future at best. But he did not forget his friends. One of his last official acts was to thank the missionaries for their help. "Be my destiny what it may," he wrote on May 28 in a nationally circulated letter, "I shall not cease to cherish for you, and for those whose condition you have so generously volunteered your services to meliorate, an ardent solicitude for your success and their welfare." He reminded the missionary societies that with the abolition of the factories they had to make new arrangements "for the transmission of . . . supplies and correspondence to the Indians, and to those who are engaged in the work of their civilization." He urged them to continue the cause. "New difficulties may arise, obstacles may multiply, and opposition itself may blacken the sky of your prospects—*but persevere.*" McKenney himself could well have used this sort of encouragement, for the next few months were to be some of the most difficult of his life.[56]

5
Political
Interlude

McKenney relished controversy, but he must have received his fill in the two years he was out of public office. Termination of the factory system disclosed such tremendous financial losses that Congress investigated McKenney's handling of the government trade. Inspired by John C. Calhoun's ambitions to become president of the United States, McKenney founded the semiweekly *Washington Republican and Congressional Examiner* and immediately became embroiled in a vicious newspaper war with the opposition presses in the District of Columbia. To further complicate his life in this period, McKenney and Treasury Department officials feuded over the settlement of his accounts as superintendent of Indian trade. Politics, however, was the common denominator, important in both the congressional investigation and the difficulty over the accounts. Calhoun's principal opponent in the early stages of the 1824 presidential campaign was William H. Crawford, the secretary of the treasury and the person ultimately responsible both for closing down the factory system and for settling McKenney's accounts.

Accusations that McKenney had mismanaged the government's trade with the Indians surfaced during the final congressional debates about the factory system. In fact, the *National Intelligencer*, on February 22, 1822, published remarks by Congressman David Trimble of Kentucky who charged that McKenney transported solid shot from Georgetown to St. Louis, where it was manufactured, and shipped furs to Ohio for sale. "I believe there was never a more abominable peculation... practised on the United States," Trimble claimed.

The remarks so incensed McKenney that he at once fired off angry denials to Trimble, Calhoun, and Thomas Metcalfe, chairman of the House Committee on Indian Affairs. "Mr. Trimble's remarks... *are entirely without foundation*," McKenney declared to Calhoun and Metcalfe in almost identical letters. "There has never been a pound of shot transported to St. Louis; nor a skin of *any sort* sent to Ohio, after arriving at Georgetown, for sale, *or for any other purpose*." To Trimble, the irate superintendent wrote: "It will be gratifying to you to learn that the information on which you felt authorised to make the remarks on the Indian Dept... was not correct." Three days later McKenney again wrote Metcalfe, demanding justice from Trimble for having "inflicted so deep a wound" and inviting a congressional investigation of his conduct as superintendent of Indian trade. "I have little in this world, except my reputation," McKenney continued. "I have endeavoured always to guard this. But it will occur to Major Trimble that I must suffer in this invaluable part by his remarks, which have gone forth to the world, unless they are contradicted."[1] At Calhoun's suggestion, McKenney sent a copy of his letter to the editors of the *National Intelligencer*, who printed it on March 7 along with a backhanded retraction by Trimble. "I believe your Reporter can neither see or hear me from my place in the House, unless he changes his position," the Kentucky congressman said, "and I presume that is the reason why the tenor and purpose of my remarks... were totally misunderstood by him."[2]

McKenney's victory was shortlived, for Trimble's comments paled in comparison with Benton's speech a month later. McKenney again asked for an investigation. "I have the honor respectfully to represent," he wrote to the president of the Senate, "that insinuations having been made in the course of debate on the bill now before the Senate, on Indian Affairs,

implicating the integrity with which I have fulfill'd the duties
of Superintendent of Indian Trade; and feeling the value of my
reputation to be enhanced by the circumstances of its consti-
tuting my only inheritance; and conscious of having executed
the duties of my office with the utmost zeal and fidelity, and
claiming the rights of an American Citizen—I do therefore respectfully solicit that a committee be appointed, with instructions to make such examinations into the manner in which I
have discharged the duties of the trust with which I have been
honored, as it may be considered proper to order." The Senate
ignored McKenney's request and instead passed Benton's bill
to terminate the factory system by June 3, 1822, under "fit and
suitable persons" other than the current officers.[3] The implica-
tion was obvious: Treasury Department appointees would un-
cover evidence of fraud, graft, and mismanagement that Mc-
Kenney and his factors would otherwise conceal.

McKenney was astounded. In vain he tried to get the order
modified. The present employees should remain at their posts,
he advised President Monroe, else "great evils relating as well
to the Supt, the Factors and to the public may result, by the
wrong management on the part of inexperienced persons who
may take charge of the property." At least allow the factors to
work with the agents appointed to close the trading houses,
McKenney pleaded. Each could check the honesty of the other.
He and his factors were bonded, he reminded the president, and
so they were responsible for government property. "I should feel
great reluctance in surrendering [my post] 'till I do thus get the
proper returns and have the evidence in my own hand of the
fulfillment of the trust with which I have been honored." When
Monroe failed to answer, McKenney appealed to Calhoun. "It
is not reasonable to expect that our bonds and oaths should be
made to involve . . . us by the acts of others," he said.[4]

Reasonable or not, this is what happened. Two days later
the fifth auditor, acting on instructions from the secretary of
the treasury, asked McKenney for the factory returns as soon
as they came in and an itemized statement of the property at
the Georgetown office. "Will you have the goodness to say if
the President have thus decided?" McKenney asked Calhoun
in disbelief. That afternoon he wrote to his factors, informing
them of their dismissal from the federal service and instructing

them to take inventory of the stock, furniture, and buildings. The work should be done in the presence of reliable witnesses, he warned, "as the property may by a possible contingency get into the hands of men who may not understand its management."[5]

McKenney had never been more prescient. Some loss was inevitable in liquidating the assets of such a far flung business, but Benton's bill giving the duty to persons unfamiliar with the trade insured maximum loss. "The factory system grew out of a national calamity, and has been one itself," the Missouri senator had declared during the final debates. Because of Benton, the system maintained its unenviable record to the end. McKenney's replacement was George Graham, perhaps the most competent of the agents hired to close out the government trade. Graham had served for a time as acting secretary of war and was familiar with the function and operations of the Office of Indian Trade. He wisely retained Jeremiah Bronaugh and Meade Fitzhugh to keep the books and merchandise in order. The other appointees, however, probably knew as little about the business as A. B. Lindsley, who replaced Jacob Varnum at Chicago for the final accounting. Varnum described him as "a hanger on about the offices for an appointment for years."[6]

Graham submitted a simple plan for closing out the factory system. Sell merchandise at the Georgetown office at 20 percent less than originally invoiced; sell goods at the factories, where the demand would be greater, at a 10 percent discount if the purchaser took the entire inventory. Merchandise still on hand at the factories in the spring of 1823 would be offered to the nearest Indian agents to use as presents and annuities; the remainder Graham planned to divide between superintendents Cass and Clark, who would receive a 3 to 5 percent commission for selling the trade goods. These sales commissions were important, Graham explained, because "prejudices now exist with many of the Indian agents against factory goods, and if they were placed in the hands of civil agents at Detroit & St. Louis, it is probable the Indian agents would find pretexts for declining to take the goods." The authority and influence of Cass and Clark would counteract these prejudices, and the sales commissions would be "a stimulus to them to dispose of the goods as expeditiously & for as good prices as possible." Graham thought his plan would enable the government to close down the factories "in less time, with less expense, and with less loss . . . than in any other mode which can be adopted. . . . With judicious management," Graham assured Crawford, "I think . . . [the factory goods] may nearly if not all of them be advantageously disposed of within two years."⁷ Crawford agreed to everything except the sales commissions.

By midsummer Graham had returns from all the factories. Total assets were $271,585.13, including buildings, furniture, furs, merchandise, and unpaid bills. Valuation of the government property ranged from $9,312 at Fort Armstrong to $49,262 at the Choctaw factory. For the Georgetown office McKenney listed $47,343 in assets, including $31,143 in merchandise, $6,856 in cash, and $9,012 in accounts receivable, of which $5,410 was owed by his brother William. Despite extensive newspaper advertising, however, in the first six months little property was sold, and only Lindsley closed a factory. Two of the newly appointed agents, in fact, died enroute to their posts, throwing the liquidation completely off schedule. By the end of December the factory system had paid back into the public treasury only $14,325, almost entirely from fur sales.⁸

Unloading the merchandise at Georgetown certainly gave Graham headaches. Although he considered the stock "generally of good quality, particularly the woollens, which are excellent," he sold nothing before the end of the year. "The absence of all demand for goods, adapted to the Indian Trade, in this District, together with the embarrassed state of its commerce, and the consequent scarcity of money make it certain that the goods cannot be sold here either at private or public sale, except at immense sacrifice," he complained to Crawford on January 22, 1823. "I should therefore suggest the propriety . . . of shipping them to New York." Accordingly, in March the packet *Abeona* accepted ninety-seven tierces valued at $31,175.28 bound for the New York auction house of J. & P. Hone & Co. Graham told the autioneers to keep the tierces themselves out of sight, "as they would be immediately recognized as United States' property by persons engaged in the Indian Trade." Then, he warned, bidders would "form combinations" to keep the prices down. Despite his precautions, the auction netted only $10,795. "I was prepared to expect considerable loss on the sale of goods," an appalled Graham admitted, "yet I must confess that the loss which has been incurred has very far exceeded any calculations which I had made upon the subject."[9]

The liquidation agents in the field fared no better. In May 1823 Graham ordered the remaining factory merchandise shipped to Detroit, New Orleans, or St. Louis where the Indian agents and superintendents were to select—at cost—suitable items to use as annuities or presents. What they did not want would then be sold at auction. This arrangement also proved unsatisfactory. Governor Cass, who had received some $12,000 worth of merchandise from the Chicago factory, refused to pay for any of it. "I was under a misapprehension respecting the provisions of the act for closing the Factory Establishment," he explained to Calhoun. Cass had thought the goods were to be given to the Indians. He had given some away; the rest he dumped in his storehouse. "These goods were selected, I presume, as the worst and most unsaleable in the factories, and certainly they well deserve this character. They are not fit for distribution, and three fourths of them in the amount are common blankets."[10]

Perhaps poor quality explains Lindsley's poor sales. Varnum left $15,400 in government property, including $709 in cash, but Lindsley returned only $1,250 in cash and $5,063 in uncollected notes. Varnum—by no means an objective observer—had another explanation. He claimed Lindsley stayed at the Chicago factory "as long as his instructions would permit without making any sale or collecting the debts, [then] he packed all the goods and shipped them to Detroit, where they were again offered for sale; and were finally auctioned off without a guarantee of any kind as to payment." The goods brought fine prices because no one intended to pay for them, while Lindsley, "a man without a single business qualification, got credit for the prompt and satisfactory manner with which he had closed the business, and subsequently received an appointment in the Custom service."[11]

On October 25, 1824, Graham submitted his final report. He had sold three of the factory buildings—Chicago, Arkansas, and Red River; the others reverted to the military post commanders. Indian debts had been turned over to their agents, who were instructed "to use their best endeavors to collect them." Many of the notes received for the government property remained unpaid, and these became the responsibility of United States district attorneys. "There is good reason, however, to believe that there will, eventually, be little or no loss in the collection of these notes," Graham assured Crawford, but he was wrong. In all, Graham had collected $56,038.15 in cash; he listed as additional assets $107,416.37 in unpaid bills, Indian debts, and unredeemed notes, almost none of which was ever collected.[12] It was a poor return on the government's twenty-seven-year investment.

McKenney, meanwhile, got his congressional investigation, but the circumstances were not of his choosing. Public indignation increased as the heavy financial losses of the factory system became known; that the government should lose money in such a lucrative business as the fur trade seemed inconceivable. To many, the explanation seemed obvious: the superintendent and factors had enriched themselves at the taxpayers' expense. McKenney was especially suspect. How else could the former "humble shopkeeper" have purchased Weston on an annual salary of only $2,000?[13] Gradually pressure mounted for an investigation of McKenney's administration of the government trade. The agitation came primarily from Crawford's followers who hoped to embarrass Calhoun; as the presidential campaign intensified, so did demands for the investigation. The *City Gazette* made the political overtones explicit. On September 14, 1822, the newspaper remarked, "there is little doubt that the next Congress will EXAMINE HIM [McKenney], and fortunate will he be if that examination leave him in condition to make his support valuable to the administration."

As the *City Gazette* predicted, early in the next session McKenney heard that the House Committee on Indian Affairs planned to investigate his conduct as superintendent of Indian trade. Specifically, the investigators wished to determine "whether any, and if any, what abuses" he committed in the purchase or sale of goods. The first hearing would be at 10:00 A.M. on February 18, Congressman Metcalfe informed McKenney. "You can attend if you think proper." No one could have kept him away. "The enquiry ... is one of the deepest interest to me," he replied. "My good name is involved ... and this I consider my all." Therefore, he hoped the investigation would be complete and thorough; the subject must be "*sifted to its very bottom*," and the satisfaction must be "*entire and complete.*" If he failed to prove the injustice of the charges against him—"*in every department of my labours*"—McKenney stood ready "to suffer the disgrace which would follow the *censure* of the committee." Otherwise, "I shall rely on *the justice* of the committee to acquit me, in the most ample and unequivocal manner by an award, freely and fully expressed, before the Congress and the world."[14]

Merchants, former factory system employees, and A. B. Lindsley testified during the two-week investigation. The committee discovered that McKenney purchased most of his goods from John Cox, a Georgetown importer whose sales to the Office of Indian Trade amounted to about $50,000 a year. Cox did not feel he had been specially favored, and he denied assisting McKenney personally beyond endorsing some notes. "I am now on Mr. M'Kenney's paper as indorser," the merchant admitted, "but am secured by his property." Jeremiah Bronaugh, who testified next, thought Cox's goods more expensive but of better quality than others McKenney bought. The former chief clerk knew Cox endorsed some of the superintendent's notes but did not think "this induced Mr. M'Kenney to purchase from him more than from others." The committee did not pursue the obvious conflict of interest. The investigators would not have been so trusting, perhaps, had they known the nature of two of the notes Cox endorsed—McKenney's $20,000 bond as superintendent of Indian trade and the $16,000 loan from the Bank of Columbia that enabled him to buy Weston.

McKenney cross-examined the witnesses and testified on his own behalf. He presented an able defense; his remarks were perceptive and demonstrated considerable mercantile acumen.

"Did you not sell . . . large amounts to my predecessor?" he asked Cox.

"I did."

"Was there . . . the least evidence of partiality shown you?" McKenney continued.

"Not that I know of," Cox answered.

"Did you not think the rigor of the inspection, and the closeness of the comparisons, I made, were sometimes too pointed?"

"I did."

Bronaugh, under McKenney's questioning, confirmed that the superintendent consistently bought the best quality goods available regardless of source.

"Were not due pains taken . . . to ascertain yearly the state of the markets, before I decided to buy the annual supplies?" McKenney asked his clerk.

"I think every necessary pains were taken."

"Did not Colonel Cox show a good deal of feeling, and often declare upon his honor, that he was not dealt as fairly by [me] as he should be, by reason of the scrutiny which was exercised in buying goods of him?"

"He did," Bronaugh admitted.

McKenney was especially effective in destroying the credibility of Lindsley, who presented samples of goods from the Chicago factory claiming that they were shoddy, overpriced, and unsuitable for the fur trade.

"Were you ever engaged in Indian trade?" McKenney asked.

"Never," Lindsley replied, "except in settling the United States factory business."

"Well then, how much should a three point N.W. blanket weigh to be good; and how long and how wide should it be?"

"I don't know," was the honest response.

McKenney followed his examinaton of the witnesses with a lengthy address to the committee. Nothing, he thought, could justify "in the smallest degree, the imputations which led to this inquiry." Because his integrity had been publicly questioned, however, he felt obliged to make a few remarks. "It is certainly very unpleasant even to appear to be one's own eulogist," he said, "but I trust to the nature of this inquiry to furnish the apology." McKenney then described in detail his mercantile background which he thought had prepared him for the superintendency and from which he had completely severed himself before taking office. He denied favoring Cox, his former business partner Joseph C. Hall, or any other merchant and challenged "the worst enemy I have upon earth to convict me in this matter." McKenney's sole concern was his reputation. "Money is not the god of my idolatry, as those who know me will attest. It had been better for me to-day, perhaps, had I worshipped a little more devotionally at this shrine." An untarnished reputation was his only legacy. "I am concerned, for its preservation," he declared proudly. "I will not, I could not disguise it; but I shall expect it to be protected, on this occasion only, on the grounds of my having demonstrated that it has been unrighteously assailed."

The committee's findings, announced March 1, 1823, exonerated McKenney. "The conductors of the Indian trade," the committee concluded, "were generally men of integrity and honor; not deficient in talent or enterprize, or any of the requisite qualifications for discharging the duties of their respective stations. And how it does happen, that ... the government should not now be able to realize a sum equal to the original capital stock, appears to be inexplicable." Perhaps the fault lay in the factory system itself. A knowledge of it, therefore, would be useful, "not only as a matter of curious history, but for the lesson it teaches to succeeding legislators."[15]

Although the factory system was now a thing of the past, McKenney's accounts remained an enormous piece of unfinished business. As a disbursing officer, the superintendent of Indian trade had to "account" for the public monies that passed through his hands; expenditures he could not justify were charged against him. Accounts of every public officer were reviewed twice in the Treasury Department—first by an auditor, then by a comptroller. However, McKenney was accountable to an extra auditor as well. The second auditor reviewed his expenditures for annuities, presents, and the ordinary business of Indian affairs; the fifth auditor examined expenditures relating to the trade itself.[16] The accountability process at best was elaborate and inflexible, but for McKenney it was a nightmare. The Treasury Department took almost two years to straighten out his accounts and another nine to settle them officially.

Keeping correct accounts was difficult even for precise and well-ordered individuals. McKenney was not such a person, but he did his best. He insisted on duplicate bills and receipts for his own records. "Whenever ... the Cash transaction is negotiated thro' me," he explained, "I become debtor [to the government] for the specific amount of the Cash part ... & I am dependent on the receipt of the agent to whom the remittance is made for a voucher to write off the charge." McKenney even claimed he kept triplicate vouchers—one set for the Treasury Department, one for his office files, and one in safekeeping. To avoid confusion, he even deposited funds in separate banks. The annuities and presents account he kept in the Bank of Columbia;

the trade funds he deposited in the United States Bank. He maintained this dual system until March 1819 when the second comptroller ordered him to keep all funds in the United States Bank as the law required.[17] McKenney's habit may have been sensible, but his large personal debt to the Bank of Columbia makes his choice of depositories suspicious.

In his *Memoirs* McKenney insisted that vindictive Treasury Department officials caused the trouble with his accounts. According to his version, he read in the newspaper one morning that the audit of his accounts would show he owed at least $120,000 to the government. McKenney rushed to the second auditor's office.

"Are my accounts settled, sir?" McKenney asked the clerk.

"They are, sir, so far as they can be," he replied. "Many of the vouchers are missing."

McKenney demanded to see his returns and found that many of the vouchers were indeed missing. Jeremiah Bronaugh, however, insisted he had delivered them to the auditor. "I saw the ties had been severed, and the whole package bore marks of mutilation," claimed McKenney, who promptly related the story to Calhoun. The secretary of war, according to McKenney, called William Lee, the second auditor, to his office and ordered him to put his whole staff to settling the accounts. The audit, when completed, cleared McKenney of any financial obligation. Nevertheless, he concluded, "I can never know, nor can anybody ever know, the extent of the mischief which this aspersion produced upon both my name and my circumstances."[18]

McKenney's tale is interesting but not entirely accurate. A week before McKenney left office in June 1822, Lee asked him for an abstract of his expenditures relating to presents and annuities. Impossible, McKenney replied; he and his staff were too busy taking the inventory. When the superintendent failed to complete his accounts, Graham gave the task to Meade Fitzhugh. The copy clerk scarcely made a dent, although he worked six weeks locating and arranging the documents. Graham, who had stretched the law to keep Fitzhugh on the payroll, dismissed him; McKenney, however, persuaded the clerk to continue, promising reimbursement when the accounts were settled. Fitzhugh worked until early autumn and then quit, convinced he would never be paid for his efforts.[19]

McKenney obviously had not kept duplicate vouchers, much less triplicate vouchers. He admitted as much to Calhoun. "I feel great solicitude respecting the adjustment of my public accounts," McKenney wrote on July 25. Would the secretary of war ask Lee to settle the accounts *as far as the vouchers go*? What was missing McKenney promised to supply later. "A practice prevails of leaving accounts open, til *every voucher, & every document necessary* to a *final* settlement are handed in," he explained. "But . . . this practice involves the liability of loss of vouchers, and lays the accounts open to erronious impressions respecting their true state."[20] Calhoun could not help, and the accounts remained open.

The second auditor, meanwhile, was diligently trying to piece together McKenney's records. By November 5, Lee completed a preliminary audit which revealed numerous discrepancies as well as the absence of key vouchers. Would the colonel provide the missing documents at his earliest convenience? Three weeks later Bronaugh delivered some hastily gathered papers that Lee studied for two days and then claimed were incomplete. Either furnish the necessary documentation or be declared a defaulter to the government, Lee announced. By now McKenney was deeply committed to his newspaper enterprise and could not spare the time to search for the information. Two months passed before he found someone else to do the work—John Hersey, the Choctaw factor, who had recently returned to his Maryland home. Hersey accepted the tedious job on McKenney's assurance he would be paid by the government for his services.[21]

The second auditor's response to the news of Hersey's assignment was not encouraging, however. Apart from the missing vouchers, Lee wrote McKenney on January 14, 1823, many of the documents already submitted were so informal that they "must be suspended, and consequently present a very large balance against you." McKenney's patience had worn thin. "I have to state that Mr. Hersey's business is to look into *the entire state of the accounts*, which from some cause, you & I have never exactly agreed in understanding," was his ill-tempered reply. "Whatever vouchers are 'informal' Mr. Hersey's business will be to have made formal. I request, therefore, that you will give him every facility in his business of adjusting my accounts. He attends in my name. I cannot see how his attention to the sett'ling of these accounts can at all effect any of your arrangements for reporting upon them." Lee answered agreeably, "every information will be cheerfully rendered him at any time he may attend."[22]

McKenney was sadly mistaken if he thought Hersey could solve his problems with the Treasury Department. The ex-factor waded patiently through hundreds of letters, lists, and scraps of paper for seventy-six days between December and March, for which he received $325 in compensation from the government. Thinking he had finished the work, Hersey gave the corrected accounts to Lee and left Washington. "Informalities" remained, however. "Could you stop by the office?" Lee asked Bronaugh on May 5. "Half an hour's conversation will bring us to a perfect understanding." The second auditor needed certified copies of certain improperly submitted vouchers. Bronaugh could not find them, and eleven days later Lee asked McKenney for the documents. "I am unwilling to make my report to the 2nd Comptroller before I receive your answer, [since I am] convinced that you may remove most of the difficulties still existing." McKenney's response was almost civil. "I see the ground on which the whole rests, & thank you for delaying your report, 'til I can present the necessary [documents] to right what *appears* now to be wrong."[23]

McKenney, of course, had no documents, and he again hired Fitzhugh to search for the elusive vouchers. The clerk, who eventually was paid $200 by the second auditor, worked on the accounts until autumn when Graham closed the Georgetown office and removed the factory system records to the Treasury Department. But the two-year dragnet for vouchers benefited McKenney very little. The final audit, stated November 24, 1823, showed a balance against him of $11,393.27.[24]

Settling McKenney's accounts with the fifth auditor was much easier. A preliminary examination found the superintendent accountable for $5,987.13, but the final audit concluded in March 1824 showed a balance in his favor of $11,318.58, which erased the charges against him on the books of the second auditor. McKenney's additional personal claim of $7,933.27 was suspended for further examination. Not until October 1833 did the Treasury Department rule he could not receive the money because he had been a salaried officer. The fifth auditor, however, did agree to cancel a charge of $2,159.62 against McKenney discovered in settling George Graham's accounts for closing the factory system.[25] With this simple transaction the treasury closed its books on McKenney's career as superintendent of Indian trade.

However muddled the story of McKenney's accounts may be, the role politics played in their settlement is clear. During the two years Treasury Department officials haggled with McKenney over incomplete and inaccurate accounts, Calhoun was engaged in a bitter contest with Secretary of the Treasury Crawford for the presidential nomination. Interestingly, concern for missing vouchers evaporated soon after Calhoun withdrew from the race.

McKenney was one of Calhoun's most outspoken and enthusiastic backers. As early as December 1821 he began enlisting support for his candidate. "What do you think of our excellent friend Calhoun for next President?" he asked Milledoler in a letter marked *private altogether sir.* "What a lodgement of power, politically, & *morally*, would be in the executive seat. *He is the man.*" The next day McKenney again wrote the clergyman. "If you would like this great result to be realized, and I am sure you would, you can, without stepping into the department of an electioneering campaign, *do much.* Write me; and tell me what you & your friends think of it."[26]

Calhoun was an attractive candidate. He was not yet forty; he had a brilliant record, charm, and growing popularity. Despite formidable opposition—from not only Crawford but also Andrew Jackson, Henry Clay, and John Quincy Adams—his chances seemed good, so good that his opponents early in 1822 renewed the economy drive of the previous Congress and directed it exclusively at the War Department. What had begun as a sincere effort to reduce federal spending because of shrinking revenues degenerated into a vicious campaign to expose Calhoun as an inefficient and wasteful administrator. Doubtless, much of the criticism directed against McKenney during the final debates on the factory system was an outgrowth of the attempt to discredit the secretary of war. Particularly abusive was Jonathan Elliot, editor of the *City Gazette* and a supporter of Crawford. In May, Calhoun complained, "the miserable paper in this place, the City Gazette, keeps a constant attack on me. I doubt

John C. Calhoun, by Charles Bird King, 1822. *Courtesy Corcoran Gallery of Art, Washington, D.C.*

Andrew Jackson,
by Ralph Eleaser
Whiteside Earl, 1815.
*Courtesy National
Portrait Gallery,
Smithsonian Institution.*

John Quincy Adams,
by Gilbert Stuart.
*Courtesy White House
Collection.*

not, however the paper is under the influence of the Treasury, which is concealed for the present to give more effect to [Elliot's] attacks."[27] Frustrated and worried that the editorials eroded his political strength, Calhoun accepted McKenney's offer to establish an opposition newspaper.

The abolition of the factory system became effective on June 3, 1822, and within the week McKenney was circulating the prospectus of the *Washington Republican and Congressional Examiner*, a semiweekly newspaper dedicated to the "support of the existing administration." McKenney's printer was James C. Dunn, whose shop in the Franklin Hotel row on Twentieth Street and Pennsylvania Avenue also served as the editorial office; his assistant was John Agg, an experienced newspaperman from New York. The *Washington Republican* would appear Wednesday and Saturday evenings and could be ordered by subscription for $5 a year.[28]

As usual, McKenney leaned on friends and acquaintances. "I have concluded to cast anchor in the bosom of my Country," he announced to Milledoler on June 8. "The accompanying prospectus's speak my views, and all that is to be done now is to procure that patronage on which the undertaking must rely for success." McKenney realized the clergyman was not "of the political arena," but he hoped Milledoler would give the blank subscription lists to "*some active friend*" for distribution. The friend in turn could enlist other equally active fellows to enroll subscribers, ensuring first that "suitable & commanding" names headed each list. "When all was done that could be accomplished," Milledoler was to return the lists to McKenney. "I have (between ourselves), a good support *at home*. I am not alienated from *the Executive*, if I am from *the Congress*. You understand this: It is for yourself. *I am entirely in favor.*"[29]

Circulars and similar instructions went to Lewis Cass. An extensive patronage was essential to the success of the enterprise, McKenney explained. Moreover, "it has, (and I am authorized to say so, to you) the sanction of our President, and *your friend* —and this is worth something, at least to me. It is a pleasure to find ones self in such good company." To keep expenses down, Cass was to return the lists of subscribers under the frank of the adjutant general. The governor needed no prodding. "I have but one moment to enclose one of Mr. McKenney's subscription papers for his new paper," he wrote Henry R. Schoolcraft, the Sault Ste. Marie Indian agent. "I have it from the *best* authority, that his plan and object are highly approved in a *certain quarter.*" Cass urged Schoolcraft to round up as many subscribers as possible because "a respectable patronage is a favourite object with *more than one person.* Exert yourself and make every man woman and child subscribe." Army officers should be particularly receptive, Cass continued, since the newspaper would support their interests "totis veribus."[30]

Not everyone was enthusiastic, however. James Madison, having "a due sensibility to your hard experience," agreed to take the *Washington Republican* for one year, but Thomas Jefferson declined. As his secretary explained, "age, debility, and an aversion to politics have for some time withdrawn him from everything of that character."[31]

Although Calhoun did not want his name associated with the *Washington Republican,* he helped solicit subscribers. "You will see by the enclosed prospectus, that Col McKenney, with whom I believe you are acquainted, proposes to edit a new paper in this place. I know him well and he is a man of the strictest honor and considerable talents," Calhoun wrote in early June to Virgil Maxcy, a Maryland lawyer. "*The cause* depends in a considerable degree on its success. I have said to the editor, that I would endeavor to enlist my friends in his support." A few weeks later Calhoun again wrote Maxcy. "The paper will appear on the 7th [of August], and I have furnished the editor with some reflections which he is to bring out in his own language in a series of Nos, commencing with this first paper. It will at once display the talents, character and the course of the paper. I have seen the first No; and think it able and well executed. It is important," Calhoun stressed, "that it should be republished and favorably noticed as far as possible."[32]

Considering their well-known association, McKenney and Calhoun fooled no one with circumspect behavior. Even before the first issue appeared, John Quincy Adams expressed candid skepticism in his diary. "I doubt much ... whether Mr. McKenney's paper will be independent. I think it originated in the War Office, and will be Mr. Calhoun's official gazette, as long as it lasts." The *City Gazette,* of course, did not hesitate to publicize its suspicions, sparking angry denunciations from the editor of the *Washington Republican.* "As to all those idle charges of the carriage of the Secretary of War stopping at the door of our office, and of his being closeted with us, they are without the shadow of the truth," McKenney insisted on September 21, 1822. Such rumors, however, prove "we must be on our guard; for it now appears, that we are sufficiently important to have placed over us a system of Treasury *espionage*, for the first time introduced into our country, by which every act and word of ours, however private and important, is to be noted and reported." Nevertheless, McKenney continued, "we do not choose to disguise our feelings on any subject; and therefore, we make a declaration which we are not bound to make. . . . For Mr. Calhoun we have a personal and political predilection, founded on long acquaintance. We know his worth. We have seen him in peace and war, the same firm, consistent patriot and statesman, always regarding, exclusively, what he considers the interest of his country, and steadily pursuing that point, without stopping to enquire what effect it may produce on his personal popularity. The very abuse which he now receives does him the highest honour. It comes, exclusively, from those who hate him for his *fidelity to the administration*, and his *energetic* support of a system of policy *truly republican and national.*"[33]

The *Washington Republican* had a short and turbulent history. Its favorite target from the first issue was Crawford, whose policies McKenney attacked so vigorously that Washington socialite Margaret Bayard Smith thought the editor "and his employers" were trying to drive the secretary from the cabinet. "The discussion is kindling personal feelings," she reported, "and the friends of these gentlemen will I fear be made hostile to each other." The *City Gazette*, Crawford's defender, countered with personal abuse. It ridiculed McKenney for being "turned out of office, by special act of Congress," and argued that the factory system had been abolished for no other reason than the superintendent's dishonesty and mismanagement.[34]

"The newspaper war between the presses of Mr. Crawford and Mr. Calhoun waxes warm," Adams noted in his diary on September 14. "This day the City Gazette has three columns of brevier type of the foulest abuse upon McKenney, and upon Mr. Calhoun personally." A week later the presidential hopeful from Massachusetts recorded that the two papers "are yet in deadly conflict, but with such unequal force, all reason, all argument, and demonstration on one side, and all scurrility and billingsgate on the other, that the National Intelligencer has been compelled to step in to the relief of the Treasury."[35]

Despite the *Washington Republican's* political soul, the newspaper strongly reflected the humanitarian interests of the editor. "I have purposely omitted any reference to our Indian concerns [in the prospectus]," McKenney wrote Milledoler, *"but the paper shall defend that noble cause.* Consider it as the pillar of its strength here; and if I am not mistaken, more good will result from it, than I had the power to confer in my former relations to the Govt." From the first issue, editorials on Indian affairs, reports on Indian civilization, and letters from missionaries reached the readers of the *Washington Republican.*[36]

McKenney did not limit himself to Indians. His newspaper staunchly supported the African Colonization Society, of which his brother Samuel was a leading figure, and the Female Orphan Asylum of Georgetown. It appealed for improvement of the District of Columbia debtors prison. In a signed editorial, McKenney advocated the establishment throughout the country of a system of Sunday schools, where would be assembled "on each returning Sabbath, (the day on which the idle and profligate, let loose from the restraints of their daily avocations, roam abroad in the indulgence of whatever propensity may be strongest,) HUNDREDS OF THOUSANDS, to whom the lessons of instructions are given, not in *letters* only, but in morality and religion also."[37]

The *Washington Republican* was also a vehicle for presenting McKenney's side of the factory system controversy. The editor refuted insinuations, accusations, and charges against his handling of the Indian trade; he printed copious extracts from letters, reports, and other official documents to prove he was the victim of circumstances; and he published the texts of congressional debates on the factory system as well as the testimony and findings of the subsequent investigation. "The public have a right to be informed of all things which relate to the conduct of their agents," McKenney announced in a signed editorial on March 22, 1823, when printing documents relating to the investigation. "I submit *all the testimony*, and in the order in which it was taken." The committee questioned the witnesses privately, he explained. "I was not present at the first examination; but had, at my request, the statements submitted to me by the Chairman of the Committee, when, at my intimation, several of the witnesses were reassembled, and the *second* examination was made, at the close of which I submitted the remarks, which I now have the honor to offer, together with the whole of the proceedings, at the bar of the public opinion."

Whatever useful purposes the newspaper served, the *Washington Republican* was not financially successful. McKenney failed to obtain federal patronage such as contracts to publish the laws of Congress, and subscribers were never numerous. Although he claimed the paper's circulation was "very extensive, reaching into the extreme parts of the Union," McKenney evidently achieved this distribution by giving complimentary copies to politically prominent individuals, as this statement by a Kentucky reader indicates: "McKinneys paper . . . is regularly sent to me as I believe it is to many others who like me are not Subscribers." As late as October 1822, both editor and patron were still actively soliciting subscriptions. "I am anxious that my . . . paper have extensive circulation," McKenney wrote Eleuthère Irénée Du Pont, the gunpowder manufacturer. "Can you push it in your quarter?" Calhoun asked Maxcy: "It ought to be remembered that two things are desirable—to obtain patronage for the editor and to diffuse light, and the former may be useful where the latter is not required."[38]

Efforts to increase income were fruitless, and by March 1823 McKenney was desperately seeking a loan to continue publishing the paper. "A thousand or even five hundred dollars would be at present important to the editors," Calhoun wrote to Maxcy on the thirteenth. McKenney had extensive property but no cash; without financial support he faced insurmountable difficulties. "If relieved now, the establishment has a fair prospect, in [the] future. I think it important." Maxcy offered to help, and Calhoun wrote him again two weeks later. "I saw Col. McKenney yesterday, who informed me that he would write you immediately. I hope the arrangement can be made." Maxcy's failure to respond to what must have been an extravagant request from McKenney prompted a third appeal from Calhoun. "The Col. feels much solicitude on the subject of the loan," the secretary of war wrote on April 15. "I have no doubt that he intended to comprehend what would enable him to make the most suitable arrangement, rather than what was absolutely necessary. I would suppose that [any] help would put him underway."[39] The loan obviously was not arranged, for McKenney resigned six weeks later.

McKenney's source of funds to launch the newspaper is a mystery. He claimed in an editorial that "our paper has been set up . . . wholly by ourselves, and with our means and credit, and is solely and exclusively, under our own direction and controul, unpledged to anyone, directly or indirectly, and without any share of government patronage." The *City Gazette* responded knowingly to this outrageous statement with an editorial that suggested Calhoun loaned McKenney the money: "Aye, the LOAN, Mr. McKenney.—Deny this *if you dare*. You *dare not;* and if you do, we will convict you before the public, *on other evidence than your own confession*. You say your paper was set up by your own means—aye, but *where did you get your means?* That is the question. The truth is, McKenney, that *we know as well as you* do; and you have not the madness— *mad as you are*—to try to gainsay it." Probably the loan came from the Bank of Columbia; McKenney's obligation to that institution increased by $3,000—to $19,650—between the time he purchased Weston in 1817 and the time he became superintendent of Indian affairs in 1824.[40]

After McKenney's resignation, the *Washington Republican* passed to Richard Houghton who continued, less effectively, to promote Calhoun's candidacy. The newspaper maintained a struggling existence until shortly after Calhoun withdrew from the race in the spring of 1824, when it was sold to Peter Force, publisher of the *National Journal*. The *National Intelligencer* noticed the demise of the *Washington Republican* with the comment that it "exhibited, we are sorry to say, to the last moment, not the least symptom of penitence for its manifold transgressions . . . *Quiescat in pace*."[41]

McKenney left the editorship in May 1823 an impoverished man. His indebtedness to the Bank of Columbia was serious enough, but he had other obligations as well. "Whilst in business," he later wrote, "I had become surety to several friends to a large amount." One of these friends was his brother William; together they owed almost $12,000 to the government on three notes due in 1822. "My brother," McKenney explained, "from various providential visitations, such as the burning of his houses and property, was not able to contribute any thing to the relief of the debt. The whole of it, therefore, bore upon me."[42]

To compound his problems McKenney could not find a job. President Monroe suggested his name as first assistant to the postmaster general, but John McLean refused to dismiss the incumbent. Monroe next nominated McKenney for the vacant post of fourth auditor, a move which drew a biting editorial from the *City Gazette* on February 28, 1824. "We can scarcely think it possible that Mr. McKenney will be nominated for the place, ... or, if nominated, that the Senate will advise and consent to this appointment." Ignoring McKenney's vindication the previous year, the newspaper continued: "He was displaced, and not suffered to wind up the [Indian trade] business, from a conviction that he had so managed the concern as to occasion a loss to the United States. It is moreover, demonstrable, that he in part so conducted affairs, as to ensure private pecuniary advantage to himself, from his official station." That McKenney would even consider a post within the Crawford stronghold shows his desperation. President Monroe saved him further embarrassment by withdrawing the nomination.[43]

Calhoun, meanwhile, had not deserted his loyal lieutenant. The secretary of war had been quietly working on the ideal solution, one that would relieve him of his political obligation to McKenney and at the same time relieve him of an unpleasant administrative burden. That solution was the establishment of a Bureau of Indian Affairs with McKenney at its head.

6

Superintendent
of Indian Affairs

S INCE THE BEGINNING of the federal government the secretary of war had been responsible for the administration of
Indian affairs. While the subordination of Indian to military affairs may have been necessary in 1789, by the third decade
of the nineteenth century it was not. The War of 1812 had
virtually eliminated the Indian threat to national security, and
an expanding network of civilian officials—the territorial governors who served as ex officio superintendents of Indian affairs
and the Indian agents answering to them—was gradually assuming responsibilities which had formerly belonged primarily
to the frontier army.[1] Since the war, moreover, the volume and
complexity of Indian concerns had increased to such an extent
that each succeeding secretary of war was less able to cope with
the administrative details.

One solution to this problem was suggested in a report on
fiscal reforms submitted to the Senate in 1816 by the secretaries
of the navy, the treasury, state, and war. Foreshadowing the
establishment of the Interior Department thirty years later, the
report advocated the formation of a Home Department to be
responsible for territorial government, the mails, patents, in-

92

ternal improvements, and Indian affairs. "It is obvious to the mind of every reflecting man that the duties imposed upon the Secretary of War in relation to the Indian Department have no rational connexion with the administration of the military," declared the secretaries, three of whom had served as secretary of war. Congress gave the proposal little consideration.[2]

A more practical solution was the recommendation McKenney made in 1818 that Congress appoint a superintendent of Indian affairs who would oversee the "whole of Indian relations" and not just matters relating to the fur trade. The official McKenney envisioned would take an oath of office, post a $10,000 bond, and administer a network of Indian agents, one to a tribe except where a number of tribes were clustered in a specific area. "It should be made the duty of the agents," McKenney wrote, "in addition to the ordinary routine of holding treaties, and paying over annuities, and dispensing presents, to keep the Superintendent regularly & constantly and truely informed, of the state and disposition of the tribe or tribes within their respective agencies, and specially so, and their oath of office ought to embrace this obligation, in whatever should relate to any infringement of the law regulating trade with the Indian tribes, and by whom."[3]

Calhoun, in office less than a year at the time, liked the idea. Between 1818 and 1824 he formally recommended at least five times that Congress appoint an official attached to the War Department at an annual salary of $3,000 to supervise Indian affairs.[4] His most detailed proposal is found in his report to the Committee on Public Expenditures in 1822 when he suggested that Congress attach the superintendent of Indian trade (McKenney) to the War Department and change his title to superintendent of Indian affairs. The reorganization, Calhoun pointed out, would entail little additional expense and that would be more than offset by introducing "a high degree of regularity, accountability, and economy" into the administration of Indian affairs. Furthermore, he warned, should Congress abolish the factory system, the appointment of a superintendent of Indian affairs would become more essential because the whole burden of the Indian trade would be added to the secretary of war's other duties.[5] Nothing was done about the recommendations.

Frustrated by congressional inaction, Calhoun decided to

establish a Bureau of Indian Affairs without legislative sanction. His choice of McKenney to administer the bureau was natural, but getting him on the payroll was not easy. Existing legislation limited the War Department clerical staff to twenty-two permanent positions. Moreover, the salary for each position, ranging from $2,000 for the chief clerk to $800 for messengers, was also fixed by law. Although Calhoun had kept his staff within the limit, primarily because he needed fewer clerks in the bounty land office, he lacked a vacancy in a position which commanded a salary that would interest McKenney. But Calhoun did not have long to wait. Nathanial Cutting, senior clerk in the bounty land office and second in grade to the chief clerk, died unexpectedly on March 7, 1824. Three days later Calhoun appointed McKenney "a Clerk in this Department at a salary of $1,600 per annum to commence from this date."[6]

At first McKenney refused the appointment. He was financially embarrassed and needed a higher salary than $1,600 if he expected to retain Weston.[7] Besides the low pay, the position itself was unattractive. Although acting as a bureau chief, he technically would be only another clerk in the War Department —quite a comedown from the independence he had enjoyed as superintendent of Indian trade. McKenney met with Calhoun three times to discuss the position; only after the secretary had assured him that both the salary and status would be improved as soon as he could persuade Congress of the importance and need for a Bureau of Indian Affairs did McKenney accept.[8]

Before McKenney could begin his new duties, his old financial obligation to the government had to be cleared, else his salary would be withheld as soon as he went on the federal payroll. The opportunity to get around the debt presented itself during a conversation with Luther Rice, treasurer of the newly chartered Columbian College. McKenney somehow persuaded Rice to underwrite the $12,000 in notes that he and his brother William owed the government. In return McKenney gave the college $658 in cash and the promise that he would pay one quarter of his salary each year toward the notes until his Indian trade accounts were settled. He assured Rice that the final audit would show that he had at least $8,000 to his credit, perhaps twice that sum. The board of directors of the college agreed to the transaction, and McKenney was free to accept Calhoun's offer.[9]

McKenney assumed a responsibility of major proportions. As superintendent of Indian trade he had taken over the administration of an organization which had been functioning for years. He only resumed where the efficient John Mason had left off. Now the situation was radically different. From a bureaucrat's viewpoint, Indian affairs were chaotic. The field service was a loosely organized network of superintendencies and agencies operating without even the benefit of a set of written regulations, and the fiscal "derangements" of Indian affairs were notorious throughout government. Nevertheless, McKenney tackled the tremendous task before him with his usual blend of optimism, dedication, and naiveté.

He turned first to the organization of his office. For the bureau Calhoun assigned McKenney a room on the second floor of the War Department building, a commodious, two-story, white-painted brick structure standing two hundred feet west of the White House on the southeast corner of Seventeenth Street and Pennsylvania Avenue.[10] McKenney was not entirely pleased with the arrangement. Two windows overlooked Pennsylvania Avenue, but the fireplace, he later grumbled, "smoked me almost blind" and the *"well trod"* carpet quickly disintegrated into a welter of patches and holes. Four years passed before he prevailed on the secretary of war to allow the purchase of a Franklin stove and rug.[11]

The Bureau of Indian Affairs opened for business on March 16, 1824. Despite Calhoun's designation for the new section, McKenney for the first few months called it the Indian Office and then consistently termed it the Office of Indian Affairs. The staff was small but capable. Calhoun assigned two experienced War Department clerks to the Indian office, Samuel S. Hamilton as chief clerk at an annual salary of $1,400 and Hezikiah Miller as recording clerk at $1,000. The messenger was named Rawlings.[12]

The structure of the daily routine was quite like that in the Office of Indian Trade. Hamilton maintained incoming correspondence by the same sort of system of registers and pigeon holes; Miller transcribed file copies of outgoing letters in bound letterbooks. Each one contains about seven hundred letters, and Miller filled six volumes during McKenney's administration. Although the regular correspondence was expedited as much as possible, maintaining the letterbooks was a tedious business always in arrears. By the end of the first year, Miller was some five hundred letters behind. He was so overworked, in fact, that McKenney obtained congressional approval in 1826 to hire Daniel Kurtz, ostensibly a bookkeeper. Kurtz spent hours copying and recording letters, and still every winter the letterbooks were two to five months behind. Several times McKenney appealed to Christopher Vandeventer, Calhoun's chief clerk, for the services of as many as a dozen other department copyists.[13]

Frequent inquiries from legislators for information relating to Indian affairs caused part of the delay. Every year from early December until Congress adjourned in March or later, senators, representatives, and committees of both houses flooded the Indian office with constituents' petitions and with requests for reports on the number of Indians in the United States, the amount of land ceded to the government by the tribes, and the status of claims. Each request involved copying documents whose length might be a few pages or a few hundred. Apologizing to Delegate Joseph M. White of Florida Territory for not responding more quickly to a request, McKenney explained, "I have to refer, in a general way to the heavy press of duties upon this office, which, with *all my time*, I am just able to get along with; and to several calls of late, by the Congress, for information, the answers to which, in the form of reports to the Secretary of War, devolved upon me."[14]

Weekly reports also contributed to the workload. War Department regulations required branch chiefs to submit to the secretary of war every Monday a report of all letters received during the previous week. Like the registers, the reports listed the name of the correspondent, the date, the subject, and the action taken on each letter. Although the reports kept the secretary of war informed of developments in the department and checked the efficiency of his clerks, McKenney considered them a waste of time. He conceded that they were "useful to check neglect in those who may be given to neglect." However, this shortcoming, he explained to Secretary of War James Barbour, did not apply to his office since "not one letter in fifty, that I act upon is ever opened except by myself." Moreover, he continued, "all such, as afterwards require your directions I hand up to you, but *hundreds* relating only to ordinary or current business, I do not trouble you with. It is therefore a waste of time "to write out a voluminous report every week, which cannot be brought to bear on any business charged against me, to shew (as the report ought) whether I had neglected it or not."[15] Although Calhoun had begun the procedure, he eventually exempted the Indian office. Calhoun's successors, however, were not so agreeable and demanded weekly reports.

The clerks spent most of their time copying replies to the routine correspondence of the Indian office. In its first three years, the office registered approximately 2,220 incoming letters. Almost invariably McKenney personally answered each one, if only to acknowledge receiving it, and his loquacity is reflected in this public correspondence. The man seldom wrote a short letter. A dozen or more pages were common, and McKenney once sent a Treasury Department auditor a forty-five-page letter.[16]

A surprising amount of the correspondence came from Indians. Leaders of the Cherokee, Chickasaw, Choctaw, and Creek nations—the "civilized tribes"—were the most prolific letter writers. Many of these leaders were intelligent, educated, and wrote with ease. Others, such as the Choctaw chief Greenwood Leflore, who informed McKenney that "good advise you give ous for our good . . . that is become industryous and Aducate our childrens and make them white hart wee will not lose any time in doing so," had more difficulty writing in English but still got their messages across.[17] A few were pure-blood Indians who dictated their letters to agents or interpreters.

The purposes of these letters varied. Some, such as a request for the removal of an agent, concerned matters the Indians felt had to be brought directly to the attention of the Indian office, the secretary of war, or the president. Many were notes thanking McKenney for kindnesses shown to the correspondents when they had been in Washington.[18] McKenney answered letters from Indians promptly, considering the attention "not only proper, but important as a measure of policy to conciliate them and increase their confidence in me." McKenney wrote in a special jargon which he presumably believed made his letters more understandable to the Indians. He addressed letters to "My Brother" or "My Children." The agent was their "Father"; Mc-

Kenney was their "Father in Washington"; Washington was the "Great Village"; the secretary of war, the "Great War Chief"; Congress, the "Great Council" or the "Council of Twenty four fires"; the president, the "Great Father"; and those who spoke against the government were "bad birds." Indians perhaps enjoyed receiving mail from their "Father in Washington," but at least one agent resented the practice, claiming that such letters undermined his influence.[19]

The field service accounted for a major portion of the correspondence of the Office of Indian Affairs. When McKenney assumed his duties in the spring of 1824, the service included almost a hundred regular employees: four superintendents, eighteen agents, twenty-two subagents, thirty-four interpreters, and twenty-one blacksmiths, gunsmiths, clerks, and farmers. Six independent agents answered directly to McKenney; the other agents were responsible to one of the four superintendents.[20] Since the field service was already well established, McKenney did not tamper with its structure. Instead he tightened its organization and gave it the attention and direction the secretary of war was unable to provide.

Superintendents had general responsibility for Indian affairs in a large geographic area, usually a territory; normally the territorial governor served ex officio as superintendent. When a territory became a state, the responsibility for the supervision of agents was transferred either to the War Department or to a neighboring governor. The St. Louis superintendency was an exception to the pattern, created in 1822 to retain the services of William Clark. In 1824 the territorial governors were James Miller of Arkansas, William P. Duval of Florida, and Lewis Cass of Michigan; Clark had charge of all Indian agents west of the Mississippi River and north of Arkansas Territory.[21]

The St. Louis and Michigan superintendencies greatly overshadowed the others in size and importance. Clark administered the Upper Missouri, Sac and Fox, Prairie du Chien, St. Peters, Kickapoo and Delaware, and Osage agencies and the Kaskaskia subagency. At least thirty-five tribes—from the Apaches, Comanches, and Kiowas in the south to the Chippewas, Ottawas, and Winnebagos in the north—lived within the limits of the St. Louis superintendency. Cass, with headquarters at Detroit, was responsible for twenty-five thousand Indians scattered among the Chicago, Fort Wayne, Green Bay, Mackinac, Piqua (Ohio), and Sault Ste. Marie agencies. Only a few bands of three tribes —the Cherokees, Choctaws, and Quapaws—resided officially within the Arkansas superintendency; the Florida superintendency was responsible for only one tribe, the Seminoles. The Chickasaw, Choctaw, Creek, Eastern Cherokee, Red River, and Six Nations agencies were independent.[22]

In some respects territorial governors made ideal superintendents. Their broad executive powers enabled them to quell local disturbances quickly and effectively. Their proximity to the agents they supervised enabled them to give instructions and answer inquiries quickly. Normally, superintendents licensed traders, entertained visiting Indians, distributed presents, and transmitted annuities. However, not every territorial governor had the experience or inclination to deal with Indians; Duval thought the superintendency an "onerous" duty.[23]

The work was sometimes unpleasant and always underpaid. Cass once complained that he was "surrounded by drunken lawless Indians, doubtful friends, secret enemies" and asked for an allowance to hire a guard. Like Clark, he received $1,500 a year for office rent, fuel, and clerical help. The Florida superintendent received $850 and the Arkansas superintendent only $750 for operating expenses. The fund was no supplement for the standard $2,000 salary of territorial governors.[24]

Indian agents fared little better. Annual salaries, fixed by acts of Congress, ranged between $1,200 and $1,800. In addition, living quarters were furnished, which was a blessing, because, as one agent grumbled, if he had to pay rent as well as buy food, "the economy of a Franklin" could not keep him out of debtors prison.[25]

Three months after he took office, McKenney asked each agent for a description of his agency. He wanted to know its exact location and the best route from Washington, the names of the tribes and number of Indians within its jurisdiction, the topography and climate, and the number of whites in the immediate vicinity.[26] The replies form a profile of the field service in 1824 and illustrate some of the problems Indian administrators faced in this period. Many of the agencies were far removed from white settlements, inaccessible except by lakes and rivers. For all practical purposes, Sault Ste. Marie, Green Bay, Prairie du

Chien, and Chicago were the ends of the earth; an exchange of letters between Washington and these stations commonly took months. The Sac and Fox agency was on Rock Island in the Mississippi River, and besides the garrison at Fort Armstrong, only eleven whites lived on the island: the sutler and his wife and an Indian trader, his wife, child, and six hired men. The next white community was more than one hundred miles away. George Gray at Red River in Louisiana had only two white families in the immediate vicinity of his agency; both operated ferryboats "for the accommodation of the Indians and Travellers."[27]

Not all agencies were lonely outposts. Henry R. Schoolcraft reported that 152 whites (of whom 69 were mixed-bloods) lived near Sault Ste. Marie; John Tipton reported a white population of more than 300 at Fort Wayne; and Jasper Parrish wrote that the Six Nations agency at Canadaigua, New York, was "more or less surrounded by white settlements."[28] The proximity of large numbers of whites to an agency was frequently undesirable for it heightened the possibility of conflict between the races. Parrish said "frequent depredations petty theft & trespasses are committed between the whites and Indians (more frequently on the part of the former)" with the result that "it causes the Agent considerable time and trouble, to settle with and satisfy the injured persons, so as to preserve our peace and friendship unbroken." Another, more serious consequence of close contact was the debauchery and degradation of the Indians, and for that reason McKenney ultimately endorsed the policy of removal of all Indians west of the Mississippi River. For temporary relief from the press of white population, McKenney in 1828 authorized the transfer of the Fort Wayne agency to a less crowded area near Logansport, Indiana.[29]

The establishment of a new agency or the relocation of an old one involved considerable expense, especially in construction costs. McKenney, always hampered by insufficient operating funds, preferred to rent or purchase buildings in the neighborhood. When a fort was the site selected for an agency, the commandant could sometimes be prevailed upon to furnish space. Having soldiers construct the necessary buildings was relatively inexpensive, but despite the extra pay and extra whiskey for each day's labor, soldiers disliked the duty and few commanding officers released their men for such work without pressure from the secretary of war.[30] When there was no other choice, Mc-Kenney would allow the agent to put up the buildings through private contract. He hesitated to do this because his subordinates seldom shared his ideas of economy. When he authorized Benjamin Reynolds to spend up to $2,000 for an agency house, Reynolds spent $1,800 for his quarters alone. "An 'agency house,' " McKenney reprimanded his Chickasaw agent, "is not understood to embrace the main building only, but all buildings necessary to the accommodation of the agent, and those who assemble there to transact business with him."[31]

McKenney allowed agents discretion to choose precise sites, but even such a small freedom was liable to abuse, McKenney learned to his chagrin. In the fall of 1826 six Chickasaw chiefs sent him a petition stating that Reynolds had located his agency "some sixty or seventy miles from the centre of the Nation" where few members of the tribe lived. McKenney dashed off a protest to the agent. "You will explain the grounds of this dissatisfaction as made known by the Chiefs," he demanded, "—and the reasons that induced so wide a Departure, on your part in the selection of the Agency, from the very generally understood policy of the Government in its agents [being] located among the Indians to whom they are sent."[32]

The Indians usually donated about one square mile of land for the agent's use. The amount was not excessive, for an agency often included a council house, stables, barns, and gardens as well as quarters for the agent and his family, subagent, interpreter, blacksmith, and slaves (when owned). Of course, not every agent had such luxurious quarters. The Upper Missouri agent, John Dougherty, complained about his "small unhewn log cabin." An agent, he acidly informed McKenney, should have a good house "not solely on account of his own comfort, but to render him respectable in the eyes of the Indians as a public agent."[33]

An agent's duties embraced the entire spectrum of Indian affairs. He arranged and negotiated treaties, filed claims, paid annuities, distributed presents, noted violations of the statutes pertaining to Indian relations, brought delegations of Indians to Washington, and reported rumors of impending hostilities. He was also ambassador, legal adviser, and protector to the Indians in his jurisdiction. He lived among and befriended them;

to be successful, he needed their respect and trust. In his hands often lay the success or failure of the Indian policy of the federal government.

Since an agent was a political appointee of the president, he frequently lacked experience in Indian affairs. Moreover, aside from a pat on the back and a few general instructions, a newly appointed agent received little preparation for his assignment. "The great object of an Indian agency," McKenney told Reynolds, "is to see to, and minister, as far as possible to the wants of the Indians." The agent was to attend faithfully to the complaints of his charges, remove intruders from their lands, prevent them from committing crimes against whites, and above all promote federal Indian policy. McKenney sent similar instructions, with slight modifications in one or two particulars, to each new agent. "There is nothing peculiar, relating to these Indians," McKenney wrote to the secretary of war concerning the appointment of an agent to the Caddo tribe. "The same, or similar duties relate to an intercourse with these, as with other Tribes, in paying annuities, moderating their excitements, in a general supervisance of their helpless condition, and in executing the provisions of the intercourse law." In a letter to a new agent, McKenney added as an afterthought, "P.S. You will keep the Department informed from time to time of the state of feelings among the Indians, and of the affairs of the agency, generally."[34]

Aside from these basic instructions, Indian agents had few guidelines to direct them in carrying out their duties. No code of regulations for the Indian service existed. Although McKenney eventually succeeded in having regulations drafted, the code was never adopted. McKenney at first furnished the agents with handwritten copies of various laws he considered essential. In February 1825, however, he directed his chief clerk to compile all the treaties and laws relating to Indian affairs still in effect. Hamilton worked until October gathering the information which was then printed and bound. McKenney ordered 150 copies of the work and presented one to each superintendent and agent.[35]

Agents could, of course, turn to McKenney for advice. William Ward reported that a white man who had been severely wounded in "a drunken frolic" with several Choctaws now wanted the government to pay his medical expenses. "The

Government," McKenney replied, "is not inclined so far to recognize the right of getting drunk, as to pay the public money to bear the consequences of such a practice." Ward later said Indians killed several old women of the tribe because the medicine men had pointed them out as witches after patients died. McKenney wrote directly to the Choctaw headmen demanding that they stop the barbarous practice, "a cheat" imposed on their people. When the Eastern Cherokee agent asked how much charity he could extend to his Indians, McKenney replied that the government would allow "the exercise of occasional bounty in actual necessaries to such poor families around the agency as may need it. But straggling & Drunken, & worthless Indians are not to be contenanced in *any* way."[36]

Although he was happy to answer questions, McKenney apparently felt Cherokee agent Hugh Montgomery abused the privilege. After a year-long barrage of administrative inquiries, the superintendent informed the agent "it is not possible for the Department at Washington to furnish decisions for the government of every matter of detail which may arise within your agency. Some discretion it is expected will be exercised by you, in the execution, at least [of] the details of cases which may occur, and require your decision, and especially if the principle in any one division or class of cases, has been established."[37]

Officials of the Indian service could also draw on their subordinates in the field for assistance. Superintendents and agents, with the approval of the Indian office, could appoint subagents. Although the salary of $500 was less than half that of agents, the duties of the subagents were essentially the same; a few had independent stations.[38] Interpreters were also important assistants because few agents could speak the languages of the tribes to which they were assigned. Generally, interpreters were uneducated traders or mixed-bloods who received stipends of $200 to $600 a year depending on the additional duties they performed at the agencies. Some ran errands, searched for stolen horses, or guarded undistributed annuities. A few served as subagents. The duties of the "assistant Interpreter & Messenger" Cass employed at Detroit were "to receive the Indians, to remove them from the town, when drunk, to make fires for them, to draw their provisions, to keep them from quarrelling, and generally to be with them to superintend their conduct."[39]

Historians have claimed that the Indian service in the nine-teenth century was rife with graft and that agents were corrupt and self-serving. The generalization is not valid for McKenney's time. Other agents could have said with Lawrence Taliaferro, "I have the sad consolation of leaving . . . public service as poor as when first I entered—the only evidence of my integrity." More typical frailties were "extreme intemperence" and "inat-tention to duties," deficiencies for which the Chickasaw subagent was dismissed.[40] Life in the Indian service was hard and lonely; devotion to duty was often rewarded by scorn and opprobrium from fellow Americans. Yet capable men like Cass and Clark served faithfully for years, and agents like Schoolcraft at Sault Ste. Marie, Taliaferro at St. Peters, John Johnston at Piqua, Pierre Menard at Kaskaskia, Jasper Parrish at New York, and George Gray at Red River were a credit to the federal govern-ment.

It also appears that at least some of the Indians appreciated the work of their agents. On several occasions when Indians heard a rumor their agent might be removed they petitioned the War Department to retain him. "I learned that our Great Father, the President, has become dissatisfied with our Agent & was about to take him away, & send a new one to us, we were all very sorry to hear that," the chiefs of the Western Cherokees wrote. "We do not wish to change our Agent for any new one— We all know him! & He knows us & is acquainted with our business." Indians at the Six Nations agency appealed directly to President Jackson. Parrish, they wrote, "possesses now as he always has done, our entire confidence." Perhaps the most poign-ant testimony was the terse statement from Thomas Dillard, interpreter at Red River, at the death of George Gray: "I have witnessed a sene of much lamentation among the Indians."[41]

McKenney had occasional but not insurmountable problems with members of the field service. He refused to pay the salary of an agent who had not reported to his post six months after his appointment. When he learned that Ward was operating a tavern on the Choctaw agency grounds, the outraged McKenney ordered him to shed his business connections immediately and to attend "exclusively to your public duties." When Georgia planters charged Gad Humphreys with speculating in runaway slaves, McKenney launched an investigation that forced the

Florida agent's resignation.[42]

McKenney may have overcome his personnel problems, but the fiscal "derangements" of the Indian department were almost his undoing. Each spring Congress voted an appropriation for Indian affairs based on a budget that McKenney had submitted to the secretary of war the previous fall. The funding provided for four of the six primary areas of disbursements relating to Indian affairs: salary of agents, salary of subagents, presents, and contingencies. Annuities and Indian civilization were covered by separate legislation. Occasionally special appropriations were made for particular objects such as Indian removal, treaties, and conferences. The Indian office in a given year might be responsible for the disbursement of up to $1,000,000.[43]

At first McKenney had little trouble obtaining from Congress the funds he requested. He asked for and received $153,000 for 1825 and 1826. But his request for $181,224 for 1827 was trimmed by Congress to $156,100. In his budget for 1828 he again asked for $181,224, insisting that the money was "not a cent more than will be absolutely required for the service of that year." Congress again authorized only $156,100. Evidently conceding to the inevitable, McKenney naively submitted a budget calling for that sum for 1829; he received instead $151,100. Rock bottom was reached with the 1830 budget when he asked for and got $150,690.[44]

These budget cutbacks were apparently fruits of continuing political animosities. Throughout John Quincy Adams' presidency, Jackson men in Congress used every ploy at their disposal to discredit the administration. They harassed the executive departments with calls for reports aimed at overburdening the clerical staffs; they introduced resolutions on retrenchment and reform intended to expose extravagance and waste; they called for investigations of the misuse of contingency funds. Because of its well-publicized problems the Indian office was a prime target, and McKenney could do little but endure it. While he was preparing his budget for 1828, Cass warned him against asking for an increased appropriation because "the times are highly inauspicious to an avowal of an excess of expenditure over appropriation. I should be apprehensive," Cass wrote, "that such an application would not only fail but be attended with injurious effects upon the character of the department."[45]

Whatever the reason for the budgetary straits, they severely hampered the effective administration of Indian affairs. The 1830 appropriation included only $15,000 for presents. This money, used at the discretion of the agents and superintendents primarily to aid sick or starving Indians, had to be divided among all the agencies and superintendencies; yet the same amount had been appropriated for that purpose in 1802 when, McKenney pointed out, "agencies were comparatively few; and the condition of the Indians better." Then the Indians "were not so impoverished, and especially not so diseased. They had more game, and in all respects suffered less." The strain on the $95,000 appropriated for contingencies was even more critical. Field officials drew on this all-purpose fund to transport and distribute the annuities to the Indians, to buy rations for Indians visiting the agencies on business, to pay for salaries of interpreters, blacksmiths, and gunsmiths (as well as iron, steel, and coal for those shops), and to meet unanticipated expenses. But, McKenney bemoaned, year after year the needs of the Indian service increased and Congress continued to appropriate $95,000 for contingencies.[46] Despite McKenney's pleas to his field officers to exercise the "utmost economy," the Indian office accumulated an enormous backlog of debts or, as they were called, arrearages: $66,000 in 1830 by McKenney's estimate; by Treasury Department calculations the figure was $144,000.[47]

After Congress passed an appropriation bill, McKenney issued the money to his agents and superintendents for their operating expenses, at first in quarterly installments after they had properly accounted for the previous quarter's funds. In later years, when so many jurisdictions operated continually in the red, McKenney paid out funds in lump sums. He did this by means of requisitions that, once endorsed by the secretary of war, the Treasury Department filled from one or more of the Indian office funds as specified in the requisition. For special reasons or to receive their quarterly salaries, agents could write bills on the War Department, but they rarely did so because banks were reluctant to accept them.[48]

As disbursing officers, the superintendents and agents had to "account" for public money, and McKenney had the responsibility of examining the accounts before transmitting them to the Treasury Department. This duty, which should have been a routine administrative chore, gave the superintendent some of his most trying moments. In 1829 McKenney wrote Secretary of War John Eaton that since the establishment of the office there had not been a *"single instance,* involving a wrong action" attributable to the Indian office proper, but *"all* the cases of difficulty do now, and have always applied to the . . . accounting officers of the Treasury, to whom the *'settlement'* of the accounts is referr'd. Here," he insisted, *"the* whole concern has been always wrong, requiring the perpetual interference and direction of the Secretary of War; and . . . it is so from the necessity of the case, and this *necessity* arises out of *the mode,* of keeping and sett'ling the accounts at the offices of *the Treasury,* to which the law refers them for settlement."[49]

McKenney examined the accounts carefully and evaluated the expenditures on the basis of appropriateness and cost. Questionable items, such as $70 for admitting Osage Indians to a circus or $44 for paving a public sidewalk, he suspended pending explanations. Generally, perhaps because of his own difficulties with the accounting officers, McKenney was lenient in his allowances. He informed Benjamin F. Smith, the Chickasaw agent, "your accounts for the 3rd. and 4th. quarters of this year are passed—but it required the most liberal interpretations of your explanations . . . to get them through."[50]

Once satisfied that the accounts were in order, McKenney transmitted them for settlement to William Lee, the second auditor, who handled the Indian office accounts. Lee scrutinized the accounts, paying particular attention to charges on the contingency fund. His examinations were so exacting that McKenney once claimed the second auditor's report could show "almost down to the nail that is driven in an Indians coffin, how this fund is disposed of." If the auditor discovered irregularities he stated them on a sheet of differences. The agent or superintendent had to either come up with a convincing explanation or reimburse the treasury from his own pocket. The second auditor forwarded the accounts to Richard Cutts, the second comptroller, who reviewed Lee's work and stated the final balances. Settlements could take years, and it was not uncommon for disbursing officers to come to Washington to defend their accounts.[51]

For the Indian office, the unwieldy accountability process

was a source of continual confusion and embarrassment. If an agent received money from five appropriations in a given year, he had to submit vouchers closing his accounts under each of them. The far-flung operations of an agency and the accumulating arrearages often made it impossible for an agent to submit all the needed vouchers on time, and, in any given year, his accounts might be closed under only two or three headings. Since an agent could not legally receive his salary, much less the funds for his agency, until his accounts were closed, the auditor would fictitiously settle them by making up the difference with money from one or more of the Indian office appropriations. Because of the arrearages, the auditor often used money appropriated for one year to pay obligations incurred the previous year. Eventually, when the agent's returns came in, an official settlement would be made and the diverted funds restored to their proper places. If, as often happened, bills or requisitions came in for payment on an appropriation which had been cleaned out by diversions, they would be either returned marked "funds exhausted" or held over until money was restored to the fund, usually the following year.[52]

Juggling the books had an adverse impact throughout the Indian service. Creditors waited months for their money, salaries were as much as two quarters in arrears, and agencies limped along with half their expected allotments.[53] In 1828 Schoolcraft declared that the "derangements in the fiscal affairs of the Indian department are in the extreme. One would think that appropriations had been handled with a pitchfork. A correspondent writes: 'For 1827 we were promised $48,000 and received $30,000. For 1828 we were promised $40,000, and have received $25,000; and, besides these promises, were all the extra expenditures authorized to be incurred, amounting to not less than $15,000. It is impossible this can continue.' And these derangements are only with regard to the north. How the south and west stand it is impossible to say." Obviously, he complained, "there is a screw loose in the public machinery somewhere." A year later Schoolcraft expressed to Cass the need and hope that "we are not long to continue in this way, and that order & punctuality, is destined to arise out of confusion & delinquencies. But such," he concluded, "can never be the result, as I have been long convinced, while the management of the Indian Bureau remains in the hands of McK[enney]."[54]

McKenney did not become fully aware of the extent of the "confusion & delinquencies" until well into 1828. When one of his requisitions was returned in March because of lack of funds, he shrugged it off as "some blunder" in the Treasury Department. The increasing frequency of such blunders aroused his suspicion. When that autumn one of the Indian agents received his pay bill back marked "funds exhausted," McKenney finally took the matter to the secretary of war. "I have to say there is manifestly *error* in this," he declared. "I have only to state that the fund for the pay of agents, is *specific*; and cannot without *a breach of law* be applied except for the pay of agents. How then," he wanted to know, "until the agents are all paid, can the fund be exhausted?"[55]

The crisis broke when McKenney learned that the requisition he had issued to Cass on September 30 had been altered in the Treasury Department. To fill the $10,900 requisition McKenney had specified that $3,900 be taken from the fund for pay of agents, $2,500 from pay of subagents, and $4,500 from contingencies. Cass was credited, instead, with $1,882.69 from pay of agents, $1,590.26 from pay of subagents, $2,327.85 from contingencies, $1,134.14 from presents, and $3,575.22 from Indian civilization. To confuse matters further the money given Cass from Indian civilization emptied that fund, and McKenney in the meantime had authorized missionaries to draw some $2,000 from it.[56]

The news of the manipulation enraged the superintendent. "I am by my commission required to make requisitions," he complained to Secretary of War Porter, "and by it I am held responsible for their correctness. But what becomes of my responsibility; and how can I keep the accounts, and regulate the drafts upon the various appropriations, if after I act here, they are thus changed elsewhere? Such a proceeding," he pointed out, "apart from its illegality destroys all responsibility, besides confusing the accounts, and making a breach in the established regulations of the Department."[57]

McKenney suggested solutions for the financial problems. Since the arrearages caused many of the troubles, he thought Porter should ask Congress for a special appropriation to pay off all the Indian office debts. In the future the office should have an arrearages account for "proper allowances for disbursements over and above the appropriation for the year." Otherwise, he warned, charging arrearages to the next year's appropriation would "stop the operations which the act of Congress meant to sustain."[58] Porter, a lame duck secretary, did nothing.

John Eaton was more sympathetic and helpful. Two days after the new secretary took office in March 1829, McKenney presented him with a lengthy letter detailing the fiscal woes of the Indian office. Within the week Eaton told the second auditor "the Indian arrearages of 1828, shall not be chargeable upon nor paid out of the appropriations for 1829. You are, therefore, desired to adopt a new mode of keeping the Books under the proper heads of expenditure, that the accounts of the two years may not be blended, but kept distinct and separate." The purpose behind this move, McKenney explained, was to force an "appropriation for *arrearages*, of the next Congress." The strategy eventually worked. Congress did pass an arrearages bill of $61,000 to clear up indebtedness in the Indian department prior to 1829 but not until January 1831.[59]

McKenney's suggested solution for the accountability problem was equally direct. The auditors should close an agent's accounts each year regardless of the condition of the various categories of disbursement under it. Failure to account properly for all money given him for presents, for example, should not affect an agent's accountability for the succeeding year. His accounts for a given year should be closed, but he should remain charged for the open balance under presents until the money was vouched for. "Nothing is more simple than this mode, and it is a wonder to me how any other could ever have been conceived of—and yet out of the existing mode, comes all that is evil and vexatious, in the Indian department," McKenney lamented.[60] His suggestion was not adopted, however.

It was, McKenney had written earlier, "unjust in any one to rail against our Indian concerns or talk about their mismanagement. We who have to do with them know well enough how slip-shod almost every thing is, but we know also it does not arise out of a lack of effort . . . but in a want of *a suitable system*." In truth, McKenney was an administrator with neither the authority nor the power to make or enforce decisions. "A suitable system" was one with "corresponding checks and balances—and a responsible head, not of Executive creation only, but one whose acts should bring him directly in contact with the Congress, and make him responsible to that body."[61]

Legally, McKenney could do nothing without the approval of the secretary of war, the result of Calhoun's failure to honor his commitment to him. Calhoun left the War Department in the spring of 1825 to become vice-president under Adams without having persuaded Congress to improve McKenney's salary and status. Therefore, the administrative discretion McKenney enjoyed depended on the degree of *"general confidence"* the various secretaries of war had in him, which in turn depended on each secretary's personality, his knowledge of Indian affairs, and his opinion of McKenney's ability and judgment.[62]

Under Calhoun, McKenney enjoyed almost complete independence. The secretary rarely questioned his superintendent's actions, and their relationship was extremely cordial. Calhoun appreciated and respected his subordinate's, administrative talent, his knowledge of Indians, and his dedication to duty. James Barbour, the former governor of Virginia who succeeded Calhoun and served as secretary of war until June 1828, initially kept a tight rein on McKenney. Shortly after taking office he told the superintendent of Indian affairs that he could transact "ordinary business" but "in all cases of novelty—of importance or responsibility you should not act without my directions." By the end of the first year, however, Barbour gave "unqualified testimony" to McKenney's "ability and industry, and promptness, and to his experience in our Indian concerns, which I esteem to be exceedingly valuable to the Government."[63]

McKenney had less luck with the secretaries of war who followed Calhoun and Barbour. Peter B. Porter knew little about Indian affairs; the old 1812 war hawk was merely a timeserver appointed to see the War Department through the waning nine months of the Adams administration. Moreover, the president himself, who had by this time suffered a great deal of congressional criticism for corruption, waste, and inefficiency, apparently finally accepted as true those charges leveled against the Indian service in general and against McKenney in particular. On the day Porter took the oath of office, Adams cautioned him to be alert to the "irregularities which had crept into practice from the illegal control over expenditures first assumed by Mr. Calhoun, and which Governor Barbour, finding established, had not entirely rectified." The president stressed particularly the "abuses in the Indian department, and the difficulty with regard to the settlement of Mr. McKenney's account."[64]

The change in administrations brought McKenney his darkest days as superintendent of Indian affairs. Andrew Jackson became president in 1829 and appointed John H. Eaton secretary of war. Jackson correctly suspected McKenney of having worked against his election, and Eaton allowed him almost no administrative discretion, relegating McKenney to what he had been officially all along—another clerk in the War Department. In fact, shortly before McKenney's dismissal, Eaton directed that all letters the superintendent wrote first be screened by him before mailing. Little wonder then that McKenney later claimed Eaton affected "official dignity" and that he was "coarse & vulgar in his office" and "not well-informed on any subject."[65]

McKenney had from the beginning viewed his lowly status within the administrative structure of the War Department as intolerable, and when Calhoun left without correcting the situation, he decided to take matters into his own hands. In November 1825 McKenney submitted to Barbour a lengthy and detailed report in which he related the steps preceding the creation of the Indian office, outlined his duties, and stressed the inadequacy of his salary and the weakness of his position. What he needed, McKenney said, was "some new modification of this Office, some creation by the Congress of a responsible head, who should be known to the laws, and to whom should be referr'd all matters arising out of our Indian Relations.[66] Only then could such evils as the chaotic fiscal condition of the Indian office be corrected.

McKenney was not alone in his concern. President Adams included in his first state of the union message his own solution for the Indian office: the establishment of a Home Department. The message was presented to Congress on December 6, 1825, and the following day the House of Representatives appointed Daniel Webster chairman of the Select Committee on the Organization of the Executive Departments.[67] Secretary of War Barbour lent his support to the idea two weeks later by writing Webster urging establishment of the new department and suggesting transferring some of his duties to it, "particularly the

whole subject of pensions—and still with more fitness our relations with the Indians." Adams' proposal met with some success,
and in May 1826 a bill to establish a new executive department
was introduced in the House. One of its provisions called for the
secretary of the new administrative unit to "exercise & perform
such duties, now exercised by the Secretary of War, as relate
to Indian Affairs."[68]

McKenney was confident that his own plan for reorganizing
the Indian office would not be lost in the concern over the new
department. As he pointed out, "it is immaterial when, whether
before or after the organization of the Home Dept.—that for the
Indians is acted upon, except that if it precede the first, it will
only have been previously made ready for the transfer in a
properly organized state, & not in a disorganized state; & if the
Home Department *be* organized, that of the Indian Department will *have to be* afterwards, as everybody knows who has
any knowledge on the subject."[69]

However, by February Barbour had not responded to his
November memorandum, and McKenney appealed to former
President Madison for help. The superintendent claimed Barbour was at that very moment writing a report on the reorganization of the Indian office to be submitted to Congress the following week. Knowing well, he said, "the impulse which is given
in such a case, coming from *such a source;* and that however
kind the feelings are that now exist, they would be made by it,
at least more *active*," McKenney asked Madison to write Adams
that he might "feel an additional interest in my prosperity." He
also wanted Madison, if it would not be too much trouble, to
write Barbour. Madison declined to trouble the president, but
he did send a note to the secretary of war.[70] McKenney probably
anticipated matters; if Barbour did write the report, no evidence
of it remains.

The pace, however, began to quicken. In March, John Cocke,
chairman of the House Committee on Indian Affairs, asked
Barbour about "a Bureau where the affairs of the Government
with the several Indian tribes appear to be transacted." He
wanted the information, Cocke said, because the committee
members "have searched in vain for the law establishing that
office." Barbour responded promptly to Cocke's letter, answering
the congressman's questions and endorsing McKenney's plan to

reorganize the Indian office. "It would certainly relieve the Department, and in my opinion promote the public interest," Barbour wrote, "if an organization of this office were made upon the basis of the other branches in this Department; and subordinate, like these, to its head."[71]

After reading Barbour's report, Cocke personally inspected the Indian office. He questioned the clerks, poked into the files, and talked at length with McKenney and Barbour. He became convinced the new bureau was essential and asked McKenney to write a bill embodying the necessary legislation. The colonel lost no time. Leaving blank the space for the salary, he routed a bill for approval to Barbour, who wrote on it in pencil, *All right—alter not a word.*" On March 31, 1826, Cocke introduced in the House the bill calling for the appointment of a "General Superintendent of Indian Affairs" who, at an annual salary of $3,000, would be responsible for keeping the records of Indian affairs, conducting all the correspondence arising out of Indian relations, handling and adjusting the financial accounts before transmitting them to the Treasury Department—in general doing everything relating to Indian affairs that formerly had been required of the secretary of war. When Cass heard the news, he exclaimed: "God grant the bill may pass . . . I shall worship Cocke for his zeal in the matter."[72] But the bill did not pass. It was read twice and then referred to the Committee of the Whole House where it received no further action. The same fate befell the bill for the Home Department.[73]

Although Cocke did not return to the next Congress, a little more than two weeks after the opening session, the House Committee on Indian Affairs introduced a resolution calling for an inquiry "into the expediency of establishing a General Superintendency of Indian Affairs at the Seat of the General Government" and on January 2, 1828, reported a bill identical in wording to the one introduced in the previous Congress.[74]

Here matters stood when General Porter became secretary of war the following summer. After a few weeks in office, he complained that no portion of his duties were "so perplexing, and . . . less welcome, than those which appertain to the Bureau of Indian Affairs." McKenney had little trouble persuading him of the need for a reorganization of the Indian office. The first step Porter took was to call superintendents Cass and Clark to

Washington to draw up a set of regulations for the administration of Indian affairs.[75]

McKenney had long stressed the need for such regulations. Section three of his reorganization bill authorized the secretary of war "to establish regulations, for the Government of the office hereby created, as soon as may be after the passage of this act, and submit the same to the next Congress for its information and approval."[76] Since the bill was now bogged down in committee, McKenney likely thought presentation of the written code might prod Congress into action. McKenney considered Cass and Clark better informed on Indian affairs than anyone else in the country. He also recognized the value of having these two highly respected and influential men in Washington while Congress was in session.

Cass, Clark, and McKenney spent most of the winter working on the regulations. The report submitted to the House for approval on February 9, 1829, was, once printed, a massive document of 113 pages. It included a bill for the "general regulation of the intercourse with the Indians" and a "code of regulations for the government of the Indian Department, and for the general administration of its affairs." It also incorporated much of McKenney's program for the reorganization of the Indian department. The report was referred to the Committee on Indian Affairs.[77]

Congress adjourned March 3, 1829, before acting on either McKenney's bill or the regulations. The following day Jackson was inaugurated president of the United States. Once again time had run out for McKenney. For four years the Democrats had accused the Indian office of waste, inefficiency, and graft; now that party had come to power. McKenney knew his days as superintendent were numbered. He lingered a year before his dismissal in August 1830.

The bill for the Bureau of Indian Affairs, subsequently introduced, passed both houses without difficulty. The measure, providing for the appointment of a commissioner of Indian affairs at an annual salary of $3,000, became law on July 9, 1832.[78] What McKenney had labored for so long and diligently was finally realized. Unfortunately he was no longer in office to enjoy the benefits.

7

Indian Visitors to Washington

S INCE THE GOVERNMENT'S relations with the native Americans were determined by treaty, much of McKenney's work as superintendent of Indian affairs concerned the preparation, negotiation, and implementation of treaties. Simply coping with the paperwork would have been enough, for treaty making was big business; thirty-nine were ratified in McKenney's six years in the Indian office. But for McKenney there was an added dimension. Some important treaties were negotiated in Washington, which meant that tribal representatives had to be housed, fed, and entertained for months at a time. The treatment accorded these visitors illustrates well a basic anomaly in federal Indian policy. Although the government stressed diplomacy in its official dealings with the Indians, it often resorted to intimidation, liquor, and bribery to make that diplomacy work.

In negotiating formal treaties with the Indians, the United States was following a procedure established by Great Britain and other colonial powers and continued by the Continental Congress. By 1789 the concept that the tribes were independent sovereign nations had become so firmly accepted that, despite the many complications the assumption caused, the federal government entered into formal compacts with the Indians covering not only all aspects of intercourse between white and red Americans but even the internal affairs of the tribes. In the early years of the republic, the treaties had been primarily pacts of friendship, whereby the tribes acknowledged and accepted American sovereignty and protection, but by McKenney's time their main purpose was the acquisition of Indian land. Nevertheless, Indian treaties were considered to have the same status, dignity, and force as agreements with foreign nations and as such required the consent of the Senate and ratification by the president. The fiction of regarding the tribes as independent nations continued until 1871 when it was ended by act of Congress.[1]

In its negotiations with Indian tribes, the federal government followed traditional principles of international protocol. Amid much pomp and ceremony, plenipotentiary commissioners of the United States would formally meet leading chiefs and warriors of the tribes; after considerable discussion, the parties would sign a solemn document detailing compensations, guarantees, and grants and then exchange gifts affirming continued friendship and loyalty.

Only under exceptional circumstances were treaty negotiations conducted in Washington; during McKenney's years in office, only five were negotiated in the nation's capital. In 1824 the Sac and Fox and Iowa tribes, in two separate treaties signed the same day, surrendered their claims to northern Missouri; the Choctaws and Western Cherokees, in separate treaties signed three years apart, exchanged their holdings in Arkansas for territory further west; and in early 1826 the Creeks, in voiding the dishonorable treaty of Indian Springs, ceded to the United States more than two-thirds of their ancestral lands in Georgia. Each of these treaties involved either important land cessions or considerable controversy; for each, unproductive negotiations in the field prompted the government to summon tribal leaders to Washington where, under pressure, they finally came to terms. Although the secretary of war served as commissioner, McKenney had a direct hand. He made all arrangements for room and board for the Indians, presided over the sessions, and drafted the treaties which he then signed as a witness.

McKenney thoroughly enjoyed taking care of the visiting Indians, although it was no light task. During the summer of 1824, for instance, scarcely a week went by in Washington without the arrival of another delegation. Only a few came to negotiate treaties. Some, especially those from distant and truculent tribes, came to see firsthand the strength and wealth of the American people, a practice McKenney firmly endorsed. "This mode of conquering these people," he explained, "is merciful, and it is cheap, in comparison to what a war with them would cost, to say nothing of the loss of human life." Other delegations came to air grievances, and a few came for no real purpose other than a little sightseeing. Since the government normally paid all the expenses for these junkets, trips in the latter category were ruled out unless the Indians themselves agreed to pay for them out of their annuity allowances. As McKenney explained to Secretary of War Barbour, "the rule of the [War] Department in regard to paying the expenses of Agents and Indians visiting the Seat of Government is this—When the object of the visit is one in which the Government is interested; and when a visit is deemed essential to a better understanding of that object, and which could be not so well had by correspondence—and when permission to make the visit is given, by the Department."[2]

The invitation to visit Washington was normally prompted by an official in the field. "I would recommend that Neamathala and a few of the [Seminole] head chiefs, should be allowed to visit Washington," wrote Florida Governor William Duval in March 1824. "Neamathala is a man of uncommon abilities and has great influence with his nation. He is one of the most eloquent men I have ever heard. If this chief could be attached warmly to our Government, it would certainly be good policy to acquire his confidence and friendship." If the secretary of war agreed that the purpose of the visit was a good one, he would permit the Indians to come. "The privilege is granted," Calhoun informed Duval a month later, "but not to exceed four [Indians] in number. You will direct them to make the visit by the most economical route, perhaps by water would be the least expensive." Accordingly, accompanied by their agent, an interpreter, and perhaps a servant or two, the Indians would arrive in Washington.[3]

Whatever the reasons behind their visits, the various dele-

Pushmataha, by Charles Bird King, 1824. *Courtesy Gulf States Paper Corp., Tuscaloosa, Ala.*

James Monroe peace medal.

Typical flag presented to leading chiefs by the federal government. *Chicago Historical Society collection. Courtesy Milwaukee Public Museum.*

Bill for lodging Benjamin O'Fallon and his Indian delegation (see p. 246) at the Indian Queen Hotel. *Courtesy National Archives.*

gations received similar treatment. McKenney would rent first-class accommodations at Jesse Brown's Indian Queen Hotel or at the equally fine inns owned by Joshua Tennison and Basil Williamson, all on Pennsylvania Avenue within walking distance of the public buildings the Indians would be expected to visit during their stay. The Indian Queen, Washington's most popular hotel in the 1820s, advertised sixty "well proportioned and well furnished" rooms. Brown welcomed stages at the curb and ushered new arrivals into the inn under the large swinging sign, a brightly painted Pocahontas. At meal times, Brown met guests at the dining room door, carved the main dishes, and helped with the serving. Room service was summoned by cords connected to rows of bells hanging behind the bar. The bartender also had to act as desk clerk, seeing that the bells were answered, receiving and delivering messages, and giving information. The cost to the Indian office for each member of a delegation was $1.25 a day, a price that included room and board but not laundry and barbering.[4]

To match these regal surroundings, the delegates received new clothes. Throughout their stay, merchants, cobblers, and tailors scurried in and out of their quarters, bringing the Indians samples of cloth and leather and measuring them for hats, shirts, vests, coats, trousers, and shoes. The Sac, Fox, and Iowa Indians received, among other things, yellow buckskin shoes with thin soles, plain calico shirts with collars, and $5 hats resplendent with silver cords, tassels, and red, blue, and green feathers. Very important chiefs, such as the renowned Pushmataha who accompanied the Choctaw delegation, might also receive military uniforms with epaulets, swords, pistols, and boots. When distributing military insignia and equipment, McKenney generally made some attempt to distinguish levels of leadership; full chiefs would be given two epaulets, half-chiefs one, and warriors none. Silver plated rifles, pipe tomahawks of polished steel, silver arm and wrist bands, earrings, crosses, and assorted trinkets completed the ensembles. Before leaving Washington each Indian was also given "a strong and light" suitcase suitable for stagecoach traveling.[5]

By far the most important gifts were peace medals and American flags. These carried the full weight of national allegiance and conferred upon the recipients added status and rank within their tribes. As superintendent of Indian affairs, it was McKenney's responsibility to have them made and distributed. French and Spanish explorers had begun the practice of giving medals to the Indians, and the British and Americans continued the custom. The solid silver American medals bore the likeness of the incumbent president, and during McKenney's tenure were made in three sizes. The largest, about three inches in diameter, were presented to the most important chiefs; smaller medals went to chiefs and warriors of correspondingly lesser rank.[6]

The Indians regarded a medal as a prized possession, to be buried with the owner when he died or to be handed down from generation to generation. Medals were such significant status symbols that important warriors were very much offended if they did not receive one. McKenney thought it would have been impossible to conduct official business without medals. "This comes of the high value which the Indians set upon these tokens of Friendship," he explained. "They are, besides this indication of the Government Friendship, badges of power to them, and trophies of renown. They will not consent to part from this ancient *right*, as they esteem it; and according to the value they set upon medals is the importance to the Government in having them to bestow."[7]

McKenney, furthermore, viewed the medals as works of art as well as instruments of policy. "They are intended," he insisted, "not for the Indians, only, but for posterity." Thus, he took special pains to see that they were designed and manufactured well. To make the dies for the John Quincy Adams medals, he engaged the services of Moritz Furst, a Hungarian immigrant who in the course of his career designed four sets of Indian peace medals and more than thirty-five commemorative medals for the United States government.[8]

Furst's other medals may have been successful, but his renditions of the Adams likeness seem to have pleased no one. After six months of work on the three dies, Furst was told that only the middle-sized one was acceptable. "There is too much projection in the point of the nose; the head and shoulders are too big, and look to belong to a very fat man. Cannot the nose and the root of the upper lip which goes out with it too far, be altered, if the shoulders &c cannot? I hope so, for indeed the impression, I fear, will not do you credit," McKenney wrote the

artist on September 10, 1825. President Adams agreed with
McKenney, for he commented in his diary after viewing the
medals: "All badly executed." Four months later Furst finally
satisfied his critics. As John Q. Adams, Jr., wrote to McKenney
after viewing the smallest and last medal: "I think it better
than the larger size; but could wish that Mr. Furst had been
more fortunate. It is however I think better than either of the
Medals for Mr. Monroe or Mr. Madison. The family generally
coincide with me in opinion."[9]

The medals were struck at the Philadelphia mint, usually in
lots of one hundred of each size. Since they would be delivered
over a period of several months, McKenney was careful to instruct the mint to send him all three sizes of medals with each
shipment. "Such is the nature of this medal business," he pointed
out, "as to make one size almost useless without the others.
Presents cannot be made of the same size to the several grades
of Indian rank without a total loss of all the results which such
gifts are intended to produce."[10]

Retaining a supply for presentation to the Indians who
visited Washington, McKenney sent the rest to his field officials.
Whether agents collected out-of-date medals and replaced them
with current ones is not clear, but they did encourage Indians
wearing foreign medals to exchange them for American ones. It
was understood that if a chief accepted an American medal he
and his people would be loyal to the Great Father and to the
United States. Agents were sometimes accused of using medals
to "make" chiefs, to bestow office on certain Indians in return
for their cooperation at treaty-making time when legitimate
tribal leaders would have no part of the contemplated agreements. McKenney himself was accused of making chiefs when
he participated in the negotiations at Butte des Morts near
Green Bay in 1827.

The flags presented with the medals McKenney purchased
from Philadelphia merchants who made them in two sizes according to his specifications. The stripes resembled those of the
official American flag, but the fields carried as a device an eagle
or stars, or both in the case of the larger flags. The device was
hand-painted on both sides of the fabric—rough bunting that,
McKenney noted, looked crude but was durable. The large flags
measured 7'6" x 4'8" and cost $12, including tassels and cord.[11]

McKenney's letter accompanying an assortment of gifts sent to Little Prince, head chief of the Creeks who was too elderly to accompany his tribe's delegation to Washington, shows how the federal government used presents to win and retain the friendship of Indians:

Brother—The Secretary of War sends to you by the Presidents directions a Cloak bound with silver lace, and a sword and twelve silver Medals, and twelve Flags. He sends them to you. The Cloak is to keep you warm and dry, and make you live long; and the sword as a badge of honor, and the Medals are sent to you to be put, by your own hands around the necks of your faithful and true chiefs—and with the Medal you will give also a flag—keeping a Medal, and flag for yourself.

Brother—This will show you what you are—and what the great men at Washington think of you. You will consider these things as fastening one of your hands in the hand of your Great Father, and the hand of the Secretary of War.[12]

Indian delegations usually remained three or four weeks in Washington and spent several more weeks visiting New York, Philadelphia, and Baltimore. If the main order of business was the negotiation of a treaty, however, a delegation might stay in the capital as long as six months. The Indians visited theaters, circuses, churches, and farms; they inspected battleships, navy yards, and forts; they met with church groups and civic organizations. During their stay, the highlight for the delegates was an audience with their Great Father, the president. In a White House ceremony that included the pomp and pageantry accorded other visiting heads of state, speeches and gifts were exchanged and the president placed peace medals around the necks of the Indians. The lighting and passing of pipes would generally end the ceremony; then wine, cake, and other refreshments would be served.[13]

Indian delegations were often invited to White House receptions and parties on other occasions, such as the 1822 New Year's Day open house, when a delegation of Pawnee, Kansa, Omaha, Missouri, and Oto Indians shared cakes and tea and rubbed elbows with the cream of Washington society: cabinet members, Supreme Court justices, congressmen, and the ambassadors of England, France, Russia, and Sweden. One guest thought the ladies, many of whom were wearing the fashionable "Scotch bonnet with a tartan crown, border and feathers," were "brilliant and attractive" as usual; but he considered most striking the dozen or so Indians. Three were wrapped in buffalo robes with brightly painted figurines, horses, and birds; one Pawnee chief wore a headdress of feathers that descended "like wings to the waist." On the faces of all was red paint "laid on from the eyebrows to the cheek bone." The interested observer considered the Indians respectful and dignified. He also noticed that the "music and hilarity of the scene occasionally relaxed the muscles of their cadaverous countenances, and in place of pensive gravity, a heartfelt joy beamed in the sullen eye of the Indian warrior."[14]

Several weeks later this same delegation again met the president under rather unusual circumstances. On Saturday, February 9, the Indians performed several of their native dances in front of the White House. Heralded in local newspapers, the spectacle attracted six thousand people. Congress adjourned for the occasion and one witness claimed that half the male population, as well as quite a few females, was there. Despite the winter weather, the Indians danced and enacted scenes of hunting and warfare for three hours wearing nothing but red flannel breechclouts. "They were painted horribly, and exhibited the operation of tomahawking in fine style," reported one observer. Another thought the exhibition one which "no person of liberal and philosophical curiosity would willingly have missed seeing, and which no one who viewed it ... would choose to witness again."[15]

Although the visiting Indians were generally on their best behavior while in the capital, the sixteen members of the Winnebago delegation of 1828 appear to have been rather boisterous. Washington socialite Margaret Bayard Smith, for one, did not appreciate their antics, particularly when several of the "ferocious Winnebagos," as she called them, took to grabbing and kissing passing ladies "till decent young women are afraid to walk out." As a self-appointed representative of the women of Washington, she stormed into the secretary of war's office and demanded that something be done about the Indians. Her mission was evidently successful, but, as she later reported, "you have no idea, what a general dread they inspired."[16]

The ladies of Washington were not the only ones happy to see the Winnebagos leave. Joshua Tennison also heaved a sigh of relief as the last one climbed aboard the stages waiting to take the delegation home. That very afternoon he sent a bill to McKenney for $250 to repair "damage to the house, bedding, carpeting, tables, &c."[17]

The attitude of Indians who came to Washington to negotiate a treaty was usually far less festive. This was certainly true of the Creek delegation which confronted President Adams in November 1825. Led by Opothle Yoholo, the distraught Creeks hoped the president would overthrow the dishonorable treaty of Indian Springs ratified earlier in the year. Two citizens of Georgia, serving as commissioners for the United States, negotiated the treaty supposedly with the entire Creek Nation, but the signatory chiefs actually represented only a small portion of the tribe. By the terms of the treaty the Creeks ceded all their lands in Georgia and agreed to move west of the Mississippi. The Senate quickly ratified the treaty by a vote of 38 to 4, and President Adams just as quickly signed it into law, even though he suspected the circumstances surrounding the treaty had not been thoroughly investigated. By the time the delegation representing the dispossessed Creeks arrived to protest, all Washington knew the treaty was a scandal.[18]

Garbed in a combination of white man's clothes and Indian dress, the Creeks and their interpreters arrived at the White House. Opothle Yoholo's appearance, like that of his eleven companions, was remarkable for its dark and settled gloom, Adams thought. The president shook hands with them all. "I am glad to see you. We should all meet in friendship."

"We are glad to be here," responded Opothle Yoholo. "Things have happened which frightened us. We hope now all will be well again."

"That is my desire also," Adams replied reassuringly. "I also have heard things that displeased me much, but I am sure the Secretary of War will be able to arrange matters to the satisfaction of all."

Adams authorized Barbour to renegotiate the controversial

treaty, but with the original terms: a complete cession of the Creek lands in Georgia. This Opothle Yoholo could not accept. The tribe would only consider ceding its holdings east of the Chattahoochee, about two-thirds of the land in question. As the weeks dragged into months, Barbour tried to pressure the delegation into accepting the government's terms; he hammered so hard for a complete cession that Opothle Yoholo, torn between the needs of his people and the American demands, tried to kill himself in his room at the Indian Queen Hotel. Learning of the attempted suicide, Adams directed Barbour to accept the Chattahoochee as a boundary.[19] This second treaty with the Creek Nation, signed in January 1826, left unresolved the question of how to remove the tribe from Georgia.

After meeting their Great Father, being showered with presents and attention, and then confronting the Great War Chief of the whites over the bargaining table, even the most sophisticated Indians came to terms eventually. Indeed, only the Choctaw delegation of 1824 left Washington confident that it had skinned the government. For McKenney the entire Choctaw episode was a personal and professional disappointment, but it illustrates well some problems of treaty negotiations conducted in the nation's capital.

The difficulties with the Choctaws dated from 1820 and the treaty of Doak's Stand. Pressured by southern planters, the government had persuaded the tribe—with threats of the loss of American friendship on one hand and nearly $5,000 in "donations" to Choctaw leaders on the other—to exchange a large section of ancestral land in southwestern Mississippi for a tract of wild country in Arkansas Territory. Elation in Washington over the successful negotiations was immediately tempered by the howl of protest from the five thousand white settlers who occupied much of the tribe's newly acquired land; they insisted the Choctaws move further west. The Choctaws then not only refused to accept another location, they refused to leave Mississippi.[20] After wrestling with the problem for three years, Secretary of War Calhoun became convinced the only solution lay in renegotiating the 1820 agreement. In 1823 he appointed two commissioners to meet the Choctaws at the agency in Mississippi. The Choctaws, however, cannily refused to talk with anyone except the "President and heads of Departments" and in August

1823 asked their agent William Ward to get permission for them to visit "the City Washington, and hold a talk with the President about the Land, beyond the Mississippi. In preference to make a Treaty with any Commissionours that may be sent." When Calhoun ignored the request, tribal leaders met in general council at the agency the following September and formally asked to visit Washington. Not only did the Choctaws agree to pay their own expenses, they added the assurance that "whatever Treaty or other Acts that may be done by us or any negotiation between the U States and this nation shall be considered as Obligatory on this nation." When four more months passed without response, Ward wrote Calhoun again. "I have heard nothing recently from you in relation to the Contemplated Treaty with the Choctaws. The Chiefs are extremely anxious to visit Washington and negotiate the Treaty." Moreover, Ward pointed out, "the expence attending their journey would be much less than a general assemblage of the whole nation." Calhoun finally agreed to hear the chiefs plead the case but warned Ward to observe "the strictest economy" in preparing for the trip east. Ward promptly reported that the delighted Choctaws planned to arrive in Washington by mid-June "so as to be at the Seat of Government at a time when the heds of Department were not crouded with business and Congress had adjourned."[21]

Although the Choctaws were willing to pay their own expenses, federal officials had no intention of allowing them to do so. Henry Conway, the Arkansas territorial delegate to Congress, explained to Calhoun, "I have thought that the views of the Government would probably be defeated unless a sufficient sum was retained to pay the expenses incidental to the Treaty," and he asked the secretary of war what he thought adequate. Ten thousand dollars, Calhoun replied. Four days later Congress passed a $10,000 appropriation "to defray the expenses of negotiating with the Choctaw Indians."[22]

At this point came the first in a series of frustrations. A week after the delegation's expected arrival, McKenney received word from Ward that the Choctaws had not yet left home. Deaths in the families of several of the delegates would prevent their departure until autumn. The most likely reason for the delay was disagreement over the composition of the delegation and the issues to be discussed in Washington. In addition to settling the boundary dispute in Arkansas, Ward warned, the Indians were anxious to press additional claims—a $6,000 annuity promised at Doak's Stand and payments to the warriors who had aided General Andrew Jackson in his Pensacola campaign of 1817. McKenney grudgingly accepted the explanation. "A good deal of inconvenience is experienced in delays of this sort," he replied. "It is now distinctly understood that the Delegation do come on in the fall, with full powers as stated, to act in the business of their Mission."[23]

When, on September 23, 1824, the ten-member delegation finally left Mississippi, it represented the finest talent the Choctaws could command, including Pushmataha, Puckshenubbe, and Mushulatubbee, the first elected chiefs of the three political districts through which the nation was democratically governed. Each of them was a proven administrator and a tested warrior. Perhaps the most articulate delegate was McKenney's protégé James L. McDonald, now an accredited lawyer practicing in Jackson, Mississippi. The Indians reached Washington the last week of October, and McKenney lodged them at Joshua Tennison's hotel on the south side of Pennsylvania Avenue between Twelfth and Thirteenth Streets, a short, refreshing walk from the War Department. The eighty-five-year-old Puckshenubbe had fallen to his death from a fog-shrouded precipice while stretching his legs at a rest stop, and some of the delegates had colds—"in common with many of us, in Washington"—McKenney reported; otherwise all were well.[24]

As expected, the negotiations were protracted and difficult. Calhoun opened discussions by asking the Choctaws to cede additional land in Mississippi as well as their holdings in Arkansas, promising in return an enlarged area west of Arkansas Territory that would be theirs permanently. The delegates refused to discuss Mississippi, and they would consider selling only that part of their Arkansas holdings most thickly populated with white settlers.[25]

"Do you want us to give up farming and become hunters?" Pushmataha asked. "Take us to the western boundary of Arkansas Territory, and you will take all our valuable land."

"Good chief," Calhoun replied, "you are contradicting yourself. When we were trying to sell you those lands in 1820 you insisted they were all rocks and hills, and that the waters were only fit to overflow the crops, put out fires, and float canoes. What is the meaning of this great change?"

"I can only say, good father, that I am imitating the white man. In 1820 we wanted to buy; now we are anxious to sell."[26]

After conferring with President Monroe, Calhoun accepted the Choctaw limitations, asking only that the delegates agree to sell a slightly larger portion of their Arkansas holdings. McDonald responded for the delegation. "In that spirit of accommodation and compromise which brought them to your city," the delegates "have determined to accede to the request of the Government," he informed the secretary of war. "The next consideration, and perhaps the most important one, is," McDonald asked, "what compensation are the Choctaws to receive?"[27]

That all depends, McKenney replied. How did the Choctaws wish to be paid—"in one payment, in limited annuities, or in annuities forever?" McKenney also wanted to know how the money would be spent. "For myself," he needlessly reminded them, "I should be much gratified to find the Choctaw Delegation so much alive to the interests of their Children, as to lay such a deep foundation for their future prosperity, as to make an appropriation of a permanent kind for their improvement in agriculture and knowledge. The act itself would be honorable to the Delegation, in the eyes of all reflecting and good men, in every part of the world." McDonald would not give McKenney a "decisive answer." First tell us what you are willing to pay, the young man responded, then the delegation "with the less hesitation" can tell you how it will be applied.[28] Three days were lost in this fruitless exchange.

On November 19, Calhoun sent the delegation the government's offer—$5,000 in cash and $6,000 annually for ten years, in other words, $65,000. The accompanying note from McKenney indicates who actually framed the offer, which ostensibly came from the secretary of war. "Mr. Calhoun approves of the inclosed proposition—But left the office before it was signed. It is sent to you now for your information, and to save time. You can send it up in the morning when it will receive his signature." The delegation found the proposal *entirely inadequate.* Unless the government made "a far more liberal offer," the negotiations would be terminated. The delegates, McDonald wrote, would frame their own terms of what they considered "just and liberal."[29]

The promised reply, signed by the entire delegation, must have jolted the secretary of war. It was lengthy, reasoned, and outrageous. The delegates reminded Calhoun that the proposed cession totaled five million valuable acres drained by the Arkansas and Red Rivers, which provided ready access to New Orleans. Even if only a third of the land were arable, at the minimum price for public lands the government would realize $2,000,000. "Is it not just and right we should receive, in annuities, a reasonable portion of that sum?" they asked. By "a reasonable portion" they meant $450,000, not including the Pensacola claims and the unpaid annuities from the treaty of Doak's Stand. That the bulk of the money would be used for educational purposes must have been of small comfort to McKenney and Calhoun.[30]

Again Calhoun conferred with President Monroe. The terms are "wholly inadmissible" he replied four days later. The government would not realize $2,000,000 even if the entire tract were sold. Unless the Choctaws were prepared to make a very great reduction in their demands, "it would be useless to attempt to conclude a treaty," Calhoun declared. Again McKenney sent with Calhoun's official letter a note of his own addressed to McDonald. "You know me well, and my feelings towards your people, I am their friend," he wrote. The delegates must realize the price they asked was simply beyond anything ever heard of before. Reconsider the government's original offer, McKenney pleaded. The money would be incalculably more valuable to them than the land would ever be, even if they held it forever. "You are to consider this not as an official, but private note," he cautioned.[31]

The delegates deliberated for three days. "Our determination is made: we cannot depart essentially from our original position," they answered. Perhaps they did ask too high a price, but they also had a great responsibility to their people, who expected an advantageous treaty or none at all. "The negotiation, therefore, comes to a close, and we shall prepare to return to our homes." Before leaving, however, they would like to settle claims unrelated to the Arkansas business; they listed them in a letter to Calhoun the following day.[32]

The hard line adopted by the delegation perplexed the federal officials, who then adopted a strategy of patient waiting. A week went by before McKenney wrote the delegates, excusing the delay on the grounds that the president was too busy to consider their grievances. The Indians heard nothing more until the end of December, a month later. There are two versions of Calhoun's letter to the delegation. One, dated December 28, remains in the Indian office letterbook but evidently was not sent. Strongly worded, it declares that the two parties were so far apart that the president "deems it unnecessary further to continue the negotiation." The second version, dated three days later and printed in the *American State Papers*, states that the president "is desirous, both on your account and that of the United States, to conclude a treaty of cession" and trusts the delegation will reconsider its position "and agree on one more reasonable."[33]

The Choctaws responded to the second version. Although they had "believed the negotiation terminated," they remained anxious to make an amicable adjustment of the difficulties between the tribe and the United States. Rather than waste time in a further exchange of notes, they asked Calhoun to make an offer which he considered *"more reasonable."* "Tell us, at once, the highest price you can give—the utmost extent to which you can go; and we can immediately determine whether to accept or reject your offer." The secretary of war promptly replied: $90,000, payable over ten years. Still too low, the delegation declared after a week's deliberation. The tribe would, however, accept a package deal for cash, annuities, and claims settlements totaling $216,000. After a hasty conference with President Monroe, Calhoun agreed to the Choctaw terms the following day, and the treaty was signed in his office on January 22, 1825, almost three months after the delegation's arrival in the city.[34]

If settling the boundary dispute cost more than anticipated, so did the delegation's living expenses which amounted to $7,463. Only about $2,000 was room and board; the rest went for clothing, $1,771; liquor, $2,149; transportation, $960; oysters and brandy, $394.75; and such incidentals as bootblacking, $75; barbering, $58; and laundry, $25. McKenney was outraged by the bill, particularly at the incredible sum spent for liquor. He insisted that the delegation pay half the bar and refectory bill, or $1,469, leaving the government share at $6,000, not including the considerable sum spent on medical care for the delegates.[35]

Few Indian delegations returned to their homes without some illness or injury; the delegates, many of whom were quite elderly, literally risked life and limb making the trips. One of the stagecoaches carrying the Creek delegation to Washington overturned, injuring most of the passengers. The Choctaws' experience was particularly tragic. Puckshenubbe's death had been followed by that of Pushmataha, who died of the croup midway through the negotiations. Too much liquor, agent Ward charged; more likely, the sixty-year-old warrior could not shake a persistent cold in the damp, chill Washington weather. He collapsed on the street early on the morning of December 23; two physicians tended Pushmataha until he died on Christmas Eve. Certain of his approaching death, the old chief called for his weapons and trophies of war and asked that "the big guns be fired over me."[36]

Pushmataha's request for a military funeral was honored the day after Christmas by the Marine Corps under the direction of the secretary of the navy and two companies of the District of Columbia militia. Two thousand congressmen, government officials, and citizens followed the cortege to Congressional Cemetery beside the Anacostia River. The minute guns that thundered on Capitol Hill were echoed by three crisp musket volleys at the graveside as America paid tribute to a fallen warrior. Far different was this service from the meager rites given Puckshenubbe, whose Kentucky funeral cost the government but $11.87—for music, shrouding, and coffin.[37]

McKenney may have wished for similar economy. The Indian office laid Pushmataha to rest in "Drilling Panteloons and 1 Ruffle Shirt" and in a mahogany coffin with a liner and case. For the funeral McKenney rented thirteen hacks, including one for the Reverend William Hawley, rector of St. John's Church, who also received $10 for conducting the service. Altogether the funeral cost $147.32. It could easily have been more, but McKenney did his best to keep expenses down. On Christmas Day James Dougherty, the physician, sent McKenney his bill for $20 for "attending to Genl Push-a-ma-ta-ha preparing and administering four injections to him while on his Death Bed—together with all other necessary attentions until he was buried." McKenney, who by this point had lost the Christmas spirit, thought the charge too much and allowed the doctor only $10.[38]

McKenney had anticipated the needs of the Choctaws by arranging for the surgeon general's office to provide medical attention to the delegates. Army surgeon John Brereton was specially charged with their care, and McKenney cautioned the Choctaws to seek his aid "and not ... any citizen physician." Evidently the delegation considered it too much trouble to visit the War Department. When Robert Cole broke out with ulcers, his comrades promptly called James Wallace, another private physician. Wallace visited Cole daily at Tennison's hotel to dress the chief's open sores, attending the aches and ills of the other delegates at the same time. Wallace charged the Indian office $2 for each visit. Despite sixty days of treatment, Cole was still unable to travel when the delegation left Washington on February 22. Unhappy at the prospect of remaining behind alone, he asked McDonald and Daniel McCurtain, another delegate, to stay until he was well enough to go home. As the other delegates prepared to board the stagecoach, they spied Doctor Wallace, and in a dramatic scene witnessed by curious spectators the Choctaws pleaded with the physician to continue treating Cole. Thus innocently began for McKenney an episode that threatened to eclipse both financially and emotionally the expenses and problems caused by the entire delegation, for it became quickly evident that Cole, McCurtain, and McDonald had no intention of leaving for Mississippi as long as money remained in the federal treasury. As the days passed into weeks and the weeks into months, McKenney's patience finally wore thin. "Do not delay this matter any longer," he snapped at McDonald on June 16. "Cole is now well enough, and wishes to be off, any further delay is an expense which it is desireable to avoid." He closed the curt note with "I wish Mr. Tennison's bill also."[39]

The innkeeper's bill, delivered the following day, showed the other delegates had been models of sobriety compared to the boon companions who remained behind. Tennison's bill for the three was $1,502.23, including $935 for liquor. McKenney was enraged. "I cannot recommend it for payment," he promptly wrote Tennison. How could the trio average $8.40 a day for liquor, he wanted to know, particularly since McDonald and McCurtain must have done most of the drinking, Cole "having been during the whole time, in the hands of the Doctor." He had warned Tennison about allowing extravagance when he received the bill for the entire delegation. McKenney did concede one point: "Enormous as the bar bill is, I am quite sure that you have charged no more than you actually furnished."[40]

McKenney sent a similar letter to the chiefs of the Choctaw Nation. The government would pay the trio's bill for room and board, McKenney explained, but would allow them only $3 a day for liquor. The tribe would have to make up the difference from its annuity. The Indian office would pay $1,340.25, the tribe $622.75. "Robert Cole has not been extravagant—He could not be so," McKenney lectured. "He was too sick. But the others have been. A liberal allowance has been made. Enough for the President of the United States, to each of them—for we wished them to live like Gentlemen. But . . . if men will be so extravagant, and act so injuriously to themselves, they must pay for it themselves."[41] No doubt a righteously indignant McKenney escorted the wayward trio to their stage and personally witnessed their departure.

Unhappily for McKenney, the physician's bill remained to be settled. Since the Choctaws had made a public spectacle of their desire for Wallace's services, McKenney had been compelled to allow it. As the delegates had shrewdly pointed out, "it is Indispensable that a patient should have confidence in his physician; and Doctr Wallace has the confidence of Col. Cole & of the Delegation." Despite the confidence in his physician, Cole had not improved, and on March 17 he changed doctors. Still the delegates were reluctant to call the surgeon general; they chose instead Nathanial P. Causin, yet another private physician, who attended Cole for thirteen weeks. When Cole finally left Washington, Causin presented McKenney a bill for $300. McKenney refused to pay more than the $2 a day he had paid Wallace, which would have entitled Causin to $182. The doctor strongly objected. The chief "never took a dose of medicine but from myself or [a] young Gentleman in my office," Causin replied, "& during the whole of that time, the most abominable ulcers, almost that were ever seen, were cleansed & dressed twice a day with my own hands." He should have added another charge of $1 or $2 daily for "nurse & dresser," he continued. The Indians were not to have private physicians,

McKenney responded weakly, but—"a *gratification* of these un-lettered people, being the object of the Department"—he had complied with their "*notions*." When Cole urged payment of Causin's bill, McKenney withdrew his objections and passed the bill to the auditor's office for payment, no doubt grateful that he could finally bring to a close the Choctaws' expense account.[42]

The boundary dispute had been settled but at an extremely high price. The government paid roughly $8,000 for expenses; the tribe absorbed another $2,000. The cost to the Choctaws was even greater, for two of the tribe's most important leaders were dead.

The difficulties experienced in concluding the Creek and Choctaw treaties were atypical. Normally, especially when nego-tiations were conducted in the Indian country, the bargaining was far less sophisticated and was completed in relatively short order. Treaty commissioners seldom had to do more than ex-plain the needs of the federal government and the payments that would be made; the assembled Indians, interested more in the presents and food than in deliberations, would usually agree to the terms with little or no comment. Certainly this was Mc-Kenney's experience when he served as a treaty commissioner to the Chippewas and Menominees.

8

Tour
of the Lakes

McKENNEY TWICE ENJOYED the privilege of serving as a treaty commissioner, making extensive tours of the Indian country with Governor Lewis Cass on both occasions. In the summer of 1826 they traveled to Fond du Lac at the western end of Lake Superior, where they negotiated a treaty with the Chippewas. The following year they met with the Menominees and Winnebagos at Butte des Morts near Green Bay. After concluding his business at Butte des Morts, McKenney, now alone, returned to Washington by way of the southern tribes, visiting the Choctaw, Chickasaw, and Creek Indians to persuade them to remove west of the Mississippi. (see Chapter 11)

Normally the most experienced and capable men would be chosen to negotiate treaties in the field. The two most competent and productive commissioners in the early nineteenth century were William Clark and Lewis Cass. During his federal career Clark negotiated thirty-seven ratified Indian treaties; Cass negotiated twenty.[1] Experienced men were chosen because, except for initial instructions, the commissioners were on their own. To their discretion were left all details of the negotiations, including the time, place, and local arrangements, a great respon-

sibility because the conferences were often elaborate and expensive affairs that required months of preparation and presented
problems of logistics similar to those experienced in moving
armies.

Sufficient food for the assembled Indians was of paramount
importance. "An Indian will not consider himself treated well
with a [daily] ration short of a pound and a half of beef, and
a pound and a half of Flour," McKenney explained. Hence, a
conference to be attended by some five thousand Indians for
thirty days required at least 225,000 pounds of each.[2] Leftovers
were distributed to the Indians. The commissioners requisitioned
supplies from military stores when possible or else purchased
them from private contractors.

Liquor was another key item. Although instructions to the
commissioners usually warned against the use of alcohol during
the negotiations, this regulation seems to have been largely
ignored. "In almost every important negotiation between the
Government & Indians," Clark claimed, "difficulties (seemingly
insurmountable) have occurred at the commencement, and have
not been fairly obviated until their cause was traced to whisky,
secretly administered to some of the principal men previous to
& pending the negotiation, by interested individuals." When
McKenney questioned an unexplained item in one expense account Cass submitted, the governor admitted the charge was
for alcohol. "You know very well," he wrote in a letter marked
"private," that "at all these treaties wine must be allowed."
To detail all the use of liquor in an account "would not only
be useless, but it would produce, and in fact has produced injurious effects." McKenney learned quickly. When he and Cass
served as co-commissioners for treaty negotiations conducted
near Green Bay in the summer of 1827, their supplies included
116 barrels of whiskey.[3]

McKenney's first appointment as a treaty commissioner was
no happy accident but the result of months of careful planning,
for the trip appears to have been part of McKenney's master
plan to establish a legitimate Bureau of Indian Affairs with himself as superintendent, for he remained, technically, only a clerk
in the War Department. In August 1825 Cass and Clark had
negotiated with representatives of the Sioux, Chippewa, and other
northwestern Indian tribes the important treaty of Prairie du

Chien which settled longstanding territorial disputes.[4] One clause in the treaty stipulated that the Chippewas would assemble in full numbers the next summer "upon some part of Lake Superior" to affirm the treaty and acknowledge the authority and jurisdiction of the United States; Cass would serve as one of the commissioners since the Chippewas were under his jurisdiction.

Shortly after Cass returned to Detroit he received a personal letter from McKenney praising "that *work of mercy* at P. D Chien" and urging him to hurry to Washington. "I want to see you & talk a great deal to you about matters & things in general, & one in particular." The superintendent needed the governor's "help in *a plan* of organization" for the proposed bureau. "I wish it to be so fitted & Join'd together as that when the building is up the eye may love to look upon it; & when its machinery works, it may be all spirit, & life, & harmony."[5] Cass, who needed little persuading, arrived in Washington shortly after Christmas and stayed a month.

Sometime during the governor's holiday, McKenney seized upon the idea of accompanying him to Lake Superior the following summer. By writing a book about his experiences, McKenney hoped to publicize the need for an Indian department equivalent to other federal agencies. Not only might a treatise on Indians be just the catalyst needed to prod Congress into establishing a Bureau of Indian Affairs, it might also enhance the author's reputation and ensure his appointment. As McKenney later confided to Cass, the book "will be a *right clever thing*, I mean in the small way."[6]

McKenney also wanted the trip for a much needed vacation. Organizing the Indian office had been so strenuous that his health had failed. "Such were my labors, so constant and oppressive, and so weighty the responsibilities which devolved on me," he claimed, "as to have very nearly cost me my life." Indeed, his health was so precarious at the beginning of the journey that the other members of the party expected him to die along the way. "It was not until some time after the expedition had entered that lake," he later discovered, "that the officers in command of the military escort gave over their more than half-made preparations to give me a magnificent burial on its shore. Of this kindness, however, I knew nothing at the time, but was often reminded of it after my health was restored."[7]

Besides rest, McKenney desperately needed the extra pay he would receive as a treaty commissioner—$8 for each day spent conferring with the Indians and $8 for every twenty miles traveled. His tendency to live beyond his means kept him in continual financial trouble, and he was now in danger of losing his beloved Weston. Aware that he could no longer maintain the expensive residence on his meager salary of $1,600, he offered the estate for rent in the spring of 1826. The $2,080 he received for the trip to Lake Superior and the $4,972 he realized from his tour the following year only forestalled the inevitable. The trustees of the Bank of Columbia foreclosed McKenney's mortgage and sold Weston at public auction on October 22, 1828.[8]

McKenney also had a political motive for making the trip. Active campaigning for the 1828 presidential election had already begun, and as a loyal member of the John Quincy Adams administration he feared Andrew Jackson's success. Since McKenney saw no harm in mixing politics with business, he planned to distribute anti-Jackson campaign literature along the way to Michigan. As he confidentially informed Cass, "I shall have some materials, I hope, that the public would not refuse to *con*, & especially as I mean not to frighten it with the *bulk*, but only invite it by the nature of the subjects, & the manner of managing them. I can say so to you."[9]

McKenney's plans were almost thwarted in early February 1826 when Congressman James Strong of New York, with the support of eight other legislators and Secretary of State Henry Clay, recommended Andrew G. Whitney of Detroit to negotiate the Chippewa treaty as co-commissioner with Cass. As soon as McKenney learned of the nomination, he scribbled a private letter to the Michigan governor asking for help in blocking Whitney's appointment. Write "direct & strong" letters to Clay and Secretary of War James Barbour asking for my appointment, McKenney urged. At the same time, Congressman Richard M. Johnson of Kentucky would submit McKenney's name as a counter-recommendation. "You see how I stand—I am *anxious* to go," he confessed. "I have many reasons for it —& I look to you. I may then *possibly* see you in the land of the Lakes."[10]

Cass wrote as McKenney directed. Rather than antagonize any congressmen, however, he simply asked that both McKenney

William Clark,
by George Catlin, 1832.
*Courtesy National
Portrait Gallery,
Smithsonian Institution.*

Lewis Cass.
A year after McKenney's
departure from the Office of
Indian Affairs, Cass became
secretary of war. He was later a
senator from Michigan, and in
1848 was the Democratic
candidate for president.
Courtesy National Archives.

Henry R. Schoolcraft.
*Courtesy National Portrait Gallery,
Smithsonian Institution.*

Big Martin
(also called The Good Martin),
by Charles Bird King
from a watercolor sketch
by James Otto Lewis, 1826.
Big Martin is shown with
the British officer's coat
he was wearing during
the treaty negotiations
at Fond du Lac.
*Courtesy
Gulf States Paper Corp.,
Tuscaloosa, Ala.*

and Whitney be named to join him in negotiating the treaty.
"It has been a common practise to appoint three Commissioners,
where the object to be attained is important, and the place of
operations remote," he reminded the secretary of war. "I should
be highly gratified, if this arrangement could be made."[11]

The strategy worked; President Adams passed over Whitney
and chose McKenney for the coveted assignment. "I am quite
skipping on the subject," McKenney excitedly wrote Cass. "You
do not rejoice at the result ... more than I do," the governor
responded. "It will be the most interesting summer, you have
passed. We shall see a thousand interesting objects, and have a
thousand interesting conversations. I will have every thing in
readiness, and if you arrive here by the first of June, it will be
in season."[12]

Although Congress had not yet appropriated the estimated
$27,000 needed to finance the treaty, preparations were well
under way by March. The site selected was Fond du Lac, an
American Fur Company outpost on the St. Louis River, twenty-
four miles from its mouth at the western end of Lake Superior.
Sault Ste. Marie, the nearest American settlement, was to be
the staging area. The garrison at Fort Brady at the Sault would
furnish the military escort, while responsibility for organizing
the expedition went to Henry R. Schoolcraft, the Indian agent
at Sault Ste. Marie. Unlike Cass and McKenney, Schoolcraft
found scant comfort in the assignment. "My hands are already
full," he grumbled in his diary. "Boats, canoes, supplies, transportation for all who are to go, and a thousand minor questions,
call for attention. A treaty at Fond du Lac, 500 miles distant,
and the throwing of a commissariat department through the lake
is no light task."[13]

Congressional tardiness in appropriating funds for the council was an unforeseen and troublesome development. Not until
May 20, two days before Congress recessed for the summer, did
the bill pass. A relieved McKenney relayed the welcome news
to Cass and urged him to proceed "as speedily as possible" with
the arrangements. McKenney need not have worried. The confident governor, wise in the ways of the bureaucracy, had already
authorized Schoolcraft to send messengers to various Chippewa
bands, inviting them to assemble at Fond du Lac by August
1826. "In your messages," Cass directed, "you will state to

them, the subject of the Council is important to them & to the United States, and that it is the wish of their great Father they should generally attend." At the same time he ordered the Fort Brady commissary officer to furnish 250 barrels of flour, 150 of pork, and "some corn" to feed the Indians, leaving to Schoolcraft the problem of getting the provisions to Fond du Lac.[14]

While Schoolcraft wrestled with his logistics, Cass and McKenney received their commissions from Secretary of War Barbour. All details attending the treaty were left to their discretion. The president, however, wished the expedition, in addition to securing Chippewa agreement to the treaty of Prairie du Chien, to "impress the Indians in that remote region, with some proper conception of our power" and "to ensure for trial and punishment" the recapture of the Chippewa warriors who had killed and scalped four Americans near Lake Pepin in 1824. Under threat of reprisals, the tribe had earlier surrendered five of the guilty men who were then sent to Michimilimackinac to await trial. Much to the government's embarrassment, the imprisoned Chippewas carved their way out of the log jail and made good their escape; the tribe, having surrendered them once, refused to do so a second time. Obviously, if the United States expected to control the northwestern Indians, the murderers had to be apprehended again. "This," Barbour stressed, "is considered to be an important object. As nothing so much encourages Savages to the perpetration of crimes, as to feel that they can commit them with impunity. A rigid infliction of justly incurred penalties is esteemed to be friendly in its effects upon the peace and security of our border population, whilst upon the other hand, mercy and kindness are due to the unfortunate Indians in all our intercourse with them."[15]

Charged with his commission and mindful of Cass' warning to "fly, or we shall be late," McKenney, accompanied by his black servant Ben Hanson, left Washington on June 1. After resting in Utica, where he had been "fairly overcome" by loss of sleep "and the other harrassing influences of quick & constant travelling," he reached Detroit sixteen days later.[16]

A week before leaving Washington, McKenney had written Cass suggesting they return from Lake Superior by way of Green Bay, meet with the Menominee Indians, and settle a boundary line left unresolved by the treaty of Prairie du Chien. "If such

a thing *be possible* both Treaties should be held this year,"
McKenney explained. "The Treaty of Prairie du Chien stipulates
for both and the Commissioners are instructed accordingly, but
if it be *impossible* it can be so reported." Cass lost little time in
convincing the novice commissioner it would be unwise to attempt both treaties on one trip. By the time they reached Green
Bay from Fond du Lac it would be much too late in the season
for the Indians to assemble and still have time for their fall hunt.
Green Bay should be postponed until the following summer.[17]

Relaying this information to the secretary of war, McKenney
for the first time revealed his intention to write a book about
his trip. "I may," he hinted to Barbour, "perhaps, find leisure
during this one thousand miles of Lake voyaging which is before
me, to trouble you with sketches of the Country thro' which I
have pass'd & I may pass. New York, the Land of Lakes—of
Canals, & of Towns—is in itself a world, fertile in the richness
of its resources, the fertility of its soils, and in the magnificence
& majesty of her scenery."[18] This is precisely the outline of
Sketches of a Tour to the Lakes which McKenney published a
few months after his return.

McKenney and Cass, a retinue of secretaries, commissary
clerks, and some thirty voyageurs left Detroit on June 23 for
Sault Ste. Marie. They arrived on the Fourth of July. Waiting
there were Schoolcraft and a company of the Second Infantry
from Fort Brady, including four musicians and army surgeon
Zina Pitcher. Schoolcraft, who finally saw the end of his time-
consuming and tedious chores, welcomed the commissioners with
open arms. "Jason could not have been more busy in preparing
for his famous expedition to Argos," he wrote in his diary.[19]

Six days later the party, now more than one hundred strong,
embarked on the final leg of the journey. The whole expedition
must have presented an imposing spectacle as it swept the five
hundred miles to Fond du Lac. The soldiers, powering three
twelve-oared barges, formed the advance; following in train were
four more barges laden with presents, provisions, and "subsistence supplies of the commissioners' table." Although Cass
chose to ride in one of the barges, McKenney, "struck with the
'coach-and-six' sort of style of this kind of conveyance," invited
himself aboard Schoolcraft's large, canopy-covered canoe manned
by ten voyageurs and equipped "with every appendage to render

the trip convenient and agreeable." Since Schoolcraft and McKenney did not feel bound to the relatively slow pace of the barges, they amused themselves by darting about in their canoe, lagging behind or dashing ahead, examining the bays and inlets of the Lake Superior shoreline.[20]

The expedition reached the treaty grounds at 2 P.M. on July 28, 1826, eighteen days out of Sault Ste. Marie. Fond du Lac consisted of six or seven log cabins clustered on the north bank of the St. Louis River; although Chippewa lodges dotted both sides of the river, most of the Indians were camped on a small island about seventy-five yards offshore directly opposite the post. At the suggestion of Governor Cass, the boats approached in formation "with flags flying, and martial music." In the van —"with characteristic presumption," thought Doctor Pitcher— were Schoolcraft and McKenney in their canopied canoe. Fifty yards behind trailed the governor's barge flanked by a score of Indian canoes. The remaining barges stretched back for a quarter of a mile. "The sight was truly interesting," McKenney recalled. The Indians, "all naked, painted, and silent, gliding over the surface in their bark canoes," were speechless as "for the first time, their ears, like their native hills and rivers, were greeted with 'Hail Columbia.' " As the commissioners stepped ashore, the musicians switched to a spirited rendition of "Yankee Doodle," while the assembled Indians saluted them with a thunderous musket volley.[21]

While the soldiers pitched their tents in the clearing between the post and the river, news-starved American Fur Company employees ushered the commissioners to their rooms in one of the cabins. McKenney found his accommodations comfortable but crowded; his servant Ben Hanson refused quarters in a tent lest a Chippewa warrior lift his scalp as he slept. The commissioners were hardly settled when chiefs of the various Chippewa bands began paying their respects. In a series of interviews that consumed the rest of the afternoon, Cass and McKenney shook hands with the visitors, announced that they had been sent by the Great Father to meet them in council, and gave each chief a twist of tobacco. The Indians invariably ended the brief ceremonies by solemnly drawing their pipes, striking fire into the bowls, and smothering the commissioners in smoke. As McKenney good-humoredly wrote Barbour, "the Governor and I can neither of us make out so well in a fog of this sort, as neither of us use tobacco in any way."[22]

The Indians may have frightened Hanson, but they fascinated McKenney. Since the negotiations were almost a week away, the superintendent had ample time to pester the Chippewas with questions about their origin, their history, their religious beliefs. He scribbled notes about their dress, their ceremonies, their folklore. He ate their food, he visited their lodges, he studied them as thoroughly as any ethnologist of a later generation would have done. Of a Chippewa burial site, he wrote: "A pole is stuck in the ground, about ten feet long. From the top of this pole is suspended the ornaments of the deceased. From this, I see hanging a strand of beads—some strips of white fur, several trinkets—six bits of tobacco, that looked like *quids*, and a little frame of a circular form with net work, in the centre of which ... is fastened *a scalp*, about three inches in diameter, the hair of which is a dark brown colour, and six inches long." McKenney's disappointment in not finding a *"man-woman"* in the encampment was more than offset by discovering a woman who had been scalped during a Sioux raid on her village. He described her scars in clinical detail: "One of the knives," he wrote, "had passed under her chin, and across her throat, cutting a deep gash, and driving in pieces of wampum, a strand of which she had about her neck at the time, and pieces of which I felt through the skin, that were then buried there, and are there now. The knife passed ... between the occiput and the crown, and there, and on opposite sides, the skin of the head is bare in an irregular kind of circle of about two inches in diameter."[23]

McKenney also collected drawings and a number of artifacts for the museum he kept in his office. The drawings were by James Otto Lewis, a young Detroit artist Cass hired—at McKenney's insistence—to portray the leading Chippewa chiefs and warriors. Lewis drew not only Indians but also graves, lodges, and whatever else struck the superintendent's fancy. Copies of these drawings later illustrated the book McKenney published about his trip. The artifacts he wrested from their Indian owners included a Chippewa woman's complete ensemble and an eagle feather "appendage" that ornamented a twelve-foot pole carried by a band of Sandy Lake Chippewas. McKenney justified his ethnological acquisitions on the grounds that the Chippewas would soon lose "their character, and their costume, if not their being."[24]

Some of McKenney's ideas and racial attitudes were remarkably progressive, and he tried to be objective—"I must reserve what I have to say of these hapless people, until I shall have looked well around me." But his experiences with the Chippewas left him disdainful of the Indian way of life. The concept of a noble savage he dismissed as a fable. "Tell me not of the happiness of the Indians—of their freedom from restraint —of their independence," he scoffed. To the patronizing and self-satisfied McKenney, what he saw at Fond du Lac easily demonstrated "the superior excellence of civilized, and polished and christian society, over that of the savage." Moreover, he seemed to delight in tearing apart the fabric of Chippewa culture, exposing as frauds its secrets and superstitions. Of the tribe's medical knowledge, he remarked: "We have all heard a great deal about the skill of Indian doctors. No doubt some of them are acquainted with the virtues of many plants, and know how to cure flesh wounds." But taken "as a body," they were as "utterly ignorant" of common illnesses and their treatment as they were "of our *Materia Medica*, or of the Harveynian system of the circulation of the blood." After witnessing a Chippewa conjurer communicate with the spirit world, McKenney wrote, "it is all a sham—Indians, although they pretend to divination, and to eat fire, are no more expert in these performances than other people. It is out of such flimsy materials as I have collected at this ceremony, that travellers sometimes manufacture facts." The superintendent's most outrageous observation followed the return of a lost pencil: "I mention this to show that Indians are sometimes honest."[25]

McKenney did not indulge his ethnological interests to the neglect of his official responsibilities. The commissioners were to impress the northwestern Indians with American power and to gain their acceptance of American sovereignty. Therefore, at their direction, Captain Elijah Boardman each morning drilled and paraded his company; the soldiers then stood inspection by Cass and by McKenney, who wore his District of Columbia militia uniform for the reviews. "The appearance of the officers and men was certainly unexpectedly fine," McKenney remarked the day after their arrival. Although weapons and accouterments had suffered on the long trip to Fond du Lac, "they appeared this morning, nevertheless, in the most perfect order. The equipment was complete, and their guns shone like silver." As anticipated, the martial displays drew large and attentive Indian audiences, who expressed both "surprize and admiration" at the soldiers' skill with their guns. "I have no doubt," McKenney reported, "but this exhibition of the military among them will prove a safeguard to many a trader and traveller."[26]

The commissioners also confirmed American sovereignty over the Chippewas by collecting British medals and flags. Whenever Cass or McKenney saw an Indian with a British medal, he would ask the owner to exchange it for an American medal. Normally, the Indian would be so startled, he would surrender it without comment. The most significant exchange of this sort occurred in the midst of the treaty negotiations, when a Chippewa warrior named Big Martin addressed the commissioners while wearing a British medal. At the conclusion of his remarks, Big Martin offered his pipe. Cass, who had discussed with McKenney the wisdom of making an issue of the medal before the assembled Indians, refused to smoke it. Was the British medal a symbol of authority or only a decoration? "If we thought you displayed it as a mark of authority, we would take it from your breast, throw it in the dust, and trample it under our feet," Cass declared. The warrior immediately removed the medal and laid it before the commissioners, saying it held no value for him. The commissioners then smoked his pipe and gave him an American medal. The next day Big Martin returned to the council with a British flag, which he also exchanged. "This may seem fastidious," McKenney explained, but "when you know that one of the chief difficulties with which the government has to contend in this quarter, is that which relates to the exercise of British influence over these people . . . you will see that our exception to a badge of this sort is all proper. It is intended, and especially in council, where so many witness it, as a protest against their taking any other side, whilst they profess to look to us for protection."[27]

After waiting an extra day for stragglers to arrive, the commissioners finally opened the council at noon on August 2. The prearranged signal, three musket volleys, was fired by a detail of Captain Boardman's Second Infantry. About 350 Indians gathered under the 18′ x 60′ bower of leaves and branches the soldiers had erected in front of the Fond du Lac trading post. The only female there was an elderly woman representing her blind and feeble husband; his peace medal worn proudly around her neck justified to all her presence at the conference. Too poor to present the commissioners the traditional gift of wampum, she offered them some porcupine quills and strands of grass carefully wrapped in a piece of bark.[28]

McKenney had eagerly anticipated this moment. Sitting with Cass behind a small table under the awning, he studied intently the bronzed and painted warriors gathered on the grass in a semicircle before him. For once he was speechless. "My service in the Indian department, and the experience I have acquired there, served to satisfy me that it is not every body who knows enough of the Indian character to conduct councils with them to a successful and harmonious conclusion," he admitted to Secretary of War Barbour in a letter written the following day. "I came here, expecting, myself, to learn much; and I felt that I was with no ordinary instructor. Few men have so intimate knowledge of the Indian character as Governor Cass. . . . I wrote him before I left home, that I should attend as a pupil—and, therefore, would expect him to conduct the whole proceedings. I do not, therefore, expect to open my lips on this occasion." Presumably Barbour, who knew McKenney well, discounted the last remark. The superintendent remained silent during the initial session, but thereafter his speeches surpassed the governor's in length and number.[29]

The council began with the smoking of the peace pipes offered by the Chippewa chiefs. After this mandatory ceremony, Cass explained the purpose of the conference in a lengthy speech. He spoke slowly and distinctly, pausing between sentences as an interpreter translated his words. At Prairie du Chien the Sioux and Chippewas had agreed to bury the tomahawk and honor a boundary line between their nations. Since the treaty site had been so far away, many of the Chippewa bands were not present at the council. Thus, Cass said, the Great Father had sent the commissioners to Fond du Lac "to state to all your people in the middle of your own country, what was transacted at the Prairie, and to express his wish, that it may be faithfully adhered to, on your part." The Great Father had other matters for them to discuss as well, continued the governor. A boundary line had to be drawn between the Chippewas and their neighbors to the east, the Menominees. Also, the Chippewas included many tribesmen who were part white, descendants of French fur traders. The Great Father wanted the Chippewas to select a place where these people of mixed-blood could settle and cultivate the land. "Give each of them a small piece," Cass directed; "they would be able then to support themselves comfortably and to assist you." The Great Father also wanted the right to search the Chippewa country for copper rock which could then be made into kettles and other useful things. In return, since the tribe was so poor, he would be willing to give them cloth each year; he would also establish a school for Chippewa children at Sault Ste. Marie. "You can think of these things and give us an answer as soon as you are ready. The Council will be opened tomorrow, and three guns will be fired, when we shall assemble." The business of the Chippewa murderers Cass left for another time.[30]

The following day, the commissioners listened patiently to a succession of responding Indian orators, including the old woman. Shingauba Wassin, a leading chief, strongly supported the governor. "Our Fathers have come here to embrace their children. Listen to what they say. It will be good for you. If you have any Copper on your lands, I advise you to sell it. It is of no advantage to us. They can convert it into articles for our use." Yellow Thunder affirmed his loyalty to the United States. Pointing to Cass, he declared: "This medal was placed on my breast by you, when you came to my village. I was then told, that such as it should attach to me would be remembered. This one, was not bought. I have worn it long. I have guarded it as my heart. I have not dishonored it." Most of the speakers pleaded for generosity—"Give us a little milk Fathers that we may wet our lips." When the fifteenth, and last, warrior had finished speaking, McKenney and Cass announced they would draft a treaty embracing the subjects mentioned at the first meeting.[31]

Two days later, at 11 o'clock on the morning of August 5, the commissioners called the chiefs and warriors to the council grounds and Cass read the treaty section by section. By signing this important document as the Great Father wished, the Chippewas recognized the authority and jurisdiction of the United States; they agreed to send a deputation to Green Bay the following summer to fix the boundary between them and their Menominee and Winnebago neighbors; they granted mineral rights to the federal government; and they agreed to provide each mixed-blood with 640 acres of land. In return, the Great Father's children would receive an annual annuity of $2,000 in goods or specie; an additional $1,000 would be provided annually for the support of a school at Sault Ste. Marie. Since the sections covering the school, annuity, and land for the mixed-bloods were inserted without presidential authorization, the commissioners made it clear that these articles could be rejected without affecting the validity of the other treaty provisions.[32]

The Chippewas accepted the terms without a murmur. Cass and McKenney promptly signed the document, the superintendent with his usual bold strokes and splendid flourish. Shingauba Wassin next stepped forward and signed; he was followed by eighty-four chiefs and warriors in what seemed to McKenney an endless procession. "It is true," he wrote, "even the cross is made for the signer, and he puts only the nib of the pen on it, but it is a short journey to travel over all the length, and the ups and downs which generally enter into the formation of an Indian's name."[33] Eleven white men, including Schoolcraft, Captain Boardman, Doctor Pitcher, and Abraham Edwards, the recording secretary, then signed as witnesses.

The most important witnesses to the treaty did not sign it. These were the traders to the Chippewas who also answered the call to assemble at Fond du Lac. With their livelihoods dependent on the tribe's fortunes, the traders had more than a casual interest in the proceedings, and the federal officials encouraged their presence. "I deem their attendance desirable as witness of what is agreed on," Schoolcraft explained to Cass, "that they may hereafter, should questions arise, explain & repeat to the Indians any Stipulations that may be entered into. We are so liable to misunderstand & be misunderstood in our Indian intercourse, that no opportunity of avoiding it ought to be neglected in our publick negotiations."[34]

After a two-hour recess, the commissioners reconvened the council to discuss the Chippewa fugitives. McKenney spoke. "We come now in the name of your Great Father, and demand of the Chippewa nation, the surrender of these murderers—that they may be tried by the same laws by which your Great Fathers children would be tried had they committed the same crime. This is that serious subject we told you we had to present to you, and your Great Father expects the great men of the Chippewa nation to stretch out their hands, and take hold of the murderers and that they will be prompt in complying with his demands."[35]

McKenney called forward Mit-talk-quis-e-ga. The Great Father had been told the warrior was one of the murderers. "As you are a warrior and a brave man, we ask you to tell us the truth," McKenney sternly said.

"A lie has been put on me," the frightened Indian replied. He had in fact been with the war party and witnessed the killings, but he had tried to prevent them. Not until much later did he know the victims were white men.

"If you are innocent, we shall not touch you. If you are guilty, we shall take you with us," answered McKenney, who then asked another Indian if the prisoner had participated in the murders.

"He did not.—The others of the party said so."

"Do you say so before the Great Spirit?"

"Am I a dog that I should lie?" replied the Indian.

Satisfied that Mit-talk-quis-e-ga was innocent, the commissioners smoked the pipe of peace with him and released him.[36]

The discussion would be continued the following day, McKenney informed the council. "It is a serious matter, and unless something is done in it by you, before we leave here, you will be visited with your Great Fathers heaviest displeasure," he warned. "No trader shall visit you—not a pound of tobacco nor a yard of cloth, shall go into your country. This is not a thing to pass away like a cloud.—If no agreement is made by you, to surrender them, the thunder and the storm will come. We will hear your answer tomorrow."[37]

When the council reconvened Mit-talk-quis-e-ga, accompanied by three other members of the Lac du Flambeau band, stepped forward and pleaded for more time to make a decision. Be patient, he told the commissioners. "We have no young men attached to us. It is very difficult for us to make an answer to you. We have first to consult our friends, and we then make answer to any question proposed to us. Father, we will see the men belonging to the War Party, and tell them they are sent for by you—When we hear what they say, we can give you our final answer."

"We are not satisfied with your answer," McKenney replied. The commissioners realized the guilty men were far away; nevertheless, they had to be delivered in the spring when the traders arrived to collect the furs from the winter hunts. "If they are not surrendered then, destruction will fall on your women and children," McKenney threatened. "Your father will put out his strong arm. Go, & think of it.—Nothing will satisfy us, but this."[38]

Mit-talk-quis-e-ga and his three companions conferred briefly then agreed. "Next spring, you may look for those young men who committed the murder," he replied. Pleased at the ease with which they had extracted the promise, Cass and McKenney quickly drafted a supplementary article to the Fond du Lac treaty which specified that the murderers "shall be brought in, either to the Sault St. Marie, or Green Bay, as early next summer as practicable, and surrendered to the proper authority; and that, in the mean time, all further measures on the part of the United States, in relation to this subject, shall be suspended."[39]

After a short break for lunch, the commissioners presented peace medals to a few of the more prominent warriors. McKenney, again flanked by a military honor guard, delivered the main address. "Friends & Brothers," he said, "the business part of our Council is closed. But we have seen who are your great men. We stand here to put medals around their necks—and smaller medals we will put round the necks of your first warriors, and best young men. All these medals have on one side of them Your Great Fathers face, and on the other side is his pipe, his peace hatchet, and his hand." McKenney advised the chiefs to obey their Great Father and "no more to advise your warriors to shed blood." Then the medals would act as lights on their breasts to which the young men could look for wisdom. To the warriors he said: "Listen to your great Chiefs—and mind their words—and if you disobey and do bad actions your medal will be a shame to you and not a badge of honor." The superintendent concluded his oration by admonishing the young men to "keep out of crooked places" and "when you get old you will be respected."[40]

McKenney then asked eleven chiefs, seven warriors, and four young men to step forward and receive their medals. As each one approached the table Schoolcraft hung a medal tied with blue ribbon around his neck.

McKenney concluded the ceremony with an even lengthier speech emphasizing the power of the Great Father and stressing the importance of bringing in the murderers as promised. If the Chippewas followed the treaty, they would have nothing to fear from the Great Father who was mild in peace and would protect and love his children. As a sign of his benevolence, the Great Father had sent them Schoolcraft, their agent. "He speaks your Great Fathers words, listen to him—Then you will be happy—and this is what your Great Father wishes you to be."[41]

The following afternoon the commissioners called the Indians together for the last time. The entire group of nearly seven hundred assembled band by band in a great semicircle around the commissioners, who distributed presents until nearly sundown—twelve hundred knives, twists of tobacco, handkerchiefs, calico for shirts, cloth for leggings, petticoats, blankets, flints, fishhooks. The final gift was the remaining stock of food. Although each Indian had received daily three-quarters of a pound of pork and a pound of flour, enough was left to feed all of them until they reached their homes.[42]

The commissioners and Indians broke camp on the morning of August 9. At sunrise, as a parting gift to the Great Father's children, the soldiers rolled a barrel of whiskey into the center of the compound and doled a cupful to each man, woman, and child. The musicians piped "strike your tents" at 8 A.M. and within the hour all gear was stowed snugly in the barges. For the return trip McKenney found himself sole master of the canopied canoe because Schoolcraft chose to ride with Cass in an equally large vessel made by the Indians during the conference. McKenney could not resist putting his craft through its paces and, as he waited for the others to embark, "took a turn with awning up and flag flying." He found the river choked with the heavily laden canoes of departing Indian families, while howling dogs raced frantically along the shore seeking lost masters.

When the governor's party reached midstream, it took the chanting of McKenney's voyageurs as a challenge to race; in an instant both vessels were wildly dashing down river. "We were victorious!" exclaimed McKenney. The governor's boat may have been impeded by the Indian canoe it rammed, he admitted, but "the truth is . . . Lake Superior has never had on its waters eight more efficient or more skillful voyageurs." Looking back, McKenney saw only the forlorn figures of the American Fur Company employees standing silent and alone on the bank, while scattered about the island and river valley were the empty frames and naked poles of scores of lodges. Near each, smoke still curled from the morning fires, making the landscape even more barren and desolate.[43]

McKenney reached Washington on October 7 after a journey marred only by the foundering of one of the military barges, which fired the Northwest with rumors that Cass, Schoolcraft, and McKenney had been lost in the wreck. Although a few soldiers got a good dunking, there had been no injuries. In McKenney's opinion, the expedition to Fond du Lac had been a signal triumph. "The hand of the government," which never before had been seen or felt in that region, had returned with bayonets unstained, while "many hearts" had been "made glad by the kindness which our government put it in our power to shew to these poor sufferers." Schoolcraft was also pleased with the outcome. He thought the treaty placed "our Indian relations in this quarter on a permanent basis" and guaranteed "the future peace of the frontier." Equally important, Schoolcraft wrote, "my agency was now fixed on a sure basis, and my influence fully established among the tribes."[44]

Less satisfied with the results was the Senate, which found fault with the treaty provisions respecting the land grants, annuities, and education. A "two weeks war" ensued before the treaty was ratified the following January. "I am told the strife was a glorious one," McKenney wrote Cass. "We have full credit for the bounty of the provisions, but they scratched them to death with their *constitutional clauses.* . . . How hard is the fate of the poor Indians! We proposed to give them bread out of their *own* ground, & those who know they were dying for lack of food will not let them have it!!! Well, every thing is in God's hands; & will go right in the end."[45]

Within a week of his return, McKenney began seeking a publisher for his *Sketches of a Tour to the Lakes, of the Char-*

acter and Customs of the Chippeway Indians, and of Incidents connected with the Treaty of Fond du Lac.[46] Fielding Lucas, a Baltimore printer whose firm remains in operation even today, eventually accepted the manuscript, and the book appeared in April 1827. Its unwieldy title notwithstanding, the format of the book is simple. The text consists of letters ostensibly addressed to Barbour between May 31 and October 6, 1826. Although the letters appear to have been written in the course of the trip, McKenney actually composed many of them from notes after he returned to Washington. He explained his literary method in a letter to Barbour from Sault Ste. Marie: "Having gathered up the pieces of paper on which my journal from Detroit to this place has been written, I enclose them herewith. I know I only send you a skeleton, and even that very clumsily articulated; but it is the best I could do; and being such, you must make the most of it." The notes, he continued, "may serve, when I return, to recall the images of the past. I will write you during my stay here, as before; and when I get on Lake Superior, shall resume my journal form again." Besides the letters, there are twenty-nine illustrations—most of them poorly done lithographs—and a lengthy appendix which includes a transcript of the official journal kept during the treaty negotiations, a copy of the ratified treaty of Fond du Lac, and a Chippewa vocabulary that McKenney had obtained at the request of Albert Gallatin who was trying to determine the origin of the American Indians through classification of their languages.[47]

Sketches of a Tour to the Lakes brought the author neither fame nor wealth and, after a flicker of public interest, was quickly forgotten. Although it failed to convince Congress of the need for a Bureau of Indian Affairs, it did find a receptive audience in the missionaries working among the Indians. They likely shared the sentiments of the reviewer who admired *Sketches* primarily for "the deep veneration which it uniformly manifests for the Christian religion."[48]

Lucas had not finished setting type for the *Sketches of a Tour to the Lakes* before McKenney began arranging his return to the lake country the next summer. Again, his plans required Cass' cooperation. On January 30, 1827, he informed the governor that he had just drawn a bill on him for $450, payable in sixty days. "Please accept it," McKenney pleaded, "& when

I see you which will be I hope early in May, or at such time as you may think I ought to be there, I will put you in cash to pay it." Or, he suggested, perhaps the governor would advance him the pay he could anticipate as commissioner, minus the $450. "At all events *honor* the bill, & in some form you will be *honorably* paid. Before I can move a peg," he explained, "I must leave my monied concerns & *my family* at ease—& this must be done in good part by *this pay to myself, as commissioner*."[49]

That very day McKenney penned a second request to the surprisingly tolerant Cass. Would the governor be willing to replace Abraham Edwards, who had served them so well as secretary at Fond du Lac, with Philip Barton Key, a college classmate of McKenney's son, William?[50] The secretary's pay of $5 for each twenty miles traveled and each day of treaty negotiations would enable the boy to make the trip; and, McKenney explained, "as I mean to take my son along I am anxious for Philip to join us, but he *cannot* go, except in this capacity." McKenney's only justification for the request was "my *feelings* are *interested* in this matter." Nevertheless, if Edwards could be left behind, "I will join you in making *some* arrangement ... as well perhaps in the money way," McKenney assured the governor. Perhaps he could offer Edwards the next vacant post as Indian agent in Michigan Territory. Edwards did not make the trip to Green Bay, but he waited two years for the promised position.[51]

Although McKenney prevailed in this case, he failed in his attempt to turn the expedition to Green Bay into an electioneering junket on behalf of the Adams administration, as he apparently did a year earlier when he carried anti-Jackson literature on his trip to Fond du Lac. He also failed in his plan to include prestigious persons among the Green Bay entourage. McKenney invited three key men to make the journey: Secretary of War Barbour, fur baron John Jacob Astor, and Stephen Van Rensselaer of Albany, New York, who had cast the deciding vote giving Adams the presidency in 1825 when the contested election had been thrown into the House of Representatives. However, by late March it was obvious that McKenney was having trouble putting together this grand excursion. He wrote Van Rensselaer: "I am just informed by Mr. Astor of a cause which may possibly deprive us of the pleasure of his company."

But Astor's absence need not discourage Van Rensselaer from going. "Drop me a line, that I may write to Gov Cass to make the preparation. I am the more anxious to hear definitely from you, because it is our wish to save you all the trouble of preparation; and that you shall find on your arrival at Detroit every thing in readiness for your accommodation up the Lake." Since the commissioners planned to leave Detroit about the first of June, McKenney hoped to be away from Washington by mid-April so he could "proceed leisurely" to the north country. Perhaps Van Rensselaer would like to meet McKenney in Albany and travel "in company" from there. "Now I wish most anxiously for one thing, & that is, that our excellent Secretary of War should accompany us. Much of the success of this desire will depend upon you. I must get you therefore to *urge* him, by letter, to go." Since Barbour planned to visit Bedford with his family about that time, "it will be easy for him to step across ... to Erie, and go from thence to Detroit in the steam boat from that place," McKenney explained. Barbour, like Astor, evidently had better things to do, which must have given Van Rensselaer reason to reconsider. In the end Cass and McKenney went alone to Green Bay.[52]

McKenney obviously was playing for high stakes here. Always anxious to curry favor with the social and political elite, he undoubtedly wished to ingratiate himself with the illustrious trio. And it is difficult not to think that the imaginative opportunist was trying to drum up interest in the hinterland for the forthcoming presidential campaign, as the Jacksonians so vehemently accused later. Besides, at the very least, prominent traveling companions would have provided excellent copy for the companion book to *Sketches*, which McKenney already planned to write.[53]

The superintendent had every reason to anticipate another delightful excursion. Funds for the negotiations at Green Bay had been included in the appropriation for Fond du Lac, there was no question of his appointment as a commissioner, and the trip would not be nearly as strenuous as his wilderness odyssey of the previous year. The entire journey from Detroit to Green Bay was to be made by steamboat. As for their official duties, Cass and McKenney had only to arrange the boundary between the Chippewas and their Menominee and Winnebago neighbors and to settle a dispute between the Brotherton Indians and the citizens of Green Bay. As part of the embryonic removal program, a few Brothertons had recently moved into Michigan Territory from New York much to the consternation of the French Canadians of Green Bay, who thought the area already overpopulated with Indians. Both sides had been invited to sit in council and explain their difficulties to the commissioners.[54]

McKenney left for the lake country on May 10, 1827, with his servant Ben Hanson, his son William McKenney, Philip Key, and a physician. In Detroit, they joined Cass aboard the *Henry Clay* for an eight-day, storm-tossed passage that left them grounded five miles above their Fort Howard destination. The vicious squall that welcomed the commissioners to Green Bay should have been an omen to McKenney that the idyllic experiences of the previous summer were not to be repeated.[55]

"Our visit here is opportune," McKenney reported in a barely legible letter to Barbour written the following day from aboard the *Henry Clay*. The commissioners found the people of Green Bay alarmed by rumors of an impending attack by the Winnebagos, who were supposedly sending war belts to all the Lake Michigan tribes seeking their participation in the uprising. Continued encroachments on Winnebago lands by lead miners—a complaint which, "so far as we can yet know, is *true*"—had inspired hostilities. Whether the rumors of war were true or not, many families in the area had already abandoned their homes and were crowding into Fort Howard for safety. The commissioners, two weeks early for the council, decided "to ascertain matters in regard to this contingency." Cass left immediately in an express canoe for Prairie du Chien, a small but strategic settlement at the terminus of the important Fox-Wisconsin waterway that linked Lake Michigan with the Mississippi River. McKenney and the ever-present Hanson reboarded the Detroit-bound *Henry Clay*, returning with it as far as Mackinac. After alerting the army garrisons there and at nearby Sault Ste. Marie, McKenney was to return by canoe in time to meet Cass for the council. "We shall get all the information we can; & if the affair be as serious as we have heard, we will stay the stroke," he wrote confidently.[56]

While McKenney enjoyed comparative tranquility aboard the *Henry Clay*, Cass discovered matters were much graver than they had originally believed. On the banks of the Fox River he encountered a small band of Winnebago Indians. They professed peace and friendship for the Americans when the governor talked with them, but as he turned to leave, one of the young men stepped across his path, leveled a musket at his ample stomach, and pulled the trigger. The weapon misfired. In a show of bravado that belied concern for his safety, the shaken Cass brushed the gun aside, stepped into his canoe, and continued on his way. He reached Prairie du Chien on the Fourth of July, having traveled the four hundred miles in six days. To his amazement he found the settlement "utterly broken up" and the inhabitants barricaded in Fort Crawford, a small post that had been abandoned only the year before in a period of military austerity. A Winnebago war party had entered the village a week earlier, murdered two men, and scalped but not killed an infant boy. Two days later and forty miles away, a much larger war party had attacked a keelboat, killing two men and wounding six others while suffering at least two fatalities of its own. "It is difficult to conceive that such decisive steps would be taken without the strongest expectation of cooperation," Cass wrote in a letter that reached McKenney a hundred miles above Green Bay.[57]

The emergency dictated a change in plans. Cass would organize the local militia; then he would descend the Mississippi, raising volunteer militia companies from the Indian agencies and mining settlements. At St. Louis he would direct General Henry Atkinson, commander of the western military district, to field his entire force. Cass would then travel to Chicago, where he hoped McKenney could meet him. Meanwhile, the governor would send runners to the Sioux, warning them against joining their Winnebago relatives, and he would invite all tribes in the area to send large delegations to the council at Green Bay. "I consider it important to detach as many Indians as possible from this confederacy, if there be one. And at all events, they are better [off] at the Bay," he reasoned, "than in the wilderness with trigger-happy frontiersmen who would not take time to determine if their victims were hostile or not. To get the Indians to go to Green Bay, Cass would promise many presents, and "I must look to you to bear me out in it. It is no time for half way measures," he warned McKenney.[58]

Midsummer storms prevented McKenney from pressing on
to Chicago as Cass had requested. He chose instead to return
to Green Bay, which he reached on the evening of July 18. "On
arriving here I found the inhabitants in a state of great excitement," he wrote the secretary of war the following day. Word
of the attacks at Prairie du Chien had been followed by an
alarming report of a Winnebago ambush of the governor's party;
the Indians had supposedly killed one man, wounded two others,
and made a prisoner of Cass. Although McKenney discounted
the rumor, he asked the Fort Howard commandant to send
forty additional soldiers to supplement the small squad guarding
the supplies at the treaty site, an Indian mound known as Butte
des Morts, or hill of the dead, located thirty-three miles above
the bay on the west bank of the Fox River.[59]

After resting a day at the fort, McKenney moved to the
treaty grounds, now an armed camp guarded by some sixty
soldiers of the Regular Army and more than a hundred Menominee warriors. "It is a beautiful spot, so far as Nature and
the Indians of olden time who erected the mound in the centre
of the ground can make it so" wrote McKenney in describing
the site to Barbour. The mound, thirty feet high and approximately ninety feet in diameter at the base and ten at the crown,
dominated a plain of upland prairie roughly three-quarters of
a mile square; skirting the plain that opened onto the river was
a thick forest of towering oaks. The soldiers chose to erect their
flag on the summit and in digging the emplacement found the
mound filled with human bones, which McKenney, of course,
examined carefully. "From their lightness and porous appearance," he wrote, the bones "have been there for perhaps a
hundred years—a period of time long enough to have mouldered
them down to dust, and which would doubtless have been affected, but for the dry and sandy soil which encloses them."
McKenney fortunately spared both Barbour and posterity a
narration of the legend that "purports to explain the fight which
terminated in such destruction of human life—its causes and
its consequences."[60]

For almost a week McKenney kept busy at Butte des Morts
supervising arrangements for the forthcoming council. One can
well imagine his pleasure in directing work crews in felling trees
and constructing storehouses, temporary quarters, and a kitchen.

The scores of Indians that arrived daily also required his attention. By July 26, some thirteen hundred Menominees, Chippewas, Winnebagos, and even a few Iroquois and Stockbridges from New York had crowded onto the grounds. This convinced McKenney that no confederation existed, although he admitted that the more suspicious whites feared the Indians were planning a surprise attack during the conference.[61]

Confederacy or not, the superintendent considered it time to deal the northwest Indians a heavy blow. Waiting for Cass, McKenney aired his opinions in two strongly worded letters that belied his Quaker background. The Winnebagos "are unlike all other Indians known to me, & are not now, & have never been worthy of the slightest trust," he declared to Barbour. McKenney hoped the Winnebagos would attack Atkinson's command as it moved through their country, giving the general an excuse "to chastise them well." Whoever struck first, "prompt movements, & a sudden throwing in among these people who are the Ishmaelites of these regions of a strong force, & fierce & spirited retaliation, will be a most happy event." McKenney recommended similar steps against the Lac du Flambeau Chippewas, who had broken their promise to deliver the escaped murderers. "It is my opinion that spirited movements upon both those points would secure the peace & quiet of this frontier for a quarter of a century, & that without them, these acts will multiply . . . just in proportion as their previous acts may have been allowed to pass unpunished." McKenney need not have worried. Even as he was writing, hastily assembled armies of frontiersmen and regulars were converging on the southwestern corner of present-day Wisconsin.[62]

The threat of a general Indian uprising had not been very great, although Red Bird, leader of a small Winnebago band residing about eighty miles above Prairie du Chien at La Crosse, had done his best to organize one. His people occupied extremely rich mineral lands coveted by speculators and lead miners. Disturbed by flagrant and constant white encroachments and provoked by a rumor that miners had clubbed two of his warriors to death, Red Bird, who mistakenly expected his raids to inspire other tribes to move against the Americans, retaliated by killing the two Prairie du Chien farmers and attacking two keelboats on the Mississippi River. Indian support failed to develop largely because the other tribes of the Northwest realized the futility of resisting the Americans without British aid and because of the timely arrival of Lewis Cass. The territorial governor assembled federal and civilian forces with such swiftness that he effectively suppressed any latent support. Thus, while Red Bird and a handful of warriors tried desperately to elude pursuing armies, their potential allies were answering Cass' call to gather at Green Bay.[63]

"I consider the difficulty at an end," McKenney announced to the secretary of war on August 4. Red Bird and his followers would soon be captured, more than eighteen hundred Indians were already at Butte des Morts nervously waiting for the negotiations, and Cass had returned safely from his month-long circuit of the territory. Since the Winnebago troubles had already forced a delay, the commissioners thought it wise to postpone the council until Monday, August 6, to allow more distant Indian bands time to arrive. The recent outbreak would of course be discussed, McKenney explained, and, if many Indians were present, the commissioners might be able to ensure, "in Treaty form," against its recurrence.[64]

In the meantime, the commissioners called a special meeting of the five hundred or so Winnebagos on the treaty grounds and urged them to persuade the hostile band to surrender. The Great Father did not want to punish the innocent, Cass warned, but if the guilty were not surrendered, the Winnebagos could expect a road to be carved through their country—"not with axes, but with guns."

At noon on Monday, the commissioners formally opened the council, the prearranged signal this year a cannon shot. Almost a thousand warriors gathered in the council square along with scores of curious spectators. Cass, McKenney, recording secretary Key, and other dignitaries sat on puncheon benches around a rude table shaded by a bower of evergreens similar to that erected at Fond du Lac.[65]

Cass spoke first. "My friend who sits by me here, & who when at home sits by our Great Father to issue his orders about his red children, & myself have been sent here to do business with you, & we will now tell you what it is." The Great Father wished the Chippewa and Menominee elders to draw a boundary line between their nations "that they may know their own country, & that there may be no dispute between them, nor between their children, nor between their children's children." Another line must be drawn to separate the Indian country from the lands occupied by American settlers along the Fox River and at Green Bay. "We want to make a straight line between us," Cass explained, "that if one of our people puts one foot over it, our father, with his long strong arm may draw him back again." Still other lines were needed between the Menominees, the Indians from New York, and the citizens of Green Bay. "We will look at all the papers & hear all the stories, & then determine the boundaries," Cass said. Since the commissioners had already warned the Winnebagos about the troubles at Prairie du Chien, nothing more would be said on that subject until Red Bird and his followers were captured.

The governor concluded his lengthy remarks with the startling announcement that the commissioners the next day would appoint a head chief for the Menominees. "There is no one to whom we can talk, as the head of the nation. If any thing happens, we want some person who has authority in the nation, to whom we can look. They appear to us like a flock of geese without a leader. Some fly one way, & some another."[66]

The following morning, the assembled Indians witnessed a remarkable ceremony. McKenney with typical verbosity claimed that the Great Father, confused by the many voices he heard from the Menominee Nation, had said: "*Go*, select from my Menominee children the best man & make him Chief. Give him good things. Put a Medal around his neck, & a robe over his shoulders, & give him a flag." The superintendent then solemnly placed a medal around the neck of a warrior named Oshkosh. "You are now the great Menominee Chief. You will take care & act like a man & not like a dog." Turning to a second warrior named Caron, McKenney presented him with a middle-sized medal, saying: "You are to speak to your great father through the mouth of your great chief. Should the great Spirit put his hand on him, you will, if you are a good man, take his place; if not, we will make another. Your great father will have no bad or foolish chiefs."[67]

The commissioners needed to conclude formal agreements with recognized leaders. Since the Menominee political structure appeared too poorly defined for them to carry out their instructions, Cass and McKenney felt they had no other alternative but to appoint suitable leaders. While irregular, their action was by no means unique in the history of federal Indian relations, but it was normally done less overtly. When a congressman later challenged McKenney for tampering with the internal affairs of the Menominees, McKenney denied wrongdoing. "I have already stated," McKenney explained to the secretary of war, "that the persons employed to hold treaties with the Indian tribes in the Territory of Michigan, during the year 1827, did not undertake to 'constitute and appoint an Indian chief.' But in conformity to immemorial usage, as well of the British and French, as our Government, the ceremony of recognizing those as chiefs who were reported by their bands as their acknowledged leaders, was observed by 'those persons' in putting medals around their necks. Further than this, and the giving of what was considered good advice, at the time, for their own and their people's government, nothing was done. All such signed the treaty, and after they received the medals."[68]

Only the boundary lines were agreed upon in the next four days. Rather than face the problem of the New York Indians, Cass and McKenney announced that the decision would be made by the Great Father after he sifted all the testimony presented at the council. The treaty was signed on Saturday, August 10. Oshkosh and Caron were the first Menominee signatories.[69]

Although McKenney was anxious to begin his southern tour, the commissioners remained at Butte des Morts several days longer, hoping they could wind up the Winnebago troubles. Red Bird had not surrendered. While waiting, the commissioners handed out $15,000 in presents and, on another day, fourteen medals in a brief ceremony; they also addressed the Winnebagos and Chippewas in separate conferences. The talk to the Chippewas was tough and to the point. If the escaped murderers were not surrendered by the following spring, the government would ban traders from the Chippewa country. "If after that, you do not give them up, we will all march into your country for them," the commissioners declared. "We want your chiefs to tell your people this as soon as they get home. They must be delivered." To the Winnebagos, Cass and McKenney were equally firm: "We have been waiting a great while—we are tired of it. We will not injure the peaceable. If they surrender the murderers at Prairie du Chien, & three or four of the principal men who attacked the keelboats, we will sit still & be satisfied. *But if they will not, we will not stop, but strike until we can get them ourselves.*"[70]

Unable to delay longer, the commissioners returned to Green Bay on August 17, where, two days later, they parted company. Cass and the rest of the official party boarded the steamboat *La Grange* for Detroit, while McKenney hired a canoe to take him and his servant Ben Hanson on the second leg of the trip. Philip Barton Key and William McKenney had originally planned to accompany the colonel on his southern tour, but at the last moment they, too, boarded the steamboat. Governor Cass evidently prompted this change in plans by asking William to carry dispatches about the treaty and the Winnebago uprising to the secretary of war.

The two college chums needed no encouragement to return to the East, and they bade the colonel a hasty farewell. McKenney not only lost their company, but later he also had to endure considerable embarrassment because William billed the War Department $300 for his services. The Treasury Department at first refused to honor the bill, claiming it was unheard of for commissioners to hire someone to deliver a treaty when it could have been mailed at considerably less expense. Cass rescued a potentially damaging situation by insisting he had sent young McKenney, without his father's prior knowledge, "in consequence of the critical state of things . . . and my anxiety that the Secretary should be speedily informed of all that had been done and was contemplated." Indeed, Cass claimed, "the mere sending of the treaty was a matter of comparatively little importance. It was taken by Mr. McKenney because he was going upon much more important business, but it never occurred to me to send him, merely that he might take it. . . ." William got his $300, but his father regretted "that the account was ever handed in; or that my son ever consented to perform the service."[71]

McKenney probably had not given his son's change in plans a second thought, for he was too busy with the emergency at hand. Although already greatly behind schedule, he tarried a few days longer in Green Bay to help organize a force of regulars, militia, and Indians to continue hunting the elusive Red Bird.

Under Major William Whistler, commandant of Fort Howard, the army was to rendezvous with General Atkinson at the Fox-Wisconsin portage, 140 miles southwest of Green Bay. Mustering the Indians was not easy. When Menominee agent Henry Brevoort visited a nearby village early on the morning of the eighteenth, he found most of the men, including three of the four chiefs, drunk. He returned at noon only to find them "in a similar, but improving state, two of the Chiefs asleep—a third not to be found." The agent sheepishly informed McKenney that the one sober chief promised to gather what force he could and join the Fort Howard expedition. Brevoort was unduly discouraged, however, for 112 Menominee warriors, shouldering new trade muskets, accompanied the 101 regulars, 28 militiamen, and 49 New York Indians who took to the field five days later. Although the muskets had to be surrendered later, each brave received for his services a pair of leggings, a breechclout, a blanket, moccasins, a paper of vermilion, and a box of clay pipes, all charged to the contingency fund of the Indian office.[72]

The command left Fort Howard by barge on August 23. Confident that his canoe would overtake the lumbering barges, McKenney, Hanson, and John Kinzie, the Prairie du Chien subagent who acted as his clerk and interpreter, delayed two days at the fort before following. Thirty miles upstream and only nine hours out of Green Bay, he overtook the little army. Three miles further he reached the Butte des Morts treaty grounds and discovered the Indians had burned all the buildings. Although thick clouds of smoke still hung in the air, McKenney could not resist stopping for a final visit.[73]

Because of the slow pace of the barges, the Fort Howard expeditionary force did not reach the portage until late on the afternoon of September 1, but even then General Atkinson was not yet at the rendezvous. Why McKenney did not press on to his business in the South remains a mystery, but his decision was fortuitous because the next day, while the colonel rested in front of his tent, a Winnebago warrior from a village about nine miles distant appeared. Squatting down, the Indian announced: "Do not strike—when the sun is there to morrow," pointing to the late afternoon sun, "they will come in."

"Who will come in?" McKenney asked through his interpreter.

"Red-Bird and We-Kaw," the two men who killed the Americans at Prairie du Chien, replied the Indian, who rose, wrapped his blanket about him, and stalked off.[74]

The following day, Red Bird, We Kaw, and more than a hundred warriors materialized on the bank of the Fox River opposite the encampment. Red Bird carried a white flag in one hand, a peace pipe in the other. Two other warriors carried American flags. Barges were sent across the river to receive the large delegation; as the unarmed Winnebagos climbed the bank from the barges they met a formation of Fort Howard soldiers and Indians. On the left flank stretched an irregular line of Menominee and New York Indians, uneasily fingering their muskets. To the right stood the musicians, slightly in advance of a line of soldiers. McKenney, Major Whistler, and a small knot of Indian agents, interpreters, and army officers formed the center, and they met Red Bird and We Kaw, who approached to within ten paces. "All eyes were fixed upon the Red Bird," McKenney later recalled; "and well they might be—for of all the Indians I ever saw, he is, without exception, the most perfect in form, in face, and gesture." Red paint marked half his face, the other half was green and white. He was dressed in his finest regalia—bleached buckskin jacket and leggings that were heavily fringed and decorated with blue beads. On each shoulder, like epaulets, was the skin of a red bird.

The ceremony of surrender was painfully brief. The musicians played Pleyel's hymn, then Major Whistler praised the Winnebagos for bringing Red Bird and his accomplices to justice —they had saved their nation from destruction. The Winnebagos could be assured the warriors would receive a fair trial under the same laws that governed the Great Father's white children. Red Bird stepped forward and spoke to the major: "*I am ready.*" Then moving a step closer, he continued: "I do not wish to be put in irons. Let me be free. I have given away my life— it is gone." With a graceful motion, he stooped, scooped up a handful of sand, tossed it in the air, and watched it fall to the ground. "I would not take it back," Red Bird said without a trace of emotion. "*It is gone.*"[75]

Immediately after the arrest of Red Bird, We Kaw, and four of their principal warriors, McKenney left for the South. He reached Prairie du Chien on the evening of September 5.

He remained three days, investigating the circumstances surrounding the Winnebago hostilities, and then proceeded down the Mississippi. Pausing only to inspect the lead mines at Fever River and the Rock Island agency, he arrived in St. Louis on the sixteenth. McKenney, still accompanied by Hanson, spent a conversation-filled week with William Clark and then boarded the steamboat *Crusader* for Memphis where he finally abandoned the waterways and began a cross-country trek to Washington by way of the Chickasaw, Choctaw, and Creek agencies.

Whatever McKenney's personal motives for making these trips, they were invaluable to him as superintendent of Indian affairs. Through them he acquired first-hand knowledge of the native Americans. Although responsible for their welfare, McKenney previously had no personal contact with Indians other than those who visited Washington. As Cass correctly wrote in the fall of 1827, "you have taken the rounds of our aborigines fully well, and have returned with a stock of practical knowledge, added to your former experience, which will enable you to preside over the affairs of the dept with more general satisfaction, than any other man in the Union."[76]

No less important to McKenney was the opportunity to inspect several Indian agencies and to see the problems his field officials faced every day. He experienced the rigors of wilderness life, irregular meals, wet clothes, and mosquito-plagued nights; and he shared the excitement of an Indian uprising. He visited the offices of the St. Louis and Michigan superintendencies and the Sault Ste. Marie, Mackinac, Green Bay, Rock Island, Chickasaw, Choctaw, and Creek agencies. McKenney reported to the secretary of war that he found the Sault Ste. Marie and Mackinac agencies in good order and the agents "attentive to their duties," but the Green Bay agency he thought might be improved in several respects. The Choctaw agency he found in "pretty good order" and the agent "well disposed ... to the duties of his place." The Creek agency, "except as to some of the forms in which I have suggested improvement," he found in excellent order and the agent "diligent and laborious in the execution of his duties."[77] These comments, although by no means critical evaluations of the field service, indicate that McKenney was at least attempting to introduce the close administrative control that the Bureau of Indian Affairs was to exercise later in the nineteenth century, and his trips can be viewed as forerunners of the elaborate inspection system the bureau later maintained. But most important, as a treaty commissioner McKenney was helping to shape Indian policy instead of simply administering it.

9

Administering the Indian Office

B Y THE TIME McKENNEY assumed his duties in the spring
of 1824, the United States had already roughly defined
its basic program for the management of Indian affairs.
Expressed in the formal treaties with the tribes and defined in
the series of federal laws known as the Indian trade and intercourse acts, the fundamental elements of the government's program were to protect Indian lands from illegal settlement, regulate the fur trade, control the liquor traffic, prevent and punish
crimes by members of one race against another, and encourage
and promote civilization and educational programs among the
Indians.[1] As superintendent of Indian affairs, McKenney had
to see that all components of this policy were carried out as
effectively and efficiently as possible.

McKenney considered the illegal settlement of Indian lands
the *"principal curse"* of the native Americans, and he exerted
every effort to prevent the further erosion of their domain. To
assist him he had a vast legal arsenal. The federal government
retained exclusive control of the disposition of tribal lands,
denying to private individuals or state governments the right
to acquire territory from Indians by any means; all treaties of

168

cession had the universal corollary guaranteeing unceded lands against encroachment. The Indian trade and intercourse acts provided the means of enforcing these regulations. The act of 1802—the one, with various amendments, in effect during Mc-Kenney's administration—specified a fine of up to $100 and imprisonment up to six months for any white man who crossed onto Indian country to hunt or to graze livestock. Settling on or surveying such lands could mean imprisonment for twelve months and a $1,000 fine. The law further authorized the president to remove intruders by whatever means necessary.[2]

Not all white settlement on Indian lands was illegal, however. Whites did not need *"expressed* consent" to live on tribal lands, McKenney explained to his agents. If the Indians knew of their presence and did not report it, the whites were not to be considered intruders. Nor were the agents to interfere with the so-called Indian countrymen—whites who lived with a tribe although they were not formally connected with it by marriage —if they first presented the agents with approved testimonials of good character. Should their conduct later become detrimental to the welfare of the Indians or should they interfere with federal policy, the agents were to order them from the Indian country.[3]

The troublesome whites were the squatters, described by agent Hugh Montgomery as "Disorderly people who hang on between the white & Red people & act as a kind of Pioneers to Civil Sosciety."[4] Operating on the premise that possession is nine-tenths of the law, these frontier farmers simply settled where they pleased, and nothing short of force could make them leave.

Fearful that squatters would provoke an Indian war, Mc-Kenney continually exhorted his field officials to be alert to their encroachments. "It is time the Indians saw we had power not only to correct them, but to control our own people," he wrote Superintendent Clark in 1828. The following year Mc-Kenney stressed to Governor Cass the "importance to allay, by all proper measures any excitements which the conduct of our Citizens may create among the . . . Indians; and when there shall be an open violation of the intercourse law to prosecute the offenders. It is by this means alone that the Indians can be made sensible of the protection of the Government; and their

confidence in it maintained." He wrote to the Choctaw agent:
"If [squatters] . . . persist in coming on the lands *you* will warn
them off within a given period—if they will not obey, report
their refusals to the Department."[5]

Coping with squatters was an endless cycle. An agent would
visit the intruders, announce that they were trespassing, and
order them to leave within a specified time. If they did not go,
the agent would return and, often with military assistance,
destroy their fences, crops, and cabins and escort the unwelcome
visitors from the Indian country. The agent tried to time the
punitive foray so that the growing season would be too far advanced for the squatters to plant another crop but not so far
advanced for them to salvage produce after the agent left. No
matter how thorough the damage, however, the squatters invariably returned close on the heels of the departing soldiers.[6]

The incident that began in October 1823 along the border
between Georgia and land belonging to the Eastern Cherokees
was a routine case. That month Cherokee leaders complained
to their agent, Joseph McMinn, about numerous squatters on
their lands. McMinn promptly sent Colonel Archibald R. Turk
and thirteen soldiers to evict them. The soldiers remained in the
field some four months, and in February 1824 Turk reported to
the secretary of war that all the intruders had been removed.[7]
Not two months later, however, McKenney heard the squatters
were back in the area and directed McMinn to remove them
without delay. In May the agent's proclamation "to the Intruders on the Cherokee Lands, within the State of Georgia"
told them they were "doomed, to be the sufferers by their own
actions," and gave them thirty days to leave. At the same time
McMinn instructed Colonel Turk to raise a volunteer force of
thirty men, to prepare them to move against squatters who ignored the edict, and to use force in case of resistance. The preparations were "judicious," McKenney said. "It is time these
complaints be hushed; and the laws of the Country in their
application to this subject be completely executed." Enforcing
the intercourse laws, he continued, "will also rid the Government
of the trouble and cost of adjusting such an accumulation of
claims of which this very violation is deemed to be the most
fruitful source."[8]

McKenney soon discovered neither cost nor trouble was

saved. The squatters were much more hostile than they had been the previous summer. Bushwhackers continually harassed Turk and his men, firing on them seven times in one day alone. Turk learned James Dickson was the leader of the resistance and took several soldiers to his cabin to arrest him. Dickson was shot in the scuffle; three others were later arrested and turned over to Georgia authorities. The prisoners escaped, Dickson died, and Turk found himself and four of his men in the superior court of Hall County, Georgia, charged with murder. By the time they were acquitted their defense had cost the federal government more than $2,000 and the better part of a year. McMinn reported the exasperating finale of the affair: when the troops left, several of the squatters had immediately returned.[9]

Despite such discouraging results, field officials seldom relaxed their efforts against the squatters—if only to prevent the Indians from acting on their own behalf. One of the most serious of such incidents during McKenney's administration took place in Randolph County, Missouri, in July 1829. A band of about fifty Iowa warriors, accompanied by women and children, chanced upon a community of squatters and ordered them to leave. The unintimidated whites raised a force of twenty-six men and pursued the Indians for fifteen miles before catching up with them. In the fight that ensued three white men were killed, four were wounded, and the rest fled; the Indian losses were unrecorded. Two Iowa chiefs and four warriors were later arrested and charged with murder. The grand jury investigation held in St. Louis the following spring cleared the Indians and, the defense lawyer said, showed that the white men were guilty "of an unprovoked and bloody murder." The verdict, however, probably did not comfort the Indian prisoners, who were near death from their long confinement.[10]

McKenney believed authorizing the Indians to remove squatters was the best solution to the problem of intruders. The Indians, he reasoned, could more effectively patrol their own country than the undermanned military garrisons on the frontier, and they had more incentive to do so. All that was needed, he pointed out, was new legislation, "duly, and rigidly enforced."[11] The federal government, however, understandably hesitated to give Indians police powers, and the problem was never adequately resolved.

Not all white men who entered the Indian country wanted land. Some were interested in furs, others in annuity money; and controlling the traders often proved more of a challenge to McKenney. Intruders who were interested primarily in land were content to leave the Indians alone. Traders, on the other hand, had continual contact with the natives, and that contact was often detrimental to the Indians' moral welfare, particularly when whiskey played a part in the trade. McKenney's service as head of the factory system had prepared him well for his duties regarding the fur trade, and at the outset he initiated a vigorous program for its more effective administration.

Private fur trade was a major business in the country's economy, with significant influence and large capital investments —more than $600,000 in 1824, McKenney estimated. However, when he became superintendent of Indian affairs, McKenney was disappointed over the lack of War Department records concerning the operations and the financial condition of the private fur trade. To rectify this unfortunate state of affairs, the superintendent urged the secretary of war to institute "a system of outfits and returns." Such returns, McKenney said, would provide the government with statistical and political data "to see the whole state, and the value of that trade." The next year he repeated his recommendation in another report to Barbour, proposing that traders be required to submit annual reports to the Indian office. The fur trade, he wrote, "is a branch of commerce highly important and interesting to the Country; and yet no means exist by which the Country can arrive at any satisfactory knowledge of its commencement or value." His recommendations were ignored. Thus, in 1829 when the Senate asked for a report on the economic condition of the fur trade within the United States, McKenney was forced to admit there was not a single document in his office on the subject. He did not miss the opportunity to point out that he had anticipated such a need from his first days in the War Department; but, he wrote, "nothing . . . was done, and there remains, as before that period, no data on which to base the information asked for."[12]

McKenney's recommendations regarding the regulation of the fur trade, however, met with more success, enabling him to score a personal triumph over the private traders that had been denied him during his years as administrator of the factory system. Licensing remained the government's principal method of regulating trade with the Indians, but the law was far more effective than the one with which McKenney had to cope when he was superintendent of Indian trade. In 1822, following the abolition of the factory system, Congress raised the bond limit for licenses to $5,000, proportionate to the trader's capital investment, and required agents and superintendents to submit to the War Department annual abstracts of the licenses they had issued, listing recipients, their bonds, and their capitalization. At the same time, the Indians were urged not to do business with unlicensed traders and to report the names of traders who visited them for comparison with the abstracts. Persons found trading on Indian lands without a license were subject to the forfeiture of their goods, one half going to the informer, the other half to the United States.[13]

Nevertheless, McKenney still considered the licensing system inadequate and weak in two respects: there was no way to keep a license out of the hands of an unreliable citizen if he had sufficient collateral to post his bond; and there was "no power any where to cancel the license, (except upon legal proof that the law is violated; and that is next to impossible where the trader is a party on the one hand, and the Indians only, on the other) when mischievous proceedings involve either the peace of the Indians or the repose and quiet of our borders." McKenney suggested modifying the law to allow Indian agents discretion in granting licenses and to allow them "on sufficient grounds, of just complaint, to cancel a grant, reserving a right of appeal to the trader, to the Department, in either case." The proposed Indian department reorganization that Cass and Clark submitted to Congress in February 1829 included these recommendations, and they were enacted in the Indian trade and intercourse act of 1834.[14]

Meanwhile, Congress had taken additional steps to strengthen the laws governing the Indian trade. On May 25, 1824, scarcely two months after McKenney took office, it enacted legislation requiring Indian agents "to designate, from time to time, certain convenient and suitable places for carrying on trade with the different Indian tribes, and to require all traders to trade at the places thus designated, and at no other place or places"—

the very law for which McKenney had lobbied so energetically during his administration of the factory system. He welcomed its passage and quickly took steps to ensure its proper implementation. He no doubt drafted the circular the War Department issued June 5. It directed the superintendents and Indian agents to put the law into effect and provided these guidelines: no more than one site was to be selected for a tribe unless compelling reasons dictated otherwise; agents were to inform the department of the sites, which, once approved, could not be changed without authorization; licenses issued thereafter were to indicate the approved site and any departure from the terms of the license was to be grounds for forfeiture of the bond.[15]

The new law was not favorably regarded by the traders, who claimed that it would ruin their business. Employees of the American Fur Company were among the most indignant. The idea of Indian agents' selecting trading sites was "truly a curiosity," wrote one company official, "unless it originated in the fertile brain of Mr. McKinnie; but if so, it is perfectly reconciliable with the rest of his blundering absurdities." McKenney attempted without success to mollify the powerful company by telling William B. Astor that, within the limits of the law, the government would extend every accommodation to "our enterprizing Citizens who are engaged in the Fur Trade and to accord to them in these locations for Indian Trade whatever facilities may be considered by them to be necessary for the promotion of their interests."[16]

The act had been in effect for a little less than two years when the traders succeeded in getting the House of Representatives to consider its repeal. In February 1826 the House Committee on Indian Affairs directed the secretary of war to report on the effects of the act and to determine whether it operated to the "injury" of the traders and the Indians. Barbour entrusted the reply to McKenney, who rose admirably to the occasion. He prepared a vigorous defense of the law, especially its usefulness in curbing the liquor traffic among the Indians. He supported his argument by citing dramatic accounts from officials in the Indian country who had apprehended whiskey smugglers. "The existing obligation to locate, and carry on trade, at places, which are known, and no others, and which are *previously designated*, does appear to me," he wrote, "to bring the evils which it is esteemed, on all hands, to be so important to remedy, more immediately, within the eye of the Officers of the Government, and the grasp of the law, than any that has been heretofore devised."[17] The House evidently agreed because a bill to modify the act, introduced in March, was not acted upon; a similar resolution introduced the following December fared no better.[18]

By the late 1820s both the political and economic importance of the fur trade had diminished considerably. The danger of foreign manipulation of the Indians through the trade was practically a thing of the past, and Astor was soon to withdraw from the business because of its financial liabilities. These developments had little effect on McKenney's duties, however, because ingenuous traders, especially those among the eastern tribes, had found a lucrative substitute for furs—money.

The tribes received money for a variety of reasons, principally for ceding land to the United States. The government indemnified the Indians for acquired land with cash, merchandise, or both. Money was also sometimes given to individuals, usually leaders who had been helpful in getting treaties signed or in keeping their tribes from the warpath. Depending on the desire of the Indians, the money could be paid in lump sums or in specified amounts over a specified number of years—in some cases in perpetuity. Occasionally money was placed in a bank and the Indians received the interest as annuity payments. The Senecas, for example, in 1797 deposited in the Bank of the United States the $100,000 they had received for surrendering their rights to certain lands in New York; the annual interest on the deposit amounted to $6,000.[19]

Money for the annuity payments was provided by special congressional appropriations. In McKenney's first year as superintendent of Indian affairs the appropriation was slightly more than $100,000; by 1832 it had climbed to $336,405. Payments were normally made in cash because it was more convenient for the government, but services and merchandise were also given. The 1826 appropriation, for example, included $10,000 to build houses for five Osage and Kansa chiefs, $2,550 to equip a blacksmith shop for the Shawnees, and $320 to buy 160 bushels of salt for the Miamis.[20]

To distribute the annuities, the agent usually summoned the

tribe to the agency and gave the money or goods to the chiefs, who in turn divided the annuities among their tribesmen. The Eastern Cherokees, however, devised a different method. Since 1816 the secretary of war had deposited the undivided annuity in the tribal treasury. Although the tribe no longer assembled at the agency to receive the annuities, the Eastern Cherokees continued to demand the $1,280 allowance for rations the government normally gave the tribe at disbursement time. McKenney put a stop to this practice in 1827, explaining to the agent that the ration money was needed for "relieving other Indians who are more in need for the favors of the Government."[21]

McKenney considered cash annuities a "radical defect" in federal policy. The practice "furnishes a lure to the avaricious —and gives the means of indulgence to these untutored people, in all their propensities to drunkenness & idleness; & is known, to have produced from the beginning, *no other fruits.*" The superintendent may have exaggerated but not much. Often at annuity disbursement time, an agency would swarm with peddlers, traders, and merchants who tempted the Indians with trinkets, plied them with liquor, and then cheated or even robbed them. Joseph Street, the Winnebago agent, told of such a swindler's harvest. In September 1830 he had paid the tribe their $3,000 annuity in cash. The next day local traders had all but $700 of it, and the Indians had in exchange a few blankets and trinkets and "much whiskey."[22]

Incensed by such occurrences, McKenney sought various ways to protect the Indians from predators. One was to urge the tribes to accept annuity payments in merchandise rather than cash. But the traders urged the Indians to do otherwise, and, McKenney lamented to Governor Duval of Florida, "if they insist on having the money, we have no right to refuse it." Equally unworkable was his idea of keeping secret the time and place of disbursement.[23] More logical but not adopted was McKenney's suggestion that Congress make it mandatory that the Indians be given "necessary and useful articles" instead of cash. "Indians are only children," he wrote the chairman of the House Committee on Indian Affairs, "and require to be nursed, and counselled, and directed as such."[24]

McKenney's attempts to control the traffic in whiskey fared

little better. As superintendent of Indian trade he had conducted a heroic but futile campaign against the problem, and
he found liquor remained to haunt him in his new position.
Moreover, the situation had not improved during his absence
from the Indian service. Thomas Forsyth, the agent at Rock
Island, wrote that along the Mississippi River "almost every
settlers house is a whiskey shop" and "truly shameful" amounts
were being sold to the Indians. When Forsyth threatened legal
action, the offenders simply retorted: "Prove it and the Justice
will fine me." Since the agent's only informants were Indians,
"no proof can be had." The Quapaw agent claimed the use of
liquor was so rampant at the Red River agency that he could
do little business with the Indians there. Several times he had
tried to assemble the Quapaws to distribute annuities, but the
"Barrells of Whisky, brought in amongst them" kept "the whole
country in an uproar." Cephas Washburn, missionary to the
Cherokee Indians west of the Mississippi, told McKenney the
"ruinous traffic" was decimating the tribe. "There has been no
pestilence, no raging epidemic here," he insisted. "The decrease
is wholly owing to the free introduction among them, of spirituous liquors."[25]

Despite his previous lack of success, McKenney once again
took up the challenge and urged his agents to ferret out and
prosecute whiskey peddlers. He told the Creek agent to enforce
the intercourse laws "vigilently, and vigoursly." To the Choctaw
agent he wrote: "Nothing short of the unwearied exertions, of
the agent, can stop the avenues to this destructive commerce.
But it is for such objects, in great part that agents are kept
among the Indians." He assured Washburn, "it is the fixed purpose here to exact of all, the utmost vigilance in preserving the
Indians from wrongs and outrages of every kind. I repeat it,
you ought not to be backward in surrendering the proof you
have against those who have at such a waste of life violated
the laws regulating trade and intercourse with the Indians."[26]

McKenney heard such unsettling reports about the wide-
spread use of whiskey by the Choctaws that he urged the agent
to persuade tribal leaders to enact laws prohibiting the sale or
use of liquor and to use the light horse, the tribal police, "to
destroy all they find, and bring it up to their Councils for punishment, all persons of their Tribe who may be found violating their

regulations." He even appealed to David Folsom, one of the leading men of the tribe, reminding him that "Choctaw Chiefs ought to be good, sensible, *sober* Men, above all things they should be *sober* men. A drunken man or a man given to drink, whether white or red, is a fool; and not fit to do business of any kind."[27]

Negligible possibly as a means of controlling the liquor traffic, but encouraging nonetheless to McKenney, was the help of those Indians aware of the evils of drink. Old Decori, a Winnebago chief, at the Prairie du Chien agency in January 1828, publicly condemned the use of liquor by his people. "Indians ought not to buy whiskey," he declared. "It is *hot in his heart for a little while*, then it is gone, the Indian is *cold*, his head is *sore*, and he does not remember what he did when the poison was in him. Whiskey is *hot-poison* for the Winnebagos. My head is like the snow with age, I have seen the ruin that it has brought upon our Nation—and I advise them, *to buy no more whiskey!*[28]

The Indian agents needed more than existing laws and McKenney's encouragement to stop the whiskey traffic. Confiscating a trader's property was not an adequate deterrent; whiskey was relatively cheap, and the possibility of quick, substantial profits more than offset the risks. Moreover, those apprehended for smuggling whiskey into the Indian country were seldom punished for their crime. In 1824 John Tipton, the Indian agent at Fort Wayne, seized goods belonging to the American Fur Company for violating the regulation against whiskey. The case was tried before the Ohio district court. The jury delivered a verdict of guilty after only fifteen minutes of deliberation, and the court ordered the trader's goods condemned. John Jacob Astor, however, appealed the case to the U.S. Supreme Court and obtained a reversal of the decision on a technicality concerning the meaning of the term "Indian Country."[29]

McKenney did close one source of liquor, scoring a minor triumph over the American Fur Company at the same time. He persuaded Secretary of War Barbour to rescind the order authorizing the company to use liquor in the Northwest. The fact that the British used whiskey in the fur trade could not justify the American policy, he reasoned. "This truly is an evil of which our Citizens have a right to complain." An elated McKenney relayed news of the change to Governor Cass. "Any discretion which may have been heretofore given not provided for by law, you will consider as withdrawn. The laws will govern." Cass objected to the new ruling, but McKenney replied that nothing short of absolute exclusion could protect the Indians. "One single license to exercise *a discretion,* as *to quantity,* you must be aware is equivalent to a universal grant. There is no controlling the evils of the practice short of *an unqualified prohibition.*"[30]

What McKenney really wanted was legislation to drive whiskey peddlers from the Indian country. "Sound policy, no less than Justice and Humanity, requires that it should be made a capital offence for any person to furnish spiritous liquor to Indians, *under any circumstances.*" This recommendation, however, was not adopted. Had it been, the government would have been in an embarrassing position, for federal officials were themselves often guilty of giving liquor to Indians. "I am in the habit of giving honest trusty Indians permission to purchase a small quantity of Whisky which I believe is customary with all Agents," the Red River agent admitted. "Granting this indulgence to Indians . . . makes them Friendly and faithful."[31]

Crimes in the Indian country also demanded much of McKenney's attention. The law specified that any person entering Indian lands to commit "robbery, larceny, trespass, or other crime" against an Indian or his property could be fined as much as $100 and imprisoned for up to twelve months; in addition he had to make restitution up to twice the value of the property stolen or destroyed. Should the injured Indian or his tribe seek revenge, however, the law was nullified.[32]

When Indians were accused of crimes against white persons, the law required only that the tribe be identified. The claimant presented the necessary evidence to the Indian agent, who in turn presented the claim to tribal leaders "for satisfaction." The Indians had eighteen months to act on the claim. If they ignored it or refused to admit their responsibility, the agent forwarded the claim to the Indian office where McKenney reviewed the documents. The sum needed to satisfy an approved claim was deducted from the next annuity payment due the tribe. If the tribe did not receive an annuity, the claimant had to apply to Congress for indemnification. Under the best of circumstances the process was time-consuming, and claims were sometimes contested for years before settlement.

McKenney was shocked to discover how little had been done to process claims before he assumed his duties. "Claims of Indians against Citizens, under the 4th Sec[tion] of the law of intercourse, and of Citizens against Indians under the 14th Section," he wrote in August 1824, "have accumulated so in the Department as to become quite a burden to the files; and none or very few of them appear to have gone thro' any of the formalities requisite to constitute a legal claim against the Government." The missing formalities were understandable. To many white men all Indians looked alike, and determining the tribes responsible for crimes could be quite difficult. Moreover, Indians were often accused of crimes they had not committed, since frontier communities suspected Indians whenever a horse or cow strayed. As McKenney explained to one claimant, the mere fact that an animal had been seen in the possession of Indians did not mean they had stolen it. They could have purchased the animal, or it could have strayed into their village.[33] Nevertheless, when McKenney rejected a claim, the petitioner inevitably appealed to his congressman for redress; many claimants, in fact, wrote directly to their congressmen, bypassing entirely the legal channels and adding to the correspondence, confusion, and delay.[34]

Indians also submitted property damage claims to the government, but few received consideration. Again, the difficulty lay in the lack of supporting evidence. Few Indians had receipts proving ownership or value of livestock. McKenney's protégé, McDonald, summarized the situation eloquently. "How easy it is for the white man to establish his claim! He is robbed; an Indian has done it—no matter what Indian;—an application to the Agent, with the proofs of the fact, restores him the value of his property. How hard the case of the Indian! ... How is he to go among a people with whose language he is unacquainted, and enter into a labyrinth of litigation in which his civilized white brothers are so frequently lost?"[35]

McDonald might also have mentioned that several states, such as Mississippi and Tennessee, did not permit Indians to testify in court, which meant that white witnesses had to act on their behalf. Few frontiersmen would risk the wrath of their neighbors to help an Indian. The Eastern Cherokee agent reported a typical case in June 1824. The Cherokee light horse brought before him a white man who had cheated a Cherokee out of $60 on tribal lands in Tennessee. The two whites who witnessed the incident refused to go to Knoxville to testify before a civil magistrate. Without the witnesses the court would have released the accused for lack of evidence. Rather than allow this, the agent turned him over to the Cherokees for punishment. They gave him thirty-nine lashes, "laid on with a very tender hand, as I understood," the agent facetiously reported.[36]

Serious crimes, such as murder, were handled less casually. When an Indian killed a white man, his tribe was asked to deliver him to federal officials. Rather than suffer the consequences of a military incursion into their country, the Indians generally complied with the demands. Frontier authorities, however, were not above holding other members of the tribe as hostages until the guilty Indian surrendered or was delivered. The accused was then taken to the nearest civil court for trial.

Court trial, McKenney discovered, did not always protect the civil rights of Indians suspected of crimes. A circuit judge might visit a frontier community only once or twice a year, meaning as much as twelve months of imprisonment for an Indian before his guilt or innocence was determined, an unfair and expensive procedure. Detained prisoners escaped, as happened when the five Chippewa murderers sawed their way out of the log jail at Michilimackinac in 1825; Indians unaccustomed to close quarters often died in jail. Furthermore, the tribes strongly opposed imprisonment. Jury trials were meaningless to them, and when they surrendered a criminal, they expected and demanded a quick death penalty.[37]

The case of Red Bird and his five followers well illustrates the problems of trying Indian criminals. McKenney, who took special interest in the proceedings because of his involvement, demanded an immediate trial after the Indians were arrested in September 1827. Yet everything worked against speedy justice. The regular session for the Prairie du Chien court was not scheduled until May 1828. Witnesses were so scattered between Prairie du Chien and Green Bay, a distance of more than four hundred miles, that it took a federal marshal to find them and

bring them to the trial. The court further needed a French-
and Winnebago-speaking interpreter. Finally, a jury had to be
selected, and, Cass pointed out, of the scarcely 450 people who
lived in the area, few were competent to serve as jurors.[38]

Meanwhile, Red Bird and his companions were jailed in
Prairie du Chien with two other Winnebago murder suspects
who had already been confined without trial for more than a
year. By January 1828 Red Bird's people began to grow restless
about the long imprisonment. They informed the Winnebago
agent that when "the murderers were delivered up to the whites,
. . . we expected they would immediately be shot. This, was our
desire. Indians do not love to know, that their fellow Indians,
are living, in confinement, with *Iron on them*, where they cannot
see the Sun in the day upon the plains, or the Moon in the
night. We are ready to hear that those who murdered white-men,
are killed—But our faces are blackened *for* sorrow—our hearts
are big with grief, & our lips are closed-up; when we come to see
our Father [the agent], and look towards the walls that hide
our fellow Indians." Long confinement took its toll, and a month
later Red Bird died. McKenney regretted his untimely death,
"as well from the previous suffering which it presupposes; as
from the loss of the example which hanging would have produced."[39]

The trial was not held until September 24, 1828, a full year
after the crime had been committed. Two of the remaining
prisoners were sentenced to death, and five were released, including the two Winnebagos held since 1826. Although evidently
guilty, they were freed after an imprisonment of two years and
five months because no witnesses appeared at their trial.[40]

"Something ought to be done to change the necessity of
keeping immured so long, Indians who commit violence, and
who ought to die for their acts," McKenney wrote to Superintendent Clark after Red Bird's death. "The forms of our Courts
in their cases ought to be changed, in so far as the nature of the
required testimony is concerned. It should suffice if an Indian
surrenders himself, or is surrendered by his Tribe for murder.
—In either case, the verdict of the Jury should be resolved into
the act of such surrenders, that act should be the proof, and
the culprit executed." But, he lamented, " 'til that is done, we
shall go on slip-shod, as we have gone on."[41]

In the converse situation, when a white man murdered an Indian, arrest and conviction were not quite so simple. Juries were less likely to punish and much less likely to execute white murderers. In fact, by McKenney's time the government ordinarily compensated the families of murdered or injured Indians with $100 or $200 in goods or money. The payment was intended to appease the Indians, not to absolve the government from its obligation to find and punish the murderers, but the practice nevertheless offended McKenney's sensibilities. Indians came to expect the payment, he felt, and once they received it seemed content to forget about the due process of law. "You will impress it upon the kindred and friends of the murdered Indians," he informed one agent who had just paid off several grieving families, "that the Govt would prefer to see them less willing to commute their loss for money, and more disposed to take the application of the law in punnishing the murderers as the satisfaction due to such deeds."[42]

Not all white men escaped retribution for their crimes against Indians, however. Three were hanged for the wanton murder in March 1824 of nine Indians in Madison County, Indiana. John Johnston, the Indian agent, informed McKenney that he arranged for fifty Indians to witness the execution of two of the white men. "The character and justice of the country will for once be vindicated in the minds of the natives," he wrote.[43]

Intertribal warfare was not covered by the provisions of the 1802 intercourse law, but federal officials tried to react swiftly to prevent its outbreak because the combatants might vent their hostilities on American citizens and because such warfare necessarily cost the lives of innocent Indian women and children. "Humanity directs that these people, who sport so with each other's lives," McKenney wrote, "should be counselled frequently, and led, if possible, to cherish the more agreeable state of peace and friendship."[44]

When one tribe committed an act of violence against another, the nearest federal official would try to intercede before the victims initiated retaliatory measures. Presents to the injured party might settle the affair immediately. Unfortunately, it was usually the case that by the time federal authorities heard of the hostile action, both tribes would be involved in at least sporadic fighting. In such circumstances, the Indian agents would try to bring the contending factions to a conference where they could threaten government intervention and dispense gifts liberally to each side. Sometimes, however, even sterner measures were needed. When warfare broke out between Sioux and Chippewa warriors in the upper Mississippi country in the spring of 1830, Governor Cass recommended that the army hold several principal chiefs from both tribes as hostages to enforce peace. McKenney strongly endorsed the idea. "It is useless to compromise by Treaty alone. This was tried in 1825 at Prairie Du Chien with those same Indians," he wrote. "Power must be employed, & they must be *commanded* to desist, & made to do so."[45]

For the most part McKenney occupied a lowly administrative post within the federal bureaucracy. His was a tedious, thankless job far less glamorous than riding in canopied canoes through the wilds of Michigan Territory. In handling claims, crimes, and the other day-to-day details of the Indian service he had to follow well-established precedents and procedures that left little latitude for interpretation or innovation. But McKenney also made significant contributions to the development of federal Indian policy. He was a major architect of the civilization and removal programs, two of the government's most important policies for the management of Indian affairs in the first half of the nineteenth century.

10

The Failure of Indian Reform

Of ALL THE PROGRAMS McKenney monitored as superintendent of Indian affairs none was as dear to him as the school system which he had launched with such hope and confidence in 1819. His pride in the schools was justified, for few of them would have been established without his encouragement and support while superintendent of Indian trade. Indeed, the schools almost did not survive his absence from office because the civilization program was not popular. Congress continually demanded progress reports, and as early as 1822 the House of Representatives tried to repeal the legislation authorizing the civilization fund.[1] The missionaries and their associates must have welcomed McKenney's return to the Indian department.

One of McKenney's first acts was to bring the school system under rudimentary administrative control. By May he had designed and sent to the school superintendents printed forms for their annual reports. He did this, he said, "to obtain the information in relation to the several schools in the Indian country in a more uniform & condensed mode." McKenney wanted the missionaries to prepare the forms "with great care" and to report "in detail, the prospects of the School, the disposition of the

185

Indians, whether more or less favourable to it, the names of
the teachers and other persons, and the kind of property belonging to the institution." They were also to note "any thing remarkable in the progress of any Indian child, accompanied by
his or her age, and the tribe to which he or she belongs; the
general health of the children, their advances in the work of
civilization with such remarks as may be deemed useful as to
the climate, soil & productions of the surrounding country."
McKenney first used the forms in the fall of 1824; and, he
proudly explained to Secretary of War Calhoun, they "produced
a system in their reports, out of which a general exhibit of all
that relates to this Branch of the Indian Department can be
furnished with facility and accuracy, at the close of each year."[2]

The returns showed that the civilization fund had fulfilled
its purpose beyond McKenney's most optimistic expectations. In
March 1819, when the bill had been passed, McKenney knew
of only four schools in the Indian country: two Cherokee schools
had a combined enrollment of 75 students; two Seneca schools
were on a reservation in New York, but McKenney did not know
their exact location or enrollment. Now in 1824 there were
thirty-two schools teaching 916 Indian children. The reports
from the superintendents convinced McKenney that "no in-
superable difficulty is in the way of a complete reformation of
the principles and pursuits of the American Indian." In fact,
on the basis of these early returns he rashly assured the secretary
of war there was "good reason to believe that an entire reformation may be effected (I mean among the Tribes bordering our
settlements, and to whom those benefits have been extended) in
the course of the present generation." All that was needed, he
concluded, was added support for the system "as its enlarge-
ment may be required" and "the same zeal and Intelligence
which have so far characterized those who superintend, and
conduct it."[3]

McKenney believed the schools were following the right
method of civilizing the Indians. He was well aware that since
the discovery of America there had been many attempts to
civilize and convert the Indians, but the failures, he thought,
had been the result of two basic mistakes. The early missionaries learned and used native languages; in the new schools the
missionaries taught the Indians English. The early missionaries

began with instruction in morality and virtue; the new system taught the Indians first of all to work for a living.[4]

McKenney considered the use of English the essential improvement. "I have always, myself, esteemed language to be the very centre of the power which is to reform and bless our Indians," he explained, "—language I mean, not only of the right sort, itself, but *rightly applied*. It is this which, after all, is to effect the change in the character and destiny of these people. It is the lever by which they are to elevate themselves into intellectual and moral distinction—And I prefer our own to be put into their hands, to any other." Although he had been impressed with the genius that George Guess displayed in inventing the Cherokee syllabary, McKenney viewed the discovery as a mixed blessing, useful perhaps to the older generation of Indians who might not be willing or able to learn English. He prohibited teaching Cherokee to the children. "I care not how soon they forget altogether their own language," he admitted, "altho' this is not necessary—they may retain both. But I believe the less of it that is taught, or spoken, the better for the Indians. There [sic] whole character, inside and out; language, and morals, must be changed."[5]

McKenney also approved of the change in subject matter. Virtue and morality were important, he believed, but they were not suitable as the first lessons for a savage people. "I am not combatting your belief that the Gospel is to do every thing," he explained to Cyrus Kingsbury. But, he declared, "I am clear in the belief that whilst the preaching of the Gospel is essential, that the *teaching*, in the arts of life, and in the means appointed for man's more certain subsistence, ought not to be neglected." Indians must first be taught to work. "Nothing is more clear than that without the *habit* of labor, man will not prosecute it. Nor will these habits keep him to his task, after his necessities shall cease to compel him. It is in man's nature to be idle. Labor is painful. Education and habit alone, can reconcile him to it. It is upon this basis the present school system rests," McKenney wrote. "It is hoped it may never be departed from, for if it shall be, the work of reformation among the Indians is lost."[6]

To assist the work of reformation, McKenney occasionally sent what he considered useful teaching aids to the missionaries. When superintendent of Indian trade, for example, he urged them to adopt the novel *No Fiction* as a textbook. Published anonymously in England in 1819, the book was a bestseller among humanitarian circles of the day. Its value, as the author wrote in the preface, lay in the "importance of its lessons, and the truth of its delineations."[7] The plot concerned a young man who rebelled against his religious training, strayed into a life of vice, and then, after several severe emotional experiences, once again embraced his religious beliefs, thereby regaining his former peace of mind. McKenney convinced Calhoun to authorize the purchase of at least two copies of the work for the Cherokee and Choctaw mission schools. Praising the book's high moral tone, McKenney assured Calhoun that *No Fiction* would show Indian children how to develop rapidly "the chief points for the government of the human passions."[8]

No Fiction was not the only book McKenney promoted. In 1827 he asked Secretary of War Barbour to send free copies of *Sketches of a Tour to the Lakes* to the mission schools. Arguing on questionable grounds that the book was "at least, part Indian," he added: "It might not be amiss to forward one to each of the agencies also." Barbour probably found more persuasive a note from McKenney's old friend Richard M. Johnson, who with three of his cronies in Congress urged the secretary of war to give *Sketches* "as a present" to the missionaries. "It is a work which will interest them, and which we consider in courtesy due to them," the congressmen claimed. Barbour bought sixty copies from the printer at $4 each. Only one clergyman acknowledged the gift; he told McKenney he found the book "very interesting" and promised to explain to his charges those parts that "exhibit your friendship for the Indian race."[9] The value of the book to the Indians is conjectural.

No doubt the missionaries found more beneficial the small medals McKenney sent to be used as "premiums" during the school year. "You will use them in your discretion," he wrote, "and give them to the most worthy." The medals fitted in nicely with the Lancasterian system of instruction, and one missionary said that he awarded them "as badges of honour to distinguish the most industrious students & intend to distribute others as marks of decided approbation among such children as may leave the school with our consent after making satisfactory progress in their studies."[10]

Occasionally more advanced students would thank McKenney personally for his interest in their welfare. Although the missionaries probably encouraged the letters, McKenney found them gratifying nonetheless. "Your letter . . . came safe to hand, and I have read it with great pleasure," he replied to David Baldwin, a student at Elliot. "You are a full blooded Choctaw—and yet, altho' some men say Indians, to learn, must have white blood in them, yet your letter proves that the Indian's blood is no blacker or thicker than the white man's. No—we are 'all made of one blood'—So says the good book, and every word in it is true." McKenney sent medals to David and to two of his classmates who had also written.[11]

Most of the mission schools were patterned after Brainerd. One that differed was the Choctaw Academy, a boarding school for Choctaw boys operated under the auspices of the Southern Baptist Association at Blue Springs, Kentucky, on the plantation of Richard M. Johnson, an ardent Baptist and a member of Congress. Because the school was not on Indian land, it was not eligible for support from the civilization fund; it was financed largely with proceeds of the sale of Choctaw lands. In the treaty of cession of 1820 the federal government had agreed to set aside fifty-four sections of land to be sold "for the purpose of raising a fund, to be applied to the support of the Choctaw schools, on both sides of the Mississippi River." An annual payment of $6,000, promised by the treaty of 1825 for the "support of schools in said nation," supplemented the fund. Shortly after ratification of the latter treaty, tribal leaders had prevailed on President Adams to allow the establishment of the school in Kentucky for Choctaw boys who had progressed beyond the elementary education offered by the mission schools in their own country, and the tribe agreed to conduct the school according to regulations established by the Indian office.[12]

The Choctaw Academy opened November 1, 1825, with an enrollment of fifty-five. The school's advanced curriculum, which included surveying, natural and moral philosophy, bookkeeping, history, algebra, and astronomy, soon attracted applications from other students. The Choctaws allowed boys from other tribes as well as a few white youths from neighboring communities to attend for $250 a year. In the fall of 1830 the Indian students at the academy consisted of fifty-eight Choctaws, thirteen Creeks, fourteen Potawatomis, three Miamis, and one Osage.[13] McKenney thought bringing these boys together was the best possible method of promoting the future peace and friendship of the tribes represented at the school; he hoped to see the day when all tribes and races could live together in one large community free from strife and jealousy. The Choctaw Academy probably did not contribute much toward this utopian goal, but the school's administrators did claim one benefit from their experiment. "We have discovered from actual observation," they reported to Secretary of War Eaton, "that when the school is composed of youths from different tribes that a laudable emulation is excited, & consequently their progress in learning is proportionably greater, and moreover, they learn to speak our language much sooner having necessarily to converse in the english language."[14]

Sons of prominent Indian leaders often did not attend mission schools. Instead they went east for their education, their expenses borne by relatives or by the government if the family was particularly important. McKenney, during his federal career, took a direct hand in educating four such boys, including James McDonald. The others were Dougherty Colbert, a Chickasaw; William Barnard, a Creek; and Lee Compere, a Uchee. McKenney's apparent success with McDonald doubtless encouraged him to accept responsibility for the other boys, who like McDonald provided excellent examples of the efficacy of the civilization program. Seldom did McKenney miss an opportunity to bring their scholarly attainments to the attention of visiting Indians, congressmen, and even the president himself. McKenney admitted that care for the boys was motivated equally by Christian charity and policy—"policy, because there is no so direct way of securing the confidence and friendship of the Indians, as to notice, and cherish their children." Although he developed a sincere regard for them, none ever enjoyed the relationship McDonald once held.[15]

Dougherty Colbert was about fifteen when his father, Levi, a prominent Chickasaw chief, brought him to Washington in December 1824 and left him with McKenney. Like McDonald, the boy lived with the McKenney family at Weston, and the colonel closely supervised his schoolwork. "You can say to [his father] . . . that Dougherty is improving now, rapidly," Mc-

Kenney wrote the Chickasaw agent a year later. "His appearance and manners are beginning to do him credit, and he is considered a promising boy at school, and much liked and attended to by all the young men. He will lose his Chickasaw language in a few years—it is slipping away from him very fast."[16]

Since Colbert wished to be a surveyor, McKenney in April 1827 sent him to the Choctaw Academy for further study. His farewell to the boy indicates the warmth of their relationship. "To morrow morning you leave me, to go to your Father. I part from you with the feelings of a sincere friend; and can never be indifferent to your welfare. For two years you have lived in my family. I have often counseled and advised you," wrote McKenney. He could not resist one last sermon: "Now, my poor boy, as we are about to part, I can do no more than urge upon you the lessons I have endeavored to teach you—and remember, the *world is wicked*. You will find but little in it to make you happy." Nevertheless, McKenney advised, "remember that God sees you in every place; be industrious, gentle, kind, for bearing, and you will prosper." An entry in President Adams' diary, dated April 2, 1827, indicates that the boy made his rounds before leaving Washington: "Colbert is a Chickasaw Indian youth about 17, who has been living two years for education with Col. M'Kenney and being now on the point of departure to return home, came to take leave."[17]

McKenney's relations with Lee Compere and William Barnard did not end as pleasantly. Lee was about ten and William thirteen when the superintendent met the boys on his southern tour in 1827. At the insistence—McKenney claimed—of parents and relatives, he brought the youngsters to Washington, placing them with the Reverend James McVain of Georgetown for schooling. They boarded with the McKenneys, who now resided in a rowhouse on First Street, until President Andrew Jackson separated them in October 1830. Following his dismissal, McKenney sought desperately to take them to Philadelphia, but Jackson refused permission despite a last-minute plea from the boys. "Great Father," wrote William in a bold, careful hand, "we are in trouble—our friend Col McKenney is going away— we want to go with him—we dont want to stay Here without him   He is our friend   we love him   he is good to us   Do not Father let us be taken away from him—we ask you to Let

us go with him   He is like a Father to us   we come from our
nation with him   when we leave him we want to go back—But
we Do not want to go back if we can go with him   We come to
see our Father with this talk—we hope he will not deny what
we come for." The boys lived with McVain for two years before
returning to Georgia with a delegation of Creeks. McKenney
never learned what became of them. "Of William," he later recalled, "I heard that he never recovered from his depression—
became desperate—and, getting into an Indian quarrel, a fight
ensued, in which some of the parties were killed ... and [he]
joined the Seminoles in Florida. Of Lee, I have never heard
anything."[18]

Despite McKenney's expectations, the civilization program
did not revolutionize Indian reform. In fact, by 1826 McKenney
began to question the value of the movement. Several considerations apparently influenced his thinking, not the least of which
was a breakdown in personal communications. Antagonism often
developed between the men of the cloth and the less idealistic
Indian agents. John Crowell, the Creek agent, thought the missionaries were wasting their time with "uninformed Savages who
neither understood their language nor believed in the truth of
their doctrines" and told one "preaching was fudge." Major
John F. Hamtramck, agent for the Osages, evidently vented his
opinions to the local missionary in somewhat stronger language.
Calling William Clark's attention to Hamtramck's views, Mc-
Kenney regretted that "such terms" had been used in the
presence of a clergyman. "It is to be hoped when Major Hamtramck shall become better acquainted with the worth of these
excellent people he may feel inclined to be more respectful to
them."[19]

McKenney thought the conflict serious enough to issue a
strongly worded circular reprimanding the agents. "It is deemed
to be of the utmost importance," he wrote, "that all agents bearing the authority of the Government, and whose personal connexion is direct with the Indians, should *sanction*, and *second*,
this plan of renovating the morals and enlightening and improving these unfortunate people, and by the observance, in
all their intercourse with them, of a conduct strictly moral."
Opponents of the civilization program in effect opposed the
government itself, bringing it into contempt in the eyes of the

Indians, the very people whom the schools were to benefit. "That the system of Indian improvement may not be subject to consequences so unfavorable, nor the Government to implications so disgraceful, as the keeping in commission Officers whose conduct tends to frustrate its own designs, the Secretary of War directs that you receive these as the views of the Department on this subject, with its determination to have them carried, in all respects, into comple[te] effect."[20]

Much to McKenney's chagrin, the missionaries often antagonized the Indians as well as the agents. Most of the missionaries were admirably motivated, but, one Choctaw pointed out to McKenney, "some will be found among them, who are inefficient, bigotted, or overzealous."[21] Missionary enthusiam appears to have been the biggest problem. The civilization act did not forbid preaching, and the proselytizing of the missionaries was a source of friction. While the Indians may have been receptive to education for their children, they balked at religious instruction.

The Creeks, for example, demanded assurances that no preaching would be done if they allowed a school to be built in their country. Despite the firm stance taken by tribal leaders, Lee Compere, the missionary to the Creeks, began conducting worship services at his home and giving religious instruction to those Indians who knew English. He preached not only to the Indians but also to their Negro slaves. Compere ignored McKenney's repeated warnings and continued the practice. One Sunday in May 1828, a band of Creek warriors entered his house during services and ransacked the rooms "under the pretence of searching for the Black people." They took the slaves they found into the yard and, Compere reported, "beat them unmercifully." The incident ended Compere's effectiveness among the Creeks and he soon left.[22]

The Passamaquoddy Indians, many of whom were Catholic, opposed their schoolteacher's efforts to make Episcopalians of their children. Tribal leaders appealed to McKenney to remove the missionary. McKenney refused, but he allowed the tribe to divide its $300 grant from the civilization fund and use $200 for maintenance of the school and $100 for support of a Catholic priest. "It is no part of the policy of the United States Government to force upon any Indians the belief in, or observance of

any of the religious creeds," McKenney assured the Passamaquoddy leaders. "If you prefer the Catholic Religion, there is
not the slightest objection against your doing so."[23]

McKenney was further discouraged by the inadequacy of
the school system. Seldom did a tribe have more than one school,
thus only a few children could be educated. These exercised
little influence on the rest of the tribe, and once removed from
the academic environment the children quickly reverted to their
former habits. McKenney wanted to expand the school system
"to embrace the entire body of Indian children to whose tribes
it may be extended. Without this," he pointed out, "they will
have to contend with opposing influences, and their progress
will be less rapid. The examples of those not embraced by it,
will be necessarily felt. It is in the nature of man to imitate,
and it being easier to imitate bad habits than good, the former
will predominate, and especially among a people where the
checks arising out of public opinion, and which apply to social
and moral actions, are less regarded than are those which demand the exercise of self-denial and the sterner virtues."[24]

McKenney also considered it imperative to make provision
for students who completed their studies. He recommended, in
advance of his time, that they be given a section of land, a house,
and an assortment "of agricultural or other implements suited
to the occupations in which they may be disposed, respectively,
to engage." Such a course would be wise and humane. Before
going to school, the Indian had been content with the wilderness
because he had known no better; once exposed to the finer
things in life he would become disillusioned, frustrated, and
discontented unless they were available to him. The student's
only alternative, McKenney claimed, "is to turn Indian again;
and too often by his improved intelligence he becomes the op-
pressor of his less cultivated brothers." With a home and business, McKenney thought, the educated Indian could be an
example to his own people and to whites, "an intermediate link
between our own citizens, and our wandering neighbors, soften-
ing the shades of each, and enjoying the confidence of both."
Despite the foresight embodied in these suggestions, they were
not adopted, although the War Department did give Kingsbury
$150 to buy tools for two Indian boys who had finished their
course of study at Elliot. The boys, Kingsbury said, had "ac-

quired a sufficient knowledge of the Mechanic Arts to understand and need the use of them."[25]

Undeniably, the lack of money to finance the school system properly was a major problem. The civilization fund quite successfully lured participants into the field of Indian education, but the $10,000 quickly proved insufficient to fill the demand. The lion's share of the fund went to the American Board of Commissioners for Foreign Missions. Of the thirty-eight schools in the Indian country in 1825, the American Board operated sixteen and received $4,350; ten other societies shared the rest. Amounts ranged from the maximum of $1,000 a year for Brainerd with its enrollment of eighty-four students to $100 a year for several schools with enrollments of a dozen or so.[26]

McKenney had presumed that after the program proved itself Congress would enlarge the appropriation. This Congress steadfastly refused to do—an outrageous development, in McKenney's view. "Numerous applications for assistance, and from the most respectable societies are now on file in this office," he complained to Barbour in the fall of 1826, "to which it has not been possible to return any other answer than that *the fund appropriated by the Congress is exhausted.*"[27]

McKenney was even angrier when, shortly thereafter, he discovered the civilization fund was oversubscribed by $3,783.33. For several years few schools asked for aid and the fund built up a surplus. When the demands for aid increased McKenney gave out the surplus as well as the basic amount. He blamed the Treasury Department for the discrepancy even though his own miscalculations probably caused the error. Regardless of who was at fault, McKenney had to inform the religious societies sharing the fund that their allotments would be reduced to make up the difference. *"Necessity,* therefore, and not choice," he explained to one missionary, "imposed this new apportionment upon the Department."[28] The societies received only $7,150 each year until 1829 when the fund recorded a surplus of $2,335.06. McKenney had learned his lesson and this time did not touch the surplus. He kept it as a contingency fund, he explained to Secretary of War Porter, "in the support of additional schools, or when necessity may require it, in meeting the wants of those now in operation."[29]

The lack of funds adversely affected the growth of the civilization program. While there had been a prospect of substantial federal support for the schools, the religious societies had been more than willing to invest their own assets in the system. Thus, in 1824 and 1825 the societies received $12,708.48 and $13,620.41 from the government, and they in turn invested $170,147.52 and $176,700.44. In the fall of 1825 the number of schools was thirty-eight and the enrollment 1,159. With the cutback in the federal contribution to the school system, however, expansion practically ceased for a time. In 1826 the number of students was 1,245, up only 86 from the year before. In 1827 enrollment dropped to 1,161. The annual report for 1828 listed forty schools but only 19 more students than the year before. When McKenney left office in 1830, there were only fifty-two schools and 1,512 students.[30]

In an attempt to salvage the education program, the ever-resourceful McKenney began casting about for other sources of revenue. Annuities were one possibility. He saw no reason why at least some of the money the tribes received could not legitimately be applied to support the school system, which, after all, had been established for their benefit.

Therefore, McKenney made a determined effort to siphon some of the annuity money off to the schools. He begged Clark to use his influence to divert to the education program one-sixth of the $60,000 the tribes in his jurisdiction received yearly. In 1830 McKenney asked the agents for the Winnebago, Chippewa, Ottawa, and Potawatomi Indians to encourage those tribes to apply some of their $34,000 to schools. He urged the Chickasaws to use $10,000 of their $35,000 annuity to educate their children. It was only necessary, he explained to the tribal leaders, to write to the president; for their convenience he enclosed for their signature a letter to Jackson making the request.[31]

On the other hand, any tribe's attempt to withdraw support from the civilization program dismayed McKenney. Early in 1829 the Chickasaws decided to stop their $2,500 annual contribution to their school. "Some evil spirit has put you up to this," McKenney protested. "Some secret bad people who want your money. Shut your ears to them both—and listen to me. . . . I appeal to your good sense. I know you. You are not fools. You will see that I reason correctly for you. No—no—you gave the annuity. Let it alone until the Government sees it is not properly applied, and then it shall be applied in some other way. I promise you this. I never yet broke my word with you."[32]

In one respect, McKenney's efforts were successful. In 1824 the Indian tribes applied about $8,750 to education. By 1830 the amount had increased to $21,000 a year, more than twice the sum provided by the civilization fund. However, by the spring of 1830 McKenney was ready to admit that the civilization program was a failure. He reached this agonizing assessment when the Senate Committee on Indian Affairs asked for a report on the success of the civilization program and the progress made in the previous decade. In addition to the annual reports from the school superintendents, McKenney turned to his field officials for summary statements of evaluation. Reading their replies must have been painful to him. Governor Cass was not aware of any improvement in the condition of the Chippewa, Ottawa, and Potawatomi Indians. "On the contrary," he wrote, "from the progress of our settlements and the greater facilities afforded for the introduction of whiskey into their Country, I believe every year adds to the moral and physical evils, which surround them." Equally depressing was the reply from John Dougherty, the Upper Missouri agent. "It may be truly said," he wrote of the tribes in his area, "that they have made no advances in any of the means of civilization . . . and as to 'education' there is not a single Indian man, woman, or child, to my knowledge, from the head of the Missouri to the mouth of the Kanzas river, that knows one letter from another."[33]

Reporting to the Senate committee, McKenney admitted that except for those relatively few Indians who had attended school, no progress had been made. For the most part, the moral and physical condition of the Indians was growing worse every year. "Of the Florida Indians," he wrote, "it may suffice to say, their condition is in all respects truly deplorable." Of the other southern tribes, only the mixed-bloods "lived well." The Indians in the north "catch fish—and plant patches of corn; dance, paint, hunt, fight, get drunk when they can get liquor, and often starve." The minor tribes, such as the Narragansetts, Biloxi, and Caddos, "are at best stationary; and the most of them are fast verging towards total extinction."[34]

Perhaps one clue for McKenney's dramatic change of heart

lies in his relationship with McDonald. Despite the colonel's great hopes, the young Choctaw never fulfilled his promise. The carefully groomed example of the potential of the educated Indian crumbled emotionally under the burden he carried. Instead of emerging as the intellectual leader of the Choctaws, the Tallyrand of the tribe, McDonald slipped into obscurity and alcoholism.

McKenney became aware of the problem in late 1824 when McDonald accompanied the Choctaw delegation to Washington. The young lawyer played an important part in wresting from the government the most favorable terms to that time given a tribe for a land cession, but McDonald paid a personal price for his tribe's triumph. As the negotiations dragged on, he drank more and more heavily. "I sought all proper opportunities to restore him," McKenney recalled. "On one occasion I detained him in my office, after the rest of the delegation had retired, and, locking the door, spoke to him on his fall with every tenderness that I could employ."

"I had looked to you as the crowning of my hopes, and trusted to see, from your continued good example, a day-star arise for the enlightening of your race," McKenney said. "Remember those days of innocence, and honor, and bliss, you enjoyed at Weston?"

"Spare me! oh, spare me!" McDonald exclaimed. "It is that thought that makes me so miserable. I have lost that sweet home, and its endearments; the veil that was so kindly placed between me and my Indian caste, has since been torn away. I have been made to see since, that I cannot, whilst such anomolous relations exist as do exist between the red and the white race, be other than a *degraded outcast!*"[35]

Not once in the seven months McDonald was in Washington did he visit Weston. In fact, after his departure in June 1825, McDonald never again saw McKenney, although the two men corresponded.

A few months after he returned to Mississippi, the young Indian tried to reassure his mentor that the drinking had been a temporary phase. "I think, Sir, that you need entertain no apprehension that my dissipation had been confirmed to habit. It was a fearful experiment; and the occasional disposition of my feelings gave to it a character of recklessness which must

have been truly painful to every judicious friend." He had
learned a valuable lesson, he explained. "We shall meet again,
I trust, under different circumstances, and under more happy
auspices. Without the hope and the expectation of yet doing
something grateful to the feelings of my friends, and honourable
to myself, life would have but few charms for me."[36]

McKenney, however, was not prepared to forgive and forget.
McDonald's public dissipation had been a keen embarrassment
—this after all the education and special favors he had heaped
on the boy. No, McKenney would not dismiss the episode as a
temporary lapse, although in the spring of 1826 McDonald
again pled for forgiveness. "I should be glad to hear from you,"
he wrote McKenney. "Your two last letters have been entirely
of an official character. They are perfectly satisfactory; but I
should be glad to hear something more of your prospects, Mrs.
McKenney's health, et caetera. I see you offer Weston for rent.
That is a spot most dearly cherished in my memory of all that
I have seen, or ever expect to see." McKenney did not reply.
The following December, in a letter to a mutual acquaintance,
McKenney wrote: "I have done all I could to save him." Mc-
Kenney could not bring himself to forgive the errant Choctaw,
perhaps because he could not accept blame himself for placing
unbearable pressure on McDonald. Patron and protégé remained
estranged until the summer of 1831 when, after a white woman
rejected his proposal of marriage, McDonald either fell or jumped
from a cliff to his death.[37]

The tragedy shocked McKenney into the realization that
civilizing the Indians involved far more than simply teaching
them English and making them into farmers. What was to
become of educated Indians? Imitating white culture was one
thing; being accepted by white society was another. Obviously
more time was needed—time for the Indians to adapt to the
complexities of a completely new way of life and time for the
Americans to accept the idea of civilized Indians with equal
rights and benefits. For this reason—to buy time—McKenney
turned to the removal program as the last best hope for the
Indians.

11
Indian Removal

THROUGHOUT THE COLONIAL period the effect of white settlement in America was to push the aborigines westward, erode their populations, and degrade their cultures. By McKenney's time many eastern tribes had already disappeared; he thought others would soon follow them into oblivion. McKenney, despite his initial optimism, soon realized the Indian propensity for acquiring the white man's vices eclipsed whatever progress the tribes made toward civilization. The Indians somehow had to undergo at their own pace the slow process of acculturation. Although McKenney never completely abandoned his civilization program or lost faith in the schools, he came to accept Indian removal—not as an alternative to civilization but as a prerequisite. On a permanent reservation west of the Mississippi River, undisturbed and isolated from the degenerating influence of the whites, the Indians could learn a new way of life.

Other pressures for Indian removal were older and less humanitarian. White planters wanted the large tracts of rich land that the powerful and populous southern tribes occupied. On April 24, 1802, Georgia ceded to the United States her claims to western lands; in return the federal government agreed to extinguish Indian titles to land within Georgia as soon as it could be done peaceably on reasonable terms. The following year President Jefferson suggested that the United States relocate the eastern tribes somewhere in newly acquired Louisiana north of 31° latitude.[1]

By the end of the Jefferson administration the government made overtures to the Cherokees to persuade them to move across the Mississippi, but the War of 1812 intervened before an adequate land exchange could be developed. Although a few Cherokees in 1817 removed to an area that two years later became part of Arkansas Territory, the Creeks and Cherokees in Georgia had no intention of leaving their homes. Georgia citizens grew more and more impatient, pressuring both the Indians and the government to comply with the 1802 compact. President Monroe, hoping to avoid a direct confrontation with the Georgians, reopened the subject of removal. In his annual message to Congress on December 7, 1824, the president suggested that all Indians residing in the eastern states be invited and persuaded to move across the Mississippi River. Monroe realized removal would be expensive, but he saw no other solution.[2]

Secretary of War Calhoun endorsed the removal proposal and directed McKenney to compile a summary list of all the Indians residing within the states and territories. The summary was to include the number of Indians east of the Mississippi River, the names of the tribes, and the amount of land each tribe claimed. McKenney determined that there were 97,000 Indians claiming some 77,000,000 acres of land; the area proposed for their relocation contained at least 134,579,000 acres of unsettled land. An equitable exchange seemed possible. Calhoun, in a report dated January 24, 1825, relayed this information to the president.[3]

A short three days later, Monroe in a special message to Congress advocated moving the Indians across the Mississippi to land that would be "satisfactory to themselves and honorable to the United States." He also recommended for the Indians "a system of internal government which shall protect their property from invasion, and, by the regular process of improvement and civilization, prevent that degeneracy which has generally marked the transition from the one to the other state." No force would be used or needed to encourage the Indians to emigrate, Monroe said. The prospect of a home beyond white interference would be inducement enough to leave the East.[4]

McKenney gave the policy his wholehearted support and immediately began to promote it. He obtained reprints of the president's message and distributed them liberally to field officials, missionaries, religious societies, and Indian leaders. "I enclose herewith the Message of the President to Congress on a subject of great interest to all Indians," McKenney wrote Cherokee chief Charles Hicks. "At present I will make no comment on it, further than, that the design is one of the kindest that has ever been perfected; and if carried into effect, would in my opinion, perpetuate the Aboriginal race, elevate it to its proper dignity; and impart to it a perpetuity of happiness."[5]

McKenney viewed removal as a great colonization venture. "It is my opinion," he wrote, ". . . that nothing can preserve our Indians but a plan well matured, and suitably sustained, in which they shall be placed under a Government, of which they shall form part, and in a colonial relation to the United States." Across the Mississippi the tribes would have time to adapt to the white man's way of life. "I once, like you, hoped for complete success," he wrote to Cyrus Kingsbury, "before I was compelled to let go the hope to which I had like you, been so long clinging, as wholly delusive. It is as much impossible to redeem the Natives *situated as they are*, and elevate their condition, and place them on a level with ourselves, as it would be for you, or I, to raise the dead."[6]

Territorial status for the colony and education for the Indians were essential components of McKenney's interpretation of the removal program. If Indian territory functioned like the other United States territories, and eventual statehood was the goal, white men could not take land away from the Indians as easily as they had in the past. Once the integrity of their lands was guaranteed, McKenney thought, the Indians could proceed along the path to civilization. "They must be placed under the operation of such a system as is that which is known from the beginning to have operated upon the white man in improving and elevating his nature," he explained to another missionary. "And this embraces all our domestic, social, relative, and political privileges—With these, and other hopes they would inspire, and in a Territory of their own to be connected with our Government like our other Territories, the Indians would be saved."[7]

McKenney did not believe all Indians were prepared for self-government, but he trusted education to remedy the defect. He proposed doubling the civilization fund; he suggested sending a "corps of educated young [white] men" into the territory to help the Indians build their houses and start their farms. McKenney thought there were enough educated Indians within each tribe to make the colonial experiment feasible. The Cherokees were especially important to his scheme. McKenney considered them the most civilized and thus best able "to impart to their Brethren in their new homes, the benefits of the Civilized state; and to enjoy under the form of Government what it has been proposed to adopt for them some of its rewards and honors."[8]

McKenney naively believed that a majority of the Indians would accept and welcome the removal program. He realized not every individual would want to leave his home, so he anticipated exceptions. Self-sufficient Indians could remain behind if they insisted. "Suitable provisions, in lands, and otherwise" as well as "the privileges and immunities of Citizens of the Republic" would be extended to those who stayed. McKenney suggested Indians judged incompetent to subsist on their own should be taken by the hand like children and led across the Mississippi. This condescending statement might be construed as evidence that he condoned the use of force. In fact, the superintendent viewed force absolutely as a last resort, an alternative to be used only after all other forms of inducement had failed. *"You will never be pushed off your land,"* McKenney assured Choctaw leader David Folsom. "If you go, it will be by your own consent, and free will. Therefore do not be uneasy. You know me. I will never deceive you. Therefore mind my words. Tell your people this. It is true the Government think it best for you to be altogether—and on lands that will be forever your own;—But you will not be forced."[9]

Whatever the inspiration for the removal program, whatever the intent of the federal government, whatever grandiose plans McKenney had in mind, the tribes unanimously rejected removal. The Cherokees, Creeks, Choctaws, and Chickasaws—the tribes toward which the program was primarily directed—were the most vehemently opposed. Between 1789 and 1825 the Cherokees had made twelve treaties with the United States surrendering lands or agreeing to new boundaries. In the same period the Creeks had made eight similar treaties, the Choctaws six, the Chickasaws four.[10] The Southern tribes now wanted to be left alone. In May 1824 the Cherokees clearly expressed their determination to remain in Georgia. Tribal leaders then in Washington told the secretary of war that Georgia should be given part of Florida if it was so important to satisfy the demand for territory; the Cherokees had "come to a *decisive* and *un-alterable* conclusion, *never* to *cede away* any more *lands*." The Creeks were equally resolute. In May 1825 they executed three of their chiefs for selling land to Georgia; a fourth chief escaped the same fate only through the aid of a kinsman and a fast horse. To better defend their interests, the Choctaws between 1825 and 1828 replaced three pure-blood chieftains with educated mixed-bloods who, the Choctaw agent informed McKenney, had "a purty good knowledge of the Laws of nations." Two treaty commissioners sent to the Chickasaws in October 1826 reported glumly that "the Nation, in Council, most positively determined that they would not sell or exchange their lands or any part of them."[11]

McKenney was not unduly dismayed by the initial failure to interest the Indians in removal. When the House of Representatives passed a resolution in December 1826 asking the War Department for a report on "the disposition of the several Tribes of Indians within the United States to emigrate West of the Mississippi," McKenney responded with a lengthy and detailed analysis of the entire Indian removal program that not only answered the resolution but also suggested means of conducting the policy successfully. "I have confined my remarks chiefly, to the four Southern Tribes," he wrote. "They are those to whom, as to policy, the greater portion of the remaining Tribes in our States and Territories look; and whatever measures the body of those Tribes may adopt, it is believed would be followed by the others." Those tribes, he admitted, were presently opposed to removal. The Choctaws and Chickasaws had given the government "a decided negative" to the proposal, and there were the "most decided indications of a like determination" on the part of the Cherokees and Creeks. "But," he hastened to point out, "these answers have been given under the same mode of application, and which it is respectfully suggested is not only the most exceptionable in their view of the subject, but will continue to be as it has been in regard to those Tribes unsuccessfull. I mean *the mode of Treating with them.*"

The opponents of removal, McKenney declared, were the educated mixed-bloods. For the most part they were men of wealth—farmers, merchants, and manufacturers with comfortable homes, slaves, livestock, and personal property. As entrepreneurs, they had valuable interests to protect and good reasons for remaining where they were. In any discussion with tribal leaders about the sale or exchange of lands, the mixed-bloods united to defeat the proposals. Before the removal program could succeed, therefore, the government had to persuade them to support the policy. If the mixed-bloods would assemble, McKenney believed, "at some suitable and central place," officials could explain "the *real views* of the Government in relation to them." The officials, McKenney stressed, should be carefully selected and "should carry with them, not only the full instructions of the Government, and its pledges but also, an influence arising out of their known friendship to the Indians." He admitted the conference would not make the mixed-bloods "favorable to a removal, *themselves.*" But if they were assured that they, as individuals, would receive "suitable and liberal portions" of the lands they occupied, McKenney was certain the mixed-bloods would see that "the interests of the great body of their people would be promoted by emigration." McKenney, in other words, was subtly advocating bribery to "disembarrass the question of removal of its chief difficulty."

In the meantime, McKenney said, the government should work out the details of the removal program. Congress would have to appropriate money to feed, clothe, and transport almost one hundred thousand Indians; this cost alone McKenney estimated at $291,000. The government would have to reimburse the Indians for improvements on the land they left behind, obtain land from the western Indians to make room for the new arrivals, provide for the missionaries to continue their work across the Mississippi, and establish the territorial government for the emigrants. "But," he concluded, "I am of opinion that the first step, and without which it would be fruitless to attempt a removal, is, to ascertain by actual examination whether a suitable Country can be had; and if so, where located, and within what limits, and which should be clearly defined in all that relates to its extent and fitness for a last home for the most unfortunate of Human beings."[12]

McKenney's report made a favorable impression. A month later, in January 1827, twelve congressmen recommended to Secretary of War Barbour that McKenney visit the southern tribes the following summer to determine their true disposition to removal. The congressmen believed McKenney "fully" informed of the views of the government with respect to the removal policy, and they also thought he possessed "more of the confidence of the Indians than any person in the United States, who could so easily be employed for this desirable object."[13]

Barbour adopted the recommendation and integrated the assignment into McKenney's already scheduled visit to Michigan Territory during the summer of 1827. After he negotiated the treaty with the Menominees, McKenney was to travel south to talk to the Chickasaws, Choctaws, and Cherokees about emigration. Use your own discretion, the secretary of war told McKenney, but "any convention you may make with them will be understood to be only conditional, and subject to the approval of the President, to be afterwards confirmed, by the more formal stipulations of Treaties."[14]

McKenney left Washington for Green Bay in May, signed the treaty of Butte des Morts in August, and reached Memphis, Tennessee, on September 28, 1827. There he bought a kettle, tea, crackers, a cooked ham, and a tongue. In his medicine chest he carried brandy, calomel, and laudanum. A wagon, saddle horse, guide, and interpreter completed his outfit. Then, with his Negro servant Ben Hanson driving the wagon, McKenney set out to visit the Indians. "There had never before left these bluffs a shabbier-looking set of travellers," he declared. "Clothing, wilderness and riverworn; faces sunburnt, hair long, horses common, and wagon, and gear, saddle and briddle, even worse than common."[15]

McKenney continued the voluminous correspondence with Barbour he had carried on during his tours to the lake country. "It will be the joy of my heart," he exclaimed enthusiastically just before leaving Memphis, "if I may succeed in realizing your views in regard to these Southern Indians. I have satisfied myself upon one important point; and that is, that there is no question but a Country well wooded, & watered, and fertile, & equal to any in the world, in every good quality, and of sufficient extent for them all, is ready, or can be made so, with ease for their occupancy—it is that which lies immediately West of the Western line of Missouri, & between the Missouri river & the Mississippi. Upon this point, which has been one of controversy, there need be no doubt. My great aim will be to get their consent *to go and see*."[16]

He met the Chickasaws first and found, he wrote the secretary of war, the subject of removal "one of extreme delicacy." Nevertheless, after McKenney stayed three days and distributed $750 worth of presents to the chiefs and their families, the tribe agreed to send a delegation the following summer to inspect the land proposed by the government for their resettlement. If the delegation approved, the tribe would exchange its present land "acre for acre" for territory west of the Mississippi.[17] The first crack had been made in the united front of the southern Indians. "One thing, I think, may be assumed as certain," McKenney wrote Barbour, "and that is, if the Chickasaws become once placed under the kind of government proposed to be given to them, the other three southern tribes will follow. It may require time, but they will all, in my opinion, with suitable management, eventually go."[18]

McKenney had less reason for optimism after he met the Choctaw leaders at their agency in eastern Mississippi on October 17. Although they agreed to send a delegation from their tribe with the Chickasaw exploring party, the Choctaws refused to consider an exchange of lands regardless of the suitability of the western country. McKenney came away from the meeting convinced that only disinterested individuals could promote and direct the removal program. "*No persons* supposed to be in any manner interested in getting these people's lands ought ever to be united in any agency for their removal. I do not speak this, in disparagement of the people of Mississippi," he wrote Barbour, "but mention it as a fact, which they may profit by. I believe the U. States are not able to tempt them by the offer of all the Wealth of the Union to give up a foot of land, if the proposition should be made by a Citizen of this State."[19]

After leaving the Choctaws, McKenney decided to skip the

Cherokees. It was already late October and winter was nearly upon him; furthermore, he had little hope of success with the Cherokees. "They will be too-longwinded, & require to be met at a thousand points," McKenney wrote, telling Barbour his decision, "—& I forsee that their own scheme of *Soverignty*, & *Independence*, &c would have first to be demolished; & this would require long & patient efforts."[20]

McKenney was saving his energies for the Creeks. The secretary of war had amended McKenney's instructions before he left Washington, directing him to "employ all proper means in your discretion, to procure of the Creeks a cession of the remaining strip of land in Georgia." McKenney considered the assignment almost impossible. The Creeks, he complained to Barbour, "wince at the bare proposition for lands, and can with difficulty be got to hear it." McKenney also knew he would have to cope with David Vann and John Ridge, two Cherokee advisers to Opothle Yoholo, one of the principal Creek chiefs. Vann and Ridge were inalterably opposed to land cessions, particularly the Creeks' last toehold in Georgia, because the Cherokees did not want to stand alone on the removal issue against the Georgians. Aware of these complexities, McKenney wrote Barbour, "I can promise nothing—yet I will not despair."[21]

McKenney sent a message from Tuscaloosa to the Creek agent, and upon arriving at the agency near Fort Mitchell, he found the chiefs of the lower towns already assembling. The superintendent met twice with the chiefs—on the afternoon of November 1 and again the following morning—but they would not commit themselves. Instead they proposed that McKenney hold a general council at their capital, Tuckabatchee. He agreed; but, he wrote Barbour, "I did not accept this invitation . . . before I had exhausted my species of reasoning to get them to act now." John Crowell, the agent, agreed to accompany him to the Creek capital. Assured of at least his help, McKenney would try to bring the business to a favorable conclusion, but he was not "too sanguine."[22]

Pessimism was justified. The Creek leaders conferred privately at Tuckabatchee three days before they allowed McKenney to address them, and then he failed to impress the Indians. Ridge later reported that the "greatest part of his talk was irrelevant to the subject matter of his object, consisting of gross Indian and disgusting flattery." When McKenney saw he was making no headway with the chiefs, Ridge continued, the superintendent "made a disconnected speech, destitute of any reason, apparently the effect of anger and disappointment." Opothle Yoholo protested that McKenney talked too much. McKenney retorted he was the judge of the length of his own speeches and would talk as much as he pleased.[23] With that exchange the council adjourned to meet again the next morning.

McKenney blamed Ridge for his troubles and planned to act decisively against him should the council reject his proposal, a course he had determined before he arrived at Tucka-batchee. He had confided to the secretary of war, "if the accomplishment of the work I have in hand shall depend upon . . . [Ridge's] overthrow, I shall not hesitate." Ridge, expecting the worst, had made his own preparations for the session. "From what had passed the preceding day," he later wrote, "I deemed it prudent to be furnished with a pipe tomahawk in the act of smoking, and to be ready to make effectual resistance, in case of assault from the white men, should they be instigated to it by Col. Crowell."[24]

When the council met the following day, the chiefs said the Creeks would not sell their Georgia holdings for any terms. McKenney immediately accused Ridge of working secretly against the government, ordered him from the council, and announced "in the name of the President of the United States, that 'no further communication of any sort, would be received from the Creeks, if John Ridge had any agency whatever in it.' " McKenney later claimed that "this broke the spell of their opposition, and the agreement (treaty) was made." The Creeks agreed to sell the Georgia land in question for $42,591 and apply $10,000 to schools and other "civilization" purposes. Leaving Crowell to work out the details, McKenney left immediately for Washington.[25]

Once McKenney was gone, the chiefs would not sign the treaty. Crowell later reported to the Indian office that the Creeks were opposed to spending the $10,000 for schools and that he could get the chiefs to sign only by bribing several with presents "to a considerable amount" and increasing the payment for the Georgia land by $5,000.[26]

Crowell's report alarmed McKenney, who feared an adverse

reaction if the details of the negotiations became public knowledge—as they would when the treaty and related documents were sent to the Senate. To avoid embarrassment, McKenney wanted to delete "selected portions" of Crowell's report. The part about the bribes had to go, because obviously not all members of the tribe knew about them. "Now these people," McKenney said to Barbour, "many of them, I mean, read—and this *would* be known. The consequence, I really think, would be *death* to those who might have received presents." McKenney also wanted to delete the account of opposition to the schools. "Humanity requires that those who are opposed to the system in the Congress, & out of it, should not have such authority with which to war upon the good that is doing. And after all, it was, as I believe, but the ravings of some foolish Indian or two—for the schools are *not* unpopular among them." Barbour, however, rejected the suggestions and transmitted the incriminating report with the treaty to the Senate.[27] The dire consequences McKenney predicted failed to materialize.

The superintendent next turned his attention to promoting the removal program in Congress. In his official report of his tour, dated November 29, 1827, McKenney urged Congress to enact a removal bill to save the Indians from destruction. The Creeks, he pleaded, "are a wretched people. Poverty and distress are visible every where, and these have become entailed upon them by habitual drunkenness. No man," McKenney wrote, "who has the feelings of a man, can go through their country and see their total abandonment to this vice, without emotions of the most painful kind. I hold their recovery from it, and from its long train of miseries, *whilst they retain their present relations to the States, to be hopeless.*" The government, in McKenney's view, must intercede to save them; removal was the only solution. The first step—choosing a site for the Indians' future home—was already half-accomplished since the Chickasaws and Choctaws had agreed to explore the western country. Congress only had to appropriate $15,000 to defray the expenses of the exploring party. "It will be time enough after the country is chosen," McKenney added, "to provide the means to extinguish the title or titles of the present occupants, and for the other objects connected with the plan of settling it, &c. as proposed."[28]

When, two weeks after McKenney submitted his report, Congressman William Haile of Mississippi introduced a resolution calling on the House Committee on Indian Affairs to consider an appropriation to enable the Choctaws and Chickasaws to explore the country beyond the Mississippi River, the superintendent probably thought the removal program was well on its way to a speedy and successful conclusion. If so, his euphoria was quickly dispelled. A month went by before a bill for the appropriation was even introduced; another month passed, yet the House took no action. McKenney's patience gave out, and on February 14, 1828, he urged William McLean, chairman of the House Committee on Indian Affairs, to push the bill through as quickly as possible. "I think it due to the importance of the measure, to state," McKenney wrote, "that these people, having trusted to the faith of my pledges, made to them in the name of the Government, may experience a shock to their confidence, if the means are not provided in time for the whole plan to be carried through *as stipulated*, part of which is that they are to leave Memphis *the first of next May*." McKenney's appeal had little effect; the bill received no notice until March 22, and then Congressman Silas Woods of Ohio amended it beyond recognition.[29] Hope for an appropriation now rested with the Senate.

Two days later, Powhatan Ellis of Mississippi introduced an exploration bill in the Senate; it passed within three weeks and on April 17 was sent to the House for concurrence. There, however, the measure languished. After two weeks, McLean received another letter from the Indian office, this one signed by Secretary of War Barbour, stressing the importance of quick action. "I am of the opinion from the tenor of their communications, on this subject, as well as the slightest tenure by which their confidence in the provisions of the Government is held," Barbour warned, "that if corresponding provision be not made on our part to carry faithfully into effect that agreement, consequences highly unfavorable will be produced thereby upon the Indians in regard to the Government; and which must act correspondingly upon this, or any other plan, which it may be esteemed proper to submit with a view to their preservation & happiness."[30]

Despite Barbour's pressure, the House did not give its attention to the exploration bill until May 21, three weeks after the exploring party was to have left Memphis, and then the measure aroused bitter debate. No doubt a desire to embarrass the Adams administration or McKenney played a part in the opposition, but, significantly, the debates revealed sectional cleavage. Opposition to the bill and to removal itself centered in New England, the Middle Atlantic states, and the Upper South—areas with little or no Indian population. Support for the measure came from the Lower South and the Northwest, where whites were anxious to rid themselves of their Indian neighbors. The bill passed the first and second reading, then Congressman John Davis of Massachusetts tried to table it. He failed, but the bill went through six more stages of parliamentary delay before it finally cleared the House by a vote of 88 to 73 on May 22, a full month behind the explorers' schedule.[31]

McKenney, meanwhile, had already prepared for the expedition and only needed congressional approval to send the Indians on their way. He had carefully selected the government representatives in the group because, he explained, "the success, or failure of the plan, will depend upon those to whom may be entrusted the business of conducting and guiding the party." George H. Kennerly, nephew of Superintendent Clark, would lead the Indians. The physician was George P. Todson, a man of "knowledge of the diseases of those regions, and qualified to render service in any emergency." Baptist missionary Isaac McCoy, a staunch advocate of removal, was treasurer. McKenney also sent along a topographic engineer to "map or sketch and bring home geographical and other information." He recommended that a small complement of soldiers accompany the explorers to protect them from "any occurrence of a disagreeable sort" which might frustrate "the great plan of colonizing these people," but this suggestion was not adopted.[32]

As soon as McKenney heard Congress had appropriated the $15,000, he relayed the news to the Indian country. He had chosen St. Louis as the starting point for the expedition and had given Clark responsibility for outfitting the group and attending to last-minute details. "It is highly important that you adopt a plan as to transportation, and provision &c, that shall embrace the utmost economy which may be consistent with the satisfaction and comfort of the party," McKenney instructed him. "All that may be necessary will readily occur to you, and to your discretion is the entire subject relating to the whole object referr'd—there being no doubt from your superior local, as well as other knowledge of the Country, and the means necessary to sustain men in traversing it, you will omit nothing that should be thought of, and add nothing that might be deemed superfluous."[33]

At the same time, McKenney wrote to other officials connected with the exploration. He told Benjamin F. Smith, the Chickasaw agent, to start the delegates from that tribe on their way to St. Louis and to send a runner to the Choctaw agent to do the same. *"Let no time be lost,"* the superintendent demanded. To McCoy, McKenney concluded his instructions with *"Move Quick."*[34] Everyone did move quickly—everyone, that is, except the Indians.

The Chickasaws no longer wanted to go. John Bell, who was to escort the delegation to St. Louis, said that the tribe was "in a state of great confusion." Some of the Chickasaws were claiming the chiefs had already "sold their country"; others were insisting it was now too late in the year to make the trip. "I am fearful," Bell wrote McKenney, "that it will be hardly possible, to induce them to set out upon this tour, until they become more settled, and the excitement subsides."[35] If the Chickasaws would not go, neither would the Choctaws.

McKenney was not to be thwarted. He dashed off an appeal to the Chickasaw chiefs. "Let a red man any where stand up and say that I promised, and did not perform. He cannot." Therefore, McKenney urged, the Chickasaws should honor their pledge to him. "Fail not—It is not too late, if you move quick." To John B. Duncan, the subagent who was to accompany the delegation, McKenney wrote: "Tell them to *go at once.*" To Bell, McKenney said: "Tell them—not to disappoint me—I am their friend, and am labouring to promote their happiness—but if they will not mind my words, I shall think they are tired of me, and want another friend."[36]

McKenney's words were effective. Bell wrote back September 17, "I attended this council, and read them your letter of the 14th of August; and was aided by the Agent, who gave them an appropriate talk on the subject, which had the desired effect. Your letter was a fortunate one," Bell assured McKenney. "It made a deep impression, and contributed much towards getting them to agree to go." Finally, on October 13 Clark informed the War Department that the Chickasaw and Choctaw delegations had arrived in St. Louis. "Some discontent had arisen among them on their way to this place which seemed for a while to threaten [again] a failure of the expedition; but," Clark wrote, "I am in hopes I have succeeded in restoring a good understanding among them." The party would leave the next morning.[37]

McKenney believed the exploring expedition would settle the removal question as far as the Chickasaws, Choctaws, and perhaps the Creeks were concerned. Already he had begun planning for the Cherokees. At the time Congress was debating the exploration bill, a delegation of Western Cherokees was in Washington regotiating boundaries of the tribe's land in Arkansas Territory. In the treaty signed May 6, 1828, the government agreed to give each head of a Cherokee family in Georgia or any other state east of the Mississippi River a rifle, blanket, kettle, and five pounds of tobacco if he agreed to join his "brothers" in Arkansas. After the negotiations were concluded, McKenney prevailed on two of the delegates, James Rogers and John Maw, to return home by way of Georgia to describe to the Eastern Cherokees the soil, climate, and prospects that awaited them in the West. As secret government agents, Rogers and Maw were to use the best methods within their discretion to induce their brethren to emigrate. "As much, if not all of [their] success, will depend upon keeping the object of [their] visit a secret," McKenney explained to Hugh Montgomery, the Eastern Cherokee agent, "you will by no means make it known." Montgomery was to follow the two Indians and sign up all the Cherokees the secret agents persuaded to emigrate.[38]

The plan backfired, probably because the secret mission did not remain secret for long. Within a month after Rogers and Maw left Washington, the Eastern Cherokees knew the two were agents of the government, and soon there were rumors of "poles erected on which to exhibit their heads." Congressman James Mitchell of Tennessee criticized McKenney for even attempting the scheme. "I think the very reverse should have been the course," he wrote the superintendent. "It is impossible to do any thing with a suspicious cunning Cherokee by secret contrivance[.] All you do must be done openly and in great

candor: for the least deceit once detected is fatal."[39] Mitchell
was almost prophetic. In October two Cherokee warriors attacked Rogers, striking his head several times with a four-pound
rock. Rogers survived, but his effectiveness as an agent was
over.[40]

Montgomery's efforts to enroll emigrants fared no better.
At first some six hundred Cherokees signed—and received the
rifle, blanket, kettle, and tobacco—but then most of the regis-
trants refused to leave. An angry McKenney pointed out to
Montgomery that the time to distribute the inducements was
when the Indians were leaving, not before. "It is however
thought prudent," he added, "for the present, not to press this
subject upon the delinquents, or to refuse them, should they
enrol again, the benefits of the present proposed outfit."[41] Under
the new rules Montgomery had considerably less success. By
October 10, 1828, he could report only four enrollees, two of
them bachelors; by the end of the month only seven more had
registered. The number grew slowly—sixty-four by the end of
November, one hundred by the end of the year, and two hundred
by February 1829, of whom only twenty-one were Georgia
Cherokees.[42]

Nevertheless, on February 12 the agent sent eleven boatloads of emigrants to Arkansas. The boats were small, however,
and, Montgomery confessed, "most of those who have emigrated
are either whitemen who maried into Cherokee familys or half
Breeds, and many of them have considerable furniture, we could
not get upon an average more than from twelve to twenty in
a boat besides servants, (not counted but victualed)." Mc-
Kenney was even more discouraged by an anonymous letter
from an informant who reported that although two or three
boatloads of Cherokees had passed near his home on the
Tennessee River, the Indians beached their boats before they
reached the Alabama border and began selling their equipment.
One group sold everything, including the boat, to a local farmer
and "made good their retreat back into the Nation." Another
group "tried hard to sell." The informant hoped in the future
the Cherokees would be given a military escort to Arkansas
"to prevent a useless waste of National wealth."[43]

McKenney continued to receive bad news. The Choctaw and
Chickasaw exploring party had returned to St. Louis on Janu-

ary 2, 1829, and although McCoy's official report was "entirely satisfactory as to the extent, and fitness of the Country," the delegates claimed they did not like the land and wanted to remain in the East.[44]

The removal program obviously was not progressing as smoothly as McKenney had expected, and there were more obstacles than the understandable reluctance of the Indians to leave their homeland. For one thing, the western tribes did not welcome the easterners with open arms as McKenney had optimistically predicted. Instead, the Comanches, Osages, and Pawnees viewed the emigrants as legitimate targets of plunder; Pawnees in one attack killed five Cherokee emigrants and wounded several others. To relatives east of the Mississippi, one emigrant wrote: "At the West there is much War.—There is no prospect of peace. What you hear of bloodshed is true."[45]

Secondly, the Indians were dissatisfied with the western lands. In 1824 a delegation of Western Cherokees had reported to the president: "Almost the whole of the country which has been surveyed & designed for the Cherokees is nothing but mountains and huge bed of rocks." They were unhappy with their new environment, and "gladly would many return to the east of the Mississippi."[46] The Cherokees were not alone in their complaints. To make room for eastern tribes in Arkansas Territory, the trans-Mississippi Quapaws were persuaded in 1824 to move southwest and join the Caddos at the Red River agency near the Louisiana border.[47] By the spring of 1827, George Gray told the War Department, at least forty Quapaw families had returned to their former homes because they disliked the Red River country. The following spring he reported that the Red River had overflowed its banks—the second time in the three years the Quapaws had been at the agency—and the crops had been destroyed. The tribe was destitute and wished to return to Arkansas. "If they had never sold their Arkansas lands," the Quapaw chief told Gray, they would "at this time be a happy people." Now they had to buy corn; before they had sold it. McKenney urged Gray to keep the Quapaws at the agency unless the people of Arkansas invited them back, an unlikely possibility. "There is no doubt the poor fellows are worse off by the change," McKenney admitted, "—and any reasonable and feasible plan of affording them permanent relief would be cheerfully adopted." Perhaps the Western Cherokees would allow the Quapaws to live with them.[48]

Another obstacle to removal was renewed white pressure on tribes that had already moved once. The Indians could not fail to question the logic of a policy that moved them from one congested area to another, as happened to the Cherokees who had settled in Arkansas in 1817. McKenney threw up his hands in exasperation when the people of Arkansas requested the government to move those Indians further west. "I confess I had hope," he wrote to Barbour in the spring of 1828, "nay I had no doubt of the final success of the policy which has been begun under such flattering auspices of sett'ling our unfortunate Indians in one last and good home, and under a suitable government &c. But if those so far in the West, are not made to feel that there is something in our pledges, I shall *despair*."[49]

Lack of funds also hindered the removal program. James Rogers, the secret agent, wrote bluntly to the secretary of war. "I would respectfully Suggest, Sir, that if there was a small quantity of Secret funds placed in the hands of the Agent or any other person that you might think proper to appoint It would be the cause of considerable liveliness to the cause." Montgomery also asked for such a fund because a number of mixed-bloods expected a payoff "for breaking the Ice." Even Congressman Mitchell joined the chorus. "Rogers and Mawe are usefull and valual men but they can do nothing without money and," he sarcastically informed McKenney, "your limitted experience with Indians ought to have taught you that long since."[50]

McKenney knew well enough money was needed. To finance properly the mechanics of removal, to pay the Indians adequately for the property they would leave behind, and to establish the form of government he envisioned for them in the West would require millions. Only Congress could provide money on that scale, and so far it had not seen fit to do so. McKenney complained to Governor Cass: "The States clamour to get rid of the Indians—agreed: but it is not possible, much as I should be gratified if it could be so, to pay the cost of all this out of the pittance, at the disposition of the Department for Contingencies." To Superintendent Clark he wrote: "The policy seems to have been, *removal*—but the ways and means are not provided."[51]

Not the least obstacle to removal was opposition from many of the missionaries working among the tribes. They objected to the policy for a variety of reasons. A few worried about the cost of rebuilding their schools in the West; some expressed concern that the government intended to withdraw its support from the civilization program; others feared the Indians would be forced to emigrate whether or not they wanted to go. McKenney insisted the government was not abandoning the civilization program. True, the government viewed removal as a necessity for the salvation of the Indians, but it had no intention of forcing anyone to emigrate. McKenney also assured clergymen that the government would reimburse them for expenses incurred as a result of removal.[52] But assurances did not satisfy the missionaries. Many of them instead viewed the policy as a violation of the Indians' natural rights to remain unmolested in their homeland and became vigorous and outspoken opponents of removal.

Some missionaries, of course, supported the program. The Reverend Cephas Washburn, a clergyman working among the Western Cherokees, said that from his first acquaintance with Indians he had considered their proximity to white settlements "the circumstance most unfavorable to their improvement." For this reason, he wrote McKenney, "I have hence felt favorably towards the policy of the government which proposes the removal of the Indians beyond the limits of the States & Territories of the Union." Isaac McCoy was the most prominent missionary who favored removal. He claimed that as early as 1823 he had "formed the resolution, providence permitting, thenceforward [to] keep steadily in view, and endeavor to promote a plan for colonizing the natives in a country to be made forever theirs, west of the State of Missouri." McCoy carried out his resolution by presenting arguments for removal to congressmen, church groups, and the general public.[53] It was no accident then that McKenney selected him to accompany the Indians who went to explore the western lands in the summer of 1828.

But the missionaries opposed to removal greatly outnumbered the Washburns and McCoys. Leading the majority was the American Board of Commissioners for Foreign Missions,

McKenney's old ally in the campaign to establish the schools in the Indian country. The American Board spoke with knowledge and conviction on Indian affairs and was therefore very effective in organizing support for the Indians among eastern and northern church groups.[54] Besides arousing public opposition to removal, the American Board probably played a part in the appearance in the spring of 1828 of the *Cherokee Phoenix*, a bilingual weekly newspaper published by the tribe at New Echota, Georgia. Edited by Elias Boudinot, a Cherokee who had been educated at the board's school in Cornwall, Connecticut, the paper stood firmly against removal, a "policy, which," it said, "if carried into effect, will prove pernicious to us."[55]

The *Phoenix* also attacked the advocates of removal, particularly McKenney. "A few years ago this Gentleman would have been welcomed into this Country on any business, as a friend of the Indians, but now, we take the liberty to say, a more unpopular Commissioner could not well be sent," the paper responded editorially in May 1828 to a rumor that McKenney was about to visit the tribe. The superintendent took the criticism to heart. "I notice, and not without regret, a spirit pervading your journal which, if not checked, cannot do else than prove extremely injurious to you," he wrote the editor. "It is the spirit of personal, and ill natured remarks against those who do not happen to think with you and your chiefs, upon the question of *what is best, under all circumstances for our red brothers to do?*" McKenney cautioned the editor to use restraint in assailing known friends of the Indians. "It is for *your sakes* and not mine, that I deplore to see the vindictive quality of your spirit," he wrote. "I advise you—think of it as you may to treat persons who are your friends, at least with civility, for you have need of all their counsels, and all their wisdom." To this the *Phoenix* retorted: "With the motives of Col. M'Kenney we have nothing to do—they may be good— he may be a 'real friend'—he may be a 'wise counsellor,' but after all we must beg leave to judge for ourselves, and choose our own friends."[56]

The *Phoenix* was as effective as it was embarrassing to McKenney. The editorials, he admitted to a New York clergyman, "may possibly be seized upon by those who do not think with us, and published. The public confidence in the wisdom and mercy of the plan, for the rescue of those hapless people, may be weakened thereby." The newspaper also hampered efforts to interest the Indians in the policy. "Enclosed I send you a Paragraph which I have cut out of the Cherokee Phoenix and which has done much against the Cause of emigration," Montgomery wrote the secretary of war. "Indeed I have not enrolled a single person since it appeared in that paper which is about two weeks [ago], and some of those who have enrolled are very much disheartened by it, and some of them I am told have declined going."[57]

McKenney's first inkling that the American Board was involved with the *Phoenix* came from an anonymous letter to the Indian office in the fall of 1828. The informant claimed that Boudinot was a figurehead. The actual editor, "from whose pen flow all the Scurility and abuse heaped upon the Govt. and its officers and distinguished Individuals of other States," was the Reverend Samuel Worcester, a member of the American Board teaching at Brainerd and nephew of the Samuel Worcester who had been so helpful to McKenney in 1818 and 1819. McKenney immediately sent an extract of the letter to Jeremiah Evarts, corresponding secretary of the American Board. "If it be true," McKenney warned, ". . . then I fear much evil may result from this kind of interference, by Mr. Worcester. It ought not, from conditions of policy, if nothing else to be allowed."[58] The letter brought quick denials. Boudinot insisted Worcester had nothing to do with the paper. Worcester also denied the charges and advised McKenney to drop the entire matter, "unless an inquiry should be instituted, which I am very ready to meet."[59]

As the government pressed its removal plans, the opponents of removal correspondingly intensified their efforts. By 1829 the campaign took on aspects of a crusade as both houses of Congress were inundated with petitions and memorials from church groups, religious societies, and civic organizations opposing removal.[60] Appeals from such respectable sources were difficult to counteract. Secretary of War Porter in his annual report in 1828 reprimanded the missionaries for opposing government policies while receiving aid from the civilization fund, but his words had little noticeable effect.[61]

Equally futile was a scheme to organize a group of churchmen and humanitarians who would publicly support removal.[62]

McKenney, presumably with the permission of the newly installed Jackson administration, began mobilizing the churchmen
in April 1829. Within a month he had persuaded the Reverend
Eli Baldwin, a minister of the Dutch Reformed Church in New
York City, to sponsor an association with the "exclusive object"
of promoting the government's Indian removal policy. Baldwin,
following McKenney's directions at every step, formally organized in New York on July 22, 1829, the Board for the Emigration, Preservation, and Improvement of the Aborigines of
America. The constitution of the board pledged cooperation
with the federal government in its conduct of Indian affairs,
promised to afford emigrant Indians all the necessary instruction in the arts of life and the duties of religion, and invited all
citizens of the United States without respect to religion or party
to support the removal program.[63] The nonpartisan appeal was
somewhat besmirched by the fact that the thirty board members were, as even McKenney admitted, "the most thorough
going Jacksonites in the nation," and the supposedly interde-
nominational character of the board was belied by the fact that
it consisted almost exclusively of members of the Dutch Reformed Church.[64]

The Indian board had a brief and ineffectual existence. It
held a poorly attended public meeting at which McKenney
spoke; it printed a few pro-removal documents in the New York
Evening Post; and, as its major accomplishment, it published in
August 1829—with the aid of $200 from federal funds—two
thousand copies of *Documents and Proceedings Relating to the
Formation and Progress of a Board in the City of New York
for the Emigration, Preservation, and Improvement of the
Aborigines of America.*[65] The forty-eight-page booklet contains
minutes of board meetings, the constitution, and letters by
McKenney, Eaton, and Jackson. The pamphlet is important
because it was the first comprehensive public statement of the
government's avowed policy of Indian removal. In its last public
act, the board in February 1830 petitioned both houses of
Congress to enact removal legislation.[66] As for its primary purpose of arousing public support for removal, the Indian board
was a complete failure. It had neither the funds, personnel, nor
motivation to combat successfully the American Board of Commissioners for Foreign Missions with its world-wide and highly

organized structure of agents and auxiliaries. Most important, however, the Indian board found little legal or moral evidence to convince anyone that the government's program would benefit the Indians.

Nevertheless, McKenney's zealous efforts on behalf of Indian removal were crowned with success. On May 28, 1830, President Jackson signed into law Senate Bill 102 providing for the removal of eastern tribes across the Mississippi River.[67] McKenney should have been jubilant, but he was not. By the time the bill passed, he had begun to wonder if removal would prove to be the blessing for the Indians he had so confidently predicted. In a frank letter to Hugh Lawson White, chairman of the Senate Committee on Indian Affairs, written shortly after introduction of the removal bill, McKenney expressed concern that the measure did not mention the many benefits he had told the Indians they would receive once they had emigrated. He asked the senator to sponsor a resolution guaranteeing subsequent legislation for the benefits. "I have taken a deep stake in this business of emigration," McKenney wrote, "and stand committed to the Indians, and the public, for a fulfillment of all that I have promised the one; and assured the other *would be done*."[68] The resolution was not made. The superintendent's letter to Kingsbury a month later reveals his further worries. If the Indians emigrate, he declared, "and are not followed by suitable benefits, and preserved, and blessed, but shall be neglected and become wretched, and finally disappear, then will the cause of mourning be with those who seek, by this mode, to save them."[69] McKenney's apprehension may have been heightened by the realization that his days as superintendent of Indian affairs were numbered. With McKenney would go the administration's leading exponent of a voluntary removal program.

12

Dismissal from Office

MᶜKENNEY WAS DISMISSED from office in August 1830. He was away from Washington when he received the brief note from Acting Secretary of War Philip G. Randolph: "A furlough to the 31st. of this month is granted you, at the expiration of which time, your services will no longer be required in connexion with the Indian Department. This course is dictated by a sense of publick duty," Randolph wrote, "and not from any consideration of private feeling." McKenney was not surprised. "The order for my dismissal was a relief," he wrote a few months later. "It was to have been from the beginning [of the Jackson administration]."[1]

The superintendent had never expected Jackson to exempt the Indian service from his plans to appoint his followers to office. John Johnston, at Piqua, Ohio, knew of at least four men who were waiting for his agency, and he was the first to be dismissed despite "upwards of thirty years in the publick service." He was quickly followed by Jasper Parrish, Thomas Forsyth, and Henry Brevoort—all capable and experienced agents the Indian service could ill afford to lose. When Jackson took office in March 1829 there were twenty Indian agents and

223

thirty-six subagents. By September 1831 he had replaced ten of the agents and nineteen of the subagents.[2]

McKenney, however, was not immediately dismissed. "How the *Colonel* stands his ground," wrote Schoolcraft in June 1829, "is a perfect mystery to me. He must be very assiduous in his attentions." McKenney no doubt was equally mystified. He had ample reason for dismay at the prospects of a Jackson presidency, and as early as October 1828 he had predicted his removal should Old Hickory be elected.[3]

The Jacksonians had not forgotten McKenney's editorial role in Calhoun's campaign in 1824. Learning of McKenney's dismissal, the *Georgia Journal* proclaimed on September 25, 1830, "This is among the best acts of gen. Jackson's administration: and it will be so considered by all those who recollect the course of the 'Washington Republican' under his auspices, even if they can see no other reason to be rejoiced on account of it." *Niles' Weekly Register* countered, "If such a severe judgment is justly rendered on Col. McKenney, how great shall be the condemnation of the distinguished gentleman by whose name the 'Washington Republican' was most commonly called, *as being his own*, when the colonel was regarded only as *his* editor, or 'organ'?"[4]

Nor was it any secret that, following the collapse of Calhoun's presidential aspirations, McKenney had become a loyal member of the Adams administration. A few months after the inauguration, McKenney had written, "we are all very happy in having such a President; & no question, I think, need be entertain'd of his re-election, if it please God to spare him, & keep his mind in its accustom'd vigor." McKenney's opinion of Adams remained high throughout his term in office. In 1828, shortly before the November election, he wrote, "I should be gratified if Mr Adams could serve out his term of Eight years. I think him worthy. He is certainly an honest man, an able politician, & is withal furnished with a soul of spotless morality." He added, unnecessarily, "I am classed with those who are call'd administration men."[5]

The Jacksonians made McKenney pay dearly for his loyalty to Adams. They seized every opportunity to discredit the superintendent and, through him, the Adams administration. "Political agitation," McKenney later wrote, "and of a sort more bitter and more fierce than any that had ever preceded it, had now become universal. Mr. Adams and his administration, the ability and economy, and purity of which, no honest and intelligent man doubted, was to come down, though it was as pure as the angels at the right hand of God."[6]

An ideal opportunity for "political agitation" came when the second comptroller rejected McKenney's accounts for his 1827 tour of the southern tribes. McKenney's appointment had specified that his compensation would be "fixed" when he returned according to the *"extent* and *value"* of his services. Accordingly, he submitted to Secretary of War Barbour a claim for $5,000, a figure including $3,172.63 for expenses and $1,827.37 pay above his regular salary. A nervous Barbour spoke personally to McKenney about the claim. "Sir," he said, "I have been thinking of this. I know the terms upon which you undertook this almost hopeless mission; and I know, also, that your services have been immensely valuable; and whilst I set an almost priceless value on them, I am compelled, that no cry of favoritism may be raised, to limit your compensation to the pay of a commissioner"—that is, $8 for every day of negotiations with the Indians and $8 for every twenty miles of travel. "I am perfectly satisfied, Sir," McKenney replied, "and will make up my accounts upon that basis." He recalculated his compensation at $4,532, an amount which reduced his "profit" to $1,244. Since McKenney had received several advances in the course of his travels, $1,344 would settle his accounts. When he sent the papers to the Treasury Department, he included a warrant for $1,344 signed by the secretary of war.[7]

Second Comptroller Richard Cutts refused to accept the figures. Cutts objected primarily to McKenney's failure to submit signed vouchers verifying expenditures, and he claimed the superintendent was asking $660 too much as travel money. McKenney then refigured his mileage, discovered he was entitled to $440 more than he had originally applied for, and submitted another account asking for the additional money. A tremendous amount of correspondence passed between the superintendent and the comptroller over several months: Cutts steadfastly refused to pass the accounts; McKenney, in turn, accused Cutts of turning his office into "an engine of oppression" in "a vain attempt to rise into favor by a sudden start into a pretended vigilance over the public purse."[8]

Eventually McKenney collected both the original $1,344 and the additional $440, but not until the Jacksonians, charging that the Adams administration was rife with corruption and inefficiency, had turned the controversy to their own advantage.[9] They claimed the southern tour had actually been a campaign junket for McKenney to distribute "Coffin Handbills" and other anti-Jackson literature. The House Committee on Retrenchment, appointed in February 1828 ostensibly to seek ways to trim government spending, accused McKenney of gross extravagance—squandering public money on the trip and overcharging the government for his services. During one hearing Congressman Charles A. Wickliffe of Kentucky said McKenney spent $5,000 on entertainment at a tavern somewhere near the Great Lakes. The committee claimed McKenney was paid more than $7,000 for the trip. Wily statisticians obtained the inflated figure by adding $800 for six months salary, $1,800 for presents agents had distributed to the Indians in McKenney's name, and $4,500 he was entitled to receive as special commissioner.[10]

On May 22, 1828, a week after the Retrenchment Committee reported its findings to the House, McKenney tried to refute the accusations in a letter to "a Friend" published in the Alexandria *Gazette*. The charge that he squandered $5,000 at the tavern McKenney passed off as an "attempt of Mr. Wickliffe, (for no cause that I know of) to wound my reputation, to be settled between his conscience, his constituents and his God." But he categorically denied any political activity in the 1828 presidential race and said he had never distributed handbills, pamphlets, or campaign literature. "As to politicks, my dear friend, I have no belief in them. I once thought I might relish them; but they are too heartless for my use." Instead, he continued, "I am here filling a humble place under the Government, but one requiring incessant labor, and which is full of responsibility, and believing my business to be with my official duties, and not with politicks, I meddle not with the latter."[11] This may have been McKenney's position in May of 1828, but he evidently meddled in 1826, and he probably did so in 1827, although there is no evidence that he ever distributed the notorious coffin handbills.

The letter did not satisfy McKenney's critics, especially Duff

Green's *United States Telegraph* which frequently referred to the superintendent as the "Kickapoo Ambassador." The *Telegraph* on June 16 claimed McKenney had duped Barbour into approving his accounts. Two weeks later the paper described the superintendent as "a clerk of a third or fourth grade, (who has obtained more money, by forty fold, than any other *scribe* of like capacity ever before received,) [and who,] instead of attending to the duties of his desk, is eternally scouting the country in search of the *picturesque and sentimental,* while the United States Treasury is the bank on which this political *Mungo Park* draws for his travelling expenses." On July 15 it accused McKenney of charging mileage "for a *constructive route*" and of writing letters "*mandatory* to the Comptroller for payment, which the then Secretary of War connived at."[12]

In late July, in another attempt to refute his critics, McKenney published *To the Public.* The fifteen-page pamphlet contains an extensive quotation from the Retrenchment Committee minority report that defended the superintendent; the petition from the twelve congressmen asking that he be sent to visit the southern tribes; a letter signed by eight congressmen who believed McKenney entitled to the compensation he had requested; a letter from Barbour to Secretary of War Eaton supporting McKenney's claim for compensation; and a long statement by McKenney explaining his actions and denying the charges made against him.[13]

McKenney distributed the pamphlet widely. "Not being in the habit of being checked in which I think *right,* I adopted this form;" he explained to Barbour, "& shall have it published, thro' my friends, in every state, & City, in the Union." No one had wanted to print it, he admitted. Gales and Seaton refused to publish the pamphlet in the *National Intelligencer* unless he deleted certain caustic remarks about Cutts; the Washington *Journal* turned it down because he had first offered it to the *Intelligencer.* But the statements, McKenney told Barbour, "were *essential* for *your defence,* as well as mine, and I would never agree to sacrifice *a jot,* under such circumstances. I believe you will be satisfied that I have met, & *conquered the enemy*—Never was there a fouler attack. You will judge of the defence."[14]

The pamphlet may not have vindicated McKenney, but it

elicited gratifying comments. Delegate Joseph M. White of Florida Territory claimed McKenney had "accomplished more in a few months for a small sum than other commissioners could have done with the public Treasury at their disposal." The usually critical James Mitchell of Tennessee hoped the pamphlet "will relieve you from the smallest censure as I believe you are deserving none." Congressman William Haile of Mississippi said, "I then, and now think you were poorly paid for that service. I hope my being a *Jackson* man, will never prevent me, from differing with the party, when duty requires it—or prevent me from doing an act of justice to any man."[15]

However, if McKenney thought his critics had been silenced, he was sadly mistaken. On April 21, 1829, scarcely a month after Jackson's inauguration, the *Telegraph* editorially revived all the charges: McKenney had acted as "an electioneering agent" on his tour; he had squandered government money ostensibly to visit the Indian tribes "for some valuable purpose, but more likely for no purpose at all."[16]

Angered by this new attack, McKenney appealed to Jackson for redress. "I avail myself of this occasion," he wrote, "respectfully to state, that whilst I deeply regret the existence of a spirit in some individuals to hunt me down, that I am prepared to meet any charge, and of any sort, that they may in the execution of their settled purpose to unoffice me, prefer—a purpose that has broken out in assertions, backed by bets that it *shall* be done—and if I am at any one point, either as an officer, or a man of honor touching either my public, or private acts, deficient, I will abide, with cheerfulness, the decision that shall pronounce me so."[17]

He followed up the letter with a request for an audience with the president, which Jackson granted. During the interview Jackson said, McKenney remembered, "I am told, and on the best authority, that you were one of the principal promoters of that vile paper, 'We the People'; as a contributor towards establishing it, and as a writer, afterwards, in which my wife Rachel was so shamefully abused. I am told further, on authority no less respectable, that you took an active part in distributing, under the frank of your office, the '*coffin hand-bills*'; and that in your recent travels, you largely and widely circulated the militia pamphlet." McKenney emphatically denied all the charges. He swore that he had had nothing to do with the paper, that he had never distributed any handbills, and he knew nothing about the militia pamphlet except what he read in newspapers. Jackson replied, "I believe every word you have said, and am satisfield that those who communicated to me those allegations, were mistaken."[18]

If McKenney was now in Jackson's good graces, the *Telegraph*, which McKenney considered the "mouth-piece of the palace," evidently did not know it because Green continued his editorial assaults on the superintendent. On August 26 the *Telegraph* asked, "does the gallant Major recollect the Committee on Retrenchment, the Columbia Bank, and the Columbian College?"[19] After the Georgetown *Columbian Gazette* rose to McKenney's defense, the *Telegraph* retorted, "we congratulate his excellency that his companions and associates . . . have undertaken to stand sponsors for his good character. Will they please to say how much money Thomas L. McKenney owes to the Bank of Columbia and, next, whether the debt was fairly and honorably created?" Two days later the *Telegraph* recommended that its readers review the correspondence between McKenney and Cutts "relative to his charges, double salary, &c. and to the dockets of our Courts for the evidence of his unworthiness." The only thing that stumped Green was why McKenney was not fired. "We can account for his retention in office so long," he concluded on September 3, "only by supposing that the Secretary [of War] is ignorant of McKenney's true character."[20]

Yet in spite of logic and the *Telegraph*, McKenney held on to his job another year, even through the spring of 1830 when he became a central figure in a scandal that implicated Sam Houston and Secretary of War Eaton, both close friends of the president. In February Houston visited McKenney at his War Department office. After a brief exchange of pleasantries, he came straight to the point. He understood that if Congress enacted a removal bill, Jackson would award the contract for furnishing rations to the emigrating Indians to a private firm. "It is my intention to make an attempt to engage in this business," Houston told McKenney. "I wish you to aid me; you can do much in accomplishing my intentions. Every body knows your acquaintance with this business, and you can have the matter attended to, pretty much as you please." The firm submitting the lowest bid to the War Department would get the contract, Houston explained. Since meat was cheaper in the West, suppliers there would be more competitive than eastern firms. He wanted the announcement advertising the contract to specify that all bids be received by the War Department within thirty days. The time limit would effectively prevent western contractors from bidding.[21]

McKenney refused to have anything to do with the scheme. Houston then drew his chair closer to McKenney's. "In a whisper," Houston offered $50,000 of his anticipated profits. "I repelled him," McKenney claimed, "and told him, from that hour, never to speak to me again upon any matter, official, or otherwise." Houston then threatened to reveal that McKenney gave a $1,500 bribe to a delegation of Cherokee Indians. McKenney retorted he had about as much authority as his doorkeeper to issue that sum to anyone. As Houston stormed out of the room, he turned, shook his finger at McKenney, and said, "you shall suffer for this."[22]

McKenney next sent Houston a "temperate, but firm" letter discussing the proposition and the accusations (but not the attempted bribe). McKenney assured Houston, "with the utmost frankness," of his own "perfect readiness to have any part of [his] . . . conduct, as an officer or a man, examined into, and acted upon."[23]

About three o'clock that same afternoon, Secretary of War Eaton gave McKenney a notice to send to the *Telegraph* for the next day's edition. The call for bids for furnishing rations to the emigrating Indians, McKenney later claimed, was in Houston's handwriting. The notice specified that each Indian was to receive daily one-and-one-half pounds of fresh beef or one pound of fresh pork and a quart of corn or eighteen ounces of flour. It further specified that bids had to be received by the secretary of war within thirty days. McKenney pointed out that distant contractors would not have enough time to submit bids, but Eaton shrugged off the objection with "Houston is waiting." The notice, dated February 18, 1830, appeared in several eastern newspapers.[24]

The department received about a dozen bids, which McKenney turned over to Philip Randolph, Eaton's chief clerk and brother-in-law. All bidders but one in Louisville were members of the Washington community. The bids ranged from $.08 to $.20 a ration; Houston came in at $.18. McKenney, figuring that some eighty thousand Indians had to be fed enroute to the West and supported for a year after their arrival, knew how important the difference of a few cents per ration was, and emphasized this point in a report to Eaton on April 7. At $.10 a ration, removal would cost the government $55 per Indian, more than $4,000,000 for all the tribes. Reducing the cost of the ration to $.06, a price McKenney thought reasonable, would keep the overall cost under $3,000,000.[25]

The March 20 deadline passed, but the War Department failed to announce the recipient of the contract. Several bidders asked McKenney why, and he in turn asked Eaton. The secretary said an announcement was unnecessary. Only one bid had been submitted—from Houston in the name of Ben Hawkins, a mixed-blood Indian. When McKenney insisted he had given several bids to Randolph, Eaton claimed they had arrived too late for consideration.[26]

Nevertheless, Houston did not receive the contract. His efforts to get it had been blatant, and he had approached several others besides McKenney. Soon his finagling was the talk of Washington. Despite the notoriety of the case, Jackson remained loyal to his friend. Houston would have had the contract if Jackson had not been dissuaded at the last minute by advisers who warned the award would injure the reputation of the administration. Jackson then withdrew the contract and gave the task of feeding the emigrating Indians to the commissary department of the army.[27]

Though Houston had lost the contract, the controversy smouldered for two years. The House of Representatives finally appointed a select committee to determine not only whether Houston and Eaton had conspired to obtain fraudulently the contract to furnish rations to the emigrating Indians but also whether President Jackson "had any knowledge of such attempted fraud, and whether he disapproved or approved of the same." Between May and July 1832 the committee, five Jacksonians and two Whigs, held several hearings at which McKenney was a key witness. Despite testimony incriminating Houston and Eaton, however, the committee by a vote of 4 to 3 found them innocent of the charges. The three dissenters—the Whigs and one Jacksonian—denounced the proceedings as an attempt to whitewash the administration. Two of them asserted Houston "did attempt, wrongfully, to obtain the contract," Eaton "did attempt, wrongfully," to give it to him, and Jackson was fully aware of the conspiracy. The third dissenter, a Whig, modified his condemnation; although he believed Houston and Eaton were guilty, he would not "undertake to impute to [Jackson] a *consciousness* of the existence of 'fraudulent' practices, and an approbation of them."[28]

By the spring of 1830, life had become very uncomfortable for McKenney. As he later explained, "I was at last met by contumetious treatment to force me, as I had reason to believe, to resign." Senator John Forsyth, a Jacksonian Democrat from Georgia, accused him of "numberless contradictions and inconsistencies" in his official reports, particularly with regard to the Indian civilization and removal programs. He implied that McKenney was a political opportunist unconcerned about the welfare of the Indians. McKenney quickly refuted the charges, claiming the supposed contradictions stemmed from reports from field officers and missionaries. Until the summer of 1827, when he visited the southern tribes and saw the situation for himself, he had believed the Indians were making progress under the civilization program. "I believe now," he said, "from personal observation, and facts, about which there can be no mistake, differently."[29]

He learned Jackson had offered his job to others. Once the prospective superintendent came to inspect the office and question McKenney about the position. Unaware of his visitor's purpose, McKenney discussed his duties at length. Then the man informed McKenney he did not want the office. "What office?" McKenney asked. "This," the man replied. "General Jackson told me this morning it was at my service, but before seeing the Secretary of War, I thought I would come and have a little chat with you first." On another occasion McKenney's chief clerk, Samuel Hamilton claimed Congressman Wily Thompson of Georgia said Jackson told him he could have the job if he wanted it; Hamilton was to remain, but all the other clerks would be dismissed to make room for the president's friends.[30]

In addition, Houston was carrying out his threat to "expose" McKenney's mismanagement of Indian affairs. Beginning June 22, 1830, under the pseudonym Talohnsky, Houston published in the *Arkansas Gazette* a series of articles detailing instances of fraud perpetrated on the Cherokee and Creek Indians in Arkansas by officials of the Indian department. Most of the misdemeanors were associated with the removal program and all were attributed to McKenney. "There is but one . . . individual to who we can look, as the praiseworthy object of these cruel and crying enormities," Houston charged. "And he will be found to be none other, than the successful diplomatist of three Administrations—the constant apologist of every delinquent Agent in the Indian Department—the complaisant sycophant of those in power—always ready to play politician agreeably to the Vicar of Bray system . . . Col. Thomas L. McKenney, at the head of the Indian Department!"[31]

McKenney undoubtedly did "play politician" to some extent, for he at first aligned himself with the rather hard line of the Jackson administration on the removal issue. The superintendent had promised the Indians they would never be forced to emigrate against their wishes, and he should have realized how untenable his position was in the face of Jackson's avowed determination to exercise a vigorous removal program. Jackson may never have used the word "force," but his constituents expected more from him than the gentle persuasion Adams had tried. McKenney's supporters recognized the discrepancy and were puzzled over his apparent immunity to this problem. Noting McKenney's efforts to organize the New York board, the *Columbian Gazette* in August 1829 stated, "We know he is ardently their friend, but we cannot see how he can take high ground in their favor, with out coming in collision with what is *said* to be the intentions of the present administration in reference to those persecuted people." To Duff Green the board was "an artifice of McKenney, to create a belief, that the department could not dispense with his *commanding* talents."[32]

McKenney obviously realized that the Jackson administration had a rigid position on the removal issue, but perhaps with his characteristic naïveté and optimism he never fully grasped the implications, or maybe he thought he could ameliorate the policy. Moreover, McKenney could not afford to lose his job;

his financial circumstances were, as usual, dismal.

Whatever McKenney's motives, Jackson nonetheless recognized the value of the superintendent's support of the removal program. Even after Congress passed the removal bill in May 1830, there remained the delicate matter of getting the Indians to agree to emigrate. As John Bell told McKenney in 1828, "However, much, an individual may labor to sink you in the estimation of [the Indians], they still rely greatly upon your word, and believe you to be their devoted friend."[33] Jackson may have been willing to retain McKenney as long as he complied with administration efforts to induce the southern tribes to accept removal. The president, despite every encouragement, did not dismiss the superintendent until he balked at the hard line the War Department adopted against the Cherokees.

Harassment of the Cherokees began soon after the removal bill passed. On June 7, 1830, Eaton notified McKenney that "the allotment of $2,560 for Missionary and School purposes amongst the Southern Indians, which has been heretofore placed under the direction of the Board of Commissioners for Foreign Missions, shall from the termination of the present quarter, cease." Ten days later McKenney was ordered to notify all Indian agents to distribute the annuities among all the members of a tribe rather than paying the chiefs. "Let this be attended to immediately as it regards the Cherokees, & instruct the agent henceforth to discontinue the payment of annuities to the Treasurer of that tribe," his instructions read. The directive had a twofold purpose, McKenney believed: circumventing the chiefs would break down tribal authority and dispersing the money would deprive tribal leaders of the large sums they had used to fight removal through activities like the *Cherokee Phoenix.*[34]

Although McKenney sent the directive to the other field officials, he refused to notify the Cherokee agent because, he claimed, he viewed the order as "a first step, intended to be well covered . . . towards the overthrow of the Cherokee government, and a consequent breaking up of the power of this people."[35] The directive, dated June 18, went to the Cherokee agent over the signature of Philip G. Randolph, who was acting as secretary of war in Eaton's absence.[36]

The next day McKenney left for New York, primarily to find a printer for his projected history of the North American

Indians (see Chapter 14), but also "to see if I could get bread outside of such service as was looked for at Washington." Soon after his return he lost his administrative independence. "All official communications from the Indian Bureau will be submitted to the Secretary of War," Randolph wrote August 5, "and no letter will be forwarded from your office, until his approval shall first have been obtained." McKenney was again in New York when he received the next note from Randolph, dated August 16, informing him that the War Department no longer required his services.[37]

McKenney asked Randolph, when he returned, the grounds for his dismissal. "Why, sir," Randolph replied, "every body knows your qualifications for the place, but General Jackson has long been satisfied that you are not in harmony with him, in his views in regard to the Indians."[38]

McKenney apparently accepted the explanation. "It was Heavens own truth. I could never have been in harmony with any *such* views, or feelings," he wrote his close friend John McLean a few months later. "It was my misfortune, perhaps," he continued, "to demur to some of the strange orders that were sent out—the sole tendency of which was to harrass, & oppress the Indians. I was frank enough to give my opinion. I was sincere. I felt deeply for the Indians, & the honor of the country. I knew, if this policy & those proceedings, were right, *all the past*, under the enlightened Administrations which had preceded this, were wrong. I could not believe this. My own judgment, however, was enough. Whatever it may be worth, I felt a reliance on it, in this matter. I *knew* all was wrong—*deeply* so."[39]

The *National Intelligencer*, reporting September 1, had the same explanation: "We learn that Col. Thomas L. McKenney has been removed from the situation at the head of the Indian Bureau, in the War Department. We do not know the precise grounds of this removal, but we believe it was the want of conformity of opinion with the Executive in regard to the policy of the Government towards the Indians, in certain particulars." The *Telegraph*, unable to resist a parting shot at McKenney, retorted: "We take upon ourselves to say, that this is wholly gratuitous, and not authorized by any one fact known to the editors. When it will be necessary for the Secretary of War or

the President, to assign *the* reasons for the removal of Mr. Mc-
Kenney, they will not call upon the Intelligencer as their mentor. These jesuitical panders who smile that they may stab,
know that public sentiment embracing *all* political parties, has
long since demanded the removal of Mr. McKenney; and that
it is now hailed by all, as an act of justice to the people and the
individual concerned."[40] Fittingly, McKenney's controversial
government career ended on a controversial note.

"Thus was my connexion with the Indian Dept. of thirteen
years duration made to cease," McKenney later wrote. "I left
Washington with . . . scarcely enough means to support myself
& family, until I could get into some business. I left public life,
poor." He may have been poor but he left a rich legacy. In six
years McKenney had turned the amorphous Indian section of
the War Department into a cohesive, centralized bureau, an
achievement preserved by three major pieces of legislation. In
1832 Congress established the position of commissioner of Indian affairs; two years later it recognized McKenney's organiza-
tional accomplishments by giving the field service a legal foundation; and it provided a written code for the administration of
Indian affairs that relied heavily on the proposals for the reorganization of the Indian department that Cass and Clark had
compiled under McKenney's direction in February 1829. Mc-
Kenney was justly proud when, in January 1831, he boasted to
McLean: "The office I was sent from is my monument—its
records, its inscriptions, I stand or fall by them."[41]

13

The Indian
Office Museum

E STABLISHING THE BUREAU of Indian Affairs was an impressive accomplishment, but McKenney also deserves equal recognition for his archives of the American Indian. It was a project he conceived early in his federal career and which he nurtured throughout his years in public office. "I have often regretted that no Archive exists in which might have been enrolled the progress of things relating to our aborigines," he wrote in 1820. Not only would such an archives be an invaluable aid for the administration of Indian affairs, he reasoned, but the accumulated information could be "preserved there for the inspection of the curious, and the information of future generations, and long after the Indians will have been no more."[1] McKenney was convinced the Indians would soon disappear as a people by assimilation into American society, and he spent considerable time, energy, and funds during his government service gathering paintings, artifacts, books, and manuscripts relating to them.

Consequently, what he established bore little similarity to a modern archives; it rather resembled an American Indian museum, its holdings more ethnological in character than archival.

While he had intended to collect only items that seemed "worthy of preservation," McKenney found anything relating to Indians irresistible. By 1830 he had accessioned so well that Jonathan Elliot, in his guide to Washington published that year, recommended that visitors to the capital see McKenney and the Indian office which "possesses much [of] interest, perhaps more than any other in the Government."[2]

Tourists who followed Elliot's suggestion and climbed the stairs to the second floor of the War Department building and walked down the broad corridor to the Indian office were treated to a unique experience. A large bark canoe hung over the doorway. Inside the office some 130 portraits of Indian dignitaries adorned the walls. Indian "curiosities"—costumes, arrows, pipes, baskets in two display cases—competed with the office furniture for floor space. Scattered rocks, animal skins, and botanical specimens rounded out the spectacle. And at his desk sat McKenney—always ready and anxious to describe at length any item in the room.

McKenney began his collection in 1817, shortly after he became superintendent of Indian trade. Lack of funds, however, limited his scale. The bankrupt condition of the factory system, especially in its late years, restricted use of the trade fund to necessary expenditures. The situation improved little after he became superindent of Indian affairs, for the secretary of war retained the purse strings of the contingency fund. The amount of money the superintendent could divert to his collection depended on the interest, or lack of it, the secretary had in McKenney's ideas. Calhoun and Barbour provided generous allowances for the archives; Porter allowed small expenditures, Eaton almost none.[3]

Apparently the first items in McKenney's collection, and probably what sparked his interest in the project, were some "Indian implements" that Acting Secretary of War George Graham gave him in the summer of 1817. The next day McKenney sent a circular to the eight factors calling their attention "to a subject which will if it serve no other end gratify my individual curiosity." The circular authorized each factor to barter as much as $100 worth of factory goods to obtain curiosities peculiar to the tribes trading at his post. Besides bows, arrows, and clothing, McKenney would welcome any "natural

War Department building, 1820s.

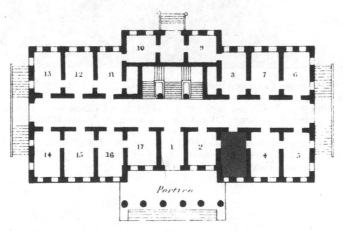

Second floor of the War Department building. Room 3 was the Office of Indian Affairs, room 10 the secretary of war's office.

An animal skin cape and a ceremonial pipe — two items from McKenney's Indian Office Museum, which are now in the custody of the Smithsonian Institution. The cape belonged to Okeemakeequid, a Chippewa chief whose portrait was painted by James Otto Lewis at Fond du Lac in 1826; McKenney later reproduced the portrait in his *History of the Indian Tribes of North America*. The pipe bears an almost illegible label in McKenney's hand that appears to read: "Presented in August 1824 to President James Monroe by Mahaskah, an Ioway Head Chief. T. L. McK."

curiosity whether of minerals, or animals, or plants." All specimens sent to the Indian office, he cautioned, were to be properly identified.[4]

The circular prompted immediate and favorable response. John Fowler, the factor at Natchitoches, said the circular gave him "much pleasure" because he had had the idea himself. "Your request," Fowler told McKenney, "together, with your permission to extend the amount to one hundred Dollars, are additional motives and will afford me the satisfaction of complying with your wishes."[5] Although at least three other factors heeded McKenney, John Johnson at Prairie du Chien was the most conscientious collector. Between 1817 and 1822 he forwarded three barrels of curiosities for which he had traded $319.59½ worth of factory merchandise. He also packed artifacts with the furs he shipped to McKenney, and when the Prairie du Chien factory was closed, the inventory listed $18.25 worth of artifacts still on hand.[6]

Johnson was not very selective in his purchases, however. McKenney informed him in 1820, "I have received a superabundance of Otter Skins & Moccasins." On the other hand, McKenney had "no Bows—two or three good Bows, & quivers, I should like to have, or indeed any thing that shall not be like those already procured." He especially wanted "Natural Curiosities . . . skins of animals well preserved which could be stuffed here—and of birds—and even a few scalps, without their being got, so as to convey the idea of their being desirable accompanied by the history of wars in which they were taken, and the persons to whom they belonged &c. &c. But," he cautioned, "these you had better get incidentally; as by telling the Indians they are disgraceful appendages & ought to be sent away, as indicating a practice which is growing to be abhorrant even amongst Indians."[7]

By 1822, when the factory system was abolished, the factors had obtained $570 worth of curiosities for McKenney. The account books list several hundred items including "2 Soo head dresses," "3 Lookfa Shootahs Tomfullen pots," "2 pr warrier garters Fox Indians," "1 Turky blanket," "1 warrior whissel," "6 Hatchicks," and "2 Indian Rattles when dancing."

Not everyone in government shared the superintendent's view of the ethnological and historical value of the collection. Graham, who liquidated the factory system holdings, auctioned off at least some of the artifacts. He advertised in a local newspaper "a number of Indian curiosities" to be sold at the Office of Indian Trade warehouse at 10 A.M. on July 1, 1822. No record of the sale has been found, but an invoice of factory goods sold at an auction later in the year lists four ornamented otter skins.[8] It is unlikely that McKenney, who followed the liquidation closely, would have allowed anything but duplicates to be sold. He preserved part of the collection by presenting "Thirty specimens Indian Dresses and Ornaments" to the Columbian Museum. The remainder of the collection probably was transferred to the War Department building; shortly after assuming his duties as superintendent of Indian affairs McKenney referred to the "Indian curiosities which are deposited here."[9]

In his new position, McKenney continued to collect. On May 22, 1824, he appealed to all the superintendents of schools in the Indian country for "specimens of birds, minerals, Indian costumes or other curiosities, which you can conveniently & without expense command & forward, also seeds of indiginous plants with their names & virtues, will be very acceptable." Other artifacts, such as a string of wampum donated by a New York clergyman, were contributed by individuals who had heard about the collection.[10]

Still another productive source was Indians visiting Washington. McKenney was responsible for them during their stay in the capital and few left without a stop at the Indian office to view his collection. The visitors were invariably impressed and often added to the assemblage from their own apparel. Unique items an Indian owner failed to offer, McKenney would attempt to purchase. He made an unsuccessful bid to buy Red Jacket's peace medal, tomahawk, and coat, probably hoping to complement the Seneca chief's portrait that hung in the gallery. On another occasion the superintendent obtained two bark canoes by giving four stranded Passamaquoddy Indians $191 in food, clothing, and cash for traveling expenses.[11]

McKenney also gathered artifacts during his two treaty-making trips. Little is known of the items he picked up in 1827 except that they included "Indian Dresses, Costumes, Minerals &c.," but those obtained in 1826 are fairly well identified because McKenney kept a diary during the trip. "After breakfast I took a ramble, alone, over this island [in Saginaw Bay]. My first direction was to its north-eastern extremity—my object was to search for mineral specimens," reads a typical entry. "The shore upon which the surf beat violently, is formed of horizontal limestone rock, in layers, not much elevated, and numerous specimens of chalcedony line it. Some of these I gathered. . . . I found also some coarse jasper, and cornelian, not much finer, and granite, out of place." Among the curiosities he collected on the 1826 trip were a model of the birchbark canoe in which he traveled, a Chippewa woman's ensemble, a British peace medal and flag, human bones he had found in a cave, an ornament made of eagle feathers, and many mineralogical and geological specimens.[12]

McKenney's collecting was not limited to inanimate objects. He brought home from his 1826 trip a pigeon he had tamed, and the following year he obtained a live elk. William Clark's letter informing him that the "Elk" had arrived safely at St. Louis and was "doing well at my cottage" was waiting for the superintendent when he returned to Washington. He promptly responded, "the Elk I am glad to hear is in your hands. Send him by the first safe conveyance to New Orleans, to some careful friend, and *by* one, if you can, to be shipped in the first vessel coming to Alexandria, '*for the Secretary of War*.' "[13] Did McKenney intend his archives to be also a zoo? Unfortunately, no other record of the elk has been found.

Manuscripts and books relating to the American Indian also formed a significant part of McKenney's collection. These he accumulated primarily for his own information and because he thought they would be useful in his work. Although he had gathered such materials from the time he first began collecting, the complex responsibilities of the position of superintendent of Indian affairs made their acquisition more urgent, particularly because he found the War Department "barren of any thing of the kind."[14] McKenney complained to Secretary of War Eaton in April 1830: "It has always appeared to me to be a desirable thing to collect periodically all that relates to the condition and prospects of these interesting but hapless people. But there has been no means that could be with propriety made applicable to defray the cost of acquiring such detailed information, at least since 1824, when this office was established. . . ."[15]

The resourceful superintendent, however, managed well enough. Just as they donated artifacts, interested citizens who knew about McKenney's archives sent information. Baptist missionary Isaac McCoy, when he wanted help in discovering the origin of the Mississippi Valley mound builders, included sketches of the mounds and a plat showing their locations. McKenney thought the sketches particularly interesting and valuable and hoped to have them engraved and circulated. He urged McCoy to continue his study of the mounds "upon the surface, and under the surface . . . turning over even their bones if necessary—in the hope of finding something there that shall tell us who they were, and when they flourished, and how, and whither they vanished."[16]

Similar appeals for help and advice from budding ethnologists, archeologists, and linguists reinforced McKenney's firm faith in the intrinsic value of his archives, and he did what he could to cooperate with correspondents. David Arnit of Lewiston, New York, hoped the Indian office would publish his history of the Six Nations. McKenney regretfully replied that the government could not purchase his manuscript. "But," he assured the author, "if it is printed you may consider me a subscriber for half-a-dozen copies for the use of the Indian Dep't." Samuel S. Conant of New York City sought assistance in the preparation of a book about Indian oratory. The helpful McKenney passed on the letter to a group of missionaries and Indian agents, asking them to send Conant, "under cover to the Secretary of War, (write on the communication Indian Affairs) such specimens of Indian Oratory as you may be able to collect, and may deem worthy a place in the work which he proposes to publish."[17]

When Congressman David Trimble of Kentucky wondered if the Indians had a cure for rabies, McKenney offered a cash award for the first tested "specific." Such cures probably existed, McKenney thought, since "we have not heard of Indians dying of Hydrophobia." The superintendent elaborated on Trimble's inquiry and asked Indian agents in addition for cures for the bites of poisonous snakes and for secret formulas for making dyes.[18]

McKenney's efforts to collect linguistic information about American Indians were considerably more complicated. "With the view of preserving in the archives of the Government what-

ever of the aboriginal man [that] can be rescued from the ulti-
mate destruction which awaits his race," he wrote missionaries
working among the tribes in August 1824, "I have to beg the
favor of you to prepare and forward to the Department, as soon
as you conveniently can, an Alphabet and Grammar, and as far
as you are able, a chapter on some subject, in the language of
the Tribe, or Tribes among whom you and your associates are
located." And, he added, "whatever may strike you as worthy
of preservation, in this, or any similar way, I will thank you to
possess me of."[19] Grammars were compiled for the Sac, Cherokee,
Shawnee, Osage, Choctaw, and Nottoway Indians. No doubt
their preparation was difficult and time consuming, and the
quality varied, of course. Some were no more than word lists.
On the other hand, the Choctaw grammar sent by the Reverend
Alfred Wright was so well done that McKenney gave him $50.[20]

The most impressive linguistic item in the archives was the
eighty-six-character Cherokee syllabary invented by George
Guess, which Charles Hicks sent McKenney in March 1825.
Although McKenney firmly opposed teaching Cherokee children
their native language in the mission schools, he did think the
syllabary was an "extraordinary discovery" that should be
shared with the American public.[21] Consequently he was receptive the following June to a missionary's suggestion that the
government print a hymnal using the syllabary. "If such a book
were printed," the missionary wrote, "it could be read by almost
every Cherokee in the nation, & would be considered by them
a very great treasure." McKenney asked him to furnish the
Indian office with a corrected copy of the syllabary and an
estimate for the cost of printing a book containing hymns and
a few chapters of the New Testament. If the cost were not too
great, McKenney assured the missionary, he would "cheerfully"
recommend to the secretary of war that the civilization fund be
used for the publication charges. McKenney also asked for a
"good likeness" of the inventor to be used as the frontispiece.
The superintendent's request that the Cherokees subscribe for
at least three hundred copies if the book were printed evidently
ended discussion of the publication.[22]

Constantine Rafinesque, professor of modern languages at
Transylvania University in Lexington, Kentucky, and Albert
Gallatin, at the time living the life of a gentleman farmer near

New Geneva, Pennsylvania, were independently trying to determine the origin of the American Indians by studying their languages. Both men—Rafinesque in 1825 and Gallatin in 1826—sent McKenney word lists they wished circulated among field officials. McKenney, intensely interested in the projects because he too was convinced that philology held the key to that "very dark subject of the origin of the Aborigines of this country," complied with enthusiasm.[23]

On August 22, 1825, McKenney sent a circular to all superintendents, Indian agents, and missionaries explaining at length the nature and significance of Rafinesque's work. "The subject increases in interest as time removes us from those to whom it relates," McKenney wrote, "but how will this be increased when antiquity shall invest it with its charms, and when the race of human beings who preceded us in the occupancy of this vast continent, will be known no more. It is for us of the present generation, if possible, to put it in the power of history to say something more of these wonderful people, than that 'they once lived.' " Although all Indian languages were important to the study, McKenney asked that particular attention be given to "any such isolated being known to you, as the 'last man' of his Tribe—to get from him the words called for. Such a man may be looked upon as the connecting link between time and eternity, as to all that regards his people; and which, if it be lost, all that relates to his Tribe is gone forever! When a preservation of it might lead to the most enlightening and gratifying results."[24]

Gallatin discussed his project with McKenney in February 1826, and a few days later a circular went out from McKenney's office. Gallatin's word list was sent to officials of the field service, to agents of the American Fur Company, to "scientific gentlemen" known to be interested in the subject, and to President Adams. McKenney considered Gallatin's work very important. "I believe," he wrote the president, "when his Ministerial labors shall have been forgotten, this vocabulary &c will remain a monument to his memory which no time can destroy."[25]

Despite McKenney's optimism, the word lists elicited few responses, probably because replies were voluntary. On May 6, McKenney sympathetically wrote Gallatin: "Nobody feels more restless than I do under *delays,* and *postponements &c, &c,*—

and I have been quite mortified, in several instances, at those which have beset and retarded your advances in the important and interesting work in which you are engaged." However, McKenney's efforts were not entirely fruitless, for he personally obtained a Chippewa vocabulary for Gallatin while on his trip to Fond du Lac in the summer of 1826. But after two years, he had little new information to share with the retired statesman. Writing in July 1828, McKenney confessed: "although I have been not so successful as I had hoped to be, I have not been unmindful of your solicitude, nor have I spared any pains to realize your wish to obtain vocabularies of our various Indian Tribes." A week later, when the Choctaw vocabulary had arrived at the Indian office, McKenney immediately sent it to Gallatin with the encouraging comment, "altho' *very slow*, we are advancing."[26]

The published works in the archives apparently were not restricted to purely American Indian subjects. A few books, such as a history of South America, a five-volume biography of the signers of the Declaration of Independence, and Webster's dictionary, McKenney acquired randomly, but most he bought through book dealers.[27] On April 25, 1825, he instructed the firm of Davis & Force to contact its agents in Baltimore, Philadelphia, New York, and Boston "for lists of the titles and numbers of volumes, and prices of such works, as relate to the Aborigines of the Country as are deemed to be standard Histories—Memoirs—Travels &c—Such as Heckewelders, Hunters, Longs, Schoolcrafts,—&c &c.—and any Theories of the Origin &c of the Indians; also such works as relate to the Geology of the Western Country &c. &c." The lists were to include a synopsis of each book. McKenney's selections were to be "bound well" and imprinted "Office of Indian Affairs" on one cover and "War Department" on the other. He reversed his procedure when, two years later, he sent the Baltimore publishing house of Fielding Lucas and Company his own list of books he wanted the firm to find. By 1828 the archives contained at least fifty-two titles purchased at a cost of more than $300.[28]

The expenditure did not go unnoticed. In the spring of 1828 the Retrenchment Committee, investigating unnecessary spending by government agencies, took exception to McKenney's archives. "If it be competent for the clerk in this office to purchase books, and pay for them out of the contingent fund for the Indian Department," reads the majority report of the committee, "it is equally within the competency and unbridled discretion of every other clerk who may desire to constitute a library in his office at public expense." Fortunately not all the members of the committee shared this narrow view. The minority even encouraged a larger library; they were "apprehensive, from its smallness, that many works of practical utility, in the office must still be wanting." Their report reads that they "would see with pleasure that care was taken, by the head of the Department, gradually to collect within the Indian Office, all such works, printed and manuscript, as are required for the intelligent and efficient discharge of its duties."[29]

Expenditures for artifacts and books were trifling compared to the sums spent on the gallery of Indian portraits that McKenney regarded as the heart of his archives. Seated in his office, surrounded by their portraits, the colonel never tired of recounting at length tales of the Indians he met on his western trips or in Washington. His enthusiasm did not escape the notice of his visitors. "I remember when I first saw him," Nicholas Biddle wrote years later, "he was surrounded by uncouth portraits of savages of both sexes, whose merits he explained with as much unction as a roman Cicerone—how nearly extremes touch when so civilized a gentleman was in contact with so wild & aboriginal a set."[30]

Charles Bird King, a local artist whose studio and gallery were on the east side of Twelfth Street between E and F, painted most of the portraits in the gallery. Although he was not an artistic genius, King established a good reputation as a portrait painter, and many prominent political figures of the period, including Calhoun, Henry Clay, and John Quincy Adams, were his patrons. The first portraits he painted for McKenney's gallery were members of a delegation of Pawnee, Omaha, Kansa, Oto, and Missouri Indians who arrived in Washington with Benjamin O'Fallon in November 1821. During the course of their stay, King did twenty-five paintings for which he received $300 from the government. Eight of the portraits were deposited in McKenney's archives; seventeen were sent home with the Indians.[31]

The paintings of the O'Fallon delegation marked the beginning of King's long and profitable association with the Indian office. Thereafter, he was regularly commissioned to paint portraits of the more prominent chiefs that came to Washington. He charged the government $20 for busts and $27 for full figures. By the time he finished his last Indian portrait in 1842, he had painted at least 143 for which he was paid more than $3,500.[32] Members of only a few important delegations received copies of their portraits, and information about the copies is tantalizingly meager. The copies given to the Creek delegation of 1825 were smaller than the 17½″ x 14″ originals, "a size," McKenney assured one of the recipients, "more convenient and portable, but just as true and perfect."[33]

McKenney also asked officials in the field to procure portraits for the gallery. Credit for the idea belongs to Governor Lewis Cass who in December 1824 sent the War Department a "striking likeness" of Tecumseh's brother, the Prophet, painted by James Otto Lewis, a young Detroit artist. Cass suggested that Lewis be allowed $200 from department funds to paint portraits of other important Indians who visited Detroit. McKenney accepted the idea but asked that Lewis enlarge his watercolor sketches to match the size of the other paintings in the Indian office. At the same time, the colonel authorized Governor Duval of Florida Territory to spend up to $100 for portraits of "a few of your most distinguished Indian Chiefs, which should be taken in the costume of the respective Tribes who may be represented by them."[34]

The exact number of paintings McKenney acquired in this manner is uncertain. The arrangement with Lewis was not entirely satisfactory, but about forty-five of his watercolors were sent to the War Department.[35] McKenney had them copied in oil for the gallery. Athanasius Ford, a Washington artist, did eleven of the copies and King evidently did the remainder. No record has been found that Governor Duval complied with the request, but McKenney did receive two portraits, which cost $10 each, from William Clark.

The gallery grew rapidly until the spring of 1827 when Secretary of War Barbour informed McKenney that "nearly all the likenesses have been collected which it is desirable to obtain." Spend no more money on portraits "unless indeed the subject be remarkable and have claims to the remembrance of posterity for some deeds of virtue or prowess; or be in figure or in costume very peculiar indeed."[36] Barbour probably was more concerned about the cost than the comprehensiveness of the gallery, for certainly the total expense for the paintings was mounting. In five years McKenney had spent more than $3,100 on the gallery alone, a considerable sum for items not easily justified as departmental necessities.

Barbour's worries were well founded. Congressman Thomas P. Moore of Kentucky was appalled at the thought of spending such sums "for the pictures of these wretches the use of which it would be impossible to tell. I believe they are hung up in Mr. McKenney's room at Washington, to gratify the curiosity of strangers."[37] The Retrenchment Committee, while attacking the library, also took exception to the paintings. Indeed, criticism of the gallery reached such proportions that McKenney felt compelled to answer the charges publicly. In a letter "To a Friend" published in local newspapers shortly after the committee's report was read in Congress, the superintendent stoutly defended the expenditures for the gallery. "Apart from the great object of preserving in some form, the resemblance of an interesting people. . . . It is the *policy* of the thing. Indians are like other people in many respects—and are not less sensible than we are to marks of respect and attention." All Indian delegations to Washington saw the collection, he pointed out. "They see this mark of respect to their people, and respect it. Its effects, as is known to me, are, in this view of the subject, highly valuable." If money was all that bothered Congress, the gallery could easily be sold for double its original cost. "And with it may go, without any regret of mine, *of a personal kind*, all the little relics which in my travels I have picked up, and at great trouble brought home with me. *It is no fancy scheme of mine.*"[38]

Again the minority members of the Retrenchment Committee defended McKenney and said he should have a larger office "in which might be more advantageously exhibited the portraits in question, and others which may be added to them, together with an ample collection of the arms, costumes, household implements, and all other articles appertaining to Indian life and manners." Not only would such an arrangement "be productive of a happy effect on the imagination and disposition of the Indian deputations, which, from time to time, repair to Washington, and with which this Government transacts very important business," but it would also "form a repository, possessing a high degree of scientific and historical value."[39]

McKenney kept the gallery, but the use of public funds for pictures practically ceased. From the time the congressional report became public until he left office more than two years later, he spent only $219 for seven more paintings, including $148 for five portraits of Winnebagos who came to Washington in the fall of 1828. When the delegation visited the Indian office, they were "highly gratified" with the portrait gallery, particularly, McKenney informed Secretary of War Porter, "at seeing so many who were known to them." But they also said: *We see no Winnebagoes here.* The superintendent asked that King be allowed to paint a few Winnebago portraits for the gallery. Porter evidently refused; a month later, as the delegation was preparing to leave the city, McKenney renewed his request. "The almost daily visits made to this office of these poor wanderers, the Winnebagoes, show an attachment so decided to the faces of those who have been painted, & that hang here; and they evince so much anxiety to have a similar respect paid to them, as to lead me to ask that you permit the likeness of Five of the principal men to be taken. . . . Yesterday they took off their bells, & ornaments, & caps, & gave me their war clubs requesting that *these* might hang up here as memorials."[40] Porter at last consented, and thus five Winnebago portraits were added to the gallery.

McKenney cherished his archives with the zeal of a modern curator and took pains to see that it was properly preserved, displayed, and publicized. King often framed his paintings before delivering them to the Indian office. Others were framed and labeled by Isaac Cooper, who also boxed and shipped the copies sent to the Indians. Two carpenters, on record only as Gaither and Wilson, hung the portraits and performed odd jobs around the office. In the spring of 1828 John Simpson installed two display cases, including one of glass that he made himself. Later the same year he worked three months "arranging and preserving from moth &c. Indian relicks; and the paintings of Indian likenesses from injury &c."[41]

After McKenney was dismissed from office in the fall of 1830, his archives passed into obscurity. Before he left Washington, he sold the items he owned personally to the War Department for $200. He claimed he wanted to prevent dispersal of the collection, but McKenney, as usual, sorely needed the money. His successors later acquired a few paintings and artifacts, but without McKenney's enthusiasm the collection attracted little attention. The books and manuscripts probably remained in the Indian office; in 1841 the curiosities and paintings were transferred to the newly organized National Institution. That organization displayed the curiosities for a while in the new Patent Office building at Eighth and G Streets and later stored them in the basement. In 1862 they were turned over to the Smithsonian Institution, where they remain today mixed with other artifacts labeled "early War Department."[42]

The fate of the paintings was paradoxically more and less fortunate. They were transferred to the Smithsonian in 1858, where the gallery was almost entirely destroyed by fire in 1865. In the meantime, however, McKenney had reproduced many of the portraits in the three-volume *History of the Indian Tribes of North America*, which he and James Hall published in Philadelphia from 1836 to 1844. The *History*, which has proven the most abiding monument to McKenney's career, occupied his attention and energies for years; his part in the project revealed his ambitions, strengths, and defects.

14
The
Indian History

How LONG McKENNEY had hoped to reproduce his gallery is unknown. He may have had the idea as early as 1822 when he persuaded Charles Bird King to do the first portraits. More likely, the idea came later in his federal career after the gallery had grown in size and excited public interest and comment. Jonathan Elliot found the portraits fascinating. "Here then is a gift to posterity," he exclaimed in his 1830 guide to Washington. "But for this gallery, our posterity would ask in vain—*'what sort of a looking being was the red man of this country?'* In vain would the inquirers be told to *read* descriptions of him—these never could satisfy. He must be *seen* to be known." How wonderful it would be, Elliot said, "to publish this interesting gallery, for the gratitude of the millions who can never see the original."[1]

Elliot was not alone in his suggestion. Jared Sparks, editor and proprietor of the *North American Review*, after seeing the gallery, casually discussed with McKenney the possibility of publishing "the rare & curious" collection. The Philadelphia printer Samuel F. Bradford was more definite; in September 1829 he offered McKenney a partnership for publication of the portraits. Although McKenney liked the proposition, he felt obliged to clear the matter with Sparks. Bradford would make the work "truly a national one" and would engrave the likenesses in "fine style," explained McKenney. The printer was a man of enterprise and great respectability; more important, he was a man of ample means. If Sparks had no "particular desire" to proceed in the business, McKenney would accept Bradford's offer. "I think I may assure you," he concluded, "that the work will fall into competent hands." Pleased that prospects for publishing the portraits were so favorable, Sparks disavowed prior claims. He asked only that the reproductions be executed with "accuracy and beauty" and that McKenney "write all that is known about the character & life of each person. Let us have a work worthy of the subject," he urged, "and honorable to the nation, & just to the Indians."[2]

"The work is to be done!" McKenney exclaimed to Sparks a month later. The portraits would be reproduced in sets of six; there would be twenty sets, or numbers, altogether. The reproductions would measure 17½" x 14", the same as the originals. Accompanying each portrait would be a biographical and anecdotal sketch based on materials "of an *authentic* character." McKenney claimed to have a great deal of biographical information already, but he had "sent out circulars for *all* I can command. The object is to make the work worthy of the nation. It will be, I think, as interesting as it will certainly be, unique," he assured Sparks.[3]

The terms were most favorable, McKenney thought. Bradford would bear printing and all other publication expenses; profits would be shared equally. "This is his own offer," he wrote. Nevertheless, "to prosecute" his part of the bargain, which was to provide the text, McKenney would need capital. Therefore, he offered Sparks half of his own share, or a quarter-interest in the project. "Every body says it will be valuable," he pointed out. In Europe, where the work would be published simultaneously, the profits would be *"beyond calculation."* He could name six noblemen in England alone who would each give $100,000 to own such a collection. If Sparks were not interested himself, perhaps he could persuade some other person in Boston to make McKenney an offer. McKenney needed only one-fourth of the money "in hand"; the rest could be made in semiannual payments. *"Nothing,"* however, could induce him to sell more than half his interest. "As to the value of the work," McKenney reiterated, "I am *sanguine.* I put a high value, of course, upon its profits. But do not think me *avaricious.* If I had been born with a *pennyweight* of this ingredient, I should not have been *obliged,* shall I say?—Yes—*obliged* to offer a fourth of such an undertaking for sale."

Sparks did not answer the letter. After a month, McKenney repeated his offer. "You are, I know, always busy," he wrote, "and I attribute my not hearing from you to the constancy of your employment and the extent of the labor which my request involved."[4] The second note also failed to move the scholar, and McKenney proceeded alone in the venture.

In the meantime, as McKenney had informed Sparks, he had asked his field officials for biographical information about various Indian leaders. The material was needed, he explained in the circular, "in anticipation to publish the Portraits of the Indians now in this office, and to accompany the work with information, historical, and biographical, so far as materials can be obtained; also to intersperse it with anecdotes of each person." John Johnston, the agent at Piqua, Ohio, promised to send facts about several Shawnee chiefs and a vocabulary of that language.[5]

McKenney also attempted to enlarge the gallery. Although congressional criticism two years earlier had forced him to stop acquiring paintings, the pending publication encouraged him to reopen the issue. The occasion presented itself with the highly publicized arrival in Washington of a party of Osage Indians. Seven of them had been taken to Europe in 1827 by an enterprising American, who then abandoned the Indians in France after exhibiting them for two years. French authorities sent them home in the spring of 1830. Three of the Osages had died of smallpox aboard ship, but the survivors, including a woman named Mohongo and her child, visited Washington before returning to Missouri.

Claiming "it is her own voluntary request," McKenney wasted little time in asking Secretary of War Eaton for permission to have Mohongo's portrait painted. "Nothing seems to delight all the Indians so much as these portraits," he wrote. "You know I am for it—& her history is so interesting, as to make it desirable; & again we have none of the Osage nation.

But you know best." Eaton replied, "if Mr. King will ... introduce the child for the usual price $20 let the Lady's request be indulged." Although King should have been paid more for a double portrait, McKenney urged the artist to accept the commission. *"Better do it*—I think it may open the door, again, for more work. The gallery is growing daily, in popularity."[6]

McKenney soon discovered to his chagrin just how popular the gallery had become. Less than three weeks later, two elderly and respected Washingtonians petitioned President Jackson for permission to copy the paintings for exhibition throughout the United States. Jackson referred the letter to Eaton, who in turn sent it to McKenney for reply. Understandably startled by this potential threat to his own unannounced plans, the superintendent refused permission. The gallery was the property of the nation, he informed the petitioners, and could not be exploited for private gain "unless it were connected with some great national object; and this could be realized only by uniting the Gallary with a work on the Aborigines of this Country, and descriptions, and history of the Tribes, and the individuals, that might be represented in the Gallary. An undertaking upon such a basis," he reasoned, "would be national." What he had outlined was, of course, his own project.[7]

The petitioners were not to be so easily denied, however. Again they wrote to President Jackson, pointing out that even monarchs allowed their subjects not only to view national works of art but also to copy them. Thus, they sneered, "it is strange that a subordinate clerk should dare to refuse to permit the Artists of the Republic to copy the public paintings for the gratification of all the Citizens who may be willing to pay the Artists for their labour in copying them and who cannot conveniently come to the Seat of Government." Again Jackson sent their request to Eaton, this time with the suggestion that "it might be well to permit them to copy the paintings if they will do so, in the Portrait room. They ought not to be taken from the room."[8] McKenney ignored the letter. After waiting two weeks for a reply, the artists asked Eaton directly. "We are old men," they wrote, "and we have learned that 'it is hard to kick against the pricks.' " Would the secretary of war intervene on their behalf?[9] Eaton did not, and there the matter ended.

Bradford, meanwhile, had returned to Philadephia in Sep-

Charles Bird King,
self-portrait, 1815.
*Courtesy Redwood Library
and Athenaeum,
Newport, R.I.*

Charles Bird King bill for 5 Indian portraits, plus frames and cases;
carries McKenney's endorsement. *Courtesy National Archives.*

The Osage Woman wishes to be painted — & hung up with the portraits. You *only* can decide. It is her own *voluntary* request. Nothing seems to delight all the Indians so much as these portraits. You know I am for it — & her history is so interesting, as to make it desirable; & again we have none of the Osage nation. But you know best.

Yrs with great respect

[signature]

Hon. J H Eaton.

15th March 1830

Letter from McKenney to Secretary of War John Eaton requesting permission to have Charles Bird King paint the portrait of Mohongo and her child, April 15, 1830. *Courtesy National Archives.*

tember 1829 with six of the Indian portraits, which he turned
over to Cephas G. Childs, who had opened a lithographic firm
a month earlier on Chestnut Street across from Independence
Hall. Although Childs was a skilled craftsman himself, the most
gifted member of the firm was his deaf-mute apprentice, Albert
Newsam, whose specialty was copying oil portraits at a reduced
size on stone; for $25 the customer received the stone and
twenty-five prints. To enhance the prestige of his firm, Childs
soon convinced Henry Inman, a noted New York portrait painter,
to become his partner. Now Childs and Inman, Lithographers,
the firm moved to the southeast corner of Fifth and Walnut
Streets in Philadelphia.[10]

Although a relatively new process—the first lithograph in the
United States had been made in Philadelphia only in 1818—
lithography made reproducing the portraits rather simple and
inexpensive. The picture was drawn with a greasy crayon on a
specially prepared stone. After the stone was dampened, the ink
adhered only to the drawing. The technique offered several advantages over the traditional wood or steel engravings: the
drawings could be made quickly; correcting them was easy; and
the stones were durable enough to provide hundreds of crisp,
clear prints. The lithographs, of course, still had to be colored
by hand.[11]

McKenney saw the first proofs of the Indian lithographs in
April 1830. He was amazed at their accuracy and quality. "I
consider the above copy, perfect, a perfect likeness of the man
who is known to me—and an exact copy of the original drawing
by King, now in the office of Indian affairs," he wrote on the
margin of one of them. A few months later, he sent a lithographed
portrait of the Seminole chief Neamathla to former President
John Quincy Adams, noting "this is a first impression, not indeed
finished, but it may serve to shew you the design, & in some
sort the skill that will be employed upon this branch of the
work." Much more enthusiastic was his letter to Nicholas Biddle.
"I confess I am delighted to see the perfection to which the
arts have risen in our Country, as exemplified in this work,"
McKenney declared. He predicted that "the engraving and
coloring" of the Indian portraits "will establish for Messers.
Childs & Inman a lasting and most enviable reputation."[12]

The partners now felt confident enough to announce publicly the plans for their "GREAT NATIONAL WORK." According to the prospectus, it would contain 120 portraits printed on fine, heavy paper "corresponding to the value and size of the work, and to its intended perpetuity." In addition to a biographical sketch of each Indian portrayed, McKenney's text would consist of an essay "calculated to throw a light upon the history of this people." The price would be $6 a number or $120 for the entire set.[13]

The project had barely been launched, however, when McKenney was dismissed from the Indian office—the first in a near endless series of setbacks. The blow could have been crippling. McKenney lost control of the gallery, the library of books and manuscripts he had so diligently collected over the years, and the franking privilege. Nevertheless, determined to see his project to completion, he and his wife moved into a boarding house at North 287 Chestnut Street in Philadelphia where, "pressed by circumstances, more than by inclination," he became editor of the *Commercial Herald*.[14]

Despite the upheaval his dismissal caused, McKenney completed a rough draft of the introductory essay by the end of the year. "*The History*, as indicated in the accompanying prospectus, is finished," he reported to his old friend John McLean in January 1831. "Mr. Sparks is here, & has read it—He promises it to be '*exactly adapted to its object*', & '*he does not see how it could be improved.*'" Sparks indeed thought highly of the manuscript. "This work will be honorable to the nation, & will illustrate the character & habits of the aborigines better than anything that has appeared," he wrote in his diary.[15]

The first proof sheet of the history was printed in September 1831. Characteristically, McKenney turned to a friend for help in correcting it. He wrote Adams, who was then living in Quincy, Massachusetts, that he wished to have "the co-operating scrutiny of more gifted minds. I do this," he admitted, "because I distrust my own ability—& fear to venture forth until *the proofs*, at least, shall pass in review before some competent intelligence." Could he send the proof sheets to Adams as they were issued "for your *close examination*, & such suggestions as you may think proper to make"? he asked. McKenney estimated the history and biographical sketches would amount to about two hundred pages.[16]

Impressed with the work's magnitude and importance, Adams agreed to read the galleys, becoming, as a result, editor of the historical narrative. "I return herewith the proof sheet of the great work which you have undertaken," he replied, "and which I trust will survive the unfortunate race of men whom we are extinguishing with merciless rapidity." Adams discussed the proof sheet in detail, commenting on both its style and content. "Now," he concluded, "if this is the sort of examination and revision which you desire to have for your work I will cheerfully give it. I may return the subsequent proof sheets more or less scarified than the present, though I shall perhaps not assign the reason for every alteration I may propose hereafter."[17]

McKenney's enthusiastic and effusive response must have overwhelmed Adams. The criticisms were *"perfectly just,"* McKenney answered. "I will be happy to incorporate whatever your Judgment & Taste may approve, into the body of the history. It is all familiar to you—you comprehend every part of this great subject—*too great for me*—and I lack not one grain of confidence in your entire power over it."[18]

The second proof sheet reached Quincy less than two weeks later; McKenney had not even taken time to read it. "Deal freely with the whole," he exclaimed in the transmittal letter. " 'Scarify' without mercy, . . . & fashion it to *your* liking." Adams made a few erasures and one or two unimportant changes.[19]

McKenney did not send the third sheet until October 10. The delay had not been by choice, he explained, "but by the tardy movement of the printer who has some little excuse, however, in the pause of the publisher, occasioned by his deliberations as to the No. of copies he will have struck off." Again, McKenney urged Adams to be "free in your use of the proofs." Adams obviously enjoyed tinkering with the galleys; he sent them back covered with questions and corrections. "The sheet I now return," he wrote four days later, "is philosophical and eloquent. Your Indian history increases in interest as it proceeds."[20] This comment so pleased McKenney he later quoted it in the advertisements announcing the first number.

McKenney may have had reasons for currying the former president's favor other than hopes for improving the history. He may have entertained the idea that Adams might try again for a second term. McKenney had been a firm supporter of the

Adams administration, and he hungered for his former post as superintendent of Indian affairs. He had much to gain if Adams would run against Jackson in 1832. McKenney obviously had this in mind when he wrote, "I have felt an itching on more occasions than one to drop *down* into Politicks—but I have spared you. I will do so yet longer.... Do you know I hate politicks—and yet," he confessed, "can with difficulty keep out of them."[21]

When, a few weeks later, illness prevented Adams from making a planned visit to Philadelphia, McKenney expressed his disappointment. "I think," he told Adams, "if you had got back, the good Citizens of this famous city would have borne testimony to the increasing estimation in which they hold your claims upon their attentions. The light in our political picture is becoming more and more visible, and as the darkness thickens, it is more & more refreshing to see the contrast." Adams, who had recently been elected to Congress from Quincy, declined the thinly veiled invitation to reenter national politics. "I have no aspirations for political fame in this world," he replied, "other than that allotted to me already. If I can discharge my duty to my constituents and my Country, I shall ask no more. I go this moment to take my seat."[22]

With a watchful eye on the political scene, McKenney attacked his history with renewed vigor, but he felt keenly his separation from the books and documents in Washington. He consumed much time asking friends to supply elusive names, dates, and facts essential to his narrative. "I am puzzled about ... that traveler," McKenney admitted to Adams, who had asked him about a missing name. "I have written to Gov Cass to look him up for me. If I fail to get him I shall have to modify the sentence but retain the *fact*." The traveler's name—Jacques Cartier—came not from Adams or Cass but from Albert Gallatin, who furnished McKenney with enough information "for a volume."[23]

Once McKenney was able to reciprocate a favor. Adams had seen and admired the portrait of Chief Justice John Marshall that the Philadelphia Bar Association commissioned from Inman. McKenney, through the generosity of Childs, sent Adams the first lithograph of the Marshall portrait to leave the city. Even for this small favor, however, he asked another of the patient Adams in return. Would the congressman ask Gales and Seaton to run a notice of the lithograph in the *National Intelligencer*? "It would be useful to Messrs Childs & Inman," McKenney said. The notice appeared six days later.[24]

Meanwhile, editor and author relieved the tedium of reviewing the fourth, fifth, and sixth proof sheets by exchanging witticisms. "If to *set* down contented is good Iroquois, it is very questionable English," Adams quipped. Replied McKenney: "I have indulged in quite a hearty laugh at my '*set* down.' " What McKenney did not find humorous was the printer's tardiness. With the sixth proof McKenney assured Adams the work would "go on faster" because the printer "promises to issue double the quantity of matter in the same time," a promise that was quickly broken. "Those printers are wonderful people," McKenney complained three weeks later. "I was promised two proofs in a week, and find it impossible to get but one—the reason assigned, is, 'The Type being scarce, and another 'job' coming in, part is taken up with that!' There is nothing like patience," he lamented. "I try, under all the circumstances of my case, to exercise what I possess, and often wish I had a larger stock."[25]

Although the pace did not please McKenney, progress was made during December. "As soon *as convenient* oblige me with the return of the proofs. I am near the close of the history except the glance I mean to take of the South Western Tribes," he wrote his editor one week into the new year. "I do not think the whole will exceed 40 pages—making 180, perhaps 200 *Octavo*." Two weeks later, McKenney sent Adams the eleventh and final proof sheet of the historical narrative. There remained, however, the biographies. Would Adams review those as well? "Many of these will be confined within a narrow compass. For, after all, what," McKenney asked, "with a few exceptions, can one say of the life of an Indian?"[26]

Much as Adams may have enjoyed helping McKenney, he could no longer do so. Once more a public servant, he found the demands on his time overwhelming. "I now receive almost every day," he wrote in his diary, "five or six letters upon subjects of inexhaustible variety and among them scarcely one in a week of the least utility to any one but the writer. Everyone opens his correspondence for purposes of his own, and if the answer is delay[ed] there comes a second or petulant complaint of

neglect." In fact, there is no evidence Adams corrected Mc-
Kenney's last four proofs. He may have returned them personally, however; Adams stayed in Philadelphia for several weeks
in the spring of 1832 while serving as a member of the special
House committee investigating the Second Bank of the United
States. During that time McKenney visited Adams on several
occasions, once accompanied by his partner Bradford.[27]

Adams was not McKenney's only editorial adviser. After
McKenney exhausted all possible sources of information about
the Uchees, a subtribe of the Creeks, he again appealed to
Gallatin. "You know, I am sure, more of these people, than
any body else," McKenney wrote. "I feel anxious to throw all
the light I possibly can upon their origin, their relations to the
Creeks, and the causes that led to them. Now, am I asking too
much of you to embody all you know respecting these people,
in the historic form, and allow me to incorporate it in my history
as *yours*?"[28] Gallatin did not answer the letter.

Furthermore, some of McKenney's friends in government
helped finance his extensive correspondence by franking his
mail. As he explained to Gallatin, "my postage is so considerable
as to be an object with me to lessen it—and I have the privilege
of using several of my friends in matters pertaining to my work
in this way." It was only fair, he rationalized, since the history
would be a contribution to the nation and should be "sustained
more practically, & extensively than this. However," he concluded, "I cannot expect more than belongs to our free institutions to grant." His obliging friends included Adams, Cass,
Richard M. Johnson, and Joseph M. White.[29]

The first hints of pessimism about the project crept into
McKenney's correspondence in May 1832. McKenney explained
to Nicholas Biddle, a subscriber, why the publication had been
so delayed. Obtaining biographical information about the Indians was much more difficult than he had anticipated. "The
very elements are scarcely less variable, or more difficult to
grasp, than are those Indians, and the incidents of their lives,"
he declared. Lack of money was another critical problem. Despite
McKenney's claim that "few works ever received a patronage
more extensive, or more honorable," he admitted that the subscription was not enough to sustain the project. "I wish I could
give these labors to the world," he said. "I would freely do it.

But I am not able to afford this."[30]

By the following spring, work on the project had ceased. McKenney blamed Bradford. "I could choke him," he exclaimed to Sparks in April 1833. Under their agreement Bradford had been responsible for the lithographs and all printing costs, leaving McKenney free to prepare the text. But the printer had been unable to bear the tremendous expense. Suspecting this, McKenney wrote, "I paused—and at last, seeing that Bradford must fail, I quit—not feeling willing to labor for the benefit of his creditors, & embarrass myself, meanwhile." McKenney claimed that practically nothing had been done on the project in more than a year and a half. Six months earlier Bradford had gone bankrupt. Although McKenney had not lost "a penny," the printer's failure had cost him dearly in time. He wished to continue the project, but to do so, he needed a partner of means. Recalling Spark's earlier interest in the paintings, McKenney again offered the scholar the opportunity to join the project and write the biographies.

Buy Bradford out, McKenney urged. The price would be minimal. The printer wanted only to be reimbursed for his expenses thus far. McKenney even offered to share future costs, assuring Sparks that credit could be had for everything—engraving, paper, and printing—and the work would pay for itself as each succeeding set of prints appeared. "A fortune awaits us," McKenney exclaimed, "if you will come into it. Now what say you?"[31]

The offer intrigued Sparks. By return mail he asked McKenney to "enlighten my mind" about the project. A grim picture emerged from the reply. In almost four years, only a dozen portraits had been lithographed. For these, however, the entire edition of four hundred copies had been struck. The forty-four folio pages of the historical narrative intended for the first number had also been printed but not a single biography. One was almost written, and there was material for perhaps five or six others, but to obtain enough biographical information about all the Indians someone would have to make a western research trip. "This you can make, or we can get Cass to send Schoolcraft through the Country on *other* business" and, through him, "get all we may want."[32]

The cost? On the first set, or number, including the narrative, $1,250 had been spent:

paper, and printing letter press	$200.00
drawing portraits on Stone, printing them, & for the paper	387.00
coloring the portraits (*6 portraits—edition 400 copies*)	600.00
Stitching & covering, estimate	63.00

Although there were only 104 subscribers, McKenney held out hopes for a large European market.

The portraits were the key to the success of the venture, and only McKenney would have permission to reproduce the War Department gallery. His friend Cass, now secretary of war, had given his personal *"assurance"* on that point. The president could overrule Cass, but McKenney had shrewdly protected himself against Jackson's *"lack of principle"* by—*"But this must be strictly confidential,"* he warned Sparks—having Inman copy in oil each Indian portrait as it arrived from Washington. The copies were *"full Portrait size"* instead of the medium size of the originals, and the effect of the thirty or forty already finished, McKenney claimed, "is more impressive than any thing I ever saw. Inman you know is a Master—& his reputation is staked on his success." By autumn, McKenney promised, *"all will be in my hands*—And I shall esteem this great gallery *a fortune.*" The lithographs could then be made from Inman's copies "at leisure" and "thus *secure* the prize."[33] This prize, which McKenney did not reveal until later, was his plan to exhibit and then sell the Inman oil portraits in Europe.[34]

"I sincerely desire to have you interested with me," McKenney concluded. "I think by yr help, every thing could be made of the work which the world would desire. *I distrust myself.*" Sparks failed to reply.

Propitiously, Edward C. Biddle and John Key, two young Philadelphia printers, bought out Bradford and saved the project. Not only did they agree to continue the Indian history, they accepted Bradford's original contract: they would bear all expenses as publishers; McKenney would provide the copy. Someone, however, still had to travel west, a trip McKenney could not make because of his *Commercial Herald* responsibilities. After only two weeks, he again wrote Sparks, this time offering to make him "joint editor." Sparks had only to "go to Washington, lay the foundation for materials, work them up—go, if necessary, West . . . and share with me my half of the proceeds of the work."[35] The scholar ignored this letter also.

Nathan Sargent, publisher of the *Commercial Herald*, agreed to join McKenney in the project—and to make the trip. On May 31, 1833, only three weeks after McKenney's last letter to Sparks, Sargent applied to Secretary of War Cass for a letter of introduction asking Indian agents to assist the project with "all the facilities in their power to [en]able me to obtain the information desired." Cass gave the request to Commissioner of Indians Affairs Elbert Herring, who promptly sent copies and strong supporting letters to several of his most knowledgeable and experienced Indian agents. "As the work will be of great interest and read with avidity, it is important that the facts contained in it should be authentic, and the information respecting the Tribes and individuals full and satisfactory," Herring wrote. "It would therefore be gratifying to the Department, if you would be pleased to comply with Mr. Sargent's request, and furnish him in the way proposed with such particulars . . . as may be in your power to give."[36]

Sargent's appeal did not go entirely unheeded. Ex-agent John Johnston replied to Herring from Piqua. "I have been requested by Col. Sargent to furnish some facts and observations, on the history of the Indians about to be published by himself and Col. McKenney, and it has been intimated to me that you would permit the manuscripts to reach their destination free of postage. With that understanding," Johnston wrote, "I take the liberty of enclosing them herewith."[37]

Although unable to venture far from his editor's desk, McKenney managed to interview some of the many Indian leaders who passed through Philadelphia, Washington, and other eastern cities as guests of the government. In January 1832 he had swallowed his pride and arranged a dinner with his former adversaries John Ridge and Elias Boudinot at the Philadelphia Atheneum, where the two Cherokees were staying. McKenney wished "to bury the Hatchet," Ridge later reported, "to which I agreed." Among other things, McKenney hoped Cherokee leader John Ross would write the biographical sketch of George Guess for the Indian history. "He is apparently as strong a friend as we have," Ridge said, relaying the message to Ross.

"He designs to publish in this City short letters addressed to the President which shall strike him as the lightning strikes the branchless pine." It was the least McKenney could do for the Cherokees: *"My Indian blood* was stirr'd when I saw them, & when I heard them tell of their sufferings," he claimed. True to his word, McKenney attacked Jackson's Indian policy in six letters published in *Poulson's American Daily Advertiser*.[38]

The following year, McKenney received permission to interview Black Hawk, the recently captured Sac chief who was being escorted through several eastern cities. Since Philadelphia was one of the scheduled stops, McKenney requested a private meeting with the celebrated warrior "of some few hours" for acquiring information not only about him but also about "other Indians with whom he may be acquainted." Accordingly, Cass instructed the army officer conducting the chief on his tour "to accommodate Col. McKenney in this particular, and to direct the Interpreter . . . to accompany Black Hawk."[39]

Other phases of the project also resumed in the following months. As McKenney had informed Sparks in April 1833, Inman had copied some thirty or forty paintings; within the next seven months the artist reproduced approximately fifty-five more. McKenney or one of his associates had been carrying the portraits back and forth between Washington and Philadelphia, but now the accelerated pace dictated the use of commercial conveyance. Freight charges were ridiculously cheap. Two boxes, each containing five portraits, were shipped in June on the "Philadelphia and Baltimore, Citizens' Union Line of Transportation, by Steam boats, via New Castle and Frenchtown Railroad" for only $.62.[40] Exchanging portraits by mail and rail did pose problems, however, particularly because the entire operation depended on the tolerance of McKenney's friends in the War Department, who allowed him to borrow the paintings, and William G. Ridgely, a clerk in the Navy Department, who acted as liaison in the transactions.

The demands of the project must have strained the best of friendships. On June 18, 1833, McKenney wrote Commissioner Herring that he had shipped ten portraits to Washington, and he asked for ten others in return—"the portrait of Eagle of delight—& the remaining 9 of those painted by King—*not* of those copied by him from Lewis." Herring replied exactly one

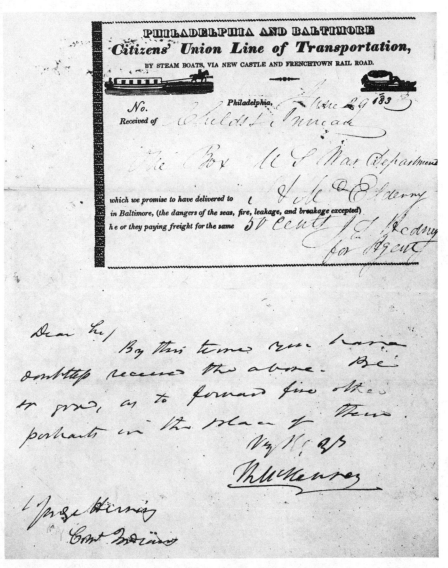

Bill of lading, dated June 29, 1833, for transporting Indian portraits from Philadelphia to Baltimore enroute to Washington. McKenney's note to Elbert Herring reads: "By this time you have doubtless received the above. Be so good, as to forward five other portraits in the place of them." *Courtesy National Archives.*

Jared Sparks, by Gilbert Stuart, 1828. In addition to editing the *North American Review*, Sparks also was for more than a decade professor of history at Harvard University and in 1849 became president there. *Courtesy New Britain Museum of American Art.*

Thomas L. McKenney, 1836. *Courtesy Lawrence Claggett, Easton, Md.*

Thomas L. McKenney, c. 1837. Engraving by Albert Newsam. The Indians in the background are taken from the McKenney-Hall *History* on which Newsam worked. This portrait served as the frontispiece for McKenney's *Memoirs*.

week later that the ten portraits had arrived and that their replacements were on their way. McKenney, meanwhile, had sent off another five asking for "five other portraits in the place of them."[41]

When, a few months later, requested paintings had not arrived speedily enough to suit him, McKenney complained to Cass. "Delays are *devouring* me. If I were there, it would be my pleasure to hasten on such things," he grumbled, "but I suppose Judge Herring is much engaged in the more important duties of his office." Herring had been away on business. When he returned, he fired back a testy reply. "There has never been any unwillingness on my part to forward Indian Portraits according to your request. They have been transmitted without delay, and with as much pleasure as you would have done the same kind office for me."[42]

Identifying the portraits also proved to be a challenge. McKenney had asked that the name of the Indian be written on the back of each portrait before it was sent to Philadelphia, but his foresight did not ensure against all mixups. He once had to send a set of lithographs to the Indian office so that Hezikiah Miller, the copy clerk, could identify the Indians. "The *stupe* of a Lithographist forgot to inscribe the name," McKenney wrote. Incredibly, a month later McKenney asked the commissioner to allow Miller, "whose pen is always ready in a good cause," to make a duplicate set of the names because he had mislaid the first.[43]

McKenney heightened the confusion by asking for nonexistent portraits. Although he claimed in April 1833 to have "a noble drawing of Black Hawk" that was not in the War Department gallery, McKenney later in the year twice asked for the Black Hawk study by King, prompting this response from Herring: "The likeness of Black Hawk is not in the Indian Office, nor has it ever been taken by order of the Department, and cannot therefore be forwarded by me."[44] On another occasion, he requested by name the portraits of six Indians of which only two—Little Crow and Waa Baa Shaw—could be found among the hundred or so that covered the walls of his old office. McKenney, however, insisted that at least one more, that of Mit-talk-quis-e-ga, was there: "The fellow with a blanket around him, whose position is over the door leading from yr room into yr Clerks—& as you go, *on the left side of the* top of the door," he told the commissioner. "The same that Miller has heard me tell a thousand times, as being at our Council at Fond Du lac asked if we thought him a dog that he should lie."[45]

Inevitably paintings went astray. "The Box containing Indian Portraits, which you say has been sent to this place, has not been delivered," Herring wrote McKenney in September 1833. McKenney responded a month later: "I am extremely anxious about the return of the box of Portraits, sent from here in the Rail Road line. Have they yet got to hand?" Although the errant portraits were later found, and despite McKenney's insistence that "there is no risque" in sending portraits by railway express, Herring later ruled that shipments would have to go in someone's care. The missionary Isaac McCoy, on a trip to Philadelphia, delivered a few to McKenney's boarding house.[46]

Meanwhile, in the spring of 1833, the project had experienced another setback: the collapse of Childs and Inman, Lithographers. Childs had anticipated a lively trade from patrons who would first have their portraits painted by Inman in his second-floor studio and then lithographed, but, except for a few important orders such as the portrait of John Marshall, the partnership never fulfilled its promise. The *United States Gazette* carried the last advertisement for the firm on April 19.[47] Before Inman returned to New York, however, he had copied in oil more than one hundred portraits from the War Department gallery. The number of Indian portraits the firm lithographed was far fewer, a dozen at most.

Childs quickly found a new partner, the landscape artist George Lehman, who had been working with the firm since 1830. As Childs and Lehman, the company struggled another year until Childs himself withdrew. He considered his lithographic career a failure. To Newsam he owed $50, an obligation that remained unpaid for eleven years; his debt to his printer, P. S. Duval, whom he had brought from France in 1831, was $750. Childs and Lehman became Lehman and Duval; the talented Newsam remained with the new firm.[48]

McKenney, by now thoroughly discouraged, temporarily shelved his project for his old nemesis, politics. He spent most of 1834 and 1835 working for the Whig party of Pennsylvania, hoping for a patronage post. It was a fruitless two years, however; McKenney failed to receive an appointment and once again turned to his Indian history for economic salvation.

McKenney found he had lost more than time during his political interlude. John Key was about to withdraw from his partnership with Edward Biddle, and Nathan Sargent had long since thought better of his agreement with McKenney. Biddle could continue alone as publisher, but McKenney desperately needed a partner with money. For once he was lucky. James Hall of Cincinnati, Ohio, a prominent jurist and a prolific writer, agreed to the same terms that McKenney had originally offered Sparks. Hall was to do the writing; Biddle was to bear all expenses. As Hall explained to the artist George Catlin, whom he unsuccessfully tried to lure into the enterprise, the work would now be known as McKenney and Hall's *History of the Indian Tribes of North America* but would still be published in twenty numbers, each consisting of six portraits and twenty or thirty pages of letterpress text. A portion of the text would be a general history, the remainder biographies of the Indians portrayed. "My materials for this part of the work are very voluminous, and of the most authentic character," the judge declared, "having been collected from a great number of the Indian agents and other gentlemen who are personally acquainted with the Indians."[49] Hall promptly left Cincinnati, arriving in Philadelphia early in February 1836.

"I became editor," Hall later wrote, "and set to work, with my usual ardor and energy (which were not small)." To his dismay, he discovered the actual situation was far different from McKenney's description. "I found the 1st No partly written—and I had to begin there, in the middle of that No and finish it." Moreover, the promised hoard of reference materials did not exist; after exhausting what little there was, he could not prevail on McKenney to gather more or to help with the writing. "I went on alone," he claimed. "The labor was Herculean. Here were a long list of Indian heroes, to be supplied with biographies —of whom we knew nothing but the names. But I was compromised to the work—and I determined to do it—and to make the work what was intended: an authentic National work." For the next eight years, he corresponded and talked with Indian agents, traders, and soldiers—"all these I took by the button, and cross examined." A few facts were gleaned from the accounts of western travelers such as Stephen H. Long and Zebulon Pike, but otherwise "nothing was compiled from books—all was collected from original sources—mostly from living and highly respectable individuals, whose testimony was examined carefully, and compared with one another. I claim therefore that this work is not only full of new and interesting facts, but that it is strictly reliable."[50]

Inspired by his new partner, McKenney resumed work on the project. On January 21, 1836, after a lapse of eighteen months, he asked Commissioner Herring to send him six more Indian portraits and to have John Ross, who was in Washington at the time, send him another copy of George Guess' biography. "Do urge it upon him," McKenney pleaded. "I really need it. I kept no copy of my draft of the life, & am in trouble for the want of it." The portraits were turned over to Lehman and Duval who also resumed their work—doubtless on credit. "I have received . . . the portraits, & the proofs," McKenney wrote the lithographers in July. "All good. I will box up, & send you two more directly. I am glad you are through your apprehensions, & can go on faster." For their deaf-mute artist, McKenney had this message: "Tell Newsam I look to him—his fame, and his name, & his honor, are all at stake. Tell him to go breast up to the work—& when I get rich I will not forget him, tho' he did run away from me in this City. Tell him he is the best fellow in the world to engrave Indians, but would not do to *fight them*."[51]

Publishing the history was only half the problem; turning a profit would require extensive sales. Biddle replaced the prospectus with two almost identical twenty-four-page pamphlets dated April 1836 and entitled *Catalogue of One Hundred and Fifteen Indian Portraits, Representing Eighteen Different Tribes, Accompanied by a Few Brief Remarks on the Character &c. of most of them.* The pamphlets urged potential purchasers to visit Biddle's shop at 23 Minor Street or the Masonic Hall on Chestnut where they could compare specimen lithographs to the Inman paintings and determine for themselves "with what fidelity the portraits are lithographed." Biddle also published a twenty-three-page pamphlet, *Recommendatory Notices of the Indian History and Biography, now Publishing by Edward C. Biddle, Philadelphia: with a List of the Subscribers, to March*

1, 1837, which contains testimonials such as the following one from Iowa subagent Andrew S. Hughes: "I think it not within the power of any artist to put on canvass a likeness of any human beings more perfect or more life-like, than are both Mohongo and her child; and I will add that, having . . . seen the lithograph copies for your work, so far as the originals are known to me, (and I know many of them,) they are as perfect as are the likenesses of Mohongo and her child."

The *History,* like many early nineteenth-century publications, could be obtained only through subscriptions sold by the publisher or his agents. Initially, John Fuller was Biddle's only authorized agent." Helping Fuller in the District of Columbia was Franck Taylor, who was associated with the project from its earliest days. In time, they were joined by subscription agents in twenty states, Canada, Great Britain, Germany, and France.[52]

A large foreign sales was essential to McKenney's plans. In May 1831 he had asked Sparks and Charles Carroll of Carrollton, among others, to write their European friends on behalf of his publication. "A great object is to convince the people over the water that the work is not a humbug," he had explained to Sparks, "that the likenesses are correct, & that it is worthy of patronage &c &c." The letters had been given to Childs, who had left for Europe that June to procure materials and pressmen for his lithographic firm. The following May, McKenney had claimed the roll of subscribers included the names of many of Europe's most distinguished citizens, "where great solicitude is expressed for a speedy and successful finish, and delivery of the work." In fact, he had admitted to Nicholas Biddle, "I am obliged to look to Europe for the greater part of the harvest which I hope to reap" from the *History.* "I have delayed, and shall continue to delay, therefore, the issuing of this first, and succeeding number until satisfactory arrangements are made for a simultaneous publication in Europe." By 1836 James M. Campbell, who had purchased for $25,000 the right to publish and sell the work in Great Britain, was acting as subscription agent in France and Germany.[53]

The first number of McKenney and Hall's *History of the Indian Tribes of North America,* the culmination of eight years of effort, was published in February 1837. Edward Biddle deposited one copy with the district court, thereby securing copyright.[54] Three days later, on March 3, McKenney presented another set of the six lithographs, inscribed "from the authors & publisher," to the American Philosophical Society. Other sets went to newspapers and magazines for review. Everyone who saw the prints was impressed. "In all the mechanical departments the work, so far as published, is faultless," reported the Philadelphia *Saturday News*. The Harrisburg *Chronicle* thought the paintings had been "lithographed with great elegance, and coloured in a manner which has never been equalled this side of the Atlantic." The Boston *Daily Advertiser and Patriot* predicted the work would be "a source of pleasure" to any subscriber and "a valuable legacy to his children."[55]

One copy of the number went to Jared Sparks, who once had said he would mention the work in the *North American Review*. "Now," McKenney wrote, "I must beg for as much of your time as will enable you to touch the subject as a reviewer, & in that periodical. I wish its effects not only for this Country, but Europe." After a year passed without the review, McKenney nudged Sparks with a not-so-subtle reminder. "You would oblige us all by the notice which you so kindly promised to take of the Indian history in the North American Review. The time, we think has arrived, when this might be done with great effect, *if done by you*." The sixth number would soon be issued; it was the ideal moment to "strike the promised blow—and give the 'shove' to the work." Sparks saw no way out and agreed to review the *History* in the April 1838 issue. "A thousand thanks to you," McKenney quickly responded. "I feel easy on that score." Except that the review did not appear until the July issue, he had no reason to be disappointed. In fifteen pages, Sparks endorsed the project and praised McKenney for "the genuine enthusiasm with which he has overcome, and continues to overcome, the many obstacles that obstruct his progress."[56]

With such favorable publicity, it is not surprising that the *History* received a substantial patronage. "Its success is wonderful," McKenney wrote Sparks in May 1838. "Over 200.000$ sold; and about 70.000$ of that within the last four months and a half—30.000$ of this in New Orleans. Were the money sluices open, it would swell out to ½ a million, as I believe." McKenney had not curbed his propensity for exaggeration, but his figures were close. The subscription book of the project lists approxi-

mately 1,250 patrons, indicating an anticipated income of
$150,000.[57]

The War Department, enrolled for fifty copies, was by far
the most important subscriber. Secretary Eaton had signed the
$6,000 order in 1830, but it was Commissioner of Indian Affairs
Carey A. Harris who found himself confronted with a $300 bill
for the fifty copies of the first set of prints that were delivered to
his office seven years later. His predicament was not eased by a
note from Congressman John Tipton of Indiana, a former Indian
agent under McKenney, who wanted to know if arrangements
had been made to pay for the subscription. If not, Tipton in-
quired, would the Indian office double its order? Harris appealed
to the Senate Committee on Indian Affairs. "The first number
of the work has been delivered, and others will be in readiness
soon," he reported. The publishers were demanding payment
and compliance with the subscription, "neither of which can be
conformed to without first obtaining from Congress an appropriation of the means." Congress answered his plea on March
3, 1837, with a $3,000 appropriation, sufficient to cover the first
ten numbers.[58]

The War Department not only honored its subscription
pledge but, a few months later, commissioned King to make
additional Indian portraits. In October 1837 a large and important delegation of Sac, Fox, and Iowa Indians arrived in
Washington. Among the delegates were Black Hawk, his son,
and Keokuk, a prominent Sac leader. King painted twenty
portraits for which the government paid him $730.[59] How Mc-
Kenney persuaded the War Department to spend so much in
enlarging the gallery is unknown, but that he was responsible
there can be no doubt. As he explained to Commissioner Harris
in October, "I supposed, when you referr'd to me the business
of having the Indians painted, that some additional celerity
would follow—and that the ceremony of transferring to canvass,
the likenesses of those selected for the artist, would be soon over.
But I was mistaken." The agent in charge of the delegation
"has a large quantity of the *snail* in him," McKenney dryly
remarked, and several of the Indians, including Black Hawk and
his son, objected to being painted. McKenney asked that as
soon as the portraits were finished they be sent to Biddle, as
well as a portrait of John Ross that the Cherokee chief had

loaned him and that was then at King's studio. "They will be put immediately in the hand of the Lithographist," McKenney assured the commissioner, "so as to have them back to you with the least possible delay."[60]

Almost nine months later, when the portraits had not been returned, King himself wrote Biddle about them. The printer blamed the delay on "the Artist in Colouring his patterns" but promised to return them all within a week, which they were. "I regret," he wrote July 7 when he shipped the five remaining portraits to Washington, "that I was obliged to retain them so long & beg of you to accept my sincere thanks for the loan of *them* & for the assistance rendered me in the prosecution of the Book itself."[61]

These seemed to be trouble-free days for the project; succeeding numbers of the *History* came out almost monthly after February 1837. An ominous sign, however, was the withdrawal of Lehman and Duval from the enterprise in August upon publication of the sixth number. J. T. Bowen of New York took their place, immediately transferring his business to Philadelphia and bringing with him Alfred Hoffy, who supplanted Newsam in the business of drawing the plates.[62]

Bowen worked on a far grander scale than the previous lithographers. At his shop on Walnut between Third and Fourth Streets, he as times employed as many as forty people on the McKenney and Hall project alone; twenty-five of them were women who did nothing but color the prints. Lehman and Duval had drawn half a dozen lithographs for numbers 7 and 8; Bowen printed and colored these and drew, printed, and colored the six plates needed to complete volume 1 of the *History*. Of the forty-eight plates which subscribers were to have bound as volume 1, Childs and Inman printed three, Lehman and Duval thirty-nine, and Bowen six. Bowen, however, printed all the plates for volumes 2 and 3 and later reissued volume 1, deleting the names of his predecessors.[63]

Although the change of lithographers appears to have been smooth, the project was foundering. Seven numbers had been published in 1837, but only three appeared in 1838. In November Biddle withdrew as publisher, although he remained with the enterprise as business agent. His place was taken by Frederick W. Greenough of Philadelphia.

Biographical information about the Indians continued to elude the authors. "I find it difficult to obtain materials for sketches of character &c of the Seminole, Creek, & Cherokee Chiefs whose portraits I am desirous of introducing into the Indian History," McKenney explained to the secretary of war in January 1839. "I have special reference, at this time, to Tucko-dee-Mothla sometimes . . . called Gov. Hicks; and Nea-mathla, both Seminoles." McKenney wondered if the correspondence of the office could be "overhawled" to determine "whether any thing is said of these two warriors that would throw a broad light upon their character, & actions." He asked if any Indian agents were visiting Washington at the time "of whom it is probable, any thing could be gleaned touching these matters." McKenney's letter was not fruitful, however. He blamed President Jackson. "I found the competent and intelligent agents were nearly all dismissed," he complained, "and ignorant partizans were in their places. I could derive no *materials* from them."[64]

Much more serious, however, were the financial problems. The developing financial plight of the publishers can be traced in their requests to the War Department for prompt payment of its subscription. "I shipped to you on the 5th . . . by Rail Road Line a box containing 50 Copies 'Indian Biography' No 11 & forwarded to your address a receipt for $300 in full for the Same," Biddle wrote Commissioner of Indian Affairs T. Hartly Crawford on February 26, 1839. "Not having heard from you in relation to their receipt, I fear the box may have miscarried." A month later he sent a less subtle appeal. "This is so different from the prompt manner in which all the former Nos sent have been paid for, that I must beg the favour of you to inform me if it arises from any noncompliance on my part, with the forms required of your office." The second auditor finally sent Biddle a check for $300 on April 9. Payment for number 12 was equally slow, forcing Biddle again to plead for quicker action. "The Scarcity of money here at this time & the heavy Expenditure involved in the publication of the 'Indian Biography' must be my apology for thus troubling you," he wrote. When number 13 was sent out in late August, publisher Greenough added his own appeal. "Do me the favour to attend to its collection & prompt remittance. Money matters are in a horrid state here."[65]

The War Department paid within three weeks, but it was too late to save the project. The depression that had followed the panic of 1837 had hit the Indian history particularly hard. Southern planters, merchants, and financiers—a group that made up more than half of the subscription list—especially suffered. "Embarrassments thickened over the land," McKenney explained. "Exchanges grew heavy against the South—until, at last, they went on from 10 to 15-20-30-40-50 pr Cent, which put a stop to our collections in those quarters, whilst many of the subscribers who were rich when they patronized the work, failed, or changed their residence, or died. Under such circumstances," he sighed, "were my cherished hopes crushed."[66]

Frustrated and bitter, McKenney became completely estranged from the project. "It seems an age since I have conversed with you & I have a deal to say, but must smother it 'till I see you," Biddle wrote him in April 1841. "Do drop me a few lines to let me know your whereabouts & inform me of your prospects. Many anxious enquiries are made by those who feel interested in your welfare; & I regret that I am unable to satisfy them."[67]

Bowen waited almost two years for the publishers to recover financially, then he resumed the project alone in an attempt to recoup something for the costly lithographic services he had provided on credit. In December 1841 he published number 14 and was immediately challenged by Biddle, who claimed the lithographer had acted without authority. Biddle asked all subscribers, including the secretary of war, not to pay for copies that were delivered. The controversy was not resolved until the following October when Biddle and Bowen agreed to transfer their publication rights to the Philadelphia printers Daniel Rice and James G. Clark, the assignees of the now bankrupt Greenough. As a result, Rice and Clark became the fifth and final publishers of McKenney and Hall's *History of the Indian Tribes of North America*. As Hall later wrote, the project was now in the hands of "a couple of Yankees."[68]

While McKenney went his separate way, the new publishers pushed the *History* to completion, with Hall writing the biographical sketches. In July 1842 they asked the War Department to loan Crouching Eagle's portrait, and during the year they succeeded in publishing numbers 15 and 16. The project had not seen the last of its troubles, however. After the publishers delivered number 16 to the War Department, the secretary informed them the government was not going to pay for numbers 14 through 20. John Eaton, the original subscriber, had recently denied ever signing for fifty copies. "To *encourage the work*," he admitted, he had allowed Bradford to announce that figure publicly, but actually he had agreed to purchase only one set. Eaton claimed a letter to that effect had been filed in the Indian office, but it was never found.[69]

Rice and Clark immediately protested the secretary of war's decision. Neither they nor the previous publishers had ever heard of such an arrangement, they declared, and to back out now, after having paid for thirteen numbers, seemed a mistake in judgment and a miscarriage of justice. "We depended entirely on the subscription to reimburse ourselves for the expense of publishing. And published *Nos.* only to complete the sets that had been commenced," they wrote. Numbers 14 to 16 would be "perfectly worthless" if the department did not claim them; the publishers did not have extra copies of numbers 1 through 13. The thirteen numbers already in government hands would be equally worthless because they were incomplete. "Besides this," Rice and Clark added, "we have incured heavy expenses to complete the remaining 4 numbers." If the War Department failed to meet its contract, the sufferers "will be ourselves & Judge James Hall of Cincinnati & no others." The secretary of war had to honor the subscription "to enable the publication to proceed, & save us from heavy losses, if not ruin." The list of subscribers had already been so reduced by failures and other causes that the project could continue only with the government's support. "We therefore hope that no obstacle, or delay, will be made by the department, to cripple us in the publication of the work, which may be called a national work, intended to perpetuate the names & character of the aborigines of our country."[70]

Rice and Clark cited McKenney, who refuted Eaton's charge, to support their case. McKenney recalled that the large subscription had been contingent on an appropriation from Congress. Eaton had agreed to this in writing. Although McKenney had seen the letter, he had not read it; nevertheless, he believed it was still in the office files. McKenney took it personally that

Eaton charged "fraud." He could not have removed the letter, he retorted vigorously; he had been dismissed from office and had no access to the files. If Eaton was trying to implicate him in wrongdoing, McKenney declared, "he does me *great injustice.*" Since no evidence could be found to support Eaton's charge, the secretary of war authorized payment, enabling the *History* to limp to completion.[71] The last number appeared in January 1844, some fourteen years after the project had begun.

The American Philosophical Society of Philadelphia has an elegant, unbound set of the *History*, and most of the original dust jackets or wrappers for these twenty numbers remain intact. The wrappers, made from heavy paper stock, folded over the portfolios from all four sides and carried advertising and the names of the sales representatives and the publishers for the *History*. From the latter listings, the changes of publishers for the McKenney and Hall project can be documented. According to the jackets, Edward C. Biddle published numbers 1 through 6; Frederick W. Greenough, with Biddle as business agent, published 7 through 13; James T. Bowen, with Daniel Rice as business agent, published number 14; and Rice and James G. Clark published 15 through 20.

The dust jacket for number 12 provided directions for binding. Numbers 1 through 8, excluding the forty-four-page historical narrative that accompanied the first three numbers, were to be bound as volume 1; numbers 9 through 16 were to be bound as volume 2; numbers 17 through 20 and the Indian history were to form the third volume. Dust jacket 17 contained further instructions. "The lives of Pocahontas and John Ross will be interwoven in the general history, and will appear in subsequent numbers." Subscribers were again reminded to bind the narrative with the last four numbers "to form a volume nearly the size of the 1st or 2nd." The dust jacket for number 20 advised subscribers to "observe the contents in No. 20, for the arrangements of the plates in volume three." Rice and Clark also offered to bind volumes for their subscribers "at lower rates and in better style than can be done elsewhere." Even plates slightly damaged, the publishers declared, "can, in most cases, be made perfect with little or no expense."

McKenney and Hall's *History of the Indian Tribes of North America* was a technological success that established J. T.

Bowen as the country's finest lithographer and proved that American lithography could rival the best European products. Its artistic achievement encouraged John James Audubon to publish in America a companion to his double elephant folio edition of the *Birds of America*. In 1839 the naturalist commissioned Bowen to provide the illustrations for a revised edition to sell in the United States for $100 in contrast to the prohibitive $1,000 of the English edition. As a reviewer in the Philadelphia *Saturday Courier* pointed out, "Audubon was truly fortunate in placing his great work in such hands, but he had seen the Indians and their admirable execution."[72]

Bowen may have realized immediate fruits from the *History*, but not the authors. Hall later groused, "McKenney & I were to have had half the profits, but got little or nothing." Even worse, they received little recognition. "The large and expensive form of the work ($120. for the whole)," he complained, "has confined it to public libraries, or to the collections of wealthy persons, so that it is not known in the literature of the country, nor has it gained me any reputation. But it is the most authentic work on the subject. And I have no doubt, that, though I may never reap any benefit from it, the day will come when some scholar whose studies shall be directed into that channel, will discover, and recognise the value of my labors."[73]

That the Indian history did not reap for McKenney the material benefit he so desperately desired was perhaps due as much to defects of character as to the high cost of the publication. Hall certainly considered McKenney a liability. Aside from "some most agre[e]able social qualities, my friend the Col. was as lazy a man as ever lived, and as unreliable a mortal as ever made big promises." The judge may have been overly critical, but even McKenney would have agreed that the charges contained a kernel of truth. "I am a regular cut out, & polished bit of laziness," he admitted, "—I always mean well, but do not act with the promptness I ought." Whatever McKenney's faults, and they were many, historians and anthropologists nevertheless owe him much. A less visionary and more disciplined man would never have begun the mammoth, tremendously expensive project, attempting on such a grand scale a venture that was barely feasible technologically. And the statement in the *Saturday Courier* that the *History* is "one of the largest and most splendid works which the literature and arts of the country have ever produced" is as true today as it was in 1842[74]

Although the lithographs received world-wide acclaim and the *History* has often been reprinted, the original oil paintings suffered a less glorious end. In June 1841, three years before publication of the final number, Secretary of War John Bell donated the entire gallery of Indian portraits to the newly formed National Institution, whose holdings were on display in the handsome Patent Office building at Eighth and G Streets. The officers of the institution, in their resolution thanking Bell, asked for a set "of the Lythographic prints and Historical sketches, having reference to these Portraits." Bell agreed that the "prints and sketches" were "properly appendages to these portraits" and donated a set of the *History* to the institution.[75] The portraits remained at the Patent Office until 1858 and were then added to the fine collection of John Mix Stanley paintings in the Smithsonian Institution. The combined exhibit, according to the secretary of the Smithsonian, formed "the most valuable collection in existence of illustrations of the features, costumes, and habits of the aborigines of this country." The priceless gallery remained on display until January 24, 1865, when fire destroyed most of the collection.[76]

Destiny was kinder to the Inman copies. In June 1839, perhaps in an attempt to secure enough capital to continue publishing the *History*, McKenney offered to sell half his interest in the Inman portraits to William D. Lewis, cashier of the Girard Bank in Philadelphia. "*I want a friend*," McKenney explained, "who shall own, jointly, with me, this valuable property, with a view to its transfer to London, &c, first for exhibition, and second for sale." With characteristic optimism, he predicted an income of $100,000 merely from exhibiting the portraits in Europe for two years; afterwards, their sale would bring another $100,000. "I have been told that the strife between Noblemen for a collection of *such paintings* . . . would run it up to an enormous sum—not less in any body's estimation, than 100,000$—For the possessor of this gallery, will be the owner of that, which *no other can own*—And you know there is a charm in this sort of ownership."[77]

Lewis asked for specific terms. McKenney wanted $5,000 for the half-interest. As security against failure of the venture, he would put up his half of the gallery. He also offered to let Lewis retain $500 to apply to "the joint expenses that may attend any steps we may agree upon for the exhibition, or sale, or both, of this gallery." McKenney then explained at length why he himself should exhibit the gallery in Europe. "My *presence* there, with the lights I could throw on the history of these interesting people would tend to multiply the profits, greatly—and then again," he pointed out, "I am there already, in the work on their race, which work has the patronage of the entire Royal Family." Concluding his "prolix" proposition, McKenney wrote: "It may, some of these days, be gratifying to you to reflect, that *you moved the enterprize* that enriched a friend; as it will be to me to reflect, that what I shall certainly esteem as disinterested, & confiding in you, has reflected back a magnificent pecuniary return."[78]

A week later McKenney sent Lewis still another note. He was leaving on a weekend trip and wanted to deposit money in the Girard bank. McKenney hoped Lewis would then "believe me *honest*" and acting in good faith regarding the portraits. "I will be back to attend to it. I go only some 20 miles off, & have no idea of an Atlantic trip," McKenney assured him, " 'till you shall say—*go*. This is in your power, at any time. When I get back we will talk about it, & about the fortune of *1, or 2 hundred thousand Dollars*, that I should be just so happy to put in yr pocket, as in mine—& strange as it may appear, I believe, *a little more so*."[79]

A letter from McKenney to Lewis written four years later indicates that the banker did not accept his offer but loaned him money. As collateral, Lewis received some of the portraits. "I have received your note," McKenney wrote on November 16, 1843. "I had forgotten that you had any of the Indian Portraits." McKenney was involved in another of his endless disputes, this time with "Doctor Clark," presumably the printer James G. Clark, who was then in the midst of the *History* and who, it appears, was holding the balance of the paintings. "What I have done in this matter ... I have done *in good faith*," McKenney avowed. Despite his reverses, he promised "to *pay what I owe—to the last dollar*."[80]

Another letter, written a week later, suggests that McKenney still hoped to profit from the paintings. "One word about the pictures," he wrote the banker. "It is this. I am free from the *taint* of avarice. A little dash of that ingredient would do me good. But I am what I am. Tho' not overanxious I wish to do the *best* with the paintings." That "best" would be to exhibit and sell them in Europe, McKenney's original proposal. Clark, however, held some of the portraits; he had to be convinced that reconstituting the gallery would benefit all concerned. McKenney, therefore, asked Lewis to give Clark the following message:

"—Col McKenney has the right as you know, to a fourth of the Indian gallery of Portraits. The design came from his head. It is right he should profit by whatever is done with them. He tells me he wishes you to have charge of all, & take them with you to Europe on an expedition of mutual benefit—That is, for him to derive out of *his* fourth that proportion of the sale of them; or whatever else you may esteem it best to do with them. *He confides in you.* Now, if the whole can be got together, *with this view*, I will deliver over those in my possession, cheerfully, to aid the Col.—"[81]

Clark evidently agreed to the proposal; the Indian portraits were ultimately again united. McKenney's profit, however, never materialized. Instead, the Inman gallery went to the firm of Tileston and Hollingsworth, a Boston paper factory, in payment of a debt. The portraits remained in the Tileston and Hollingsworth families until November 1882 when most were given to the Peabody Museum of Archaeology and Ethnology at Harvard University. There they remain, a reminder of America's Indian heritage and a memorial to McKenney, who had written in 1833: "This great gallery [is] like wine, the longer it is kept, the better. The further off we get from the Indians, & they from us, the greater interest all the public [will] feel in them."[82]

15
The
Last Decades

T HE YEARS BETWEEN his dismissal from office and his death
in 1859 were troubled, lonely, and financially difficult for
McKenney. The Indian history was a drain that forced
him to grasp at anything that might turn a dollar. He tried
business, politics, lecturing, writing. Nothing worked. His needs
always outstripped his income, and he was continually in debt.
He borrowed heavily and often, usually from friends. His wife,
Editha, died in 1835; his wastrel son, William, disappeared soon
after. McKenney's brothers and sisters had long since gone their
separate ways. William, a chaplain in the U.S. Navy, moved
to Norfolk and out of McKenney's life. Samuel, a prosperous
and prominent Georgetown industrialist, was embarrassed by
his older brother and had as little to do with him as possible.
After Editha's death, McKenney lived out of suitcases, keeping
one step ahead of the bills that pursued him relentlessly as he
made the circle of hotels that were home to him—the Chestnut
Street boarding house in Philadelphia, the Willard Hotel in
Washington, the Fremont House in Boston, the Lyceum House
in Brooklyn. No matter how bleak his circumstances, however,
he maintained a facade of affluence and never lost confidence

281

that one day would come the recognition and prosperity he craved.

One of McKenney's more promising business ventures was the Indian Emporium "for the supply of all articles used in the Indian Trade, and for the sale of Furs, Peltries, &c &c" that he established in New York City in March 1831. His extensive experience as head of the factory system and Bureau of Indian Affairs, he felt, uniquely qualified him to direct such an enterprise. As he pointed out in his announcement, "those only who have experience in this branch of commerce know any thing of the peculiar nature of the articles with which it is carried on, or the very great difficulty which those who are engaged in the Trade, experience, in obtaining them." To merchants and traders McKenney offered his services in purchasing and shipping supplies and, "at the usual rates of Commission," in receiving and selling furs. When Schoolcraft at the Sault Ste. Marie agency received the circular announcing the emporium, he knowingly commented in his diary, "this appears to me to be a striking mistake of judgement. The colonel, of all things, is not suited for a merchant." Schoolcraft may have been right, but bad timing as much as bad judgment doomed the emporium. McKenney entered the fur trade in its decline. Moreover, the government no longer purchased the enormous quantities of trade goods for the Indians, who now wanted their annuities in specie. "Unfortunately for the Indians, and for me," McKenney grumbled to Governor Cass three years later, "the great bulk of their annuities is payable in money."[1]

McKenney's political pursuits proved equally fruitless. In 1833 his good friend John McLean became a candidate for the 1836 Whig presidential nomination. He was joined a few months later by William Henry Harrison, another friend. McKenney, a loyal Whig, convinced a party victory would mean his return to the Bureau of Indian Affairs, spent most of the next two years working for the overthrow of the Democrats. His major campaign contribution was to publish in 1835 a series of thirty articles in the *Pennsylvania Enquirer* under the pseudonym "Aristides." The articles, later reprinted as a booklet entitled *Essays on the Spirit of Jacksonism, as Exemplified in its deadly hostility to the Bank of the United States, and in the Odious Calumnies employed for its destruction,* told *"the truth"* about "the war waged by *Jacksonism* against the Bank of the United States."[2]

How effective the essays were in furthering the Whig cause is conjectural. The party failed nationally but had some success in Pennsylvania where the Whig gubernatorial candidate, Joseph Ritner, upset his Democratic opponent, who was seeking a third term. McKenney promptly sought to capitalize on his campaign services by seeking a state patronage appointment and asked Nicholas Biddle to write Governor Ritner on his behalf. "My friends have, as you know, moved for me," McKenney explained. "Base your note, if you please, on that fact, & not on my application—for in my soul I loathe the *seeming*, ever, to be among those whose *acts* say—'*I have been true— now pay me for it.*' " Biddle complied, but McKenney received no appointment.[3]

Four years later McKenney was again in the field, stumping at his own expense the states of Delaware, New Jersey, and Pennsylvania. When the Whigs swept to victory, McKenney wanted and expected only one reward—his recall to the Bureau of Indian Affairs. Leaving nothing to chance, however, he urged friends and acquaintances across the country to support his claim. Typical was his appeal to the corresponding secretary of the American Board of Commissioners for Foreign Missions. McKenney wanted the board to pass a formal resolution asking for his recall. "My friends tell me I must go out of my exile & return to my former home & duties," he wrote with his usual blend of blarney and sincerity. "I have not thought it worth while to collect letters to Genl Harrison, or any one, who, it is likely may form his cabinet. I am known to them all.—But my friends say it will be better for public opinion, emanating from respectable sources, in which public men live, & by which they are mostly moved, to speak for me."[4]

The American Board politely refused to endorse his candidacy. Nevertheless, President Harrison and the members of his cabinet received scores of letters and petitions pleading for McKenney's return to office. "You know him as well as I do," Biddle wrote Secretary of State Daniel Webster. "He has been living for many years in Phila[delphia]—always on the side of good conduct & good feelings & good principles & very active & efficient in the last campaign." Writing to Secretary of War

John Bell, another Pennsylvanian declared: "No hope or confidence in the course of the administration is surer set in the hearts of the great mass of the people who have supported and sustained it, in these Districts than that the 'old White Hawk' as they affectionately term the Colonel, should be restored to his former post at Washington." The citizens of Bristol claimed "Col M'Kenney has been the fearless, zealous, and uncompromising opponent of the misrule of Jackson and Van Buren, and certainly rendered most important services to the Whig party in Pennsylva[nia] and New Jersey by his spirited and eloquent speeches at various public meetings—and to his exertions are those now in power largely indebted."[5]

Despite these testimonials, McKenney did not get the post. He said Harrison promised it to him but died before he could make it official. His claim, however, is refuted by a presidential aide who, shortly after the inauguration, confided: "McKenney *won't* do for anything but a subordinate station with limited definite powers." An attempt was made to persuade President John Tyler to appoint McKenney to the Indian office, but it also proved futile.[6]

McKenney was stunned. For ten years he had hungered for the defeat of the Jacksonians and restoration to the office he created. Now it was denied him. Scandalmongers, he rationalized, must have resurrected the lies about his mismanagement of Indian affairs. "Some insidious enemy started the insinuation that I had made improper use of the public money, and had left the [Indian] Department *rich*. And anon, another no less designing whisperer, charged me with being *embarrassed in my pecuniary affairs, therefore, not to be trusted*," he wrote to Walter Forward, congressman from New York. McKenney believed he was the victim of a smear campaign and reacted in typical fashion—he attacked. "I must reverse the order of *defences*, & bring forth *the charges*," he explained to Forward. "I fear *no* enquiry. I challenge it. But I do fear the secret, designing, wily enemy."[7]

McKenney sent a thirteen-page letter to cabinet officers, members of Congress, and friends. "I mean that you shall know me," he said, launching into a personal and poignant description of his early life and years in public office. While superintendent of Indian trade, he swore, "I never employed, or derived a dollar's benefit,—*not a cent*—more, or less, directly, or indirectly, in the passage through my hands of the millions that did pass, tho' I might not only have relieved my embarrassments, brought on me, by my friends, ... but enriched myself, without the loss of a dollar to the Government." He had accepted Calhoun's call to organize the Bureau of Indian Affairs "*upon the express condition* that I should receive the pay of an Auditor—viz: 3,000$," which he had never received. "The omission ... *embarrassed me. I feel it to this hour.*" To compound the injustices against him, he was thrown out of office for thwarting Sam Houston's illegal attempt to get the rations contract. "I had, like Bellisarious, faithfully given my time to the public service, and like him was rewarded by having my eyes torn out."

Since then, McKenney continued, "I never ... relaxed my efforts, thro' the presses of the Country, as a volunteer, to break down a party that had broken down the Country. Success, at last, crowned our cause." With Harrison's triumph there had been an outpouring of public opinion "calling for my restoration to the head of the Indian Department," he claimed. "I have yet to see the first man who did not expect my instant recall. —and I have seen thousands, and from every State, & Territory of the Union. The Indians rejoiced in the prospect of once more having me to preside over their affairs." But all this fell like water upon the sand because he was poor. "My pecuniary circumstances are such as to make the income of the Indian Commissioners pay, desireable. But I can, with God's blessing live with[out] it."

One of the autobiographical letters went to the secretary of war. "Rumor has for some time past been sending in the direction of my ears, charges implicating my official integrity," McKenney explained in his covering note. "Feeling the sting of these flying rumors, as any sensitive soul would, I determined to address [this] letter. ... You will, I am sure, appreciate my motive. It is vindicatory, wholly—and the poorest of the free, are respected in the exercise of this privilege."[8] Whatever McKenney's motive, the letter did not work and he remained unemployed.

Having failed in business and politics, McKenney next tried public speaking. The idea was not new. He had appealed to

John Quincy Adams as early as 1836 for help in developing a series of lectures about the American Indian. "The very great kindness you have manifested, in complying with several requests of mine, encourages me to add one more to their number," McKenney had written in November of that year. "I am solicited to deliver a course of lectures on Indian History, Character &c —Both my will and my wants prompt me to a compliance— But I am timid. I fear I may not be adequate to the task. It is one thing coolley to write out a case of history &c, and another to adjust it to a popular illustration." Would you do it for me? McKenney asked. "What I want is a *programme*, embracing all the points which it would be proper to touch, with as much of filling up as might be convenient. I know no one living, or dead, that could cast *a form* of such a design as well as yourself. To have your guidance, & aid in this matter, would give to me all the confidence which the undertaking would require." McKenney promised to make no suggestions. "I prefer to leave it all open, and will gladly, and confidently rely on the excellence of any you may propose; and as far as I may be able to adopt, & execute it."[9] Adams had more common sense than to do McKenney's work. He ignored the letter.

McKenney the same day sent a similar request to Jared Sparks. "I am strongly urged to deliver a course—rather, I would call them discourses, and I feel timid & doubtful of my own Judgement not only as regards the framework, but the filling up &c. Now if I could have a *skeleton* only from you it would give me confidence; & all the filling up that you could impart, would add to my pleasure in giving over the course. I have thought of dividing the course into 12 parts. But let me hear from you."[10] Sparks likewise ignored the appeal.

Six years later McKenney, unemployed and broke, approached Adams once again. "I am solicitted, often, to deliver addresses in connexion with our Indian relations," McKenney wrote in October 1842. In fact, he had just the evening before given a speech that was received "with much applause." His friends urged him to continue but still he lacked confidence. "I feel that the suggestions of your mind might be of great use to me, in framing a sett of discourses; & in the arrangement of the points to be made and illustrated." McKenney reminded the Massachusetts congressman of his earlier request; his needs were now better defined, he thought. "It would do me great service, to have divisions marked out, by you, with such suggestions as you may have the leisure to make."[11] Adams again kept his silence.

Somehow McKenney developed his lecture series: two discourses normally delivered on consecutive evenings. The first lecture, in which McKenney relied heavily on the published works of Antoine Du Pratz, John Ledyard, and others for much of his material, traced the origins and early history of the American Indians.[12] They were descendants, McKenney believed, of Tartars who migrated across the Bering Strait. "In what numbers they came, or how long they continued to cross over, we know nothing." As the Tartars spread across this continent they met a superior civilization, either Mexican or Peruvian, which they overwhelmed and destroyed. All that remains to prove its existence are the mounds that dot the North American landscape. "Few things are more certain," McKenney insisted, "than that this country was inhabited by a race, prior to the coming into it of those from whom the present race of Indians are descended . . . and that *that* race was advanced in civilization and the arts, *especially in the art of fortification*." The Tartars could not have built the mounds— "the result of skill so consummate and labor so immense"— because contemporary Indians had no oral tradition of their having done so. Furthermore, "their intellectual acquirements were as low as they are recorded to have been among any people on the face of the earth. They had no letters and no learning." Even as late as the discovery of America, McKenney continued, "I presume there was scarcely an Indian on the continent, who could comprehend an abstract idea; and at this day, the process is neither common nor easy."

In his second discourse McKenney waxed eloquent about the unhappy history of relations between Indians and white men. He highlighted his story with personal experiences; he punctuated it with melodrama and rhetoric. "Was it the purpose of the merciful God to introduce one race of men upon this continent, though they were destined to make the wilderness blossom as the rose, and to ornament it with all that was refined in the civilized, and adorn it with all that is captivating in the Christian state, at the mighty cost of annihilation?" he

asked. "Never! Never!" Americans had a Christian obligation
to preserve and reform the Indian. "Physically, intellectually,
and morally, he is, in all respects, like ourselves; and there is
no difference between us, save only in the color, and in our
superior advantages." Others had tried to help the Indians,
but their plans were incomplete and ill conceived. No one,
moreover, had tried to reform and civilize them as a race.

McKenney proposed to change all this. Why not establish
an Indian Territory, "giving to the Indians the same free-simple
title to the soil, and the same privileges ... that are enjoyed
by the Citizens of Iowa, and were possessed by the citizens of
Michigan and other Territories, when occupying a territorial
relation to the Union?" The removal program in effect had already created such a territory. More than one hundred thousand
Indians now occupied a strategic block of land west of the
states of Missouri and Arkansas. Perhaps it seemed unwise in
retrospect to congregate so many Indians in such a small area.
Should they organize, "a war more costly, and more bloody,
will ensue, than any that has ever yet been inflicted upon this
country. Philip, and Pontiac and Tecumthe, and Osceola, have
read us lessons on the capacity of Indians to revenge themselves; but never in all their history did they occupy a position
so formidable as that which is now held by their successors."
This misfortune would never occur if the Indians were made
citizens of the United States. "A new and hitherto unfelt impulse would be at once given to all the higher and nobler elements of their nature," McKenney promised, "which could not
fail of raising them in a very short time, *as a race*, upon the
same platform with ourselves. Our destiny, in a word, would
be their destiny."

The territorial plan was not new. When he was in office,
McKenney had viewed it as a second phase of the Indian removal program. A bill calling for the establishment of "the
Western Territory" had been introduced in the House in 1834
but had met severe opposition and was not acted upon.[13] Its
failure also meant the failure of the humanitarian philosophy
behind removal. McKenney knew this, but the idea was good
and he continued to advocate it. Perhaps he hoped a sympathetic administration would return him to office to implement
the program.

McKenney delivered his lectures in cities and towns along the eastern seaboard from Maine to Maryland. His purpose, he claimed, was "to awaken in the public mind an interest in behalf of the Indian race, and their destiny; to give impetus to public opinion in regard to what ought to be done, and done speedily for their welfare; and when that opinion should be fully formed, bring it to bear on Congress, in connection with a plan for the preservation and well-being of the remnants of this hapless people."[14]

Even for his lectures, however, McKenney expected friends to do much of his work. Always he couched his requests in terms of Indian welfare. "Your views are just such [as] I have long entertained, and preached to the people, as the only views which Philanthropists & Christians should adopt, who seek in earnest to save the remnants of the Indian race from annihilation, and elevate them in the scale of intelligent Beings," he wrote in June 1843 to Henry Alexander Scammell Dearborn of Boston when asking him to handle the local arrangements for a visit. Dearborn was not only to select the site but also to invite McKenney formally. The colonel could speak on behalf of Indians, the blind, orphan asylums, Sunday Schools, "or *any* other . . . [subject] that may be selected."[15]

The following autumn, McKenney made a similar request of Charles Brewster, editor of the *Portsmouth Journal of Literature and Politics*, asking him to prepare and distribute handbills. "I will be here (*Deo Volente*) on Wednesday next," wrote McKenney on October 7, 1843. "If you approve, [I] will discourse to the people on the Indian subject, on *that*, and the next evening (Thursday); and, if you approve, at ½ *past 7 O Clock*; and wish to leave one half the proceeds of sales of tickets in aid of yr Howard Association." Brewster should price the tickets "at just what you think will best promote the two-fold object of securing an audience, and bringing in aid to yr charity." Were not his expenses heavy, McKenney claimed, "I would be . . . happy to say—*keep all*."[16]

The same day Brewster printed a notice in his journal of McKenney's forthcoming appearance. "Col. McKenney will give his first Lecture on Wednesday evening next," the editor informed his readers. "As there is no man in our country so well acquainted with the interesting subject, who can speak

from personal acquaintance and observation—we trust the opportunity will be improved. His lectures have been received with
interest wherever they have been given. Aside from their intrinsic value, as half of the net proceeds go to our Howard
Benevolent Society, we have no doubt the attendance will be
full." Despite the low price of admission—$.12½—and exten-
sive advertising, the people of Portsmouth failed to "improve"
the opportunity. "We regret that the public seemed not aware
of the value of the lecture given by Col. McKenney," Brewster
reported the following week. "The attendance . . . was small,
but those who did attend were richly repaid. The lecturer has
every qualification as a good writer and eloquent speaker, to
chain the attention of an audience, and no man could have
presented a better exhibition of the early history, the character,
and the present state of the Indian tribes."[17]

No matter what McKenney tried, he could never make ends
meet. Inevitably he turned to friends, and two of the most
charitable were Eleuthère Irénée Du Pont and Jared Sparks.

McKenney had known Du Pont, whose works supplied gunpowder to the factory system, from his days as superintendent
of Indian trade. Although the friendship was more imagined on
McKenney's part than real, Du Pont had more than casual acquaintance with the colonel. Nevertheless, it is difficult to understand why the wealthy manufacturer suffered McKenney's demands, usually to get notes discounted. To borrow money
McKenney had to sell, or "discount," a personal note, which
was simply his promise to repay the loan within a specified time,
normally three or four months. The discount was the interest
rate, which the lender determined. The greater the risk the
greater the discount.[18] If Du Pont acted as his broker, Mc-
Kenney received a much lower discount than he could otherwise
command. Du Pont, who handled at least two or three notes a
year for McKenney, received nothing but thanks. "If it will not
put you to too much inconvenience," McKenney wrote on
March 30, 1833, "you would oblige me by letting me have, as
you have heretofore, so kindly done, the proceeds of the above
[note]." Inconvenient or not, Du Pont four days later sent
McKenney "a check to your order on the Philadelphia Bank
for $344.82 being the proceeds of your note [for] $350 discounted at the Bank of Delaware."[19]

Only once—in February 1831—did McKenney tell Du Pont why he needed a loan. His son, William, "a noble youth ... who is not so provident as I hope he will be," was about to embark on a two-year cruise aboard the U.S.S. *Potomac*. The ship's surgeon had agreed to let William accompany him as an unpaid assistant, and McKenney needed $350 to buy a suitable wardrobe for the boy. McKenney thought the regimen of a man-of-war would teach his son much-needed self-discipline. William never learned. "How extremely baff'ling are the incidents, & hopes of Human life," McKenney wrote Du Pont two years later. "You were kind enough to interest yourself for my Son, and ... I was indulging in the fondest hopes that William was prosecuting his voyage, and deriving benefit from the *system* of the ship, in all things pertaining to his habits." But McKenney's plans were for naught. William jumped ship overseas, sold his wardrobe, and booked passage to New York aboard a whaler. "How much this circumstance afflicts me I have not language to express," McKenney confessed. "It was the *very last resort*. Every thing else had been tried—Councils—money —any thing, but plunge, after plunge, he continued on, until he went on board the Potomac. And now here he is again, in a condition, I fear, worse than before."[20]

After the elder Du Pont died in 1834, McKenney asked his son Alfred to continue discounting notes. "On several occasions when my affairs required it, I availed myself of the friendship of one of the noblest, and best of men, your Father, who, with his characteristic cheerfulness, would get me a discount on my note, & remit me the proceeds," wrote McKenney at his florid best. "I hope I may be excused for asking of the son of my friend, a like facility—which I do, only on the ground of its being perfectly agreeable." Alfred firmly told the suppliant to take his request elsewhere, which McKenney did for six years. When he tried again he used what for him was an indirect approach. McKenney was marketing a stave cutting machine he considered ideal for the Du Pont company. "The printed paper which accompanies this, will explain the contrivance," McKenney wrote disarmingly on December 3, 1841. "It has been *tested*, and *proven* to be all that is said of it." McKenney understood the powder works used two hundred kegs a day; his machine could cut enough staves for three hundred. "If you would like to know more of this machine, or to own one, and will write me ... your views, or wishes shall be attended to." Du Pont was interested. Could the machine cut convex staves small enough for powder kegs? McKenney assured him it could and offered to arrange a demonstration. In the meantime, however, he needed a favor. Now that they were practically business associates, would Du Pont discount a note drawn on Nevins and Townsend in New York? He selected that firm, McKenney explained, because the proprietors were friends—especially Nevins—and because "I do not owe him, or his house, a Dollar."[21]

Du Pont must have groaned inwardly, "We are here in a dreadful state as regards money; the failure of the Girard Bank has caused a complete panic and the Penn[sylvani]a papers by inflammatory articles cause so much distrust that some other Banks will hardly maintain themselves," he replied. "Under such circumstances it is impossible to obtain discounts." Nevertheless, Du Pont agreed to hold the note a few days. When a week passed without further word from the industrialist, the impatient McKenney wrote again. "I apprehend my ... [letter] has miscarried," he explained. "If you can, on the receipt of this oblige me by the remittance as requested you will do me a kindness. I *infer* a miscarrage of my last only because I have not heard from you." McKenney had gone too far. Already annoyed, Du Pont simply returned the note, terminating forever McKenney's connection with the Du Pont family.[22]

McKenney's financial relationship with Jared Sparks was considerably less formal. When the colonel found himself in need of a few dollars, he simply asked the New England journalist for a loan on the basis of their *"old fashioned friendship,"* and Sparks always obliged. "I find I *may* have occasion, before a remittance reaches me from the South, for some Fifty Dollars, and not wishing to be entirely empty, among strangers, have thought of you, & as an old friend, as likely to have the means to minister to such a case," wrote McKenney in May 1843 from Cape Elizabeth, Maine. "My resources will not have ripened for some Thirty Days," he explained. "I *may* want the use of Fifty Dollars that long; but I may not, for half that time." Sparks on May 29 sent a check to McKenney for $50 drawn on the New England Bank of Boston.[23]

McKenney repaid the loan, later than promised, during a trip to Boston. "I regret that I should be behind the time in returning your obliging favor," he wrote in apology. "It is owing to an informality in the paper, which required it be sent back for correction—an affair over which I could have no control. Excuse it." Sparks also had to excuse the trouble of going to the Fremont House for his money. McKenney recognized the imposition, but his engagements would not permit returning the money personally. "Besides," he said "I shall leave Town tomorrow, & regret not having had the opportunity of a long talk with you."[24]

The following October McKenney again asked Sparks for money. "I arrived here yesterday, from Lowell—and was met by just such a circumstance as that which turned my attention to your friendly agency, some months back. A letter, that *should* have brought me a remittance deferr'd *'til the 20th Inst—, or thereabouts.'* " McKenney had an immediate need for $40. He was leaving the next morning for Portsmouth and wished "to square up some matters here." McKenney gave Sparks little option; he told the messenger to wait for the money. "I would go over, for the double purpose of saying this—and of seeing yourself & Lady," McKenney apologized, "but had the bad luck to damage my right knee, which makes it painful for me to use it. By the help of Leaches, & a little rest, it will soon be itself again." Sparks understood. "Oct. 5, sent $40. J.S."[25]

This time, however, McKenney was slower to repay. "I am mortified," he wrote on November 3. The expected funds had not yet arrived. From Portsmouth he had returned to Boston, hoping the money would be at the Fremont House, but it was not there. From Boston he went to Worcester where he spoke "to about 1500 of the Citizens about our poor Indians." Instructing the Worcester postmaster to forward his mail, McKenney left for Hartford. "No letters, yet!" He was now in New Haven, where the evening before he had addressed a few of the citizens—"the editor, professors, parsons &c, and some Fifty ladies." He would speak again that night and then leave for Philadelphia. *"But no letter!!!* I have outrun it, or, it has outrun me. We shall meet in Phil doubtless—I mean my means —& myself, when I shall remit. *But it mortifies me!"*[26]

"At last!" McKenney announced two weeks later when re-

paying the loan. Through a postal oversight the check had been at the Fremont House. "*How* very *annoying* are such things! *You* will know how to excuse the delay."[27]

Anxious not to abuse a good thing, McKenney let almost a year pass before approaching the indulgent Sparks for another loan. "I am convinced that it affords you pleasure to oblige *any body*, and yet, with this certainty, it gives me pain to tax your kindness," he wrote from Maine in September 1844. He had just repaid a rather large obligation that "took the very scrappings of my wallet to cover," yet there were still "some matters to square off hereabouts" before he could leave for Philadelphia. "I find I am *minus* some Fifty Dollars, & in this *fix*, write to say, you will, if entirely convenient, do me a favor, by obliging me with that sum, and as early after you receive this as possible, as I only wait for the *lift* to be off." McKenney suggested the money be sent via Hale's Express.[28]

McKenney borrowed money from Sparks for the last time in November 1845 when, without permission and in desperate need of $50, he cashed a check in the journalist's name. "I could not, without loss of character, put off the payment I had to make, *today*; & the presence of the Gentleman who does business in Boston, a Mr Adams, & the assurance I felt that you would allow me the privilege thus to lean on you, produced the action which I have made on the case," McKenney explained weakly. "I trust to your kindness & confidence to honor the call—as you may on its return, at the very earliest moment, after I receive the dues I have coming to me here."[29]

McKenney's boldness dampened the friendship, and his failure to repay the debt promptly did not help. Sparks waited patiently until July 1846 when, visiting New York, he left his card at the Lyceum House. McKenney got the hint. "Instead of your card, I did not know but I might be served with a Sheriffs summons!" he responded in embarrassment. "I beg pardon, I *did* know, this could 'not be, because the control of such a matter was in *your* hands." Several misfortunes had prevented him from repaying the money, McKenney explained. "There fell on me enough of financial thunder to crush giants. *Every week* since, I have been hoping to compass some of my dues, that I might restore to you your own: But to this hour I have not been able to realise this hope: But I shall soon."[30] The debt was repaid, but McKenney borrowed no more money from Sparks.

In 1844 McKenney temporarily quit the lecture circuit for the more contemplative life of a writer. Although his previous literary endeavors had not been financially rewarding, he sequestered himself on the Maine coast near Cape Cottage to write his memoirs. By early February 1845, he had completed a rough draft, which he sent to Sparks for criticism. "I send the confused mass—confused in the order of arrangement, & in its execution," he wrote February 27. "I know it is a tax; but you have a heart that knows how to excuse each trespass. Deal freely—& frankly with every thing. Tell me like a Brother what to lop off, & what to add. That you have *amended* or in any way *endorsed* the thing, shall remain between us," he promised.[31]

After a week McKenney asked about the manuscript. "Do not suppose this little message is designed to prompt you," he lied. "It is intended, only, to say, that as I *design* leaving Boston tomorrow, it would be gratifying to be able to take my *bantlings* home with me; but if your time has been so occupied, as to prevent your inspection of the (*very sad* I fear) condition of the papers, why then only hold on." Sparks could leave the edited manuscript with the proprietor of the Fremont House, who would gladly forward it. "I know & feel, the tax levied upon you by me, is a heavy one."[32]

Sparks returned the manuscript in early summer and by autumn McKenney had struck a bargain with Paine and Burgess of New York City for its publication. "I am here, & shall be here, in re-adjusting (till I finish it) the work, upon the basis you recommend," he wrote when thanking Sparks for his "practical, & Judicious" suggestions. "I shall follow you out, in all the particulars—approving, as I do, the whole of them. What is loose, or careless, or written in haste, I will try and correct, & amend. When the work is finished, I will have the pleasure of sending you a copy."[33]

The memoirs, which appeared in late summer 1846, are actually two separate volumes bound together. Volume one, entitled *Memoirs, Official and Personal; with sketches of Travels among the Northern and Southern Indians; Embracing a War Excursion, and description of Scenes Along the Western Borders,* is more official than personal, and at first glance it is disappointing; McKenney made no mention of his family, private life, or activities following his dismissal from office. Roughly half of the 284 pages he devoted to his tour of 1827, drawing on notes he took during his travels among the northern and southern tribes. McKenney originally had hoped to use the material in a companion volume to *Sketches of a Tour to the Lakes*, but the limited success of *Sketches* spoiled his plans. Except for anecdotes and asides, such as his description of the battle of Bladensburg and the attack on Washington during the War of 1812, the rest of volume 1 is a defense of his public career in which McKenney repeats the grievances and injustices he outlined in his autobiographical letter of 1841. Much of this text comes from letters, reports, and other official records of the Office of Indian Trade and the Bureau of Indian Affairs, which McKenney altered slightly to fit his narrative. A fifty-five-page appendix consists entirely of documents that support statements in the text.

The second volume is less important than the first. Entitled *On the Origin, History, Character, and the Wrongs and Rights of the Indians, with a Plan for the Preservation and Happiness of the Remnants of That Persecuted Race*, it is little more than an expansion of his discourses, which McKenney admits in the preface, he based heavily on published works. Moreover, he did not credit his sources. "It not having been in my view, at the time of preparing these Discourses, to publish them, I was not particular in making, always, quotation marks, or marks of reference to authors whom I consulted; and it sometimes happened, when their language was better than mine, I employed it." McKenney had no reason to be sensitive on this point, he believed, because other writers had taken similar liberties with his own published material.

Although written some twenty years after the events discussed, the memoirs are surprisingly accurate. Often it is possible to compare printed letters or documents with the originals; except for minor differences, they are identical. Not everything, of course, can be taken as gospel; as John Quincy Adams once remarked, McKenney tended "to magnify his office." The affable colonel may have rubbed elbows with the Washington elite, but it is unlikely he moved in the inner circles as he wanted his readers to think. McKenney also colored his role in controversial issues. He may not have carried anti-Jackson literature on his 1827 tour, but he admitted doing so on his trip to Fond du Lac the year before. Whatever its weaknesses, however, the *Memoirs* provide valuable insights into the workings of federal Indian policy in the first quarter of the nineteenth century. Jared Sparks, who reviewed the work in the October 1846 issue of the *North American Review*, went even further. "It is the tribute," he wrote, "of a sincere philanthropist to a cause which he has given not fair words alone, but the substantial efforts and costly sacrifice of many years."[34]

Not everyone, even then, concurred in Spark's kind assessment of the work. Publication of the *Memoirs* sparked a brisk and angry pamphlet war between McKenney and Kosciuszko Armstrong, son of General John Armstrong who was secretary of war when the British burned Washington in 1814. According to McKenney, the attack succeeded because Armstrong was inadequately prepared. McKenney never considered the secretary of war a traitor, although others at the time had thought so. Armstrong's mistake had been the lack of foresight to realize the nation's capital might be a target of the invaders. The popular outcry following the assault forced the secretary's resignation and led to the appointment of James Monroe in his place.

Kosciuszko Armstrong replied in a twenty-page *Review of T. L. M'Kenney's Narrative of the Causes which, in 1814, led to General Armstrong's Resignation of the War Office.* "Imagination and memory are so blended in our author," the son charged, "that it is impossible to say where the operations of the one cease, or of the other begin." The pamphleteer, who claimed to be writing a biography of his father, accused McKenney of having been part of a conspiracy to get Monroe appointed secretary of war. Armstrong admitted he could present no evidence "*directly*" contradicting McKenney's tales, since all principals but the author were dead. Nevertheless, he proposed "to furnish a chain of evidence sufficiently strong to support the inference, that the witness has misrepresented what passed, and that the opinions which he assumes to have heard, are such as could not have been expressed," especially the inference that General Armstrong had been a traitor. "Treason!

why, the foul suspicion was never breathed in any circle of honest men; and the admission that [McKenney] heard it, is a damning proof of the filthiness of his associations at that period."[35]

McKenney, ready as usual to enter a controversy, responded immediately. A card entitled *An Opening Reply to Kosciusko Armstrong's Pamphlet* and dated December 18, 1846, asked readers to withhold judgment until McKenney could "communicate with witnesses at Washington, and elsewhere, by whom I promise to prove my narrative *true*." His *Reply to Kosciusko Armstrong's Assault upon Col. McKenney's Narrative of the Causes that led to General Armstrong's Resignation of the Office of Secretary of War in 1814* appeared the following February. The twenty-eight-page pamphlet vindicated McKenney, who had found five witnesses to verify the accuracy of his statements. "How far my 'narrative' can be, with justice, tortured into an 'attack' upon General Armstrong, is . . . referred to the decision of the public."[36]

Armstrong remained unconvinced. A month later he published an *Examination of Thomas L. McKenney's Reply to the Review of his Narrative, &c.*, the final shot in the exchange. Armstrong congratulated the ex-superintendent of Indian affairs "on having at last discovered the propriety of supporting his statement of facts, by evidence, derived from other and more respectable sources," but he refused to change his opinion of McKenney or his book.[37] The twenty-page pamphlet, although sprinkled with extracts from letters evidently gathered for the biography that never appeared, did little to damage McKenney's reputation or to change the verdict of history on the incompetence of General Armstrong. In fact, the exchange seems to have served only one useful purpose. Paine and Burgess printed a second edition of McKenney's *Memoirs*.

Armstrong's charges actually angered McKenney more than his rather mild reply would indicate. "I do not know whether you saw Kos. Armstrong's pamphlet," he wrote Sparks in March 1847, "but if you did, you saw the most malignant work that has issued from the press for a long time—the coarsest, & most personally abusive. I believe I am the only writer that ever ventured to screen his Father from the effect of the imputations that were so universally cast upon him—and for which

the son undertook to denounce &, I may say, blackguard me."
In return, McKenney continued, "I treated him mildly—but
saught to take myself, & my book out of the categories in which
he saught to involve both: That is I saught to prove my narrative, *true*." Although McKenney had not yet seen the second
pamphlet, he was not worried. A mutual acquaintance thought
it was only for circulation among Armstrong's friends "—to
break the force of his fall, with them." McKenney was not so
sanguine about his *Memoirs*, however. "It has been *profitless*
so far," he complained.[38]

Profit may not have been McKenney's only concern. Convinced that lies and lack of knowledge about his accomplishments had kept him from office in 1841, he probably hoped the
Memoirs would refurbish his public image, silence his critics,
and pave the way for his restoration to office. If this was his
intent, he failed. In 1848 Zachary Taylor, another Whig, was
elected to the presidency. Despite the *Memoirs* and an effort
to arouse popular support in his behalf like the one he organized
eight years earlier, McKenney received no appointment.[39]

McKenney made one more effort to project himself into the
administration of Indian affairs. Early in 1850 he tried to give
Commissioner of Indian Affairs Orlando Brown, whom he knew
slightly, unsolicited advice about paying annuities to the Indians. "Have you concluded what to do about these cash payments—these dozes *of arsnick*, which kill, annually, so many of
the Red Race?" McKenney asked on January 21. Brown ignored
him, but McKenney was not to be put off. Three months later
he posed it again. "Will you tell me what steps have been taken,
if any, towards rescuing the Indians from the hands of those
who first brutalize, & then *rob* them of *the specie*, sent to pay
their annuities?" asked McKenney, who may have entertained
thoughts about resurrecting his long-defunct emporium. "I
cannot but hope," he continued, "that you will not stop, till
you right these wronged people, by obtaining their consent to
take goods, & other useful articles, in place of silver. The *in-
humanity* of permitting this outrage to be so long perpetuated
upon the Indians is a stain upon the Justice—(to go no further
—) of the Government. *Wipe it out*, and thus bless the Indians,
and yourself."[40]

The commissioner evidently did not share McKenney's concern. His polite response did not mention annuities. "I am a savage, am I?" retorted McKenney good-naturedly. "Then, Brother of the Red Race, shake hands. Not one word can I get out of you touching the *saliant* parts of my letters—no, not a word. You fly off & talk about my heart, and the place it occupies; and my letting go my claim upon the Anglo Saxon stock." What about the annuities? When Brown again ignored him, McKenney lost his temper. "Will you move in this matter? Or have you? Tell frankly. If you do not see your way clear, why then," McKenney threatened, "I must see what I can do with that master power, *public opinion*, in its application to Congress."[41] History was spared another McKenney crusade by Millard Fillmore's timely removal of Brown from office.

Except for a few details, the records are silent about the last decade of McKenney's life. He apparently remained financially hard-pressed, because he immediately signed over to creditors the bounty lands he received as a veteran of the War of 1812. Through the bounty land law of 1852 he received 40 acres near Mineral Point, Wisconsin, which he transferred to Cyrus Woodman; three years later he transferred to John L. Armstrong the 120 acres of Iowa farm land he received through the bounty land law of 1855. Nevertheless, a magnificent portrait of McKenney painted three years before his death shows the old hawk had lost none of his spirit. Pride and bitterness are etched in the ruddy, deeply furrowed face dominated by a sharply hooked nose and framed by unruly, almost lionlike, white hair.[42]

Death found McKenney at age seventy-three in a Brooklyn boarding house on February 20, 1859. A short obituary in the Washington *National Intelligencer* noted simply, "he was a man of active mind and philanthropic heart, and was always a zealous and true friend to the amelioration and advancement of the aboriginal people."[43]

Appendix:
Factories and
Factors, 1816-22

I N THE SPRING of 1816, when Thomas L. McKenney became
superintendent of the Office of Indian Trade, there were
eight factories in operation (indicated by asterisks in listing
below). By 1822, when Congress abolished the factory system,
nine other factories had been opened as branches or continu-
ations of the eight McKenney inherited. The list on the following two pages summarizes the dates, locations, and factors of
the seventeen factories operating or established during McKenney's tenure of office (see opposite p. 14 for map of factories).

Dates for establishing and terminating factories and for the
appointment of factors are taken, where possible, from the official correspondence of the Office of Indian Trade, but it should
be noted that considerable time often elapsed between the
signing of a document and the occurrence of the action specified.
The termination of a factory is a case in point; although it
might have been officially terminated on a certain date, it often
continued to operate for months to enable the factor to collect
outstanding debts and to sell off remaining merchandise and
equipment. This was especially true in 1822-1823; although the
act abolishing the factory system specified June 3, 1822 as the
official closing date for all factories, some remained open for
over a year.

*Green Bay
Established: 1815. *Terminated:* Nov. 3, 1821.
Factor: Mathew Irwin.†

*Chicago
Established: 1805. *Terminated:* Oct. 30, 1821.
Factor: Jacob B. Varnum.

St. Peters
Established: Oct. 30, 1821, as a consolidation of Green Bay and
Chicago factories, with Varnum as factor, but the factory
system was abolished before St. Peters could open.

*Prairie du Chien
Established: 1815. *Terminated:* June 3, 1822.
Factor: John W. Johnson.

Fort Johnson (Le Moin)
Established: Oct. 31, 1817, as a branch of Prairie du Chien
factory. *Terminated:* March 18, 1819; moved to Fort Edwards.
Factor: Robert B. Belt.

Fort Edwards (Le Moin)
Established: March 18, 1819, as a continuation of Fort Johnson
factory. *Terminated:* June 8, 1821; moved to Fort Armstrong.
Factor: Belt.

Fort Armstrong
Established: June 8, 1821, as a continuation of Fort Edwards
factory. *Terminated:* June 3, 1822. *Factor:* Belt.

*Fort Osage
Established: 1808. *Terminated:* June 3, 1822.
Factor: George C. Sibley.

Marais des Cygnes
Established: July 28, 1820, as a branch of Fort Osage factory;
Marais des Cygnes later became an independent factory.
Terminated: June 3, 1822. *Factor:* Paul Ballio.

*Chickasaw Bluffs
Established: 1802. *Terminated:* May 19, 1818.
Factor: Isaac Rawlings.

Spadra Bayou (Arkansas River)
Established: May 19, 1818. *Terminated:* June 3, 1822. *Factor:*
Rawlings opened the factory and served for over a year before
retiring from federal service; Mathew Lyon† appointed June 19,
1820 to succeed Rawlings.

*Natchitoches
Established: 1805. *Terminated:* Feb. 5, 1817.
Factor: John Fowler.

Sulphur Fork (Red River)
Established: Oct. 25, 1817, as a continuation of Natchitoches
factory. *Terminated:* June 3, 1822. *Factor:* Fowler, until his death
in 1820; William McClellan appointed Feb. 17, 1821 and served
until the factory system was abolished, when he retired from
federal service; Barak Owens, McClellan's assistant, served as
acting factor until Feb. 1823, when the Treasury Department
appointee arrived to liquidate the holdings.

*Fort St. Stephens (Choctaw)
Established: 1802. *Terminated:* Aug. 3, 1818.
Factor: George S. Gaines.

Fort Confederation (Choctaw)
Established: Oct. 13, 1819, as a continuation of Fort St. Stephens
factory. *Terminated:* June, 3, 1822. *Factor:* John Hersey.

*Fort Hawkins
Established: 1808. *Terminated:* June 1, 1817.
Factor: Daniel Hughes.

Fort Mitchell
Established: Sept. 30, 1816, as a continuation of Fort Hawkins
factory. *Terminated:* Aug. 16, 1819. *Factor:* Hughes.

---

† In many printed sources, e.g., *ASP: IA*, Irwin's and Lyon's first names are
  Matthew; however, in the original handwritten letters they are spelled
  with only one "*t*"—Mathew.

Notes

ABBREVIATIONS USED IN NOTES

IA LR	Office of Indian Affairs, Letters Received, RG 75, NA
IA LS	Office of Indian Affairs, Letters Sent, RG 75, NA
IT LR	Office of Indian Trade, Letters Received, RG 75, NA
IT LS	Office of Indian Trade, Letters Sent, RG 75, NA
MS LR	Office of the Michigan Superintendent, Letters Received, RG 75, NA
SA LS	Office of the Second Auditor, Letters Sent, RG 217, NA
SW IA LR	Office of the Secretary of War, Letters Received Relating to Indian Affairs, RG 75, NA
SW IA LS	Office of the Secretary of War, Letters Sent Relating to Indian Affairs, RG 75, NA
SW LR	Office of the Secretary of War, Letters Received, RG 107, NA
SW LS	Office of the Secretary of War, Letters Sent, RG 107, NA
ASP: IA	*American State Papers: Indian Affairs*
U.S. Stat.	*U.S. Statutes at Large*

NOTE ON FORMAT

Quotations from nineteenth-century sources are quoted verbatim, retaining the original spellings, punctuations, capitalizations, and italics or underlinings (in the case of quotations from manuscripts or unpublished letters, underlinings have been typeset as italics). A single exception has been made: One particular word that McKenney often misspelled has been corrected in his quotations—simply a concession to unambiguous readability.

304

Chapter 1 Preparation for Office

1 Charles Francis Adams, ed., *Memoirs of John Quincy Adams, Comprising Portions of His Diary from 1795 to 1848,* I, 544; Washington *National Intelligencer,* March 6, 1809.
2 James Sterling Young, *The Washington Community, 1800-1828,* 44.
3 Unless cited otherwise, the biographical and genealogical information in this chapter is taken from John McKenney, "McKenney Family History" (Hall of Records, Annapolis, Md.).
4 Undated poem by Thomas L. McKenney to Joseph Parrish, Simon Gratz Collection (Historical Society of Pennsylvania).
5 Thomas L. McKenney, *Sketches of a Tour to the Lakes, of the Character and Customs of the Chippeway Indians, and of Incidents Connected with the Treaty of Fond Du Lac,* 336; McKenney to John H. Sherburne, Jan. 21, 1842, enclosed with Sherburne to the Secretary of War, Jan. 26, 1842, SW LR.
6 McKenney to Walter Forward, Nov. 3, 1841, Gratz Collection.
7 "Obituary to Editha Gleaves McKenney," by Thomas L. McKenney, undated, unidentified newspaper clipping found among papers at the Goldsborough House, Centreville, Md.
8 McKenney to Forward, Nov. 3, 1841, Gratz Collection.
9 Militia Appointments, April 27, 1808, vol. 2, p. 63 (Hall of Records, Annapolis, Md.); T. L. McKenney, May 29, 1813, War of 1812 Manuscripts, 2828/5, Records of the Office of the Secretary of War, Record Group 107, National Archives (henceforth RG 00, NA); the rank of major dated from Jan. 1, 1814, McKenney to John C. Calhoun, March 1, 1825, Adjutant General's Office, Letters Received, Records of the Adjutant General's Office, RG 94, NA.
10 Frederick P. Todd, "The Militia and Volunteers of the District of Columbia, 1783-1820," *Records of the Columbia Historical Society,* LX (1952), 402; Washington *National Intelligencer,* July 2, 1825. That McKenney may have held the rank of colonel in the District of Columbia militia is indicated by this entry from the diary of John Quincy Adams: "*July* 4th. [1825] McKenney, Colonel T. L., Aid to General Walter Smith, came to mention the arrangements of the volunteer militia companies, which passed in review in front of my house." Adams, *Diary,* VII, 31.
11 Henry R. Schoolcraft, *Historical and Statistical Information Respecting the History, Condition, and Prospects of the Indian Tribes of the United States,* VI, 404.
12 McKenney to David Daggett, June 16, 1814, David Daggett Papers (Yale University Library); statement by Edward Hall, Nov. 12, 1817, *ASP: IA,* II, 424.
13 Thomas Gholson to James Monroe, March 20, 1816, Applications and Recommendations for Public Office during the Administration of James Madison, 1809-1817, L-M, General Records of the Department of State, RG 59, NA. Secretary of War William H. Crawford received a petition signed by "many persons" recommending McKenney for the position of superintendent of Indian trade. The petition has not been found, but the entry is in volume 9, Register of Letters Received, March 29, 1816, M-96, RG 107, NA.
14 Crawford to McKenney, April 2, 1816, SW LS, vol. C, p. 318; McKenney to Crawford, April 4, 12, 1816, SW LR, M-105, M-114(9).

15 Surety bond for Thomas L. McKenney, April 12, 1816, Records of the Bureau of Accounts (Treasury), RG 39, NA.
16 Prayer written by Thomas L. McKenney, April 12, 1816, Miscellaneous Manuscripts (Huntington Library).

Chapter 2　Superintendent of Indian Trade

1 Published material on the factory system is sparse. Most satisfactory is Chapter IV, "The Factory System," in Edgar B. Wesley, *Guarding the Frontier: A Study in Frontier Defense from 1815 to 1825.* See also Katherine Coman, "Government Factories: An Attempt to Control Competition in the Fur Trade," *Bulletin of the American Economic Association,* 4th Ser., No. 2 (April 1911), 368-88; and Royal B. Way, "The United States Factory System for Trading with the Indians, 1796-1822," *Mississippi Valley Historical Review,* VI (Sept. 1919), 220-35. Ora Brooks Peake, *A History of the United States Indian Factory System, 1795-1822,* is the only published full-length treatment of the subject, but it reflects poor style, organization, and scholarship. Aloysius Frederick Plaisance, "The United States Government Factory System, 1796-1822" (Ph.D. dissertation, St. Louis University, 1954), is a poorly written but otherwise adequate discussion of the factories.
2 Report of the Committee on Indian Affairs, Dec. 1, 1794, *ASP: IA,* I, 524; *U.S. Stat.* I, 443.
3 Francis Paul Prucha, *American Indian Policy in the Formative Years: The Indian Trade and Intercourse Acts, 1790-1834,* 44; Wesley, *Guarding the Frontier,* 32-33.
4 Quoted in Coman, "Government Factories," 388.
5 T. Tackle to Earl of Bathurst, Nov. 24, 1812, printed in Reuben Gold Thwaites, ed., "The Fur Trade in Wisconsin, 1812-1825," *Wisconsin Historical Collections,* XX (1911), 4-5.
6 An excellent, brief survey of the laws controlling the system and of the factories that were established can be found in Wesley, *Guarding the Frontier,* 35-41.
7 Calhoun to Thomas Montgomery, Feb. 12, 1822, Reports to Congress by the Secretary of War, vol. 2, p. 219, RG 107, NA.
8 *ASP: IA,* I, 763; *U.S. Stat.* II, 402-04, 652-55. The accounting procedures were as complex and confusing as the administration of Indian affairs in the early years of the republic. Originally one auditor and one comptroller reviewed the financial records of the federal government, but, because of the tremendous workload, Congress in 1817 had to increase the fiscal corps to five auditors and two comptrollers. Each auditor had responsibility for one or more government departments or bureaus, such as State, War, Navy, Customs, Attorney General, and the Indian trade; the two comptrollers reviewed the work of the five auditors. The War Department's operations were so extensive that the fiscal records of its various bureaus were divided between the second and third auditors. McKenney's financial records, as indicated in the text, were also divided. Those relating to the trade itself went to the fifth auditor's office for approval and then to the second comptroller's office for review, in effect another audit, the final one. McKenney's records concerning annuities, presents, education, and the

like went to the second auditor and then to the second comptroller.

9 "Schedule exhibiting a condensed view of the United States Indian trade during the four years preceding the 31st of March, 1815 . . . ," *ASP: IA*, II, 68.

10 *U.S. Stat.* III, 332-33; quote from Hiram M. Chittenden, *The American Fur Trade of the Far West,* I, 16.

11 John Mason to the Directors of the Bank of Columbia, Dec. 3, 1807, IT LS, vol. A, p. 12; Georgetown Assessment Records, 1818-1819, p. 4, Records of the Government of the District of Columbia, RG 351, NA.

12 *Register of Officers and Agents, Civil, Military, and Naval, in the Service of the United States, on the 30th of September, 1819,* 214; Thomas L. McKenney, *Memoirs, Official and Personal; with Sketches of Travels among the Northern and Southern Indians,* I, 22-23.

13 Second Auditor's Accounts (first series), No. 7541-A, Records of the General Accounting Office, RG 217, Washington National Records Center, Suitland, Md. (henceforth WNRC).

14 McKenney to Peter P. Porter, Aug. 4, 1827, IA LR, Michigan Superintendency.

15 McKenney to William Lee, Feb. 14, 1820, IT LS, vol. E. p. 397; McKenney to Graham, April 20, 1816, *ibid.,* vol. D, p. 8; McKenney to Mason, Jan. 20, 1818, Second Auditor's Accounts (first series), No. 7541-A, RG 217, WNRC.

16 McKenney, *Memoirs,* I, 28; McKenney to George C. Sibley, Oct. 21, 1816, IT LS, vol. D, p. 154; McKenney to Lewis Cass, June 21, 1816, *ibid.,* pp. 65-66; McKenney to George Gaines, June 10, 1817, *ibid.,* p. 327; an abstract of the statement by Cass is in enclosure D, McKenney to Crawford, Sept. 9, 1816, SW LR, M- 285(9).

17 McKenney to B. Wells, March 25, 1820, IT LS, vol. E, pp. 423-24; McKenney to S. G. Hunt, May 8, 1818, *ibid.,* p. 33.

18 McKenney to James C. Neilson, April 20, 1820, *ibid.,* pp. 439-40; McKenney to Graham, May 28, 1820, *ibid.,* p. 316.

19 McKenney to Sibley, May 2, 1817, *ibid.,* vol. D, p. 293; McKenney to Joseph Lopez Diaz, Aug. 11, 1818, *ibid.,* vol. E, p. 110.

20 McKenney to Henry Simpson, Jan. 6, 1817, *ibid.,* p. 193; McKenney to Sibley, July n.d., 1817, *ibid.,* pp. 368-69.

21 See Appendix for summary of the factories—their locations, dates, and factors—during McKenney's tenure of office.

22 Second Auditor's Accounts (first series), No. 7541-A, RG 217, WNRC; McKenney, *Memoirs,* I, 21.

23 Second Auditor's Accounts (first series), No. 7541-A, RG 217, WNRC; McKenney to John W. Rich, May 9, 13, 1817, IT LS, vol. D, pp. 300, 305.

24 See for example, John Morrison to Henry Clay, Feb. 18, 1821, printed in James F. Hopkins and Mary W. M. Hargreaves, eds., *The Papers of Henry Clay,* III, 43; McKenney to Thomas Speed, April 8, 1818, IT LS, vol. E, p. 15; McKenney to G. Robertson and to Walter Lourie, March 5, 1821, *ibid.,* vol. F, pp. 147, 148.

25 McKenney to Calhoun, Oct. 15, 1821, IT LS, vol. F, p. 268; McKenney to James Kennerly, Feb. 22 and Jan. 22, 1817, *ibid.,* vol. D, pp. 245, 227; McKenney to Sibley, Feb. 18, 1818, *ibid.,* p. 498.

26 McKenney to Thomas Posey, Oct. 1, 1817, *ibid.,* p. 423; McKenney to Abraham Woolley, Feb. 25, 1820, *ibid.,* vol. E, p. 403; McKenney to Kennerly, Oct. 29, 1819, *ibid.,* p. 352; McKenney to Joseph Saul, May

16, 1820, *ibid.,* p. 474.
27 McKenney to John C. Spencer, Nov. 4, 1841, Gratz Collection.
28 McKenney to Calhoun, March 20, 1820, IT LS, vol. E, pp. 426-27; McKenney to Walter Leake, April 19, 1820, *ibid.,* pp. 412-13; Mc- Kenney to Josiah Butler, March 31, 1820, *ibid.,* p. 425; John W. Johnson to Sibley, April 28, 1817, quoted in Wesley, *Guarding the Frontier,* 23.
29 Johnson to McKenney, June 28, 1820, IT LR; McKenney to William McClellan, July 31, 1821, IT LS, vol. F, p. 235; McKenney to Sibley, Sept. 4, 1820, *ibid.,* p. 46.
30 McKenney to Graham, July 8, 1816, IT LS, vol. D, p. 77; Graham to McKenney, July 12, 1816, SW LS, vol. C, p. 408; McKenney to Mathew Irwin, Oct. 21, 1816, IT LS, vol. D, pp. 154-55; John Fowler to the Commanding Officer at Natchitoches, May 23, 1820, enclosed with McKenney to Calhoun, July 7, 1820, SW LR, M-30(14).
31 McKenney to Graham, March 24, 1817, IT LS, vol. D, p. 263; Mc- Kenney to Irwin, Aug. 10, 1816, *ibid.,* p. 107; McKenney to Calhoun, May 13, 1818, *ibid.,* vol. E, pp. 40-41.
32 Coman, "Government Factories," 381.
33 McKenney to Cass, April 12, 1826, IA LS, vol. 3, p. 26; McKenney to Kennerly, April 6, 1819, IT LS, vol. E, p. 251.
34 Second Auditor's Accounts (first series), No. 7541-A, RG 217, WNRC; "Sales Book" (Nov. 30, 1812-Oct. 31, 1822), and "Day Book G," p. 222, Records of the Office of Indian Trade, RG 75, NA.
35 McKenney to Fowler, June 30, 1817, IT LS, vol. D, p. 350; McKenney to Mathew Lyon, May 18, 1821, *ibid.,* vol. F, p. 197; McKenney, *Memoirs,* I, 19.

Chapter 3   The Factories and Indian Reform

1 Federal Population Census, District of Columbia, 1820, Records of the Bureau of the Census, RG 29, NA.
2 McKenney to Calhoun, Dec. 5, 1821, IT LS, vol. F, p. 284; Elijah Hicks to McKenney, July 1, 1824, IA LR, Eastern Cherokee Agency; David Folsum to McKenney, May 27, 1826, IA LR, Choctaw Agency.
3 McKenney to Calhoun, Oct. 17, 1818, SW LR, M-357(11).
4 McKenney to Calhoun, Feb. 18, 1819, SW IA LR.
5 Charles B. Hicks to McKenney, Dec. 9, 1819, SW LR, M-135(13).
6 Samuel Worcester to Elias B. Caldwell and McKenney, Feb. 7, 1818, Papers of the American Board of Commissioners for Foreign Missions (Houghton Library, Harvard University); McKenney to Calhoun, Feb. 13, 1818, IT LS, vol. D, pp. 493-94; Calhoun to McKenney, Feb. 16, 1818, SW IA LS, vol. D, p. 119; Worcester to McKenney, Feb. 24, 1818, Papers of the American Board.
7 McKenney to Elias Cornelius, July 26, 1817, IT LS, vol. D, p. 375.
8 McKenney to Philip Milledoler, Jan. 29, 1820, IT LR; McKenney to Milledoler, Nov. 9, 1821, Philip Milledoler Papers (New-York His- torical Society).
9 McKenney to Agents and Factors, June 18, 1816, IT LS, vol. D, pp. 63-64; William Cocke to McKenney, Sept. 29, 1817, enclosed with McKenney to Calhoun, April 30 and Aug. 18, 1818, SW LR, M-183(11) and M-278(11); Calhoun to Andrew Jackson, Aug. 18, 1818, printed

in W. Edwin Hemphill, ed., *The Papers of John C. Calhoun*, II, 40.

10 McKenney to Robert B. Belt, June 2, 1821, IT LS, vol. F, p. 210; McKenney to Lyon, May 18, 1821, *ibid.*, p. 197.

11 McKenney to Calhoun, Dec. 5, 1821, *ibid.*, p. 284.

12 McKenney to A. H. S. Livingston, May 18, 1821, *ibid.*, p. 193; Worcester to McKenney, March 29, 1819, Papers of the American Board; Jeremiah W. Bronaugh to James Scull, Feb. 2, 1821, IT LS, vol. F, p. 116.

13 McKenney to William Clark, May 4, 1819, IT LS, vol. E, p. 260; McKenney to Fowler, Sibley, and Isaac Rawlings, May 12, 1819, *ibid.*, pp. 260-61; Lewis Edwards to Superintendents and Agents, May 12, 1819, *Papers of John C. Calhoun*, IV, 59.

14 Milledoler to McKenney, Jan. 27, March 29, and April 7, 1820, Milledoler Papers.

15 McKenney to Calhoun, April 10, 1820, SW LR, M-229(13); Calhoun to McKenney, April 13, 1820, *Papers of John C. Calhoun*, V, 31-32.

16 McKenney to James T. Miller, Indian Agents, and David Brearly, May 3, 1820, IT LS, vol. E, pp. 447-48.

17 McKenney to the Chiefs of the Osages, *ibid.*, pp. 448-50.

18 Clark to Calhoun, June 5, 1820, *Papers of John C. Calhoun*, V, 167-68; McKenney to Worcester, July 5, 1820, Papers of the American Board.

19 McKenney to Calhoun, July 5, 1820, IT LS, vol. E, pp. 494-96.

20 Calhoun to McKenney, July 17, 1820, *Papers of John C. Calhoun*, V, 263-64; Zechariah Lewis to Calhoun, Aug. 5, 1820, *ibid.*, 308; McKenney to Milledoler, Aug. 9, 1820, IT LS, vol. F, p. 34.

21 *A Register of Officers and Agents, Civil, Military, and Naval, in the Service of the United States, on the 30th of September 1823*, 88; Nathaniel B. Dodge to Calhoun, Nov. 20, 1822, SW IA LR; William F. Vaill to Calhoun, Oct. 30, 1821, and Oct. 1, 1823, *ibid.*

22 Cyrus Kingsbury to Crawford, May 2, 1816, and Crawford to Kingsbury, May 14, 1816, *ASP: IA*, II, 477-78.

23 Kingsbury to Calhoun, May 15, 1818, enclosed with Return J. Meigs to Calhoun, June 10, 1818, SW IA LR. The school was named for David Brainerd, Protestant missionary to the Indians in the 1740s.

24 Robert F. Berkhofer, Jr., *Salvation and the Savage: An Analysis of Protestant Missions and American Indian Response, 1787-1862*, 25-26.

25 Kingsbury to Calhoun, May 15, 1818, enclosed with Meigs to Calhoun, June 10, 1818, SW IA LR.

26 *House Journal*, Dec. 3, 1816, 14 Cong., 2 Sess., 13; McKenney to Isaac Thomas, Dec. 14, 1816, IT LS, vol. D, p. 201.

27 McKenney to Thomas, Dec. 14, 23, 1816, and Jan. 3, 1817, *ibid.*, pp. 200-09, 209-15, 217-25.

28 McKenney to Thomas, Dec. 14, 23, 1816, *ibid.*, 207-08, 214.

29 Georgetown Assessment Records, 1808-1812, p. 156, and *ibid.*, 1815, p. 32, RG 351, NA; McKenney to Thomas, Dec. 28, 1816, HR14A-C5.1, box 183, Records of the United States House of Representatives, RG 233, NA. Generally speaking, a salary in the early government bureaucracy stood for years without change. McKenney's predecessor had the same salary McKenney had for his entire tenure—eight years. McKenney was counting on his increased duties to justify his raise— if Congressman Thomas' bill passed.

30 *House Journal*, Feb. 4, 1817, 14 Cong., 2 Sess., 339; Original Bill 103, HR14A-B1, RG 233, NA.

31 Liber AP-40, 1817, pp. 126-29 (Recorder of Deeds, Washington, D.C.); Liber AR-42, 1818, *ibid.*
32 *Circular to the Indian Agents, as accepted by a Committee of the Board, S.T.C.S.,* [1817], HR15A-G6.2, RG 233, NA.
33 McKenney to Indian Agents, July 7, 1817, IT LS, vol. D, pp. 371-73; McKenney to Cass, Clark, and Ninian Edwards, *ibid.,* pp. 369-71.
34 McKenney to Cornelius, July 26, 1817, *ibid.,* pp. 373-74.
35 McKenney to Samuel Trott, Aug. 29, 1817, *ibid.,* pp. 394-96; Worcester to McKenney, Oct. 14, 20, 1817, IT LR; McKenney to Worcester, Oct. 30, 1817, Papers of the American Board.
36 *House Journal,* Dec. 3, 1817, 15 Cong., 1 Sess. (Serial 4), 13-14, 20.
37 McKenney to Henry Southard, Jan. 15, 1818, IT LS, vol. E, pp. 99-100.
38 *House Journal,* Jan. 22, 1818, 15 Cong., 1 Sess. (Serial 4), 169; Original Bill 50, HR15A-B1, RG 233, NA.
39 McKenney to Henry R. Storrs, Jan. 22, 1818, IT LS, vol. D, pp. 480-81; McKenney to George M. Troup, Jan. n.d., 1818, *ibid.,* vol. E, pp. 103-04.
40 McKenney to Worcester, Feb. 14, March 4, 1818, Papers of the American Board.
41 *House Journal,* April 3, 1818, 15 Cong., 1 Sess. (Serial 4), 417.
42 Philip E. Thomas to Calhoun, Feb. 16 and March 23, 1818, *Papers of John C. Calhoun,* II, 142, 207; McKenney to Calhoun, March 26, 1818, SW LR, M-117(11).
43 McKenney to Isaac Tyson and Andrew Ellicott, March 27, 1818, IT LS, vol. E, pp. 4-5.
44 McKenney, *Memoirs,* II, 111; Second Auditor's Accounts (first series), No. 7541, RG 217, WNRC; Fifth Auditor's Accounts (first series), No. 378, *ibid.*
45 McKenney to John McKee, April 15, 1818, IT LS, vol. E, p. 18; McKenney to Calhoun, April 15, 1818, SW LR, M-153(11).
46 A copy of the circular, dated July 4, 1818, is enclosed with McKenney to Worcester, July 29, 1818, Papers of the American Board.
47 McKenney to Worcester, July 29, 1818, *ibid.*
48 HR15A-G6.2, RG 233, NA.
49 *House Journal,* Jan. 18, 1819, 15 Cong., 2 Sess. (Serial 16), 188; McKenney to the Secretary of the American Board, Feb. 5, 1841, Papers of the American Board.
50 *Senate Journal,* Feb. 19, 1819, 15 Cong., 2 Sess. (Serial 13), 288; *U.S. Stat.* III, 516-17.
51 McKenney to Worcester, March 25, May 3, 1819, Papers of the American Board.
52 McKenney to Calhoun, Aug. 14, 1819, IT LS, vol. E, pp. 298-304. Copies of the circulars, dated September 3, 1819, and February 29, 1820, are pasted on the inside front cover of a volume entitled "Indian Office, Indian Civilization, Volume A," RG 75, NA.
53 McKenney to Calhoun, Aug. 10, 1819, SW LR, M-33(13); James L. McDonald to McKenney, Aug. 9, 1819, enclosed *ibid.*
54 Second Auditor's Accounts (first series), No. 3661, RG 217, WNRC.
55 McDonald to McKenney, Aug. 9, 1819, enclosed with McKenney to Calhoun, Aug. 10, 1819, SW LR, M-33(13).
56 McKenney to Calhoun, Nov. 20, 1820, *ibid.,* M-111(14).

Chapter 4   Defending the Factories

1 Adams, *Diary*, V, 237-38.
2 *ASP: IA*, II, 246; Jacob Varnum to Irwin, Dec. 5, 1818, quoted in Irwin to Jedidiah Morse, n.d., printed in Jedidiah Morse, *A Report to the Secretary of War of the United States on Indian Affairs*, 46; Henry Atkinson to Calhoun, April 7, 1820, *Papers of John C. Calhoun*, V, 12-13.
3 *Wisconsin Historical Collections*, XX (1911), xiv.
4 Belt to McKenney, June 18, 1820, IT LR; McKenney to Belt, July 28, 1820, IT LS, vol. F, p. 16.
5 McKenney to Irwin, May 28, 1817, IT LS, vol. D, pp. 318-19; *ASP: IA*, II, 533-34.
6 McKenney to Rawlings, Sept. 25, 1819, IT LS, vol. E, p. 329; McKenney to McKee, Sept. 30, 1819, *ibid.*, p. 321.
7 McKenney, *Memoirs*, I, 19.
8 Johnson to McKenney, May 25, 1820, enclosed with McKenney to Calhoun, July 29, 1820, SW LR, M-43(14); McKenney to Calhoun, Aug. 19, 1818, IT LS, vol. E, pp. 134-35; Fowler to McKenney, Aug. 10, 1818, enclosed with McKenney to Calhoun, Sept. 25, 1818, SW LR, M-352(11).
9 Prucha, *American Indian Policy*, 108; Johnson to McKenney, May 25, 1820, SW LR, M-43(14); Irwin to McKenney, n.d., printed in Lyman C. Draper, ed., "The Fur Trade and Factory System at Green Bay, 1816-21," *Wisconsin Historical Collections*, VII (1876), 278.
10 Robert Stuart to William B. Astor, April 25, 1825, American Fur Company Letter Books (originals at Astor House, Mackinac Island; photostatic copies at State Historical Society of Wisconsin), vol. III, p. 165.
11 McKenney to Calhoun, Aug. 19, 1818, IT LS, vol. E, p. 134; McKenney, *Memoirs*, I, 92-93; McKenney to Southard, Jan. 7, 1820, printed in Washington *National Intelligencer*, Feb. 25, 1820.
12 Kenneth Wiggins Porter, *John Jacob Astor: Business Man*, II, 710-14; *Wisconsin Historical Collections*, XX (1911), xv; John Hersey to McKenney, Oct. 30, 1820, IT LR.
13 McKenney to Calhoun, July 17, 1818, IT LS, vol. E, p. 85; *Wisconsin Historical Collections*, XX (1911), xv.
14 *U.S. Stat.* III, 332-33; Prucha, *American Indian Policy*, 78; McKenney to Isaac Thomas, Jan. 3, 1817, IT LS, vol. D, p. 219; Johnson to McKenney, Oct. 28, 1816, HR14A-C5.1, RG 233, NA; John Jacob Astor to William Irving, Dec. 23, 1816, *ibid.*
15 House Report of Feb. 4, 1817, HR14A-C5.1, RG 233, NA; Original Bill 103, HR14A-B.2, Bills and Resolutions Originating in the House, RG 233, NA.
16 Ramsay Crooks to John J. Astor, [March or April 1817], American Fur Company Letter Books, vol. I, p. 12.
17 Porter, *John Jacob Astor*, II, 727n57; Calhoun to Cass, March 25, 1818, SW IA LS, vol. D, pp. 130-31.
18 McKenney to Varnum and to Irwin, Aug. 3, 1818, and to Johnson, Aug. 7, 1818, IT LS, vol. E, pp. 93, 94; McKenney to Calhoun, July 29, 1820, *ibid.*, vol. F, p. 15.
19 McKenney, *Memoirs*, I, 20; McKenney to Calhoun, May 9, 1818, IT LS, vol. E, p. 32.

20 McKenney to Sibley, April 7, 1821, IT LS, vol. F, p. 175; McKenney to Sibley, May 2, 1817, *ibid.,* vol. D, p. 294; McKenney to Sibley, Oct. 21, 1816, *ibid.,* pp. 153-54; McKenney to Johnson, Nov. 11, 1816, May 20, 1817, *ibid.,* pp. 165-66, 295.

21 McKenney to Johnson, June 24, 1817, *ibid.,* vol. D, p. 348; McKenney to Calhoun, July 17, 1818, *ibid.,* vol. E, pp. 85-86; Irwin to Jedidiah Morse, n.d., printed in Morse, *A Report to the Secretary of War,* 46.

22 *U.S. Stat.* II, 142; McKenney to Southard, Jan. 7, 1820, printed in Washington *National Intelligencer,* Feb. 25, 1820.

23 William Bowen to McKenney, April 27, 1817, SW LR, M-234(10); Irwin to McKenney, n.d., printed in *Senate Doc.* No. 60, 17 Cong., 1 Sess. (Serial 59), 52-53; Fowler to McKenney, June 14, 1819, SW LR, M-74(13).

24 McKenney to Isaac Thomas, Dec. 23, 1816, HR14A-C5.1, box 183, RG 233, NA; Bronaugh to Woolley, Feb. 5, 1817, "History of Transportation" volume, Records of the Office of Indian Trade, RG 75, NA.

25 McKenney to Southard, March 9, 1818, IT LS, vol. E, pp. 104-09.

26 *House Journal,* Feb. 4, 1817, 14 Cong., 2 Sess., 339; Original Bill 103, HR14A-B2, RG 233, NA; *House Journal,* Jan. 22, 1818, 15 Cong., 1 Sess. (Serial 4), 169; Original Bill 50, HR15A-B1, RG 233, NA.

27 Crooks and Stuart to John J. Astor, Jan. 24, 1818, *Wisconsin Historical Collections,* XX (1911), 26, 28, 31.

28 John J. Astor to Calhoun, March 4, 1818, *Papers of John C. Calhoun,* II, 191-92.

29 *House Journal,* April 4, 1818, 15 Cong., 1 Sess. (Serial 4), 420.

30 McKenney to Calhoun, Aug. 19, 1818, IT LS, vol. E, pp. 130-44.

31 Calhoun to Clay, Dec. 5, 1818, *Papers of John C. Calhoun,* III, 341-55; quote appears on p. 347.

32 *House Journal,* March 3, 1819, 15 Cong., 2 Sess. (Serial 16), 351; McKenney to Daniel Hughes, March 29, 1819, IT LS, vol. E, p. 250.

33 McKenney to Factors, Jan. 26, 1820, IT LS, vol. E, pp. 401-02.

34 McKenney to Southard, Jan. 7, 1820, printed in Washington *National Intelligencer,* Feb. 25, 1820.

35 Calhoun to Leake, Jan. 31, 1820, *Papers of John C. Calhoun,* IV, 621-22.

36 *Senate Journal,* 16 Cong., 1 Sess. (Serial 25), 159, 180, 193, 197; Engrossed Bill (S 36), 16 Cong., 1 Sess., March 1, 1820, Records of the United States Senate, RG 46, NA.

37 William Woodbridge to Cass, March 20, 1820, printed in Clarence E. Carter, ed., *The Territorial Papers of the United States,* XI, 20; Crooks to John J. Astor, March 22, 1820, American Fur Company Letter Books, vol. I, p. 285.

38 Anon., *A Letter Addressed to Thomas L. M'Kenney, Esq. Superintendent of Indian Trade, March, 1820: in reply to his Report of January, 1820,* copy in custody of the Boston Public Library.

39 Crooks to John J. Astor, May 30, 1820, American Fur Company Letter Books, vol. I, pp. 305-06; McKenney to Sibley, March 8, 1820, IT LS, vol. E, p. 419.

40 McKenney to Irwin, Dec. 19, 1820, IT LS, vol. F, p. 88.

41 McKenney to Southard, Nov. 30, 1820, *Senate Doc.* No. 19, 16 Cong., 2 Sess. (Serial 42), 5-8.

42 Anon., *On the Indian Trade, by a Backwoodsman,* copy in custody of the New Hampshire Historical Society.

43 *House Journal,* March 3, 1821, 16 Cong., 2 Sess. (Serial 47), 331;
McKenney to Southard, March 17, 1821, IT LS, vol. F, p. 153.
44 McKenney to Sibley, June 21, 1821, IT LS, vol. F, p. 223; McKenney
to Calhoun, July 5, 1821, *ibid.,* pp. 226-27; McKenney to Irwin, July
5, 1821, printed in *Wisconsin Historical Collections,* VII (1876), 281.
45 McKenney to Milledoler, Feb. 13, 1821, Milledoler Papers; McKenney
to John Emory, March 13, 1821, IT LS, vol. F, p. 156.
46 McKenney to Milledoler, Nov. 9, 1821, Milledoler Papers; memorial
from the "Inhabitants of Philadelphia," Jan. 14, 1822, HR17-F6.1,
RG 233, NA.
47 Crooks to John J. Astor, Nov. 30, 1821, American Fur Company
Letter Books, vol. II, p. 177; Porter, *John Jacob Astor,* II, 714; Thomas
Hart Benton, *Thirty Years View or a History of the Working Government for Thirty Years from 1820 to 1852,* I, 13.
48 *House Journal,* Dec. 10, 1821, 17 Cong., 1 Sess. (Serial 62), 35. The
rough draft of McKenney's letter, dated December 12, 1821, is in IT
LR; a signed copy can be found in the Milledoler Papers.
49 The petitions can be found in HR17A-G8.1, RG 233, NA, and in
SEN17A-G6, RG 46, NA.
50 McKenney, *Memoirs,* I, 36.
51 McKenney to Henry Johnson, Dec. 27, 1821, *Senate Doc.* No. 10, 17
Cong., 1 Sess. (Serial 59), 1-12; quote appears on p. 8.
52 "Documents Relative to Indian Trade. Submitted to the Senate by
the Committee on Indian Affairs. February 11, 1822," *Senate Doc.*
No. 60, 17 Cong., 1 Sess. (Serial 59), 1-62; Crooks to Russell Farnham,
Feb. 10, 1822, American Fur Company Letter Books, vol. II, p. 218.
53 *Annals of Congress,* 17 Cong., 1 Sess., I, 1821-22, 235-36, 317-31; Milo
M. Quaife, *Chicago and the Old Northwest, 1673-1835,* 306.
54 *Annals of Congress,* I, 339, 342, 354, 355.
55 *House Journal,* May 4 and 6, 1822, 17 Cong., 1 Sess. (Serial 62), 555,
589; Crooks to Stuart, May 10, 1822, American Fur Company Letter
Books, vol. II, p. 274.
56 McKenney to "the corresponding secretaries of the several societies
in the United States, for the promotion of Indian civilization," May
28, 1822, printed in *Niles' Weekly Register,* June 8, 1822.

Chapter 5   Political Interlude

1 McKenney to Thomas Metcalfe, Feb. 22 and 25, 1822, IT LS, vol. F,
pp. 332, 333-34; McKenney to Calhoun, Feb. 22, 1822, SW LR, M-
282(15); McKenney to David Trimble, Feb. 23, 1822, IT LS, vol. F,
pp. 332-33.
2 Calhoun to McKenney, Feb. 27, 1822, SW IA LS, vol. E, p. 220;
McKenney to Gales and Seaton, March 4, 1822, printed in Washington *National Intelligencer,* March 7, 1822; Trimble to Gales and
Seaton, *ibid.*
3 McKenney to the President of the Senate, March 28, 1822, SEN17A-
D7, RG 46, NA; *U.S. Stat.* III, 683.
4 McKenney to Monroe, May 18, 1822, IT LS, vol. F, pp. 346, 348;
McKenney to Calhoun, May 20, 1822, *ibid.,* pp. 348.
5 McKenney to Calhoun, May 22, 1822, SW LR, M-374(15); McKenney
to Factors, *ibid.,* IT LS, vol. F, p. 353. See Chapter 2, note 11 for

discussion of the government's five auditors and two comptrollers.

6 Varnum is quoted in Quaife, *Chicago and the Old Northwest,* 308.

7 Graham to Crawford, June 18, 1822, IT LS, vol. G, pp. 1-3.

8 *ASP: IA,* II, 532; Graham to Thomas Swan, Sept. 20, 1822, IT LS, vol. G, pp. 24-25; Graham to Crawford, Dec. 21, 1822, *ibid.,* pp. 45-46.

9 Graham to Clark, Nov. 7, 1822, *ASP: IA,* II, 535; Graham to Crawford, Jan. 22, 1823, IT LS, vol. G, p. 55; Graham to Hone & Towns, March 11, 1823, *ibid.,* p. 87; J. & P. Hone & Co. to Graham, May 5, 1823, *ASP: IA,* II, 537; Graham to J. & P. Hone & Co., May 16, 1823, IT LS, vol. G, p. 102.

10 Cass to Calhoun, July 18, 1822, *Territorial Papers,* XI, 253-54.

11 *ASP: IA,* II, 538; Varnum is quoted in Quaife, *Chicago and the Old Northwest,* 308-09.

12 *ASP: IA,* II, 532-41.

13 Washington *City Gazette,* Feb. 28, 1824, reprinted in Washington *National Intelligencer,* March 19, 1824.

14 Metcalfe to McKenney, Feb. 16, 1823, printed in *Washington Republican and Congressional Examiner,* March 22, 1823; McKenney to Metcalfe, Feb. 19, 1823, *ibid.*

15 "Report of the Committee on Indian Affairs, in relation to the execution of the Act of last Session, abolishing the Indian Trading Establishments. March 1, 1823," *House Report* No. 104, 17 Cong., 2 Sess. (Serial 87), 1-29, *passim.*

16 Robert Mayo, *The Treasury Department and Its Various Fiscal Bureaus, Their Origin, Organization, and Practical Operations,* II, 87-88, 111-15, 154-55.

17 McKenney to Edwards, Aug. 2, 1819, IT LS, vol. E, p. 295; McKenney to Joseph Anderson, March 13, 17, 1819, *ibid.,* pp. 228-29.

18 McKenney, *Memoirs,* I, 26-27.

19 Lee to McKenney, May 24, 1822, SA LS, vol. 7, p. 362; McKenney to Lee, May 25, 1822, Second Auditor's Accounts (first series), No. 7541, RG 217, WNRC; Bronaugh to Meade Fitzhugh, July 7, 1824, voucher B-18, Fifth Auditor's Accounts (first series), No. 1515, RG 217, NA.

20 McKenney to Calhoun, July 25, 1822, Second Auditor's Accounts (first series), No. 7541, RG 217, WNRC.

21 Lee to McKenney, Nov. 5, 29, 1822, SA LS, vol. 8, pp. 134, 169; Bronaugh to Lee, Nov. 27, 1822, Second Auditor's Accounts (first series), No. 7541, RG 217, WNRC.

22 McKenney to Lee, Jan. 14, 15, 1823, Second Auditor's Accounts (first series), No. 7541, RG 217, WNRC; Lee to McKenney, Jan. 14, 17, 1823, SA LS, vol. 8, pp. 234, 238.

23 Payment to Hersey for settling McKenney's accounts, July 1, 1824, voucher B-15, Fifth Auditor's Accounts (first series), No. 1515, RG 217, NA; Bronaugh to Fitzhugh, July 7, 1824, voucher B-18, *ibid.;* Lee to Bronaugh, May 5, 1823, SA LS, vol. 8, pp. 397-98; Lee to McKenney, May 16, 1823, *ibid.,* p. 417; McKenney to Lee, May 19, 1823, Second Auditor's Accounts (first series), No. 7541, RG 217, WNRC.

24 Bronaugh to Fitzhugh and Fitzhugh to Crawford, July 7, 1824, voucher B-18, Fifth Auditor's Accounts (first series), No. 1515, RG 217, NA; Lee to McKenney, Feb. 26, 1824, SA LS, vol. 9, p. 269.

25 Stephen Pleasanton to Anderson, Dec. 11, 1823, Fifth Auditor's Report Books, vol. 2, pp. 499-507, RG 217, NA; Pleasanton to McKenney,

March 10, 1824, Second Comptroller, Letters Sent, vol. 2, p. 11, *ibid.;* Fifth Auditor's Accounts (second series), No. 3284—Oct. 5, 1833, *ibid.*
26 McKenney to Milledoler, Dec. 12, 13, 1821, Milledoler Papers.
27 Harry Ammon, *James Monroe: The Quest for National Identity,* 493-94; Calhoun to Virgil Maxcy, May 31, 1822, Galloway-Maxcy-Markoe Papers (Manuscript Division, Library of Congress).
28 Prospectus of the *Washington Republican and Congressional Examiner,* June 4, 1822, copy in the custody of the American Antiquarian Society, Worcester, Mass.; D. L. Corbitt, "John C. Calhoun and the Presidential Campaign of 1824," *The North Carolina Historical Review,* XII (Jan. 1935), 29n24; Wilhelmus B. Bryan, *A History of the National Capital,* II, 169.
29 McKenney to Milledoler, June 8, 1822, Milledoler Papers.
30 McKenney to Cass, June 14, 1822, MS LR; Cass to Henry R. Schoolcraft, July 7, 1822, *Territorial Papers,* XI, 252.
31 James Madison to McKenney, n.d., Miscellaneous Manuscripts (Historical Society of Pennsylvania); [Thomas Jefferson to McKenney], July 2, 1822, Miscellaneous Manuscripts (Huntington Library).
32 Calhoun to Maxcy, June 9, Aug. 2, 1822, Galloway-Maxcy-Markoe Papers.
33 Adams, *Diary,* VI, 47; *Washington Republican and Congressional Examiner,* Sept. 21, 1822.
34 Margaret Bayard Smith, *The First Forty Years of Washington Society,* ed. Gaillard Hunt, 160-61; Charles M. Wiltse, *John C. Calhoun,* I, 258.
35 Adams, *Diary,* VI, 63, 66.
36 McKenney to Milledoler, June 8, 1822, Milledoler Papers; for examples of editorials about Indian affairs, see *Washington Republican and Congressional Examiner,* Aug. 7, 17, 1822; Nov. 16, 1822; April 12, 1823.
37 *Washington Republican and Congressional Examiner,* Aug. 7, 10, 1822; Dec. 18, 1822; May 14, 1823; Jan. 3, 1824.
38 *Ibid.,* Nov. 27, 1822; Langdon Cheves to Clay, Nov. 9, 1822, *The Papers of Henry Clay,* III, 316; McKenney to Eleuthère Irénée Du Pont, Oct. 14, 1822, Du Pont Papers, Series B, Letters Received (Eleutherian Mills Historical Society, Wilmington, Del.); Calhoun to Maxcy, Oct. 28, 1822, Galloway-Maxcy-Markoe Papers.
39 Calhoun to Maxcy, March 13, April 1, April 15, 1823, Galloway-Maxcy-Markoe Papers.
40 *Washington Republican and Congressional Examiner,* Sept. 21, 1822; Washington *City Gazette,* Sept. 24, 1822; Liber WB-8, 1823-24, pp. 267-69, Recorder of Deeds, Washington, D.C.
41 Washington *National Intelligencer,* July 12, 1824.
42 "Report of the Committee on the District of Columbia," Feb. 14, 1828, *Sen. Doc.* No. 103, 20 Cong., 1 Sess. (Serial 165), 7, 11. McKenney's explanation for the notes is vague. He claimed they "had been originally given for value received, for so much of a debt, as is believed, as was then due the United States by the Messrs. Johnsons of Kentucky," *ibid.,* 7. Richard M. Johnson, however, stated that "in the year 1820, as agent for James Johnson, and John Hanna, I had the charge of collecting certain debts due to them in this City [Washington]. Among other debts, one was due from Grayson Orr, from whom I received two houses and lots, which I sold to Luther

Rice, upon condition that he would obtain from the Treasury Department, an order on the Farmers and Mechanics Bank of Cincinnati, which was indebted to the Government for deposits . . . I made a similar arrangement with the Secretary of the Treasury, for a debt due from Thomas L. McKenney, for upwards of $10,000 . . . . ," *ibid.*, 2-3. McKenney's brother, William, had purchased goods and furs from the Office of Indian Trade and owed the government $11,867.12 for the merchandise. Thomas McKenney had cosigned or endorsed the three notes covering his brother's debt. It was this financial obligation to the government that in 1824 proved a temporary obstacle to his accepting the position of superintendent of Indian affairs. (See Chapter 6)

43 McKenney, *Memoirs,* I, 50-53; Washington *City Gazette,* Feb. 28, 1824, reprinted in Washington *National Intelligencer,* March 19, 1824.

Chapter 6   Superintendent of Indian Affairs

1 Leonard D. White, *The Jeffersonians: A Study in Administrative History, 1801-1829,* 506-07. In 1827, in reply to a rumor that the administration of Indian affairs would be turned over to the army, McKenney wrote: "No man who knows his Alphabet in Indian concerns can listen to it. Officers of the Army to manage Indians! It might do well enough if they were *permanent*—But, surely, not otherwise. This single objection will, I should judge, defeat the plan." McKenney to Cass, Dec. 14, 1827, IA LS, vol. 4, pp. 180-81.

2 *American State Papers: Miscellaneous,* II, 396-99; White, *The Jeffersonians,* 171.

3 McKenney to Calhoun, Aug. 19, 1818, IT LS, vol. E, pp. 141-43.

4 "Report of the Secretary of War of a System Providing for the Abolition of the Existing Indian Trade Establishments, December 5, 1818," *House Doc.* No. 25, 15 Cong., 2 Sess. (Serial 17), 7; Calhoun to Thomas Montgomery, Feb. 12, 1822, Reports to Congress by the Secretary of War, vol. 1, p. 219, RG 107, NA; Calhoun to John Cocke, Dec. 12, 1823, *ibid.,* p. 274; Calhoun to Thomas W. Caleb, Dec. 16, 1823, *ibid.,* p. 275; Calhoun to McKee, March 8, 1824, SW LS, vol. 6, p. 1.

5 Calhoun to Montgomery, Feb. 12, 1822, Reports to Congress, vol. 2, p. 219, RG 107, NA. Silas Woods, chairman of the Committee on Expenditures in the Department of State, on April 3, 1822, proposed that the House Committee on Indian Affairs be instructed to inquire into the expediency of establishing a department of Indian affairs, but "it was determined in the negative." *House Journal,* April 3, 1822, 17 Cong., 1 Sess. (Serial 62), 426.

6 *U.S. Stat.* III, 446; Calhoun to the President of the Senate and the Speaker of the House, Jan. 13, 1825, Reports to Congress, vol. 2, p. 310, RG 107, NA; Calhoun to McKenney, March 10, 1824, SW LS, vol. 12, p. 33.

7 That the salary indeed was insufficient for him to maintain Weston is evident from the following advertisement: "Weston—*For Rent.* I will rent, *to a good tenant,* who will enter into stipulations to preserve the property, this healthful and beautiful situation. Possession to be had immediately. Tho. L. McKenney." Washington *National Intelli-*

gencer, Feb. 25-March 6, 1826. From Weston McKenney moved to a row house on First Street owned by Walter Smith. Benjamin Homans, *The Georgetown Directory for the Year 1830,* 10.

8 McKenney to Barbour, Nov. 15, 1825, *House Doc.* No. 146, 19 Cong., 1 Sess. (Serial 138), 10.

9 *U.S. Stat.* III, 668; Robert B. Semple to Gersham Powers, Feb. 18, 1830, *House Report* No. 290, 21 Cong., 1 Sess. (Serial 200), 2-3.

10 *Papers of John C. Calhoun,* II, xlvi; Robert Mills, *Guide to the National Executive Offices and the Capitol of the United States,* floor plan facing p. 15.

11 Calhoun to Philip P. Barbour, Dec. 2, 1822, Reports to Congress, vol. 2, p. 251, RG 107, NA; McKenney to Porter, Oct. 28, 1828, IA LR, Miscellaneous.

12 Calhoun to McKenney, March 11, 1824, SW LS, vol. 12, p. 33; McKenney to James H. Hook, June 2, 1825, IA LS, vol. 2, p. 31.

13 McKenney to Henry W. Dwight, Feb. 28, 1826, IA LS, vol. 2, p. 454; Barbour to Cocke, March 24, 1826, *House Doc.* No. 146, 19 Cong., 1 Sess. (Serial 138), 5; McKenney to Eaton, March 18, 1829, IA LS, vol. 5, p. 359.

14 McKenney to Joseph M. White, Jan. 8, 1827, IA LS, vol. 3, p. 302. See also, McKenney to Thomas H. Benton, May 20, 1825, *ibid.,* vol. 2, p. 20; McKenney to Samuel Smith, May 24, 1825, *ibid.,* p. 27; McKenney to Isaac McKim, May 24, 1825, *ibid.;* McKenney to Henry W. Conway, Dec. 5, 1825, *ibid.,* p. 282; McKenney to Clay, March 29, 1826, *ibid.,* 484; McKenney to Cocke, March 31, 1826, *ibid.,* p. 489.

15 McKenney to Charles Nourse, April 17, 1827, vol. 4, p. 20; McKenney to Barbour, April 18, 1827, *ibid.,* p. 22.

16 Register of Letters Received by the Office of Indian Affairs, Jan. 1, 1824-Dec. 31, 1826, RG 75, NA. The forty-five-page letter, McKenney to Richard Cutts, Aug. 5, 1828, can be found in Second Auditor's Accounts (first series), No. 14289, RG 217, WNRC. During times of heavy correspondence, when a clerk's outgoing copy of a McKenney draft might not get done until days later, the letter carried the date of the original draft, regardless of when it was transcribed and mailed.

17 Greenwood Leflore to McKenney, Dec. 15, 1827, IA LR, Choctaw Agency. See also, David Brown to McKenney, Dec. 17, 1828, *ibid.,* Eastern Cherokee Agency; Elijah Hicks to McKenney, July 1, 1824, *ibid.;* McDonald to McKenney, April 27, 1826, *ibid.,* Choctaw Agency.

18 McKenney to John Jolly, Nov. 22, 1828, IA LS, vol. 5, p. 198; Samuel S. Hamilton to the King and Chiefs of the Chickasaw Nation, Oct. 4, 1827, *ibid.,* vol. 4, pp. 132-33; McKenney to John Ross and Others, April 7, 1824, *ibid.,* vol. 1, p. 27; Templin W. Ross to McKenney, Feb. 16, 1827, IA LR, Eastern Cherokee Agency; Brown to McKenney, Dec. 17, 1828, *ibid.;* Hicks to McKenney, *ibid.*

19 McKenney to Porter, Jan. 13, 1829, IA LS, vol. 5, p. 268.

20 McKenney to Barbour, Nov. 15, 1825, IA LS, vol. 2, p. 236; "Names and Pay of all the Persons Employed in the Indian Department," Calhoun to the Speaker of the House of Representatives, April 11, 1822, *ASP: IA,* II, 364-66; *"List of Indian agents now in service . . . showing to what tribes they are agents, and the amount of compensation (which is fixed by law) paid to each,"* Calhoun to Cocke, Jan. 12, 1824, *ibid.,* 450.

21 Wesley, *Guarding the Frontier,* 23; *U.S. Stat.* III, 683; *ibid.,* IV, 35.

22 Edward E. Hill, *Historical Sketches for Jurisdictional and Subject Headings Used for the Letters Received by the Office of Indian Affairs, 1824-80* (National Archives, 1967), sketches for St. Louis, Michigan, Arkansas, and Florida superintendencies.

23 McKenney to William P. Duval, Jan. 6, 1827, IA LS, vol. 3, p. 300.

24 Cass is quoted in White, *The Jeffersonians,* 508; McKenney to Porter, Feb. 7, 1829, IA LS, vol. 5, p. 294.

25 *ASP: IA,* II, 365; *U.S. Stat.* III, 428, 461; John Jamison to Calhoun, Sept. 30, 1818, quoted in Wesley, *Guarding the Frontier,* 28.

26 McKenney to Indian Agents, June 19, 1824, IA LS, vol. 1, p. 117; McKenney to Superintendents, June 21, 1824, *ibid.,* p. 118.

27 Thomas Forsyth to McKenney, Aug. 28, 1824, IA LR, Prairie du Chien Agency; George Gray to McKenney, Oct. 1, 1824, *ibid.,* Red River Agency.

28 Schoolcraft to McKenney, Aug. 4, 1824, *ibid.,* Sault Ste. Marie Agency; John Tipton to McKenney, Nov. 13, 1824, *ibid.,* Fort Wayne Agency; Jasper Parrish to McKenney, Oct. 11, 1824, *ibid.,* Six Nations Agency.

29 Parrish to McKenney, Oct. 11, 1824, *ibid.,* Six Nations Agency; Barbour to Adams, April 30, 1828, IA LS, vol. 4, pp. 425-26; Hill, *Historical Sketches,* Fort Wayne Agency.

30 McKenney to Calhoun, Jan. 28, 1825, IA LS, vol. 1, p. 329; McKenney to Clark, Feb. 2, 1825, *ibid.,* p. 337; Francis Paul Prucha, *Broadax and Bayonet: The Role of the United States Army in the Development of the Northwest, 1815-1860,* 118-19.

31 McKenney to Eaton, July 6, 1829, IA LS, vol. 6, p. 40.

32 McKenney to Benjamin Reynolds, Oct. 13, 1826, *ibid.,* vol. 3, p. 187.

33 McKenney to Joseph McMinn, May 10, 1824, *ibid.,* vol. 1, p. 68; McMinn to Calhoun, Sept. 10, 1824, IA LR, Eastern Cherokee Agency; McKenney to McMinn, Sept. 24, 1824, IA LS, vol. 1, p. 201; John Dougherty to McKenney, Feb. 1, 1830, IA LR, Upper Missouri Agency. In a letter to Secretary of War Porter, Dougherty wrote that he had "a cabin, built with rough logs, a puncheon floor, and a clap-board roof, consisting of two small rooms 18 feet long, by 14 wide: and I have no other dwelling either for myself or Interpreters, and no other Council house to receive the Chief's and their numerous followers; who visit me on business almost daily," Dougherty to Porter, Nov. 18, 1828, Consolidated Files of the Quartermaster General, box 263, "John Dougherty," RG 92, NA.

34 McKenney to Reynolds, June 7, 1830, IA LS, vol. 6, p. 458; McKenney to Justus Ingersoll, Sept. 21, 1829, *ibid.,* vol. 6, p. 90; McKenney to Porter, Jan. 31, 1829, *ibid.,* vol. 5, p. 287; McKenney to Thomas Griffith, March 26, 1829, *ibid.,* p. 370.

35 McKenney to Henry B. Brevoort, June 6, 1825, *ibid.,* vol. 2, p. 34; Calhoun to Hamilton, Feb. 9, 1825, *ibid.,* vol. 1, p. 347; McKenney to Hamilton, Oct. 6, 1825, *ibid.,* vol. 2, p. 179; McKenney to Cass, Oct. 31, 1826, *ibid.,* p. 209; McKenney to agents, *ibid.;* McKenney to Griffith, March 26, 1829, *ibid.,* vol. 5, p. 369.

36 McKenney to William Ward, April 7, 1824, IA LS, vol. 1, p. 26; McKenney to Ward, Sept. 28, 1825, *ibid.,* vol. 2, p. 169; McKenney to Chiefs and Headmen of the Choctaw Nation, Sept. 28, 1825, *ibid.,* p. 168; McKenney to McMinn, June 11, 1824, *ibid.,* vol. 1, p. 107.

37 McKenney to Hugh Montgomery, April 29, 1826, IA LS, vol. 3, p. 57.

38 *ASP: IA,* II, 365; Wesley, *Guarding the Frontier,* 20.

39 McKenney to Barbour, Nov. 12, 1825, IA LS, vol. 2, pp. 230-31; Cass to McKenney, Jan. 5, 1828, IA LR, Michigan Superintendency.

40 Taliaferro's statement is quoted in Everett Dick, *Vanguards of the Frontier: A Social History of the Northern Plains and Rocky Mountains from the Earliest White Contacts to the Coming of the Homemaker,* 122; McKenney to Benjamin F. Smith, April 6, 1824, IA LS, vol. 1, p. 23.

41 Cherokee Chiefs of Arkansas to Eaton, June 8, 1829, IA LR, Western Cherokee Agency; Young King, Pollard, and Others to the President, July 20, 1829, *ibid.,* Six Nations Agency; Thomas Dillard to Porter, Nov. 4, 1828, *ibid.,* Red River Agency.

42 McKenney to McClellan, Oct. 15, 1825, IA LS, vol. 2, p. 189; McKenney to Ward, Feb. 23, 1825, *ibid.,* vol. 1, pp. 371-72; McKenney to Porter, Nov. 1, 1828, *ibid.,* vol. 5, pp. 165-67; McKenney to Alexander Adair, Dec. 18, 1828, *ibid.,* p. 242.

43 The Indian office disbursements in 1824 amounted to $424,978.50; in 1825 $671,470.59; and, for 1826, McKenney estimated they would be $1,082,474.68. McKenney to Barbour, April 21, 1826, *ibid.,* vol. 3, pp. 44-45.

44 McKenney's budget requests can be found in the annual reports of the Bureau of Indian Affairs for 1825 to 1829; Nov. 30, 1825, *Senate Doc.* No. 2, 19 Cong., 1 Sess. (Serial 125), 89-90; Nov. 20, 1826, *Senate Doc.* No. 1, 19 Cong., 2 Sess. (Serial 144), 507-08; Nov. 24, 1827, *Senate Doc.* No. 1, 20 Cong., 1 Sess. (Serial 163), 144-45; Nov. 1, 1828, *Senate Doc.* No. 1, 20 Cong., 2 Sess. (Serial 181), 92-93; Nov. 17, 1829, *Senate Doc.* No. 1, 21 Cong., 1 Sess. (Serial 192), 160-61.

45 Samuel Flagg Bemis, *John Quincy Adams and the Union,* 56-57, 131-33; Cass to McKenney, Oct. 28, 1827, IA LR, Michigan Superintendency.

46 McKenney to Eaton, Oct. 29, Nov. 17, 1829, IA LS, vol. 6, pp. 145, 160.

47 McKenney to Clark, March 17, 1827, *ibid.,* vol. 3, p. 450; McKenney to Cass, April 9, 1825, *ibid.,* vol. 1, p. 444; McKenney to Cass, May 26, 1830, *ibid.,* vol. 6, p. 433.

48 McKenney to McMinn, July 31, 1824, *ibid.,* vol. 1, p. 159; Hugh Montgomery to Eaton, March 6, 1829, IA LR, Eastern Cherokee Agency.

49 *U.S. Stat.* III, 723; Porter to McKenney, July 29, 1828, General Accounting Office, Letters Received, RG 217, NA; McKenney to Eaton, June 6, 1829, IA LS, vol. 5, p. 468.

50 McKenney to Clark, May 2, 1827, *ibid.,* vol. 4, p. 44; McKenney to Clark, May 7, 1824, *ibid.,* vol. 1, p. 67; McKenney to Benjamin F. Smith, Oct. 28, 1825, *ibid.,* vol. 2, p. 214.

51 McKenney to Barbour, Jan. 4, 1828, *ibid.,* vol. 4, p. 230. A discussion of how the accountability process functioned in general for all federal agencies in this period can be found in White, *The Jeffersonians,* 163-65.

52 McKenney to Eaton, March 18, 1829, IA LS, vol. 5, pp. 354-59, is a detailed report of the methods, and their effects, used by the accounting officers to settle the accounts relating to Indian affairs.

53 Henry Deringer, the rifle manufacturer, informed McKenney that "I am ashamed to see any of my creditors come anymore." Henry Deringer to McKenney, May 16, 1828, IA LR, Miscellaneous. Agent Montgomery wrote that the "business of the agency and the credit

of the Government is suffering" for the lack of funds. Montgomery to Porter, Oct. 20, 1828, IA LR, Eastern Cherokee Agency. See also McKenney to Porter, Dec 5, 1828, IA LS, vol. 5, pp. 218-19; McKenney to Eaton, Dec. 4, 1829, *ibid.,* vol. 6, p. 179; Montgomery to Eaton, March 3, 1829, IA LR, Eastern Cherokee Agency.

54 Henry R. Schoolcraft, *Personal Memoirs of a Residence of Thirty Years with the Indian Tribes on the American Frontier,* 319; Schoolcraft to Cass, Feb. 14, 1829, MS LR.

55 McKenney to Philip Lindsley, March 1, 1828, IA LS, vol. 4, p. 317; McKenney to Porter, Nov. 26, 1828, *ibid.,* vol. 5, pp. 205-06.

56 McKenney to Cass, Sept. 30, 1828, *ibid.,* p. 139; McKenney to Porter, Nov. 22, 1828, *ibid.,* p. 197; McKenney to Porter, Nov. 21, 1828, *ibid.,* p. 193.

57 McKenney to Porter, Nov. 22, 1828, *ibid.,* p. 196.

58 McKenney to Porter, July 14, 1828, *ibid.,* pp. 38-39.

59 McKenney to Eaton, March 11, 1829, *ibid.,* pp. 328-31; Eaton to Lee, March 16, 1829, *ibid.,* p. 345; McKenney to Duval, March 28, 1829, *ibid.,* p. 379.

60 McKenney to Eaton, June 6, 1829, *ibid.,* p. 471.

61 McKenney to Pierre E. Du Ponceau, Oct. 1, 1828, *ibid.,* pp. 140-41.

62 McKenney to Barbour, Nov. 15, 1825, *House Doc.* No. 146, 19 Cong., 1 Sess. (Serial 138), 7.

63 Barbour to McKenney, Aug. 5, 1825, IA LR, Miscellaneous; Barbour to Cocke, March 24, 1826, *House Doc.* No. 146, 19 Cong., 1 Sess. (Serial 138), 5.

64 Adams, *Diary,* VIII, 38-39.

65 McKenney, *Memoirs,* I, 200-06, 222-23; McKenney to John McLean, Jan. 29, 1831, John McLean Papers (Manuscript Division, Library of Congress).

66 McKenney to Barbour, Nov. 15, 1825, IA LS, vol. 2, p. 235.

67 *House Journal,* Dec. 6, 7, 1825, 19 Cong., 1 Sess. (Serial 130), 24-25, 30.

68 Barbour to Daniel Webster, Jan. 21, 1826, Reports to Congress by the Secretary of War, vol. 2, p. 340; Original Bill 279, HR19A-B1, RG 233, NA; *House Journal,* May 22, 1826, 19 Cong., 1 Sess. (Serial 130), 640.

69 McKenney to Cocke, Jan. 8, 1827, HR19A-D9.1, RG 233, NA.

70 McKenney to Madison, Feb. 4, 1826, James Madison Papers (Manuscript Division, Library of Congress); Madison to McKenney, Feb. 10, 1826, *ibid.;* Madison to Barbour, *ibid.*

71 Cocke to [Barbour], March 21, 1826, *House Doc.* No. 146, 19 Cong., 1 Sess. (Serial 138), 3; Barbour to Cocke, March 24, 1826, *ibid.,* 5.

72 McKenney, *Memoirs,* 1, 58; Original Bill 195, HR19A-B1, RG 233, NA; *House Journal,* March 31, 1826, 19 Cong., 1 Sess. (Serial 130), 394; Cass to McKenney, April 24, 1826, IA LR, Michigan Superintendency.

73 *House Journal,* March 31, 1826, 19 Cong., 1 Sess. (Serial 130), 394; *House Journal,* Jan. 19, 1827, 19 Cong., 2 Sess. (Serial 147), 182.

74 *House Journal,* 20 Cong., 1 Sess. (Serial 168), 25, 72-73, 105; Original Bill 29, HR20A-B1, RG 233, NA.

75 Porter to Cass, July 28, 1828, IA LS, vol. 5, p. 56; Report of the Secretary of War, Nov. 24, 1828, *Senate Doc.* No. 1, 20 Cong., 2 Sess. (Serial 181), 20-21.

76 Original Bill 195, HR19A-B1, and Original Bill 29, HR20A-B1, RG

233, NA.

77 *House Doc.* No. 117, 20 Cong., 2 Sess. (Serial 186).

78 *Senate Journal,* 22 Cong., 1 Sess. (Serial 211), 155, 309-10, 313; *House Journal,* 22 Cong., 1 Sess. (Serial 215), 819, 820, 823, 1029, 1092.

Chapter 7   Indian Visitors to Washington

1 Felix S. Cohen, *Handbook of Federal Indian Law with Reference Tables and Index,* 33; *U.S. Stat.* XVI, 566. For a study of the United States treaty making process, see Ralston Hayden, *The Senate and Treaties, 1789-1817.*

2 McKenney to Barbour, Jan. 24, 1828, IA LS, vol. 4, p. 267; McKenney to Barbour, April 7, 1825, *ibid.,* vol. 1, p. 441.

3 Duval to Calhoun, March 19, 1824, IA LR, Florida Superintendency; Calhoun to Duval, April 8, 1824, IA LS, vol. 1, p. 30.

4 McKenney to Barbour, April 21, 1826, *ibid.,* vol. 3, p. 45; McKenney to Gad Humphreys, May 7, 1826, *ibid.,* p. 62; Washington *National Intelligencer,* Nov. 22, 1821; Benjamin Perley Poore, *Perley's Reminiscences,* I, 42-44.

5 See for example, Clark to McKenney, July 25, 1824, St. Louis Superintendency; McKenney to Captain Noyes, July 26, 27, 1824, IA LS, vol. 1, pp. 151, 152; Calhoun to McKenney, July 25, 1820, SW IA LS, vol. D, p. 473.

6 McKenney to Eaton, Dec. 21, 1829, IA LS, vol. 6, p. 199; McKenney to Barbour, May 5, 1825, *ibid.,* vol. 2, p. 2. For a comprehensive treatment of peace medals, see Francis Paul Prucha, *Indian Peace Medals in American History.*

7 McKenney to Eaton, Dec. 21, 1829, IA LS, vol. 6, p. 199.

8 McKenney to Samuel Moore, Oct. 13, 1825, *ibid.,* vol. 2, p. 188; Francis Paul Prucha, "Early Indian Peace Medals," *Wisconsin Magazine of History,* XLV (Spring, 1962), 284-85.

9 McKenney to Moritz Furst, Sept. 10, 1825, IA LS, vol. 2, p. 147; Adams, *Diary,* VII, 53; John Adams, Jr., to McKenney, Dec. 20, 1825, IA LR, Miscellaneous.

10 McKenney to Eaton, March 13, 1829, IA LS, vol. 5, pp. 339-40; McKenney to John Vaughan, March 27, 1821, IT LS, vol. F, p. 168.

11 McKenney to Simpson, July 29, 1824, IA LS, vol. 1, p. 154; McKenney to Clark, March 26, 1827, *ibid.,* vol. 3, pp. 474-75.

12 McKenney to Little Prince, Feb. 20, 1828, *ibid.,* vol. 4, pp. 304-05.

13 For a fuller discussion of the treatment accorded Indian delegations, see Herman J. Viola, "Portraits, Presents, and Peace Medals: Thomas L. McKenney and Indian Visitors to Washington," *American Scene,* XI (June 1970).

14 Washington *Gazette,* Jan. 2, 1822.

15 Philadelphia *Franklin Gazette,* Feb. 11, 1822; Washington *National Intelligencer,* March 7, 1822; William Faux, *Faux's Memorable Days in America, 1819-1820,* reprinted in Reuben Gold Thwaites, ed., *Early Western Travels, 1748-1846,* XII, 51.

16 Hunt, *The First Forty Years of Washington Society,* 245.

17 *House Doc.* No. 129, 20 Cong. 2 Sess. (Serial 186), 4-5.

18 Bemis, *John Quincy Adams,* 80-81.

19 Adams, *Diary,* VII, 61-62, 106.

20 Arthur H. DeRosier, Jr., *The Removal of the Choctaw Indians,* 70-77.

21 Ward to Calhoun, Aug. 12, 1823, SW LR, W-79(17); extract of resolutions of Sept. 29, 1823, enclosed with Ward to Calhoun, Oct. 10, 1823, *ibid.,* W-156(17); Ward to Calhoun, Feb. 11, 1824, *ibid.,* W-250(17); Calhoun to Ward, Jan. 29, 1824, SW IA LS, vol. E, p. 36; Ward to Calhoun, March 12, 1824, IA LR, Choctaw Agency.

22 Conway to Calhoun, May 22, 1824, IA LR, Choctaw Agency; Calhoun to Conway, May 22, 1824, IA LS, vol. 1, p. 79; *U.S. Stat.* IV, 35.

23 Ward to Calhoun, May 28, 1824, IA LR, Choctaw Agency; McKenney to Ward, June 24, 1824, IA LS, vol. 1, p. 120.

24 McKenney to Kingsbury, Nov. 5, 1824, IA LS, vol. 1, p. 221.

25 Calhoun to Christopher Rankin and Thomas H. Williams, Nov. 15, 1824, *ibid.,* p. 230.

26 Quoted in Charles Lanman, *Recollections of Curious Characters and Pleasant Places,* 211-12.

27 McDonald to Calhoun, Nov. 16, 1824, Documents Relating to the Negotiation of Ratified and Unratified Treaties with Various Tribes of Indians, 1801-69, Treaty No. 124 (hereafter cited as Treaties, No. 00), RG 75, NA.

28 McKenney to McDonald, Nov. 16, 1824, IA LS, vol. 1, p. 234; McDonald and Folsom to Calhoun, Nov. 17, 1824, *ASP: IA,* II, 551.

29 McKenney to Choctaw Delegation, Nov. 19, 1824, IA LS, vol. 1, p. 236; McDonald and Folsom to Calhoun, Nov. 20, 1824, *ASP: IA,* II, 551.

30 Choctaw Delegation to Calhoun, Nov. 22, 1824, *ASP: IA,* II, 551-52.

31 Calhoun to Choctaw Delegation, Nov. 27, 1824, *ibid.,* 552; McKenney to McDonald, Nov. 27, 1824, IA LS, vol. 1, p. 242.

32 Choctaw Delegation to Calhoun, Nov. 30, 1824, *ASP: IA,* II, 553; Folsom and McDonald to Calhoun, Dec. 1, 1824, Treaties, No. 124, RG 75, NA.

33 McKenney to Choctaw Delegation, Dec. 8, 1824, IA LS, vol. 1, p. 258; Calhoun to Choctaw Delegation, Dec. 28, 1824, *ibid.,* p. 274; Calhoun to Choctaw Delegation, Dec. 31, 1824, *ASP: IA,* II, 553.

34 Choctaw Delegation to Calhoun, Jan. 3, 1825, *ASP: IA,* II, 553; Calhoun to Choctaw Delegation, Jan. 5, 1825, *ibid.,* 553-54; Choctaw Delegation to Calhoun, Jan. 14, 1825, *ibid.,* 554.

35 Expenses of Choctaw Delegation, n.d., 1825, IA LR, Choctaw Agency.

36 Thomas L. McKenney and James Hall, *The Indian Tribes of North America with Biographical Sketches and Anecdotes of the Principle Chiefs,* ed. by Frederick Webb Hodge, I, 70.

37 "Funeral Expenses of one of the Indian Chiefs [Puckshenubbe] in Company with Col Fulsom," n.d., 1824, IA LR, Choctaw Agency.

38 Second Auditor's Accounts (first series), Nos. 8412, 8373, RG 217, WNRC; McKenney to Joseph Lovell, Dec. 25, 1824, IA LS, vol. 1, 247.

39 McKenney to Folsom, Dec. 2, 7, 1824, IA LS, vol. 1, pp. 248, 256; McKenney to McDonald, June 16, 1825, *ibid.,* vol. 2, p. 48.

40 McKenney to Joshua Tennison, June 17, 1825, *ibid.,* vol. 2, p. 50.

41 McKenney to Choctaw Chiefs, June 17, 1825, *ibid.,* pp. 48-49.

42 Choctaw Delegation to Calhoun, Feb. 20, 1825, Treaties, No. 124, RG 75, NA; Nathaniel Causin to McKenney, June 21, 1825, IA LR, Choctaw Agency; McKenney to Causin, June 21, 1825, IA LS, vol. 2, pp. 57-58; McDonald to McKenney, June 22, 1825, IA LR, Choctaw Agency.

Chapter 8   Tour of the Lakes

1 For the ratified treaties negotiated by Clark, see Charles J. Kappler, comp. and ed., *Indian Affairs: Laws and Treaties,* vol. 2, *Treaties,* 110-17, 119-23, 126-31, 132-33, 138-40, 156-61, 167-68, 207-09, 217-25, 250-55, 262-64, 305-10, 365-67, 370-72, 376-77, 382-83, 468-70; for ratified treaties negotiated by Cass, see *ibid.,* 105-07, 145-55, 162-64, 168-74, 185-89, 198-201, 250-55, 268-84, 292-97, 341-43.
2 McKenney to Eaton, March 28, 1829, IA LS, vol. 5, pp. 381-82.
3 Clark to Eaton, Sept. 22, 1830, IA LR, St. Peters Agency; Cass to McKenney, April 19, 1827, *ibid.,* Michigan Superintendency; Cass to McKenney, Dec. 15, 1826, Consolidated Files of the Quartermaster General, Box 144, "Lewis Cass," RG 92, NA.
4 Kappler, *Treaties,* 250-55.
5 McKenney to Cass, Oct. 29, 1825, MS LR.
6 *Ibid.,* Jan. 30, 1827.
7 McKenney, *Memoirs,* I, 59.
8 Second Auditor's Accounts (first series), No. 12036, RG 217, WNRC; McDonald to McKenney, April 25, 1826, IA LR, Choctaw Agency; Washington *National Intelligencer,* Oct. 1, 1828.
9 McKenney to Cass, Feb. 15, 1826, MS LR.
10 *Ibid.,* Feb. 10, 1826.
11 Cass to Barbour, March 2, 1826, IA LR, Michigan Superintendency.
12 McKenney to Cass, Feb. 15, 1826, MS LR; Cass to McKenney, March 11, 1826, Michigan Superintendency.
13 Schoolcraft, *Personal Memoirs,* 242.
14 *U.S. Stat.* IV, 182; McKenney to Cass, May 22, 1826, MS LR; Cass to Schoolcraft, May 19, 1826, Letters Received by the Sault Ste. Marie Agent, RG 75, NA.
15 Barbour to Cass and McKenney, May 24, 1826, IA LS, vol. 3, pp. 95-96.
16 Cass to McKenney, April 24, 1826, IA LR, Michigan Superintendency; McKenney to Barbour, June 16, 1826, *ibid.,* Miscellaneous.
17 McKenney to Cass, May 29, 1826, IA LS, vol. 3, p. 106; McKenney to Barbour, June 16, 1826, IA LR, Miscellaneous.
18 McKenney to Barbour, June 16, 1826, IA LR, Miscellaneous.
19 McKenney, *Sketches,* 170-71; Schoolcraft, *Personal Memoirs,* 243.
20 Schoolcraft, *Personal Memoirs,* 243-44.
21 Journal of Zina Pitcher, n.d. (Burton Historical Collection, Detroit Public Library); McKenney, *Sketches,* 274-5.
22 McKenney, *Sketches,* 299, 275.
23 *Ibid.,* 283-84, 296.
24 *Ibid.,* 320.
25 *Ibid.,* 279, 287, 298, 330, 292.
26 *Ibid.,* 284, 294.
27 "Journal of the Commissioners, appointed to hold a treaty with the Chippeways, on Lake Superior, in 1826," Aug. 3, 1826, p. 17, Treaties, No. 145, RG 75, NA; McKenney, *Sketches,* 313-14.
28 McKenney, *Sketches,* 310, 314.
29 *Ibid.,* 312-13.
30 "Journal of the Commissioners," Aug. 2, 1826, pp. 11-13.
31 *Ibid.,* Aug. 3, 1826, pp. 13, 21-22, 31.
32 The ratified version of the Treaty of Fond du Lac appears in Kappler, *Treaties,* 268-73, and as an appendix to McKenney, *Sketches.*

33 McKenney, *Sketches,* 324.
34 Schoolcraft to Cass, June 14, 1826, MS LR.
35 "Journal of the Commissioners," Aug. 5, 1826, pp. 33-34.
36 *Ibid.,* pp. 34-35.
37 *Ibid.,* pp. 35-36.
38 *Ibid.,* Aug. 6, 1826, p. 38.
39 *Ibid.,* p. 38; Kappler, *Treaties,* 271.
40 "Journal of the Commissioners," Aug. 6, 1826, pp. 42-44.
41 *Ibid.,* pp. 44-46.
42 McKenney, *Sketches,* 331-32, 335.
43 *Ibid.,* 344, 346-47.
44 J. Marsh to Cass, Nov. 20, 1826, MS LR; McKenney, *Sketches,* 342-43; Schoolcraft, *Personal Memoirs,* 244-45.
45 McKenney to Cass, Jan. 30, 1827, MS LR.
46 McKenney to Peter Force, Oct. 16, 1826, Peter Force Papers (Manuscript Division, Library of Congress).
47 McKenney, *Sketches,* 175. Many of Lewis' original watercolors remained in the custody of the Baltimore firm, now known as Lucas Bros., Inc., Stationers, Printers, Engravers, but they were stolen in the spring of 1974.
48 Unidentified reviewer quoted in *Niles' Weekly Register,* Dec. 29, 1827.
49 McKenney to Cass, Jan. 30, 1827, MS LR.
50 Philip Barton Key was the nephew of Francis Scott Key, author of "The Star-Spangled Banner."
51 McKenney to Cass, Jan. 30, 1827, MS LR. Edwards was appointed subagent to the Potawatomi and Ottawa Indians of the St. Joseph's country at an annual salary of $500. Porter to Abraham Edwards, Feb. 26, 1829, IA LS, vol. 5, p. 322.
52 McKenney to Stephen Van Rensselaer, March 21, 1827, Gratz Collection.
53 McKenney mentioned his plan to Barbour, following the review of his book in the *North American Review.* "I have another set of materials for a book as big as that, but unless the right be ceeded to me to strike off into such a track as my fancy may indicate as most agreeable to myself, without being obligated to conform to the routine of book-making, why I shall give it up—which will be, as you know no great loss." McKenney to Barbour, Oct. 30, 1827, IA LR, Miscellaneous.
54 Barbour to Cass and McKenney, March 27, 1827, MS LR; McKenney to Cass, March 15, 1827, *ibid.*
55 McKenney, *Memoirs,* I, 63-65.
56 McKenney to Barbour, June 29, 1827, IA LR, Miscellaneous.
57 Cass to McKenney, July 4, 1827, *ibid.*
58 *Ibid.*
59 McKenney to Barbour, July 19, 1827, *ibid.,* Michigan Superintendency.
60 McKenney to Barbour, Aug. 4, 1827, *ibid.* For an account of the Butte des Mortes mound, see Publius V. Lawson, "Summary of the Archeology of Winnebago County, Wisconsin," *Wisconsin Archeologist,* II (1903), 45-49. Increase A. Lapham, Wisconsin's pioneer archeologist, visited the site twenty-four years after McKenney and concluded, with apparent foreboding: "There is neither necessity nor excuse for its destruction.... It is to be hoped that a monument so conspicuous, and so beautifully situated, may be for ever preserved as

a memento of the past." (*Antiquities of Wisconsin*, p. 61) In 1863 the mound was destroyed by railroad construction before any archeological work had been done.

61 McKenney to Barbour, July 26, 1827, *ibid.;* Schoolcraft, *Personal Memoirs,* 266.

62 McKenney to Barbour, July 19, 26, 1827, IA LR, Michigan Superintendency.

63 Prucha, *American Indian Policy,* 178-79; McKenney to Barbour, July 19, 1827, IA LR, Michigan Superintendency; McKenney to Barbour, Sept. 17, 1827, SW LR, M-128(22).

64 McKenney to Barbour, Aug. 4, 1827, IA LR, Michigan Superintendency.

65 McKenney, *Memoirs,* I, 81-82.

66 "Journal of the proceedings at the Treaty held by Gov. Cass & Col. McKenney with the Indians at Butte des Morts—near Green Bay— 1827," Aug. 6, 1827, pp. 2-4, Treaties, No. 148, RG 75, NA.

67 *Ibid.,* Aug. 7, 1827, pp. 5-6.

68 McKenney to Barbour, March 24, 1828, IA LS, vol. 4, pp. 362-63.

69 Kappler, *Treaties,* 281-83.

70 "Journal of proceedings," Aug. 14, 15, 1827, pp. 25-27, 24, 28.

71 Cass to Hamilton, Dec. 26, 1827, IA LR, Michigan Superintendency; McKenney to Barbour, Dec. 9, 1827, *ibid.;* Second Auditor's Accounts (first series), No. 11339, RG 217, WNRC.

72 Brevoort to McKenney, Aug. 18, 1827, IA LR, Miscellaneous; McKenney to Capt. Smith, Sept. 1, 1827, *ibid.*

73 McKenney, *Memoirs,* I, 95-97.

74 *Ibid.,* 104-05.

75 *Ibid.,* 106-12.

76 Cass to McKenney, Oct. 28, 1827, IA LR, Michigan Superintendency.

77 McKenney to Barbour, Dec. 1, 1827, IA LS, vol. 4, pp. 158, 161-62.

Chapter 9   Administering the Indian Office

1 For the Indian trade and intercourse acts, see: act of July 22, 1790, *U. S. Stat.* I, 137-38; act of March 1, 1793, *ibid.,* 329-32; act of May 19, 1796, *ibid.,* 469-74; act of March 3, 1799, *ibid.,* 743-49; and act of March 30, 1802, *ibid.,* II, 139-46. The act of 1802 was intended to be permanent and was the one that governed McKenney in his administration of Indian affairs. It remained in force, with amendments, until passage of the act of June 30, 1834, *ibid.,* IV, 729-35, which was the last of the Indian trade and intercourse acts and which embodied the best of the preceding laws and added a few new regulations as well. For a thorough discussion of these acts and how they evolved, see Prucha, *American Indian Policy.*

2 McKenney to Calhoun, Feb. 18, 1819, *Papers of John C. Calhoun,* III, 585-86; *U.S. Stat.* I, 138, 330-31, 472, 476; *ibid.,* II, 141-43.

3 McKenney to Barbour, March 10, 1827, IA LS, vol. 3, p. 429; McKenney to Montgomery, April 9, 1829, *ibid.,* vol. 5, p. 401; McKenney to Indian Agents, Feb. 17, 1829, *ibid.,* pp. 309-10.

4 Montgomery to McKenney, April 23, 1825, IA LR, Eastern Cherokee Agency.

5 McKenney to Clark, Aug. 30, 1828, IA LS, vol. 5, p. 108; McKenney

to Cass, July 2, 1829, *ibid.,* vol. 6, p. 35; McKenney to Ward, Feb. 23, 1830, *ibid.,* p. 284. See also, McKenney to Benjamin F. Smith, July 1, 1825, *ibid.,* vol. 2, p. 71; McKenney to Barbour, Jan. 30, 1827, *ibid.,* vol. 3, p. 348; McKenney to Montgomery, May 9, 1825, *ibid.,* vol. 2, p. 8; McKenney to Joseph McMinn, May 3, 1824, *ibid.,* vol. 1, p. 64.

6 McMinn to Calhoun, July 9, 1824, IA LR, Eastern Cherokee Agency. Prucha, *American Indian Policy,* devotes an entire chapter (pages 139-87) to the problem of intruders on Indian lands. The problem was endemic everywhere on the frontier where Indians possessed lands coveted by whites; and, as Prucha writes, the "procedure of moving the illegal settlers off became almost a game and was never completely effective." (163)

7 Path Killer, Ridge, and John Ross to McMinn, Oct. 11, 1823, enclosed with McMinn to Calhoun, Jan. 17, 1824, IA LR, Eastern Cherokee Agency; McMinn to Archibald R. Turk, Oct. [n.d.], 1823, enclosed with McMinn to Calhoun, April 16, 1824, *ibid.;* Turk to Calhoun, Feb. 22, 1824, *ibid.*

8 McKenney to McMinn, June 11, 1824, IA LS, vol. 1, p. 107; proclamation, May 24, 1824, enclosed with McMinn to Calhoun, May 25, 1824, IA LR, Eastern Cherokee Agency; McMinn to Calhoun, July 9, 23, 1824, *ibid.*

9 McMinn to Calhoun, July 9, 1824, IA LR, Eastern Cherokee Agency; Turk to Calhoun, Sept. 29, 1824, *ibid.;* Turk to Calhoun, Jan. 6, 1825, *ibid.;* McKenney to Thomas F. Foster, May 6, 1825, IA LS, vol. 2, p. 5.

10 Nathaniel Richardson and Augusta Gatewood to Clark, July 20, 1829, enclosed with Clark to Eaton, Nov. 30, 1829, IA LR, St. Louis Superintendency; Clark to Eaton, Dec. 9, 1829, *ibid.;* Andrew S. Hughes to Clark, March 14, 1830, enclosed with Clark to Eaton, March 22, 1830, *ibid.*

11 McKenney to Eaton, April 6, 1830, IA LS, vol. 6, p. 376.

12 McKenney to Barbour, Nov. 15, 1825, *ibid.,* vol. 2, p. 238. McKenney to Barbour, Feb. 14, 1826, *ibid.,* p. 426. McKenney to Porter, Jan. 3, 1829, *ibid.,* vol. 5, p. 252.

13 *U.S. Stat.* III, 682.

14 McKenney to Eaton, Jan. 31, 1830, IA LS, vol. 6, pp. 237-38; *House Doc.* No. 117, 20 Cong., 2 Sess. (Serial 186), 27; *U.S. Stat.* IV, 729.

15 *U.S. Stat.* IV, 36; McKenney to Calhoun, Aug. 19, 1818, IT LS, vol. E, pp. 141-43; Calhoun to Superintendents and Indian Agents, June 5, 1824, IA LS, vol. 1, pp. 96-97; McKenney to Ward, Sept. 29, 1824, *ibid.,* p. 207.

16 Stuart to John J. Astor, June 4, 1825, American Fur Company Letter Books, vol. 3, p. 178; McKenney to William B. Astor, July 22, 1825, IA LS, vol. 2, p. 99.

17 *House Journal,* Feb. 7, 9, 1826, 19 Cong., 1 Sess. (Serial 130), 236, 240; McKenney to Barbour, Feb. 14, 1826, IA LS, vol. 2, pp. 422-29 (quote appears on p. 425).

18 *House Journal,* March 29, 1826, 19 Cong., 1 Sess. (Serial 130), 388; Original Bill 189, HR19A-B1, Bills and Resolutions Originating in the House, RG 233, NA; *House Journal,* Dec. 11, 1826, 19 Cong., 2 Sess. (Serial 147), 38-39.

19 Kappler, *Treaties,* 1027-28; McKenney to the President of the Farmers and Mechanics Bank of Georgetown, Jan. 3, 1825, IA LS, vol. 1, p. 278.

20 *U.S. Stat.* IV, 37, 182-83, 526; Dick, *Vanguards of the Frontier,* 111.

21 McKenney to Philip G. Randolph, June 17, 1830, IA LR, Miscellaneous: McKenney to Montgomery, March 24, 1827, IA LS, vol. 3, p. 467.

22 McKenney to Duval, Dec. 26, 1825, IA LS, vol. 2, p. 330; McKenney to Eli Baldwin, Oct. 8, 1829, *ibid.,* vol. 6, p. 105; Dick, *Vanguards of the Frontier,* 111.

23 McKenney to Cass, March 6, 9, 1827, IA LS, vol. 3, pp. 419-20, 427; McKenney to Duval, Dec. 26, 1825, *ibid.,* vol. 2, p. 331; McKenney to Gray, March 24, 1827, *ibid.,* p. 470. See also McKenney to Benjamin F. Smith, Jan. 10, 1826, March 21, 1827, *ibid.,* vols. 2, 3, pp. 360, 460-61.

24 McKenney to Cocke, Jan. 23, 1827, *ibid.,* vol. 3, p. 328. McKenney made the same recommendation to Congress when he served as superintendent of Indian trade. McKenney to Alexander Armstrong, Aug. 15, 1821, IT LS, vol. F, pp. 248-49.

25 Forsyth is quoted in Clark to Calhoun, May 10, 1824, IA LR, St. Louis Superintendency; Gray to Porter, Aug. 11, 1828, *ibid.,* Red River Agency; Cephas Washburn to McKenney, Feb. 2, 1830, *ibid.,* Western Cherokee Agency.

26 McKenney to John Crowell, April 7, 1824, IA LS, vol. 1, p. 29; McKenney to Ward, Nov. 3, 1825, *ibid.,* vol. 2, p. 221; McKenney to Washburn, May 17, 1830, *ibid.,* vol. 6, p. 421. See also McKenney to Cass, Sept. 17, 1825, *ibid.,* vol. 2, pp. 156-57; McKenney to Ward, Nov. 3, 1825, *ibid.,* pp. 221-22; McKenney to the Indian Agent for the Cherokee West of the Mississippi, Aug. 6, 1830, *ibid.,* vol. 7, p. 7.

27 McKenney to Ward, Nov. 3, 1825, *ibid.,* vol. 2, pp. 221-22; McKenney to Folsom, Nov. 1, 1826, *ibid.,* vol. 3, pp. 210-11.

28 Quoted in Street to Barbour, Jan. 8, 1828, IA LR, Praire du Chien Agency.

29 Tipton to Calhoun, Jan. 25, 1825, *ibid.,* Fort Wayne Agency; Prucha, *American Indian Policy,* 119-20.

30 McKenney to Barbour, Feb. 14, 1826, IA LS, vol. 2, pp. 427-28; McKenney to Cass, Feb. 20, 1827, *ibid.,* vol. 3, p. 390; Cass to McKenney, March 25, 1827, IA LR, Michigan Superintendency; McKenney to Cass, April 19, 1827, IA LS, vol. 4, p. 24; McKenney to Clark, April 13, 1827, *ibid.,* p. 15.

31 McKenney to Barbour, Feb. 14, 1826, IA LS, vol. 2, pp. 424-25; Gray to Barbour, April 6, July 30, 1826, IA LR, Red River Agency.

32 *U.S. Stat.* II, 141.

33 McKenney to Benjamin F. Smith, Aug. 5, 1824, IA LS, vol. 1, pp. 164-65; McKenney to William Hendricks, May 12, 1826, *ibid.,* vol. 3, pp. 74-75.

34 See for example, McKenney to James Standefer, Jan. 11, 1825, *ibid.,* vol. 1, p. 293; McKenney to Houston, Feb. 4, 1826, *ibid.,* vol. 2, p. 405; McKenney to Conway, Feb. 4, 1826, *ibid.,* p. 404; McKenney to George W. Owen, Feb. 29, 1828, *ibid.,* vol. 4, pp. 314-16; McKenney to H. Hubbard, Feb. 3, 1830, *ibid.,* vol. 6, p. 252.

35 McDonald to McKenney, Nov. 9, 1824, IA LR, Choctaw Agency.

36 McMinn to Calhoun, June 9, 1824, *ibid.,* Eastern Cherokee Agency.

37 George Johnston to Schoolcraft, Nov. 2, 1825, IA LR, Michigan Superintendency; Street to Barbour, Jan. 8, 1828, *ibid.,* Prairie du Chien Agency.

38 Cass to Barbour, Jan. 7, 1828, *ibid.,* Michigan Superintendency.

39 Quoted in Street to Barbour, Jan. 8, Feb. 17, 1828, *ibid.,* Prairie du

Chien Agency; McKenney to Clark, April 10, 1828, IA LS, vol. 4, p. 395.
40 Street to Porter, Sept. 26, 1828, IA LR, Prairie du Chien Agency.
41 McKenney to Clark, April 10, 1828, IA LS, vol. 4, pp. 395-96.
42 Prucha, *American Indian Policy,* 198-202; McKenney to John Johnston, May 11, 1824, IA LS, vol. 1, pp. 69-70.
43 John Johnston to Calhoun, April 28, 1824, IA LR, Piqua Agency; John Johnston to McKenney, May 24, 1825, *ibid.* For a thorough discussion of this incident, see George Chalou, "Massacre on Fall Creek," *Prologue,* IV (Summer 1972), 109-114.
44 McKenney to Eaton, Nov. 17, 1829, IA LS, vol. 6, p. 166.
45 McKenney to Eaton, April 2, 1830, endorsement on Cass to McKenney, March 11, 1830, IA LR, Michigan Superintendency.

Chapter 10   The Failure of Indian Reform

1 Prucha, *American Indian Policy,* 222.
2 McKenney to School Superintendents, May 22, 1824, IA LS, vol. 1, pp. 79-80; McKenney to Calhoun, Nov. 24, 1824, *ibid.,* p. 238.
3 McKenney to Calhoun, Aug. 14, 1819, IT LS, vol. E, pp. 298-99; McKenney to Calhoun, Nov. 24, 1824, IA LS, vol. 1, p. 238.
4 McKenney to Kingsbury, April 10, 1826, *ibid.,* vol. 3, pp. 20-21.
5 McKenney to John Pickering, April 18, 1826, *ibid.,* p. 39; McKenney to William Chamberlain, July 25, 1825, *ibid.,* vol. 2, p. 103; McKenney to Kingsbury, April 10, 1826, *ibid.,* vol. 3, p. 20.
6 McKenney to Kingsbury, April 10, 1826, *ibid.,* vol. 3, pp. 21-22.
7 [Andrew Reed], *No Fiction; or, the Test of Friendship; a Narrative Founded on Recent and Interesting Facts,* xii. The book was published anonymously because its author, a well-known minister and philanthropist, did not want to capitalize on the popularity of his name and wished it to be read on its own merits. J. Grant, *The Metropolitan Pulpit; or Sketches of the Most Popular Preachers in London,* II, 267.
8 McKenney to Calhoun, June 12, 1821, IT LS, vol. F, p. 218; Calhoun to McKenney, June 14, 1821, SW IA LS, vol. E, p. 117.
9 Richard M. Johnson, William McLean, William R. King, and Thomas Hendricks to Barbour, n.d., IA LR, Miscellaneous; McKenney to Barbour, Oct. 30, 1827, *ibid.;* Lee Compere to McKenney, Feb. 28, 1828, *ibid.,* Creek Agency.
10 McKenney to Elijah Kellogg, Dec. 15, 1829, IA LS, vol. 6, pp. 195-96; McKenney to Kingsbury, April 2, 1828, *ibid.,* vol. 4, p. 384; McKenney to Cephas Washburn, Nov. 18, 1828, *ibid.,* vol. 5, p. 190; Compere to McKenney, Feb. 28, 1828, IA LR, Creek Agency.
11 McKenney to David Baldwin, Robert Turnbull, and William Trahern, April 2, 1828, IA LS, vol. 4, pp. 385, 386, 387.
12 Kappler, *Treaties,* 193, 212; Thomas Henderson to Eaton, May 1, 1829, IA LR, Schools.
13 Henderson to Eaton, May 1, Nov. 1, 1829, Oct. 31, 1830, IA LR, Schools.
14 McKenney to Richard M. Johnson, Dec. 11, 1829, IA LS, vol. 6, pp. 188-89; Board of Trustees to Eaton, Nov. 17, 1829, IA LR, Schools.
15 McKenney to Barbour, Dec. 1, 1827, IA LS, vol. 4, p. 162.
16 McKenney to James Corcoran, Dec. 22, 1824, IA LS, vol. 1, p. 272;

McKenney to Benjamin F. Smith, Jan. 10, 1826, *ibid.*, vol. 2, p. 360.
17 McKenney to Levi Colbert, March 17, 1828, *ibid.*, vol. 4, p. 340;
McKenney to Dougherty Colbert, April 3, 1827, *ibid.*, p. 3; Adams,
manuscript diary, MF, p. 165, Massachusetts Historical Society.
18 William Barnard and Lee Compere to [Andrew Jackson], n.d., IA
LR, Schools; McKenney, *Memoirs,* I, 187-90.
19 John Crowell to Calhoun, March 18, 1824, IA LR, Creek Agency;
McKenney to Clark, July 22, 1828, IA LS, vol. 5, p. 48. See also,
McKenney to John Johnston, Aug. 9, 1824, *ibid.*, vol. 1, p. 179; Mc-
Kenney to William Capers, May 24, 1824, *ibid.*, pp. 80-81.
20 McKenney to Superintendents and Indian Agents, Aug. 7, 1824, *ibid.*,
vol. 1, p. 170.
21 McDonald to McKenney, April 25, 1826, IA LR, Choctaw Agency.
22 Compere to McKenney, May 20, 1828, *ibid.*, Creek Agency; Mc-
Kenney to Samuel Southard, June 4, 1828, IA LS, vol. 4, p. 483;
McKenney to Lucius Bolles, July 22, 1828, *ibid.*, vol. 5, p. 49. For
examples of similar difficulties between missionaries and the Indians,
see McKenney to Ward, Jan. 7, 1826, *ibid.*, vol. 2, p. 350; McKenney
to Ingersoll, Feb. 23, 1830, *ibid.*, vol. 6, pp. 283-84; McKenney to
Parrish, April 9, 1824, *ibid.*, vol. 1, p. 32.
23 McKenney to Leaders of the Passamaquoddy Tribe of Indians, Aug.
12, 1828, *ibid.*, vol. 5, pp. 82-83; McKenney to Eaton, Dec. 12, 1829,
ibid., vol. 6, pp. 184-85.
24 McKenney to Barbour, Dec. 13, 1825, *ibid.*, vol. 2, p. 304.
25 McKenney to Barbour, Nov. 20, 1826, *ibid.*, vol. 3, p. 231; McKenney
to Porter, Nov. 28, 1828, *ibid.*, vol. 5, pp. 209-10; McKenney to Kingsbury, March 14, 1826, *ibid.*, vol. 2, p. 466.
26 McKenney to Barbour, Nov. 30, 1825, *Senate Doc.* No. 2, 19 Cong.,
1 Sess. (Serial 125), pp. 89-92, statement B.
27 McKenney to Barbour, Nov. 20, 1826, IA LS, vol. 3, p. 230.
28 *Ibid.;* McKenney to Herman Lincoln, March 8, 1827, *ibid.*, p. 425.
29 McKenney to School Superintendents, Feb. 9, 1827, *ibid.*, p. 379;
McKenney to Porter, Nov. 28, 1828, *ibid.*, vol. 5, pp. 208-09.
30 Data compiled from the annual reports of the Office of Indian Affairs,
1825-30.
31 McKenney to Clark, May 4, 1830, IA LS, vol. 6, p. 404; McKenney
to Joseph Street, April 13, 1830, *ibid.*, vol. 6, pp. 384-86; McKenney
to Chiefs and Headmen of the Chickasaw Nation, Feb. 16, 1829, *ibid.*,
vol. 5, pp. 307-08.
32 McKenney to Chiefs and Headmen of the Chickasaw Nation, Feb. 16,
1829, *ibid.*, vol. 5, pp. 306-08; George Dewey Harmon, *Sixty Years of
Indian Affairs, Political, Economic, and Diplomatic, 1789-1850,* 380.
33 McKenney to Superintendents and Indian Agents, Jan. 29, 1830, IA
LS, vol. 6, p. 247; Cass to McKenney, Feb. 11, 1830, IA LR, Michigan
Superintendency; Dougherty to McKenney, Jan. 30, 1830, *ibid.*, Upper
Missouri Agency.
34 McKenney to Eaton, March 22, 1830, IA LS, vol. 6, pp. 349-53.
35 McKenney, *Memoirs,* I, 116-17.
36 McDonald to McKenney, Jan. 31, 1826, IA LR, Choctaw Agency.
37 McDonald to McKenney, April 25, 1826, *ibid.;* McKenney to Henderson, Dec. 22, 1826, IA LS, vol. 3, p. 268; McKenney, *Memoirs,*
II, 118-19.

Chapter 11   Indian Removal

1 For a detailed analysis of Indian removal, see Annie Heloise Abel, "History of Events Resulting in Indian Consolidation West of the Mississippi," *Annual Report of the American Historical Association for the Year 1906,* I (1908), 233-450.

2 James D. Richardson, ed., *A Compilation of the Messages and Papers of the Presidents, 1789-1897,* II, 261.

3 The reports by McKenney and Calhoun are printed in *House Doc.* No. 64, 18 Cong., 2 Sess. (Serial 116), 7-13.

4 Richardson, *Messages and Papers,* II, 280-83.

5 McKenney to Charles B. Hicks, March 29, 1825, IA LS, vol. 1, p. 433. McKenney to Calhoun, April 11, 18, 1825, *ibid.,* pp. 445-46, 456, contain lists which indicate that he gave at least 657 reprints of the report to thirty-two individuals and societies. Not all recipients are on these lists, however, as is indicated by McKenney to Madison, April 7, 1825, Madison Papers.

6 McKenney to Porter, Jan. 31, 1829, IA LS, vol. 5, pp. 289-90; McKenney to Kingsbury, March 8, 1830, *ibid.,* vol. 6, p. 315.

7 McKenney to T. L. Ogden, Jan. 2, 1828, *ibid.,* vol. 4, p. 223.

8 McKenney to Barbour, Dec. 27, 1826, *ibid.,* vol. 3, pp. 284, 280.

9 McKenney to Porter, Nov. 28, 1828, *ibid.,* vol. 5, p. 208; McKenney to Barbour, Nov. 29, 1827, *ibid.,* vol. 4, p. 155; McKenney to Folsom, May 9, 1826, *ibid.,* vol. 3, p. 66.

10 Kappler, *Treaties,* 25-217, *passium.*

11 George Lowery, Elijah Hicks, and Major Ridge to Calhoun, Feb. 11, 1824, IA LR, Eastern Cherokee Agency; Montgomery (Alabama) *Republican,* May 6, 1825, reprinted in Washington *National Intelligencer,* May 25, 1825; Ward to Porter, Oct. 11, 1828, IA LR, Choctaw Agency; Thomas Hinds and John Coffee to Barbour, Nov. 2, 1826, IA LR, Chickasaw Agency.

12 McKenney to Barbour, Dec. 27, 1826, IA LS, vol. 3, pp. 279, 273-75, 283-85.

13 Richard M. Johnson, Thomas B. Reed, William H. Harrison and others to [Barbour], Jan. 25, 1827, IA LR, Miscellaneous.

14 Barbour to McKenney, March 28, 1827, IA LS, vol. 3, pp. 484-85.

15 McKenney to Barbour, Sept. 29, 1827, IA LR, Miscellaneous; McKenney, *Memoirs,* I, 64, 153-54.

16 McKenney to Barbour, Sept. 29, 1827, IA LR, Miscellaneous.

17 McKenney to Barbour, Oct. 10, 1827, Chickasaw Nation, *Senate Doc.* No. 1, 20 Cong., 1 Sess. (Serial 163), 23-24.

18 McKenney to Barbour, Oct. 10, 1827, Mayhew Station, *ibid.,* 185.

19 McKenney to Barbour, Oct. 15, 1827, IA LR, Choctaw Agency; McKenney to Barbour, Oct. 17, 1827, *Senate Doc.* No. 1, 20 Cong., 1 Sess. (Serial 163), 193-95; Choctaw Chiefs to McKenney, Oct. 17, 1827, *ibid.,* 195-96; McKenney to Barbour, Oct. 17, 1827, IA LR, Choctaw Agency.

20 McKenney to Barbour, Oct. 15, 1827, IA LR, Choctaw Agency.

21 Barbour to McKenney, April 10, 1827, IA LS, vol. 3, p. 493; McKenney to Barbour, Oct. 28, 1827, Treaties, No. 150, RG 75, NA; McKenney to Barbour, March 24, 1828, IA LS, vol. 4, p. 362. A complete discussion of the signing of the Creek treaty can be found in Richard J. Hryniewicki, "The Creek Treaty of November 15, 1827,"

Georgia Historical Quarterly, LII (March 1968), 1-15.

22 McKenney to Barbour, Oct. 28, 1827, Treaties, No. 150, RG 75, NA; McKenney to Barbour, Nov. 2, 1827, *ibid.*

23 *Cherokee Phoenix,* June 25, 1828.

24 McKenney to Barbour, Nov. 2, 1827, Treaties, No. 150, RG 75, NA; *Cherokee Phoenix,* June 25, 1828.

25 McKenney to Barbour, March 24, 1828, IA LS, vol. 4, pp. 360-61, 355; McKenney to Barbour, Nov. 17, 1827, *Senate Doc.* No. 1, 20 Cong., 1 Sess. (Serial 163), 197-98. The treaty is printed in Kappler, *Treaties,* 284-86.

26 Crowell to Barbour, Jan. 7, 1828, IA LR, Creek Agency.

27 McKenney to Barbour, [Jan. 1828?], *ibid.*

28 McKenney to Barbour, Nov. 29, 1827, IA LS, vol. 4, pp. 153-57. The quotes are taken from pp. 154, 157.

29 Original Bill 55, HR20A-B1, RG 233, NA; *House Journal,* Jan. 7, 1828, 20 Cong., 1 Sess. (Serial 168), 34, 129, 318; McKenney to William McLean, Feb. 14, 1828, IA LS, vol. 4, pp. 293-94.

30 Original Bill 126, S20A-B1, RG 46, NA; *Senate Journal,* March 24, April 17, 1828, 20 Cong., 1 Sess. (Serial 162), 252, 305-06; Barbour to William McLean, April 29, 1828, IA LS, vol. 4, p. 423.

31 *House Journal,* May 21, 22, 1828, 20 Cong., 1 Sess. (Serial 168), 811-29.

32 McKenney to Gabriel Moore, Jan. 22, 1828, IA LS, vol. 4, p. 264; McKenney to Clark, June 10, 1828, *ibid.,* vol. 5, pp. 7-8; McKenney to Samuel Southard, June 5, 1828, *ibid.,* vol. 4, p. 488.

33 McKenney to Clark, June 10, 1828, *ibid.,* vol. 5, p. 8.

34 McKenney to Benjamin F. Smith, June 10, 1828, *ibid.,* p. 9; McKenney to Isaac McCoy, *ibid.,* p. 11; McKenney to John Bell, *ibid.,* p. 10; McKenney to Ward, *ibid.;* McKenney to Luther Blake, June 12, 1828, *ibid.,* p. 15; McKenney to Crowell, *ibid.;* McKenney to George P. Todson, *ibid.,* p. 14.

35 Bell to McKenney, July 22, 1828, IA LR, Chickasaw Agency.

36 McKenney to Levi Colbert, George Colbert, Tish-ho-Mingo, and Others, Aug. 14, 1828, IA LS, vol. 5, p. 85; McKenney to John B. Duncan, *ibid.,* p. 88; McKenney to Bell, *ibid.,* p. 86.

37 Bell to McKenney, Sept. 17, 1828, IA LR, Chickasaw Agency; Clark to Porter, Oct. 13, 1828, *ibid.,* St. Louis Superintendency.

38 McKenney to James Rogers, May 31, 1828, IA LS, vol. 4, p. 477; McKenney to Montgomery, May 27, 1828, *ibid.,* p. 466. The treaty with the Western Cherokee, dated May 6, 1828, is printed in Kappler, *Treaties,* 288-92. The treaty included a provision paying Rogers $500 for a lost horse and "for services rendered by him to the United States," *ibid.,* 291. See also Rogers and Thomas Mawe to Eaton, June 23, 1830, IA LR, Cherokee Emigration.

39 *Cherokee Phoenix,* Aug. 27, Oct. 15, 1828; James C. Mitchell to McKenney, Aug. 17, 1828, IA LR, Cherokee Emigration.

40 Montgomery to Porter, Oct. 31, 1828, *ibid.,* Eastern Cherokee Agency. Rogers evidently did not work out as well as expected. By July McKenney was asking the secretary of war not to pay Rogers any more money until his services could be properly evaluated. "He took with him 500$, I think," McKenney wrote, "and [he] received 500$, besides on Treaty Stipulations—and it has done him harm it appears instead of good. He's been drunk, it seems, and with plenty of money

an Indian will keep so. To support him now, and pay him according to his services when ascertained, would be to ensure better services, and these more faithfully performed." McKenney to Porter, July 26, 1828, IA LS, vol. 5, p. 54.

41 Montgomery to Porter, Aug. 30, 1828, IA LR, Eastern Cherokee Agency; McKenney to Montgomery, Oct. 1, 1828, IA LS, vol. 5, p. 140.

42 Montgomery to Porter, Oct. 10, 31; Nov. 24, Dec. 26, 1828; and Jan. 23, Feb. 12, 1829, IA LR, Eastern Cherokee Agency.

43 Montgomery to Porter, Feb. 12, 1829, *ibid.*; "A Republican" to Porter, Feb. 9, 1829, Cherokee Emigration. Getting the Indians to Arkansas Territory evidently was only half the problem as the agent in charge of the arriving emigrants indicates. After one year he had received but 225 emigrants at the agency and of those, he claimed, "The male adults consist almost entirely of White Men and Quateroon Cherokees, one of whom is more troublesome in all relations and intercourse than fifty full blooded Indians." E. W. DuVal to Eaton, Jan. 1, 1830, *ibid.*

44 McKenney to Porter, Jan. 31, 1829, IA LS, vol. 5, p. 289; McKenney to Levi Colbert and Chiefs of the Chickasaws, Oct. 21, 1829, *ibid.*, vol. 6, pp. 127-28.

45 *Cherokee Phoenix*, July 15, 1829; The Glass to all Cherokee, Aug. n.d., 1828, printed *ibid.*, Oct. 29, 1828.

46 Rogers, Samuel MacKey, and David Brown to the President, March 3, 1824, IA LR, Western Cherokee Agency.

47 The treaty with the Quapaw was signed November 15, 1824, and the Indians moved the following year. Kappler, *Treaties,* 210-11. According to Abel, very little thought was given to the western tribes until after passage of the removal bill. President Monroe "did not tell the would-be emigrants that there were no red men in the West to dispute their entry; but he acknowledged the indigenous occupancy claim and prepared to extinguish as much of it as was necessary to locate the eastern tribes. Hence, at this time treaties were signed only with the Quapaw and Osage." Abel, "History of Events," n286-87.

48 Gray to Barbour, April 1, 1827, June 30, 1828, IA LR, Red River Agency; McKenney to Gray, Aug. 18, 1828, IA LS, vol. 5, p. 90.

49 McKenney to Barbour, April 12, 1828, IA LS, vol. 4, pp. 403-04.

50 Rogers to Porter, Oct. 24, 1828, IA LR, Cherokee Emigration; Montgomery to Porter, Oct. 2, 1828, *ibid.*, Eastern Cherokee Agency; Mitchell to McKenney, Aug. 8, 1828, *ibid.*

51 McKenney to Cass, Dec. 14, 1827, IA LS, vol. 4, p. 182; McKenney to Clark, March 17, 1827, *ibid.*, vol. 3, pp. 450-51.

52 Jeremiah Evarts to McKenney, Feb. 14, 1825, Papers of the American Board; McKenney to James C. Crane, Dec. 30, 1824, IA LS, vol. 1, pp. 276-77; McKenney to Bishop Soule, March 31, 1825, *ibid.*, p. 434; McKenney to Bolles, Dec. 20, 1828, *ibid.*, vol. 4, p. 201.

53 Washburn to McKenney, Feb. 2, 1830, IA LR, Western Cherokee Agency; quote by McCoy is taken from Berkhofer, *Salvation and the Savage,* 101. For a comprehensive discussion of McCoy and his work, see George A. Schultz, *An Indian Canaan: Isaac McCoy and the Vision of an Indian State.*

54 Francis Paul Prucha, "Thomas L. McKenney and the New York Indian Board," *Mississippi Valley Historical Review,* XLVIII (March 1962), 636.

55 The prospectus of the *Cherokee Phoenix* came out in October 1827. The first issue of the paper, from which the quote is taken, is dated February 21, 1828.

56 *Cherokee Phoenix,* May 21, 1828; McKenney to Editor, Oct. 8, 1829, printed *ibid.,* Nov. 11, 1829; Editor to McKenney, *ibid.*

57 McKenney to Eli Baldwin, Oct. 8, 1829, IA LS, vol. 6, p. 104; Montgomery to Porter, Dec. 5, 1828, IA LR, Eastern Cherokee Agency.

58 Ross to Porter, Nov. 22, 1828, IA LR, Eastern Cherokee Agency; McKenney to Evarts, Dec. 11, 1828, Papers of the American Board.

59 Elias Boudinot to McKenney, Jan. 10, 1829, IA LR, Eastern Cherokee Agency; Samuel Worcester to McKenney, Feb. 4, 1828 [1829], *ibid.*

60 S21A-C8, RG 46, NA. See the indexes to the House and Senate journals, 21 Cong., 1 Sess., for the presentation of the petitions and memorials. Many are printed in the serial set of congressional documents.

61 Porter to Adams, Nov. 24, 1828, *Senate Doc.* No. 1, 20 Cong., 2 Sess. (Serial 181), 22.

62 Prucha, "McKenney and the New York Board," 635-55, is a detailed account of McKenney's efforts to enlist church support for Indian removal. The article, however, implies that the controversy arose only after Andrew Jackson became President, overlooking the fact that the clergy spoke out against removal from the policy's inception. The article also isolates McKenney's efforts on behalf of removal, failing to consider them in the light of all his other efforts to promote passage of the removal bill. There can be no doubt that McKenney viewed the New York Board as a means to secure his position with the Jackson administration.

63 McKenney to Baldwin, May 21, 1829, IA LS, vol. 5, p. 439. The constitution is printed in *Documents and Proceedings Relating to the Formation and Progress of a Board, in the city of New York, for the Emigration, Preservation, and Improvement, of the Aborigines of America, July 22, 1829,* 22-23.

64 McKenney to Eaton, Wednesday [July 22, 1829], IA LR, Miscellaneous. According to an article in the *Cherokee Phoenix* the New York Board was composed of twenty-two members of the Dutch Reformed Church, three Scotch Presbyterians, one Episcopalian, and one Moravian. *Cherokee Phoenix,* May 1, 1830.

65 The meeting was held in New York City on Aug. 12, 1829. McKenney to Eaton, Thursday [Aug. 13, 1829], IA LR, Miscellaneous. The documents appeared in the New York *Evening Post,* Oct. 15, Nov. 5, 1829. The war department gave money to the board to pay "such bills as are, or may be created in its preliminary operations." McKenney to John Clark, Sept. 16, 1829, IA LS, vol. 6, p. 87. The War Department received 1,750 copies of the booklet. Bill of Lading from Vander Poole and Cole, Sept. 28, 1829, IA LR, Miscellaneous.

66 Prucha, "McKenney and the New York Board," 651-52.

67 *U.S. Stat.* IV, 411.

68 McKenney to Hugh Lawson White, Feb. 26, 1830, IA LS, vol. 6, p. 294. Before the bill was passed McKenney sent White another letter on the same subject. McKenney to White, April 9, 1830, *ibid.,* p. 381.

69 McKenney to Kingsbury, March 8, 1830, *ibid.,* p. 315.

Chapter 12   Dismissal from Office

1 Philip G. Randolph to McKenney, Aug. 16, 1830, SW LS, vol. 13, p. 9; McKenney, *Memoirs,* I, 262; McKenney to John McLean, Jan. 29, 1831, McLean Papers.

2 Adams, *Diary,* VIII, 103; Johnston to McLean, March 2, 1829, IA LR, Piqua Agency; *Register of Officers and Agents, Civil, Military, and Naval, in the Service of the United States, on the 30th of September, 1829,* 82-85; *Register of Officers and Agents . . . on the 30th of September, 1831,* 95-98.

3 Schoolcraft to Cass, June 16, 1829, MS LR; writing to the editor of the New York *Commercial Advertiser* shortly before the 1828 election, McKenney claimed that all he feared should Jackson be elected President was "the separation from friends in the Administration who are my friends!" McKenney to William Leetes Stone, Oct. 28, 1828, Miscellaneous Papers (Manuscript Division, New York Public Library).

4 The statement from the *Georgia Journal* is quoted in *Niles' Weekly Register,* Oct. 9, 1830; the rejoinder by the *Register* appears in the same issue.

5 McKenney to J. Bailey, Nov. 17, 1825, Miscellaneous Papers (New-York Historical Society); McKenney to Stone, Oct. 28, 1828, Miscellaneous papers (New York Public Library).

6 McKenney, *Memoirs,* I, 193.

7 McKenney to Barbour, Dec. 26, 1827, IA LS, vol. 4, pp. 209-12; McKenney, *Memoirs,* 1, 192; McKenney to Lee, May 22, 1828, IA LS, vol. 4, p. 460. See Chapter 2, note 11 for discussion of the government's five auditors and two comptrollers.

8 The correspondence relating to this episode is scattered. The bulk of the material is found in SW LR, I-149(22), and Second Auditor's Accounts (first series), No. 14289, RG 217, WNRC. The latter file contains a forty-five-page letter from which the quote is taken (McKenney to Cutts, Aug. 5, 1828, p. 43).

9 Certificate dated June 19, 1830, Second Auditor's Accounts (second series), No. 14289, RG 217, WNRC; certificate dated Nov. 14, 1833, *ibid.,* No. 17702.

10 See the "Address of Thomas R. Moore to His Constituents," June 27, 1828, printed in the Louisville *Public Advertiser,* July 19, 1828; "On Retrenchment. May 15, 1828," *House Report* No. 259, 20 Cong., 1 Sess. (Serial 179), 117, 132.

11 McKenney to "a Friend," May 15, 1828, printed in the Alexandria *Gazette,* May 22, 1828, and in the Washington *National Intelligencer,* May 31, 1828.

12 *United States Telegraph,* July 1, 14, 15, and Sept. 20, 1828, and Aug. 6 and Sept. 1, 1829.

13 Thomas L. McKenney, *To the Public* (n.p., 1828). A copy of the pamphlet can be found with the Papers of James Madison (Rare Book Room, Library of Congress).

14 McKenney to Barbour, July 24, 1828, James Barbour Papers (Manuscript Division, New York Public Library).

15 White to Eaton, July 8, 1828, IA LR, Florida Superintendency; Mitchell to McKenney, Aug. 17, 1828, *ibid.,* Cherokee Emigration; William Haile to McKenney, Aug. 28, 1828, *ibid.,* Miscellaneous.

16 *United States Telegraph,* April 21, 1829.

17 McKenney to Jackson, April 23, 1829, IA LS, vol. 5, p. 417.

18 McKenney, *Memoirs,* I, 202, 203-04.

19 *United States Telegraph,* Aug. 26, 29, 1829. The reference to the "Major" is a jab at the fact that the highest military rank McKenney held was that of major and hence had no legitimate claim to the title of colonel; cf. Chapter 1, note 10.

20 Georgetown *Columbian Gazette,* Sept. 1, 1829; *United States Telegraph,* Sept. 1, 1829.

21 "Rations to Emigrating Indians. July 5, 1832," *House Report* No. 502, 22 Cong., 1 Sess. (Serial 228), 9; McKenney, *Memoirs,* I, 209.

22 McKenney to Forward, Nov. 3, 1841, Gratz Collection; *House Report* No. 502, 22 Cong., 1 Sess. (Serial 228), 10; McKenney, *Memoirs,* I, 223.

23 McKenney to Sam Houston, Feb. 18, 1830, *House Report* No. 502, 22 Cong., 1 Sess. (Serial 228), 10.

24 "Proposals for Supplying Emigrant Indians with Rations, West of the Mississippi," Feb. 18, 1830, IA LS, vol. 6, p. 278; *House Report* No. 502, 22 Cong., 1 Sess. (Serial 228), 11; McKenney, *Memoirs,* I, 210. The notice, with instructions to print it three times weekly until March 15, was sent to the Richmond *Enquirer,* Baltimore *Republican,* Philadelphia *Gazette,* Cincinnati *Republican,* Washington *National Intelligencer, Ohio State Bulletin,* and the Louisville *Advertiser.* [McKenney to Editors, Feb. 18, 1830], IA LS, vol. 6, p. 278.

25 McKenney, *Memoirs,* I, 211, 216; McKenney to Eaton, April 7, 1830, IA LS, vol. 6, pp. 374-75.

26 *House Report* No. 502, 22 Cong., 1 Sess. (Serial 228), 13.

27 *Ibid.,* 62-63; McKenney to Forward, Nov. 3, 1841, Gratz Collection.

28 *House Report* No. 502, 22 Cong., 1 Sess. (Serial 228) 1-3. The Jacksonian Democrats on the committee were William Stanbery, William Drayton, James Moore Wayne, Henry P. Muhlenberg, and Henry Hubbard; the Whigs Isaac Chapman Bates and John Leeds Kerr.

29 McKenney to John McLean, Jan. 29, 1831, McLean Papers; McKenney to John Forsyth, April 1, 1830, IA LS, vol. 6, p. 361.

30 McKenney, *Memoirs,* I, 205, 222-23.

31 Houston to Eaton, June 13, 1830, printed in Amelia W. Williams and Eugene C. Barker, eds., *The Writings of Sam Houston, 1813-1863,* I, 152-53; the articles, dated June 22, July 7, Aug. 14, and Sept. 8, 1830, are printed, respectively, *ibid.,* 155-57, 157-63, 164-70, and 170-77; the quotes appear on 162, 161, 168.

32 Georgetown *Columbian Gazette,* Aug. 25, 1829; *United States Telegraph,* Aug. 29, 1829.

33 Bell to McKenney, Sept. 17, 1828, IA LR, Chickasaw Agency.

34 Eaton to McKenney, June 7, 1830, IA LS, vol. 6, p. 459; McKenney to Evarts, *ibid.,* p. 456; Randolph to McKenney, June 17, 1830, IA LR, Miscellaneous; McKenney, *Memoirs,* I, 260-61.

35 McKenney to Indian Agents, June 18, 1830, IA LS, vol. 6, p. 486; McKenney to Superintendents, *ibid.;* McKenney, *Memoirs,* I, 260-61. McKenney did not refuse immediately, however. At the foot of Randolph's letter to him, McKenney noted his objection to the new ruling but then wrote: "If however you desire such an order to be given, it is my business to comply, & I will issue it." McKenney to [Randolph], June 17, 1830, IA LR, Miscellaneous.

36 Randolph to Montgomery, June 18, 1830, IA LS, vol. 6, p. 487.
37 McKenney to McLean, Jan. 29, 1831, McLean Papers; Randolph to McKenney, Aug. 5, 1830, SW LS, vol. 12, p. 504; Randolph to McKenney, Aug. 16, 1830, *ibid.,* vol. 13, p. 9.
38 McKenney, *Memoirs,* I, p. 262. Essentially the same statement is found in McKenney to McLean, Jan. 29, 1831, McLean Papers.
39 McKenney to McLean, Jan. 29, 1831, McLean Papers.
40 *Tri-Weekly National Intelligencer,* Sept. 1, 1830; *United States Telegraph, ibid.*
41 McKenney to Forward, Nov. 3, 1841, Gratz Collection; *U.S. Stat.* IV, 564, 735-38, 729-35; McKenney to McLean, Jan. 29, 1831, McLean Papers.

Chapter 13   The Indian Office Museum

1 McKenney to T. Lewis, Nov. 22, 1820, IT LS, vol. F, p. 81; McKenney, *Sketches,* 320.
2 McKenney to School Superintendents, Aug. 9, 1824, IA LS, vol. 1, p. 173; Jonathan Elliot, *Historical Sketches of the Ten Miles Square Forming the District of Columbia; with a Picture of Washington, Describing Objects of General Interest or Curiosity at the Metropolis of the Union,* 165.
3 It appears from surviving fiscal records that between 1816 and 1830 at least $4,300 of public money was spent on the archives. Records indicate that McKenney spent at least $530 while superintendent of Indian trade (see note 6) and at least $3,770 while superintendent of Indian affairs. Although the records for the Bureau of Indian Affairs period appear to be complete, those for the factory system are not. During the administrations of the four secretaries, 1824-30, the amounts spent were as follows: Calhoun, $744.75; Barbour, $2,793.86; Porter, $160.50; and Eaton, $71.00. For the funds spent between 1824 and 1830 see, Second Auditor's Accounts (first series) Nos. 5724, 5810, 8062, 8100, 8106, 8358, 8447, 8668, 9130, 9444, 9445, 9513, 9570, 9873, 9953, 9955, 10163, 10210, 10509, 10584, 11442, 11679, 11904, 12910, 12923, 15437, RG 217, WNRC.
4 McKenney to Graham, July 21, 1817, IT LS, vol. D, p. 379; McKenney to Factors, July 22, 1817, *ibid.,* pp. 376-77.
5 Fowler to McKenney, Sept. 9, 1817, Letter Book of the Natchitoches-Sulphur Fork Factory, p. 122, Records of the Office of Indian Trade, RG 75, NA.
6 Journal of the Prairie du Chien Factory for quarters ending Dec. 31, 1817; June 30, Sept. 30, 1818; June 30, 1819; June 30, 1820; Dec. 31, 1820; March 31, 1821; and June 30, 1822. Inventory of the Green Bay Factory for quarter ending Dec. 31, 1819; Inventory of the Choctaw Factory for quarters ending March 31, 1818; Sept. 30, Dec. 31, 1818, Records of the Office of Indian Trade, RG 75, NA.
7 McKenney to John W. Johnson, Aug. 26, 1820, IT LS, vol. F, p. 38.
8 *Metropolitan and Georgetown National Messenger,* June 25, 1822; Sales Book, Oct. 31, 1822, Records of the Office of Indian Trade, RG 75, NA.
9 "Additions and Donations to the Columbian Museum, since its commencement in this City," Washington *National Intelligencer,* April

7, 1824; McKenney to James V. S. Ryley, April 18, 1825, IA LS, vol. 1, p. 451.

10 McKenney to School Superintendents, May 22, 1824, IA LS, vol. 1, p. 80; McKenney to Ryley, *ibid.*, p. 451.

11 McKenney to Porter, Dec. 9, 1828, IA LR, Miscellaneous; McKenney to Ingersoll, Feb. 27, 1830, IA LS, vol. 6, p. 295; McKenney to Eaton, March 13, 1829, *ibid.*, vol. 5, p. 340; McKenney, *Memoirs,* II, 29.

12 Second Auditor's Accounts (first series), No. 14418; McKenney, *Sketches,* 412, 201, 240, 243, 248, 299, 313, 314, 315, 393, 429.

13 McKenney, *Sketches,* 353, 425, 440; Clark to McKenney, Nov. 2, 1827, IA LR, St. Louis Superintendency; McKenney to Clark, Dec. 15, 1827, IA LS, vol. 4, p. 188.

14 McKenney to Lewis, Nov. 22, 1820, IT LS, vol. F, p. 79; McKenney to Samuel S. Conant, Jan. 5, 1825, IA LS, vol. 1, p. 284.

15 McKenney to Eaton, March 22, 1830, IA LS, vol. 6, p. 352.

16 McKenney to McCoy, May 5, 1827, *ibid.*, vol. 4, p. 48; McKenney to John S. Skinner, *ibid.*, pp. 48-49.

17 McKenney to David Arnit, Sept. 28, 1824, IA LS, vol. 1, p. 205; McKenney to Conant, Jan. 5, 1825, *ibid.*, p. 284; the circulars, dated Jan. 12, 1825, were sent to Cass, Clark, Sibley, McDonald, Vaill, Kingsbury, Kellogg, McCoy, James B. Finley, John Gambold, Robert Belt, T. C. Stuart, *ibid.*, p. 299.

18 Barbour to David Trimble, Feb. 6, 1827, *ibid.*, vol. 3, p. 368; McKenney to Superintendents and Indian Agents, Feb. 7, 1827, *ibid.*, p. 369.

19 McKenney to School Superintendents, Aug. 9, 1824, *ibid.*, p. 173.

20 Thomas Forsyth to Barbour, June 15, 1826, IA LR, Sac and Fox Agency; McKenney to John Pickering, April 18, 1826, IA LS, vol. 3, p. 39; Johnston to McKenney, Nov. 3, 1829, IA LR, Piqua Agency; McKenney to Benton Pixley, March 26, 1825, IA LS, vol. 1, p. 427; Barbour to Mary Randolph, Oct. 17, 1826, *ibid.*, vol. 3, p. 197; McKenney to Wright, Aug. 9, 1828, *ibid.*, vol. 5, p. 79.

21 McKenney to Charles Hicks, March 29, 1825, *ibid.*, vol. 1, p. 432; Hodge, *Handbook of Indians,* II, 510; McKenney to Barbour, Dec. 13, 1825, IA LS, vol. 2, p. 304.

22 McKenney to Chamberlain, July 25, 1825, IA LS, vol. 2, p. 103.

23 George Harvey Genzmer, "Constantine Samuel Rafinesque," Johnson and Malone, eds., *Dictionary of American Biography,* XV, 323; David S. Muzzey, "Albert Gallatin," *ibid.*, VII, 108; McKenney to Superintendents of Indian Affairs, School Superintendents, and Indian Agents, Aug. 22, 1825, IA LS, vol. 2, p. 129.

24 McKenney to Superintendents of Indian Affairs, School Superintendents, and Indian Agents, Aug. 22, 1825, IA LS, vol. 2, pp. 129-30.

25 Hamilton to Albert Gallatin, June 9, 1826, *ibid.*, vol. 3, p. 118; Hamilton to James Rochelle, Aug. 14, 1826, *ibid.*, p. 157; McKenney to Adams, May 30, 1826, *ibid.*, p. 110.

26 McKenney to Gallatin, Feb. 18, 1826, *ibid.*, vol. 2, p. 437; McKenney to Gallatin, May 6, 1826, *ibid.*, vol. 3, p. 61; McKenney to Gallatin, July 31, 1828, *ibid.*, vol. 5, p. 70; McKenney to Gallatin, Aug. 9, 1828, *ibid.*, p. 79.

27 For the books mentioned, McKenney paid $2, $15, and $20, respectively. Second Auditor's Accounts (first series), Nos. 9931, 10397, and 12470, RG 217, WNRC.

28 McKenney to Davis and Force, April 28, 1825, IA LS, vol. 1, p. 472;

McKenney to Fielding Lucas, April 10, 1827, *ibid.,* vol. 4, p. 9; the bill of sale from Davis & Force contains a list of the titles which they furnished McKenney, the cost for each, and the total cost. Second Auditor's Accounts (first series), No. 9130, RG 217, WNRC; "On Retrenchment. May 15, 1828," *House Report* No. 259, 20 Cong., 1 Sess. (Serial 179), 30.

29 "On Retrenchment, May 15, 1828," *House Report* No. 259, 20 Cong., 1 Sess. (Serial 179), 30, 181.

30 Nicholas Biddle to Webster, March 2, 1841, SW LR, M-1841.

31 Herman J. Viola, "Invitation to Washington," *American West* (Jan. 1972), 18-31.

32 Second Auditor's Accounts (first series), Nos. 5724, 8062, 8100, 8668, 9445, 9955, 10163, 10584, 11679, 12910, 12923, 15437; (second series), Nos. 1154, 1421, 7071, RG 217, WNRC.

33 McKenney to Clark, Dec. 10, 1824, IA LS, vol. 1, p. 260; Second Auditor's Accounts (first series), No. 8646, RG 217, WNRC; McKenney to Clark, April 14, 1825, IA LS, vol. 1, p. 447; McKenney to Ridge, Dec. 14, 1825, *ibid.,* vol. 2, p. 309.

34 Cass to Calhoun, Dec. 15, 1824, IA LR, Michigan Superintendency; McKenney to Cass, Jan. 11, 1825, IA LS, vol. 1, p. 298; McKenney to Duval, Feb. 21, 1825, *ibid.,* vol. 1, p. 361.

35 "I sent you the other day Lewis' account, agreeably to the intimation you gave me respecting it. I do hope you will have it paid. You must not wholly cast off the poor fellow, although in reality he perhaps deserves but little commiseration. I have urged and reurged him to complete the unfinished drawings, since his return from the Wabash, within a few days, but a paralysis seems to have seized him. He has been, I fear, attacked with the old mania. Still he appears to dread the loss of your esteem, as one of the greatest misfortunes, which could befal him. He will probably apply himself to business after a few days." Cass to McKenney, Nov. 27, 1826, IA LR, Michigan Superintendency; Second Auditor's Accounts (first series), Nos. 9444, 9513, RG 217, WNRC; Hodge, *Indian Tribes of North America,* I, xxxiv-v.

36 McKenney to Clark, May 3, 1827, IA LS, vol. 4, p. 45.

37 "Address of Thomas R. Moore to His Constituents," June 27, 1828, printed in the Louisville *Public Advertiser,* July 19, 1828; "On Retrenchment. May 15, 1828," *House Report* No. 259, 20 Cong., 1 Sess. (Serial 179), 31.

38 McKenney to "a Friend," May 15, 1828, printed in Alexandria *Gazette,* May 22, 1828, and Washington *National Intelligencer,* May 31, 1828.

39 "On Retrenchment. May 15, 1828," *House Report* No. 259, 20 Cong., 1 Sess. (Serial 179), 187.

40 McKenney to Porter, Nov. 3, 1828, IA LS, vol. 5, p. 169; McKenney to Porter, Dec. 9, 1828, IA LR, Miscellaneous.

41 Second Auditor's Accounts (first series), Nos. 5810, 8106, 9570, 9953, 10509, 11679, 10210, 11901, RG 217, WNRC.

42 *Ibid.,* No. 14418; Miscellaneous File 113 (Smithsonian Institution Archives); John Bell to J. J. Abert, A. O. Dayton, and Francis Markoe, June 21, 1841, SW LS, vol. 23, p. 458; Appendix to the Report of the Secretary of the Smithsonian Institution, Dec. 31, 1858, *House Misc. Doc.* No. 57, Pt. 1, 35 Cong., 2 Sess. (Serial 1016), 52-53; "Annual Report of the Board of Regents of the Smithsonian Insti-

tution Showing the Operations, Expenditures, and Condition of the Institution for the Year 1865," *House Ex. Doc.* No. 102, 39 Cong., 1 Sess. (Serial 1265), 14, 16; "Annual Report ... for the Year 1862," *House Misc. Doc.* No. 25, Pt. 2, 37 Cong., 3 Sess. (Serial 1172), 56.

Chapter 14 The Indian History

1 Elliot, *Historical Sketches of the Ten Miles Square Forming the District of Columbia,* 167, 168.
2 McKenney to Jared Sparks, Sept. 22, 1829, Jared Sparks Papers (Houghton Library, Harvard University); Sparks to McKenney, Sept. 27, 1829, *ibid.*
3 McKenney to Sparks, Oct. 26, 1829, *ibid.*
4 McKenney to Sparks, Nov. 27, 1829, *ibid.*
5 McKenney to Clark, Oct. 20, 1829, copy in Lawrence Taliaferro Papers (Minnesota Historical Society); Johnston to McKenney, Nov. 3, 1829, IA LR, Piqua Agency.
6 McKenney to Eaton, March 19, 1830, IA LR, Miscellaneous. Eaton replied on the same letter. McKenney to Charles Bird King, April 3, 1830, Miscellaneous Manuscripts (New-York Historical Society).
7 Lewis Clephane and John Gardiner to Jackson, April 22, 1830, IA LR, Miscellaneous; McKenney to Clephane and Gardiner, April 26, 1830, IA LS, vol. 6, p. 393.
8 Clephane and Gardiner to Jackson, April 27, 1830, IA LR, Miscellaneous. Jackson's endorsement is dated April 28, 1830.
9 Clephane and Gardiner to Eaton, May 7, 1830, *ibid.*
10 Nicholas B. Wainwright, *Philadelphia in the Romantic Age of Lithography,* 13-14; John Sartain, *The Reminiscences of a Very Old Man, 1808-1897,* 161-62.
11 Wainwright, *Philadelphia,* 1.
12 McKenney's notation is on the lithographic portrait of Mahaska (White Cloud) which is in the custody of the Library Company of Philadelphia. McKenney to Adams, Sept. 7, 1831, Adams Family Papers (Massachusetts Historical Society); McKenney to Biddle, May 19, 1832 (Manuscripts Division, University of Virginia Library).
13 The partners evidently did not name their "great national work" until quite later. On February 2, 1832, Bradford registered with the clerk of the District Court for the Eastern District of Pennsylvania the title: "History of the Indian Tribes of North America, with Biographical Sketches and Anecdotes of the Principal Chiefs. Embellished with one hundred and twenty Portraits from the Indian Gallery in the Department of War, at Washington. By Thomas L. McKenney, Late of the Indian Department, Washington." Copyright Records, Eastern District of Pennsylvania, Library of Congress. A copy of the prospectus can be found in the Adams Family Papers.
14 McKenney to Forward, Nov. 3, 1841, Gratz Collection; McKenney to Milledoler, Aug. 22, 1831, Milledoler Papers.
15 McKenney to McLean, Jan. 29, 1831, McLean Papers; manuscript diary of Jared Sparks, Feb. 4-6, 1831, photocopy at the American Philosophical Society.
16 McKenney to Adams, Sept. 7, 1831, Adams Family Papers.
17 Adams to McKenney, Sept. 12, 1831, *ibid.*

18 McKenney to Adams, Sept. 16, 1831, *ibid.*
19 McKenney to Adams, Sept. 23, 1831, *ibid.;* Adams to McKenney, Sept. 27, 1831, *ibid.*
20 McKenney to Adams, Oct. 10, 1831, *ibid.;* Adams to McKenney, Oct. 14, 1831, *ibid.*
21 McKenney to Adams, Oct. 25, 1831, *ibid.*
22 McKenney to Adams, Dec. 2, 1831, *ibid.;* Adams to McKenney, Dec. 5, 1831, *ibid.*
23 McKenney to Adams, Oct. 25, 1831, *ibid.;* McKenney to Gallatin, Nov. 15, 1831, Albert Gallatin Papers (New-York Historical Society); McKenney to Adams, Dec. 2, 1831, Adams Family Papers.
24 McKenney to Adams, Dec. 2, 3, 1831, Adams Family Papers; Adams to McKenney, Dec. 17, 1831, *ibid.;* Washington *National Intelligencer,* Dec. 9, 1831.
25 Adams to McKenney, Dec. 17, 1831, Adams Family Papers; Mc-Kenney to Adams, Dec. 17, 1831, and Jan. 9, 1832, *ibid.*
26 McKenney to Adams, Jan. 9, 1832, *ibid.*
27 Adams manuscript diary, Jan. 15, 1832, *ibid.*; for McKenney's visits, see entries for March 22, 28, and April 3, 1832, *ibid.*
28 McKenney to Adams, Dec. 2, 1831, *ibid.;* McKenney to Gallatin, Dec. 18, 1831, Gallatin Papers.
29 McKenney to Gallatin, Dec. 18, 1831, Gallatin Papers.
30 McKenney to Biddle, May 19, 1832 (Manuscript Division, University of Virginia Library).
31 McKenney to Sparks, April 11, 20, 1833, Sparks Papers.
32 Sparks to McKenney, April 16, 1833 *ibid.;* McKenney to Sparks, April 20, 1833, *ibid.*
33 McKenney to Sparks, April 20, 1833, *ibid.*
34 In addition to the contemplated European venture, McKenney probably had more immediate and concrete reasons for having Inman copy the King portraits. For one thing, although the Philadelphia lithographer usually had enough time to do his initial work from the King portraits borrowed from Washington, his employees needed considerably more time to complete the coloring of the printed lithographs. Thus, the Inman copies probably served as models for the artists after McKenney returned the King originals to Washington. The Inman portraits may also have been McKenney's hedge against any future challenge to his right to do the lithograph project. If President Jackson or any other government official claimed McKenney did not have permission to reproduce the King portraits in portfolio form, the colonel could reply that his lithographs were made from the Inman portraits, not King's work.
35 McKenney to Sparks, May 7, 1833, Sparks Papers.
36 Nathan Sargent to Cass, May 31, 1833, IA LR, Miscellaneous; Elbert Herring to John H. Kinzie, John Dougherty, P. L. Chouteau, Pierre Menard, June 1, 1833, IA LS, vol. 10, pp. 394-95.
37 Johnston to Herring, Feb. 8, 1834, IA LR, Miscellaneous.
38 John Ridge to John Ross, Jan. 12, 1832, John Ross Papers (Thomas Gilcrease Institute of American History and Art); McKenney to Adams, Jan. 23, 1832, Adams Family Papers; *Poulson's American Daily Advertiser,* Jan. 18, 19, 20, 21, 23, 25, 1832.
39 Sargent to Cass, May 31, 1833, IA LR, Miscellaneous; Herring to John Garland, June 3, 1833, IA LS, vol. 10, p. 400; Herring to Mc-

Kenney, *ibid.,* p. 401.

40 McKenney to Herring, June 18, 1833, IA LR, Miscellaneous.

41 *Ibid.;* Herring to McKenney, June 25, 1833, IA LS, vol. 11, p. 15; McKenney to Herring, June 29, 1833, IA LR, Miscellaneous.

42 McKenney to Cass, Sept. 15, 1833, IA LR, Miscellaneous; Herring to McKenney, Sept. 21, 1833, IA LS, vol. 11, p. 200.

43 McKenney to Herring, Oct. 21, 1833, Dec. 24, 1835, and Jan. 28, 1836, IA LR, Miscellaneous.

44 McKenney to Sparks, April 20, 1833, Sparks Papers; McKenney to Herring, Sept. 5, 1833, IA LR, Miscellaneous; McKenney to Cass, Sept. 15, 1833, *ibid.;* Herring to McKenney, Sept. 21, 1833, IA LS, vol. 11, p. 200.

45 McKenney to Herring, Jan. 21, 1836, IA LR, Miscellaneous; Hezikiah Miller to McKenney, Jan. 19, 1836, enclosed with Miller to McKenney, Jan. 23, 1836, *ibid.;* McKenney to Herring, Jan. 28, 1836, *ibid.*

46 Herring to McKenney, Sept. 21, 1833, IA LS, vol. 11, p. 200; McKenney to Herring, Oct. 21, 1833, IA LR, Miscellaneous; McKenney to Herring, Jan. 21, 1836, *ibid.;* Miller to McKenney, March 8, 1836, *ibid.;* Miller to McCoy, March 14, 1836, *ibid.*

47 Sartain, *Reminiscences,* 161-62; Wainwright, *Philadelphia,* 25.

48 Albert Newsam to P. S. Duval, March 22, 1864, Library Company of Philadelphia; Newsam to John A. McAlister, March 21, 1865, *ibid.;* Wainwright, *Philadelphia,* 26.

49 According to the copyright book of the U.S. District Court for the Eastern District of Pennsylvania, Key and Biddle registered their last book on May 6, 1836, Copyright Records (Rare Book Room, Library of Congress); James Hall to George Catlin, Feb. 12, 1836, printed in Hodge, *Indian Tribes of North America,* I, xxix-xxxii.

50 David Donald, "The Autobiography of James Hall, Western Literary Pioneer," *The Ohio State Archaeological and Historical Quarterly,* LVI (1947), 301-02.

51 McKenney to Herring, Jan. 21, 1836, IA LR, Miscellaneous; McKenney to Lehman and Duval, July 20, 1836, Coryell Papers, vol. 3, p. 31 (Historical Society of Pennsylvania).

52 Information on subscription agents is found on the wrappers of the various numbers. An almost complete set of wrappers is in the custody of the American Philosophical Society.

53 McKenney to Sparks, May 16, 1831, Sparks Papers; McKenney to Charles Carroll, May 30, 1831 (Maryland Historical Society); McKenney to Nicholas Biddle, May 19, 1832 (Manuscript Division, University of Virginia Library); McKenney to Sparks, Nov. 24, 1836, Sparks Papers.

54 Biddle registered volume one on February 16, 1837, but did not deposit the first number until February 28. Copyright Records.

55 Edward C. Biddle, comp., *Recommendatory Notices . . . ,* 10, 14, 16.

56 McKenney to Sparks, Nov. 24, 1836, Dec. 6, 1837, Jan. 31, 1838, Sparks Papers; [Jared Sparks], "History of the Indian Tribes of North America . . . ," *North American Review,* XLVII (July 1838), 135-36.

57 McKenney to Sparks, May 11, 1838, Sparks Papers; Subscription Book (New-York Historical Society).

58 Tipton to Carey A. Harris, Feb. 13, 1837, IA LR, Miscellaneous; Harris to the Secretary of War, Feb. 17, 1837, enclosed with the

Secretary of War to Hugh S. White, Feb. 18, 1837, HR24-A-D23.4, Senate Papers relating to Indian Appropriations, House of Representatives Committee on Ways and Means, RG 233, NA; *U.S. Stat.* V, 161, 299.

59 Second Auditor's Accounts (second series), Nos. 1154, 1421, RG 217, WNRC.

60 McKenney to Harris, Nov. [Oct.] 30, 1837, IA LR, Miscellaneous.

61 Edward C. Biddle to Harris, July 10, 17, 1838, *ibid.*

62 Biddle to Harris, April 11, June 23, Aug. 7, 1837, *ibid.*; Wainwright, *Philadelphia,* 50.

63 Wainwright, *Philadelphia,* 50.

64 McKenney to the Secretary of War, Jan. 24, 1839, IA LR, Miscellaneous; McKenney to Forward, Nov. 3, 1841, Gratz Collection.

65 Edward C. Biddle to Thomas Hartley Crawford, Feb. 26 and March 23, 1839, IA LR, Miscellaneous; Second Auditor's Accounts (second series), No. 2981, RG 217, WNRC; Biddle to Crawford, June 12, 1839, IA LR, Miscellaneous; Frederick W. Greenough to Franck Taylor, Aug. 24, 1839, enclosed with Second Auditor's Accounts (second series), No. 3595, RG 217, WNRC.

66 McKenney to Forward, Nov. 3, 1841, Gratz Collection.

67 Edward C. Biddle to McKenney, April 24, 1841, SW LR, M-1841.

68 Bowen, listing himself as proprietor, registered number 14 in the Pennsylvania District Court on December 20, 1841. Biddle wrote to the War Department on December 31, 1841 (registry entry B-1841, Registers of Letters Received, Bureau of Indian Affairs, RG 75, NA). The documents surrounding the controversy are in Second Auditor's Accounts (third series), No. 7963, RG 217, WNRC. Donald, "Autobiography of James Hall," 302.

69 Charles C. Stratton to Crawford, July 16, 1842, IA LR, Miscellaneous; Daniel Rice and James G. Clark to John C. Spencer, Dec. 31, 1842, *ibid.*

70 Rice and Clark to Spencer, Dec. 31, 1842, *ibid.*

71 McKenney to Rice and Clark, quoted *ibid.*; Crawford to Spencer, Jan. 12, 1843, Report Books, vol. 3, 355-56, RG 75, NA; Crawford to Rice and Clark, Jan. 19, 1843, IA LS, vol. 33, p. 240.

72 Wainwright, *Philadelphia,* 50, 54; *Saturday Courier,* Jan. 4, 1840.

73 Donald, "Autobiography of James Hall," 302.

74 *Ibid.,* 301; McKenney to Sparks, May 11, 1838, Sparks Papers; *Saturday Courier,* April 2, 1842.

75 J. J. Abert, Francis Markoe, and A. O. Dayton to John Bell, June 18, 1841, IA LR, Miscellaneous; Bell to Abert, Markoe, and Dayton, June 21, 1841, SW LS, vol. 23, p. 458.

76 *House Misc. Doc.* No. 57, 35 Cong., 2 Sess. (Serial 1016), 41-42; *House Ex. Doc.* No. 102, 39 Cong., 1 Sess. (Serial 1265), 14-16.

77 McKenney to William D. Lewis, June 11, 1839, Miscellaneous Manuscripts (Huntington Library).

78 McKenney to Lewis, June 13, 1839, *ibid.*

79 McKenney to Lewis, June 20, 1839, *ibid.*

80 McKenney to Lewis, Nov. 16, 1843, *ibid.*

81 McKenney to Lewis, Dec. 13, 1843, *ibid.*

82 Hodge, *Indian Tribes of North America,* I, lvi; McKenney to Sparks, April 20, 1833, Sparks Papers.

Chapter 15   The Last Decades

1 A copy of McKenney's circular announcing the "New York Indian Emporium" can be found in the Schoolcraft Papers, Library of Congress; Schoolcraft, *Personal Memoirs,* 343; McKenney to Cass, Dec. 19, 1843, IA LR, Miscellaneous.
2 Aristides, *Essays on the Spirit of Jacksonism . . . ,* 5, 6.
3 McKenney to Nicholas Biddle, [Dec. 13, 1835?], letters received, vol. 108, Nicholas Biddle Papers (Manuscript Division, Library of Congress); Biddle to McKenney, Dec. 14, 1835, vol. 118, p. 417, letters sent, *ibid.*
4 McKenney to the Corresponding Secretary of the American Board, Feb. 5, 1841, Papers of the American Board.
5 Biddle to Webster, March 2, 1841, SW LR, M-1841; J. Hall Bready to John Bell, March 4, 1841, *ibid.*; Citizens of Bristol to Bell, April 1841, *ibid.*
6 McKenney to William D. Lewis, Aug. 28, 1841, Miscellaneous Papers (Huntington Library); Charles MacAlester to Charles S. Todd, March 19, 1841, William Henry Harrison Papers, box 1805-41, Benjamin Harrison Collection (Manuscript Division, Library of Congress); Barbour to John Tyler, April 6, 1841, SW LR, P-275(56).
7 McKenney to Forward, Nov. 3, 1841, Gratz Collection.
8 McKenney to John C. Spencer, Nov. 3, 1841, *ibid.*
9 McKenney to Adams, Nov. 24, 1836, Adams Papers.
10 McKenney to Sparks, Nov. 24, 1836, Sparks Papers.
11 McKenney to Adams, Oct. 28, 1842, Adams Papers.
12 The discourses form volume two of McKenney's *Memoirs.*
13 Prucha, *American Indian Policy,* 272-73.
14 McKenney, *Memoirs,* II, v.
15 McKenney to Henry Alexander Scammell Dearborn, June 24, 1843, Morristown National Historical Park.
16 McKenney to Charles W. Brewster, Oct. 7, 1843, *ibid.*
17 Portsmouth *Journal of Literature and Politics,* Oct. 14, 1843.
18 Peter Temin, *The Jacksonian Economy,* 32.
19 McKenney to Eleuthère Irénée Du Pont, March 30, 1833, Du Pont Papers (Eleutherian Mills Historical Society); Du Pont to McKenney, April 3, 1833, *ibid.*
20 McKenney to Du Pont, Feb. 9, 1831, and March 22, 1833, *ibid.*
21 McKenney to Alfred Du Pont, Jan. 26, 1842 (two letters of the same date), and Jan. 31, 1842, Du Pont Papers, *ibid.*
22 Alfred Du Pont to McKenney, Jan. 29 and Feb. 5, 1842, and McKenney to Du Pont, Feb. 4, 1842, *ibid.*
23 McKenney to Sparks, Oct. 5, and May 20, 1843, Sparks Papers.
24 McKenney to Sparks, June 22, 1843, *ibid.*
25 McKenney to Sparks, Oct. 5, 1843, *ibid.*
26 McKenney to Sparks, Nov. 3, 1843, *ibid.*
27 McKenney to Sparks, Nov. 16, 1843, *ibid.*
28 McKenney to Sparks, Sept. 30, 1844, *ibid.*
29 McKenney to Sparks, Nov. 3, 1845, *ibid.*
30 McKenney to Sparks, July 13, 1846, *ibid.*
31 McKenney to Sparks, Feb. 27, 1845, *ibid.*
32 McKenney to Sparks, March 5, 1845, *ibid.*
33 McKenney to Sparks, Nov. 3, 1845, *ibid.*

34 *North American Review,* LXIII (Oct. 1846), 481.
35 Kosciuszko Armstrong, *Review of T. L. McKenney's Narrative of the Causes which, in 1814, Led to General Armstrong's Resignation of the War Office,* 9, 6, 19.
36 Thomas L. McKenney, *An Opening Reply to Kosciusko Armstrong's Pamphlet;* Thomas L. McKenney, *Reply to Kosciusko Armstrong's Assault Upon Col. McKenney's Narrative . . . ,* 4.
37 Kosciuszko Armstrong, *Examination of Thomas L. McKenney's Reply to the Review of His Narrative, &c.,* 3.
38 McKenney to Sparks, March 9, 1847, Sparks Papers.
39 McKenney to Bishop Whittingham, May 7, 1849, Duke University Library; J. P. Kennedy to T. Ewing, May 24, 1849, Appointments Division, Commissioner of Indian Affairs, Records of the Office of the Secretary of the Interior, RG 48, NA.
40 McKenney to Orlando Brown, Jan. 21 and April 29, 1850, Orlando Brown Papers, The Filson Club.
41 McKenney to Brown, May 9 and May 25, 1850, *ibid.*
42 Land Warrants 36483/1852 and 16903/1855, Records of the Bureau of Land Management, RG 49, WNRC. The portrait of McKenney was painted in 1856 by Charles Elliott and is in the custody of the Corcoran Gallery of Art, Washington, D.C.
43 Certificate of Death, Municipal Archives and Records Center (New York, NY); Washington *National Intelligencer,* March 10, 1859.

Bibliography

RECORDS IN THE NATIONAL ARCHIVES

Record Group 29. Records of the Bureau of the Census.
>Federal Population Census, District of Columbia, 1820.

Record Group 39. Records of the Bureau of Accounts (Treasury).
>Surety Bonds of Officials Responsible for Collection and Disbursement of Public Monies, 1783-1925.

Record Group 46. Records of the United States Senate, Fifteenth through Twenty-second Congresses (1816-30).
>Bills and Resolutions Originating in the Senate.
>Committee Reports and Papers.
>Petitions and Memorials, Resolutions of State Legislatures, and Related Documents.
>President's Messages—Indian Relations.

Record Group 48. Records of the Office of the Secretary of the Interior.
>Appointments Division, Commissioner of Indian Affairs.

Record Group 49. Records of the Bureau of Land Management.
>Land Entry Papers.

Record Group 59. General Records of the Department of State.
>Domestic Letters of the Department of State, 1816-30.
>Miscellaneous Letters of the Department of State, 1816-30.
>Applications and Recommendations for Public Office during the Administrations of James Madison, James Monroe,

John Quincy Adams, and Andrew Jackson.

Record Group 75. Records of the Bureau of Indian Affairs.
  Records of the Office of Indian Trade,
    Letters Sent, 1816-30.
    Letters Received, 1816-24.
    Factory Records, 1816-22.
  Records of the Office of the Secretary of War Relating to
    Indian Affairs,
    Letters Sent, 1816-24.
    Letters Received, 1816-23.
  Records of the Bureau of Indian Affairs,
    Registers of Letters Received.
    Letters Received, 1823-44.
    Letters Sent, 1824-44.
  Records of the Michigan Superintendency of Indian Affairs,
    Letters Received, 1816-31.
    Letters Sent, 1816-31.
  Documents Relating to the Negotiation of Ratified and
    Unratified Indian Treaties, 1816-30.

Record Group 92. Records of the Office of Quartermaster General.
  Consolidated Files of the Quartermaster General.

Record Group 94. Records of the Adjutant General's Office.
  Letters Received, 1824-30.

Record Group 107. Records of the Office of the Secretary of War.
  Registers of Letters Received.
  Letters Received, 1816-48.
  Letters Sent, Military Affairs, 1816-30.
  Reports to Congress by the Secretary of War, 1816-30.
  Manuscripts Relating to the War of 1812.

Record Group 217. Records of the United States General Accounting
  Office.
    Second Auditor's Accounts, 1816-40.
    Second Auditor's Office, Letters Sent, 1824-30.
    Second Comptroller's Office, Letters Sent, 1822-24.
    Fifth Auditor's Accounts, 1816-40.
    Fifth Auditor's Report Books, 1822-24.

Record Group 233. Records of the United States House of Representatives, Fifteenth through Twenty-second Congresses (1816-
  30).
    Bills and Resolutions Originating in the House.
    Committee Reports and Papers.
    Petitions and Memorials, Resolutions of State Legislatures,
      and Related Documents which were Referred to
      Committees.

Record Group 351. Records of the Government of the District of
  Columbia.
    City of Georgetown Assessment Records, 1808-12, 1815, 1818.

MANUSCRIPTS

Adams Family Papers (microfilm edition). Massachusetts Historical
    Society.
American Board of Commissioners for Foreign Missions Papers.
    Houghton Library, Harvard University.
American Fur Company Letter Books, 1816-30 (photostatic copies).
    State Historical Society of Wisconsin.
James Barbour Papers. Manuscript Division, New York Public
    Library.
Nicholas Biddle Papers. Manuscript Division, Library of Congress.
Orlando Brown Papers. The Filson Club (Louisville, Ky.).
Carroll-McTavish Papers. Maryland Historical Society.
Copyright Records. Rare Book Room, Library of Congress.
Lewis S. Coryell Papers. Historical Society of Pennsylvania.
David Daggett Papers. Yale University Library.
Peter Force Papers. Manuscript Division, Library of Congress.
Albert Gallatin Papers. New-York Historical Society.
Galloway-Maxcy-Markoe Papers. Manuscript Division, Library of
    Congress.
Simon Gratz Collection. Historical Society of Pennsylvania.
William Henry Harrison Papers (Benjamin Harrison Collection).
    Manuscript Division, Library of Congress.
"Journal of Proceedings of the National Institution." Miscellaneous
    File 113. Archives of the Smithsonian Institution.
Lewis-Nielson Papers. Historical Society of Pennsylvania.
Longwood Manuscripts. Eleutherian Mills Historical Library
    (Wilmington, Del.).
James Madison Papers. Manuscript Division, Library of Congress.
Thomas L. McKenney certificate of death. Municipal Archives and
    Records Center, New York, N.Y.
Thomas L. McKenney letter. Manuscript Division, University of
    Virginia Library.
Thomas L. McKenney letters and documents. Miscellaneous Manu-
    scripts, Henry E. Huntington Library (San Marino, Calif.).
Thomas L. McKenney letters. Manuscript Collection, Morristown
    National Historical Park (Morristown, N.J.).
Thomas L. McKenney letters. Miscellaneous Papers. Manuscript
    Division, New York Public Library.
Thomas L. McKenney letters. Miscellaneous Papers, New-York
    Historical Society.
John McLean Papers. Manuscript Division, Library of Congress.
Militia Appointments. Maryland Hall of Records (Annapolis, Md.).
Philip Milledoler Papers. New-York Historical Society.
Albert Newsam Folder. Library Company of Philadelphia (Historical
    Society of Pennsylvania).
Recorder of Deeds Records, Washington, D.C.

John Ross Papers. Thomas Gilcrease Institute of American History and Art (Tulsa, Okla.).

Henry R. Schoolcraft Papers. Manuscript Division, Library of Congress.

Jared Sparks Papers. Houghton Library, Harvard University.

Subscription book for *History of the Indian Tribes of North America.* Manuscript Division, New York Public Library.

Lawrence Taliaferro Papers (microfilm edition). Minnesota Historical Society.

William Whittingham Papers. Manuscript Department, Duke University Library.

CONGRESSIONAL DOCUMENTS

"Report of the Secretary of War, of a System, Providing for the Abolition of the Existing Indian Trade Establishments of the United States, and Providing for the Opening of the Trade with the Indians to Individuals, under Suitable Regulations." December 5, 1818. *House Doc.* No. 25, 15 Cong., 2 Sess. (Serial 17).

"Letter from the Superintendent of Indian Trade, to the Chairman of the Committee on Indian Affairs, Communicating a Report in Relation to Indian Trade." December 13, 1820. *Senate Doc.* No. 19, 16 Cong., 2 Sess. (Serial 42).

"Communication from Thomas L. McKenney, Superintendent of Indian Trade, to the Chairman of the Committee on Indian Affairs." January 14, 1822. *Senate Doc.* No. 10, 17 Cong., 1 Sess. (Serial 59).

"Documents Relative to Indian Trade. Submitted to the Senate by the Committee on Indian Affairs." February 11, 1822. *Senate Doc.* No. 60, 17 Cong., 1 Sess. (Serial 59).

"Report of the Committee on Indian Affairs, in Relation to the Execution of the Act of Last Session, Abolishing the Indian Trading Establishments." March 1, 1823. *House Report* No. 104, 17 Cong., 2 Sess. (Serial 87).

"Message from the President of the United States, Transmitting Sundry Documents in Relation to the Various Tribes of Indians within the United States, and Recommending a Plan for their Future Location and Government." January 27, 1825. *House Doc.* No. 64, 18 Cong., 2 Sess. (Serial 116).

"Documents from the Department of War." December 1, 1825. *Senate Doc.* No. 2, 19 Cong., 1 Sess. (Serial 125).

"Documents Submitted by the Chairman of the Committee on Indian Affairs, Accompanied by a Bill for the Establishment of a General Superintendency of Indian Affairs in the Department of War." March 31, 1826. *House Doc.* No. 146, 19 Cong. 1 Sess. (Serial 138).

"Documents from the War Department, Accompanying the Presi-

dent's Message to Congress." November 28, 1826. *Senate Doc.*
No. 1, 19 Cong., 2 Sess. (Serial 144).

"Documents from the War Department, Accompanying the President's Message to Congress." November 26, 1827. *Senate Doc.*
No. 1, 20 Cong., 1 Sess. (Serial 163).

"Bill for the Relief of the Columbian College." February 14, 1828.
Senate Doc. No. 103, 20 Cong., 1 Sess. (Serial 165).

"On Retrenchment." May 15, 1828 *House Report* No. 259, 20 Cong.,
1 Sess. (Serial 179).

"Documents Accompanying the President's Message. Report of the
Secretary of War." November 24, 1828. *Senate Doc.* No. 1, 20
Cong., 2 Sess. (Serial 181).

"Letter from the Secretary of War, Transmitting the Information
Required by a Resolution of the House of Representatives of the
15th Ultimo, in Relation to our Indian Affairs Generally." February 10, 1829. *House Doc.* No. 117, 20 Cong., 2 Sess. (Serial
186).

"Documents Communicated to Congress by the President . . . Accompanying the Report of the Secretary of War." November 30,
1829. *Senate Doc.* No. 1, 21 Cong., 1 Sess. (Serial 192).

"Columbian College." March 12, 1830. *House Report* No. 290, 21
Cong., 1 Sess. (Serial 200).

"Rations to Emigrating Indians." July 5, 1832. *House Report* No.
502, 22 Cong., 1 Sess. (Serial 228).

"Annual Report of the Board of Regents of the Smithsonian Institution Showing the Operations, Expenditures, and Condition of
the Institution for the Year 1858." *House Misc. Doc.* No. 57,
35 Cong., 2 Sess. (Serial 1016).

"Annual Report of the Board of Regents of the Smithsonian Institution . . . for the Year 1862." *House Misc. Doc.* No. 25, 37 Cong.,
3 Sess. (Serial 1172).

"Annual Report of the Board of Regents of the Smithsonian Institution . . . for the Year 1865." *House Ex. Doc.* No. 102, 39 Cong.,
1 Sess. (Serial 1265).

House Journals. Fifteenth through Twenty-first Congresses. (Serials
4, 16, 30, 47, 62, 75, 92, 112, 130. 147, 168, 183, 194, 205).

Senate Journals. Fifteenth through Twenty-first Congresses. (Serials
1, 13, 25, 41, 58, 72, 88, 107, 124, 143, 162, 180, 191, 202).

OTHER GOVERNMENT PUBLICATIONS

American State Papers: Indian Affairs. 2 vols. Washington, 1832-34.
American State Papers: Miscellaneous. 2 vols. Washington, 1834.
Annals of Congress. 17 Cong., 1 Sess., vol. 1, 1821-22. Washington,
1855.
Carter, Clarence E., ed. *The Territorial Papers of the United States.*
26 vols. Washington, 1934-62.

Cohen, Felix S. *Handbook of Federal Indian Law with Reference Tables and Index*. Washington, 1941.

Hill, Edward E. *Historical Sketches for Jurisdictional and Subject Headings for the Letters Received by the Office of Indian Affairs, 1824-80*. Washington, 1967.

Hodge, Frederick Webb, ed. *Handbook of American Indians North of Mexico*. 2 vols. Washington, 1907, 1910.

Kappler, Charles J., comp. and ed. *Indian Affairs: Laws and Treaties*. vol. 2, *Treaties*. Washington, 1904.

Martin, John H., comp. *List of Documents Concerning the Negotiation of Ratified Indian Treaties, 1801-1869*. National Archives Special List No. 6. Washington, 1949.

Mayo, Robert. *The Treasury Department and Its Various Fiscal Bureaus, Their Origin, Organization, and Practical Operations, Illustrated*. 2 vols. Washington, 1847.

A Register of Officers and Agents, Civil, Military, and Naval, in the Service of the United States, on the 30th of September, 1819. Washington, 1820.

A Register of Officers and Agents, Civil, Military, and Naval, in the Service of the United States, on the 30th of September, 1823. Washington, 1824.

A Register of Officers and Agents, Civil, Military, and Naval, in the Service of the United States, on the 30th of September, 1829. Washington, 1830.

A Register of Officers and Agents, Civil, Military, and Naval, in the Service of the United States, on the 30th of September, 1831. Washington, 1831.

U.S. Statutes at Large.

PUBLISHED CONTEMPORARY WORKS

Adams, Charles Francis, ed. *Memoirs of John Quincy Adams, Comprising Portions of His Diary from 1795 to 1848*. 12 vols. Philadelphia, 1874.

Anon. *On the Indian Trade, by a Backwoodsman*. Washington, 1821. New Hampshire Historical Society.

Aristides [Thomas L. McKenney]. *Essays on the Spirit of Jacksonism, as Exemplified in its Deadly Hostility to the Bank of the United States, and in the Odious Calumnies Employed for its Destruction*. Philadelphia, 1835.

Armstrong, Kosciuszko. *Review of T. L. M'Kenney's Narrative of the Causes which, in 1814, Led to General Armstrong's Resignation of the War Office*. New York, 1846.

——————. *Examination of Thomas L. McKenney's Reply to the Review of His Narratives*. New York, 1847.

Benton, Thomas Hart. *Thirty Years View or a History of the Work-*

ing Government for Thirty Years from 1820-1852. 2 vols. New York, 1854-1856.

Biddle, Edward C., comp. *Recommendatory Notices of the Indian History and Biography, now Publishing by Edward C. Biddle, Philadelphia: with a List of Subscribers, To March 1, 1837.* Philadelphia, 1837.

Calhoun, John C. *The Papers of John C. Calhoun.* W. Edwin Hemphill, ed. 5 vols. to date. Columbia, S.C., 1959—.

Clay, Henry. *The Papers of Henry Clay.* James F. Hopkins and Mary W. M. Hargreaves, eds. 4 vols. to date. Lexington, Ky., 1963—.

Documents and Proceedings Relating to the Formation and Progress of a Board, in the city of New York, for the Emigration, Preservation, and Improvement, of the Aborigines of America, July 22, 1829. New York, 1829.

Draper, Lyman C., ed. "Fur Trade and Factory System at Green Bay, 1816-21." *Wisconsin Historical Collections,* vol. 7. Madison, 1876.

Elliot, Jonathan. *Historical Sketches of the Ten Miles Square Forming the District of Columbia; with a Picture of Washington, Describing Objects of General Interest or Curiosity at the Metropolis of the Union.* Washington, 1830.

Grant, J. *The Metropolitan Pulpit; or Sketches of the Most Popular Preachers in London.* 2 vols. London, 1839.

Homans, Benjamin. *The Georgetown Directory for the Year 1830.* Georgetown, D.C., 1830.

Houston, Sam. *The Writings of Sam Houston, 1813-1863.* Amelia W. Williams and Eugene C. Barker, eds. 8 vols. Austin, 1938-43.

Lanman, Charles. *Recollections of Curious Characters and Pleasant Places.* Edinburgh, 1881.

Lapham, Increase A. *The Antiquities of Wisconsin.* Washington, 1855.

A Letter Addressed to Thomas L. McKenney, Esq. Superintendent of Indian Trade. n.p., 1820. Boston Public Library.

McKenney, Thomas L. *An Opening Reply to Kosciusko Armstrong's Pamphlet.* New York, 1846.

―――――――. *Memoirs, Official and Personal; with Sketches of Travels among the Northern and Southern Indians.* 2 vols. in one. New York, 1846.

―――――――. *A Narrative of the Battle of Bladensburg in a Letter to Henry Banning, Esq., by an Officer of Gen. Smith's Staff.* n.p., 1814.

―――――――. *Reply to Kosciusko Armstrong's Assault Upon Col. McKenney's Narrative . . . .* New York, 1847.

―――――――. *Sketches of a Tour to the Lakes, of the Character and Customs of the Chippeway Indians, and of Incidents Connected with the Treaty of Fond Du Lac.* Baltimore, 1827.

——————. *To the Public.* n.p., 1828. James Madison Papers. Rare Book Room, Library of Congress.

McKenney, Thomas L., and Hall, James. *History of the Indian Tribes of North America, with Biographical Sketches and Anecdotes of the Principal Chiefs. Embellished with One Hundred and Twenty Portraits, from the Indian Gallery in the Department of War, at Washington.* 3 vols. Philadelphia, 1836-44.

——————. *The Indian Tribes of North America with Biographical Sketches and Anecdotes of the Principal Chiefs.* Frederick Webb Hodge, ed. 3 vols. Edinburgh, 1933.

Mills, Robert. *Guide to the National Executive Offices and the Capitol of the United States.* Washington, 1841.

Morse, Jedidiah. *A Report to the Secretary of War of the United States on Indian Affairs.* New Haven, 1822.

Poore, Benjamin Perley. *Perley's Reminiscences.* 2 vols. Philadelphia, 1886.

Reed, Andrew. *No Fiction; or, the Test of Friendship; a Narrative Founded on Recent and Interesting Facts.* 3rd. ed. Baltimore, 1821.

Sartain, John. *The Reminiscences of a Very Old Man, 1808-1897.* New York, 1899.

Schoolcraft, Henry R. *Historical and Statistical Information Respecting the History, Condition, and Prospects of the Indian Tribes of the United States.* 6 vols. Philadelphia, 1851-57.

——————. *Personal Memoirs of a Residence of Thirty Years with the Indian Tribes on the American Frontier.* Philadelphia, 1851.

Smith, Margaret Bayard. *The First Forty Years of Washington Society,* Gaillard Hunt, ed. New York, 1906.

Sparks, Jared. Review of Thomas L. McKenney and James Hall's *History of the Indian Tribes of North America. North American Review,* XLVII (July 1838), 134-48.

——————. Review of Thomas L. McKenney's *Memoirs, Official and Personal. North American Review,* LXIII (October 1846), 481-96.

Thwaites, Reuben Gold, ed. "The Fur Trade in Wisconsin, 1812-1825." *Wisconsin Historical Collections,* vol. 20. Madison, 1911.

NEWSPAPERS

Cherokee Phoenix and Indian Advocate (New Echota, Ga.), February 1828-January 1831.

City Gazette (Washington, D.C.), September 1822-February 1824.

Columbian Gazette (Georgetown, D.C.), July 1829-December 1830.

Daily National Intelligencer (Washington, D.C.), 1809-1859, *passim.*

Evening Post (New York), October-November 1829.

Metropolitan and Georgetown National Messenger, January 1820-June 1822.
Niles' Weekly Register (Baltimore), June 1822-October 1830.
Paulson's American Daily Advertiser (Philadelphia), January 1832.
Portsmouth Journal of Literature and Politics, October 1843.
United States Telegraph (Washington, D.C.), July 1828-October 1830.
Washington Republican and Congressional Examiner, August 1822-July 1824.

BOOKS AND ARTICLES

Abel, Annie Heloise. "History of Events Resulting in Indian Consolidation West of the Mississippi." *Annual Report of the American Historical Association for the Year 1906,* I (1908), 233-450.
Ammon, Harry. *James Monroe: The Quest for National Identity.* New York, 1971.
Bemis, Samuel Flagg. *John Quincy Adams and the Union.* New York, 1956.
Berkhofer, Robert F., Jr. *Salvation and the Savage: An Analysis of Protestant Missions and American Indian Response, 1787-1862.* Lexington, Ky., 1965.
Bryan, Wilhelmus B. *A History of the National Capital.* 2 vols. New York, 1914-16.
Chalou, George. "Massacre on Fall Creek." *Prologue,* IV (Summer 1972), 109-114.
Coman, Katherine. "Government Factories: An Attempt to Control Competition in the Fur Trade." *Bulletin of the American Economic Association,* 4th ser. (April 1911), 368-88.
DeRosier, Arthur H., Jr. *The Removal of the Choctaw Indians.* Knoxville, 1970.
Dick, Everett. *Vanguards of the Frontier: A Social History of the Northern Plains and Rocky Mountains from the Earliest White Contacts to the Coming of the Homemaker.* New York, 1941.
Donald, David. "The Autobiography of James Hall, Western Literary Pioneer." *Ohio State Archaeological and Historical Quarterly,* LVI (1947), 295-304.
Harmon, George Dewey. *Sixty Years of Indian Affairs. Political, Economic, and Diplomatic, 1789-1850.* Chapel Hill, 1941.
Hay, Thomas Robson. "John C. Calhoun and the Presidential Campaign of 1824." *North Carolina Historical Review,* XII (January 1935), 20-44.
Hayden, Ralston. *The Senate and Treaties, 1789-1817.* New York, 1920.
Hryniewicki, Richard J. "The Creek Treaty of November 15, 1827." *Georgia Historical Quarterly,* LII (March 1968), 1-15.

Lawson, Publius V. "Summary of the Archeology of Winnebago County, Wisconsin." *Wisconsin Archeologist,* II (January 1903), 45-49.

Peake, Ora Brooks. *A History of the United States Indian Factory System, 1795-1822.* Denver, 1954.

Porter, Kenneth Wiggins. *John Jacob Astor: Business Man.* 2 vols. Cambridge, Mass., 1931.

Prucha, Francis Paul. *American Indian Policy in the Formative Years: The Indian Trade and Intercourse Acts, 1790-1834.* Cambridge, Mass., 1962.

——————. *Broadax and Bayonet: The Role of the United States Army in the Development of the Northwest, 1815-1860.* Madison, Wis., 1953.

——————. "Early Indian Peace Medals." *Wisconsin Magazine of History,* XLV (Spring 1962), 279-89.

——————. *Indian Peace Medals in American History.* Madison, Wis., 1971.

——————. "Indian Removal and the Great American Desert." *Indiana Magazine of History,* LIX (December 1963), 299-322.

——————. "Thomas L. McKenney and the New York Indian Board." *Mississippi Valley Historical Review,* XLVIII (March 1962), 635-55.

Quaife, Milo M. *Chicago and the Old Northwest, 1673-1835.* Chicago, 1913.

Schultz, George. *An Indian Canaan: Issac McCoy and the Vision of an Indian State.* Norman, Okla., 1972.

Temin, Peter. *The Jacksonian Economy.* New York, 1969.

Todd, Frederick P. "The Militia and Volunteers of the District of Columbia, 1783-1820." *Records of the Columbia Historical Society,* L (1952), 379-439.

——————. "Thomas L. McKenney and the New York Indian Board." *Mississippi Valley Historical Review,* XLVIII (March 1962), 635-55.

Viola, Herman J. "Invitation to Washington." *American West,* IX (January 1972), 18-31.

——————. "Portraits, Presents, and Peace Medals: Thomas L. McKenney and the Indian Visitors to Washington." *American Scene,* XI (June 1970).

——————. "Washington's First Museum: The Indian Office Collection of Thomas L. McKenney." *Smithsonian Journal of History,* III (Fall 1968), 1-18.

Wainwright, Nicolas B. *Philadelphia in the Romantic Age of Lithography.* Philadelphia, 1958.

Way, Royal B. "The United States Factory System for Trading with the Indians, 1796-1822." *Mississippi Valley Historical Review,* VI (September 1919), 220-35.

Wesley, Edgar B. *Guarding the Frontier: A Study in Frontier Defense from 1815 to 1825.* Minneapolis, 1935.

White, Leonard D. *The Jeffersonians: A Study in Administrative History, 1801-1829*. New York, 1951.
Wiltse, Charles M. *John C. Calhoun*. 3 vols. Indianapolis, 1944-51.
Young, James Sterling. *The Washington Community, 1800-1828*. New York, 1966.

UNPUBLISHED WORKS

McKenney, John. "McKenney Family History." Maryland Hall of Records.
Plaisance, Aloysius. "The United States Government Factory System, 1796-1822." Ph. D. dissertation. St. Louis University, 1954.
Viola, Herman J. "Thomas L. McKenney and the Administration of Indian Affairs, 1824-30." Ph.D. dissertation. Indiana University, 1970.

Acknowledgments

M Y RESEARCH ON Thomas L. McKenney was aided by a grant from the Penrose Fund of the American Philosophical Society. Brief portions of this book appeared previously in the *Smithsonian Journal of History* (Fall 1968) and the *American Scene* (Summer 1970) and in the introductions to McKenney's *Memoirs, Official and Personal*, reprinted in 1973 by the University of Nebraska Press, and McKenney's *Sketches of a Tour to the Lakes*, reprinted in 1972 by the Imprint Society.

All historians must acknowledge their reliance on others, and I am in debt to many, especially Francis Paul Prucha, S.J., who first suggested McKenney to me as a topic in his graduate seminar in 1962 and who encouraged me to write this book. Thanks are also due to Frank L. Klement, who urged me to enter graduate school, and to the late O. O. Winther, who directed my doctoral studies. Others to whom I would like to express appreciation for helping me with my work on McKenney are Donald F. Carmony, Erminie Wheeler-Vogelin, Clifford Evans, John C. Ewers, William C. Sturtevant, Patricia Andrews, Sara Jackson, Charles South, Albert H. Leisinger, Jr., Whitfield

Bell, W. Edwin Hemphill, John and Maria McKenney, Leonard Rapport, Ralph E. Ehrenberg, Eleanor McKenney Gibson, James R. Bentley, Edmund Berkely, Jr., Albert U. Blair, Lyman H. Butterfield, Lawrence G. Clagget, Betty Bridge Low, Samella T. Anderson, Richard C. Crawford, John D. Macoll, and Shelley C. Bailey.

The collections and staffs of numerous libraries and manuscript depositories have served me well. I wish to acknowledge specifically my debts to the following institutions: the National Archives and Records Service, the Library of Congress, the Smithsonian Institution, the Gilcrease Institute of American History and Art, the Henry E. Huntington Library and Art Gallery, the Massachusetts Historical Society, the Detroit Public Library, the Cincinnati Historical Society, the Filson Club, the Redwood Library and Athenaeum, the Maryland Hall of Records, the Houghton Library of Harvard University, the American Philosophical Society, the Historical Society of Pennsylvania, the Eleutherian Mills Historical Library, the New-York Historical Society, the New York Public Library, and the Corcoran Gallery of Art.

I also wish to acknowledge the considerable help of Robert M. Kvasnicka, who knows so well the records relating to the American Indians at the National Archives, and Jan Shelton Danis, whose editorial advice has meant so much to me.

Without doubt my greatest debt is to my wife Susan. But for her patience and support this book could not have been written.

H. J. V.

Index

Italic numeral indicates illustration following that page.

358

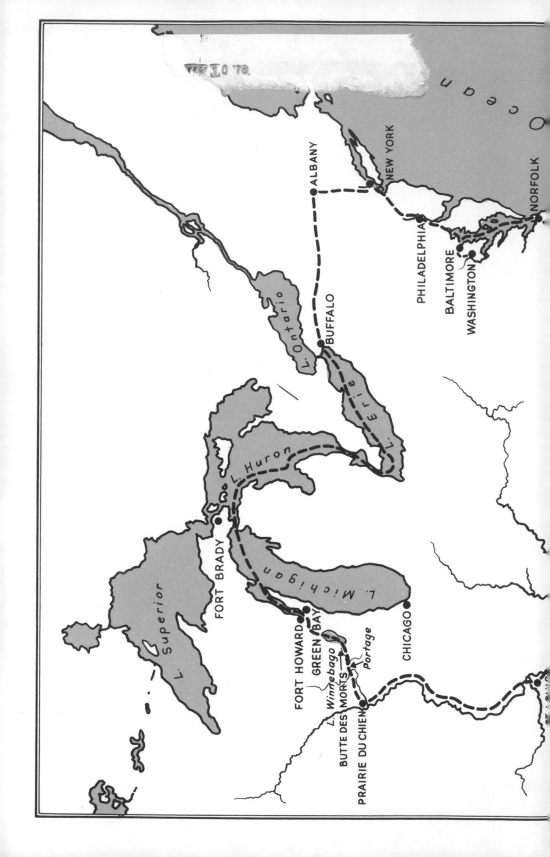